America Firsthand

VOLUME ONE

Readings from Settlement
to Reconstruction

TENTH EDITION

America Firsthand

VOLUME ONE

Readings from Settlement to Reconstruction

Anthony Marcus
*John Jay College of Criminal Justice of
the City University of New York*

John M. Giggie
University of Alabama

David Burner
*Late of the State University of
New York at Stony Brook*

bedford/st.martin's
Macmillan Learning
Boston | New York

For Bedford/St. Martin's

Vice President, Editorial, Macmillan Higher Education Humanities: Edwin Hill
Publisher for History: Michael Rosenberg
Senior Executive Editor for History: William J. Lombardo
Director of Development for History: Jane Knetzger
Developmental Editor: Jennifer Jovin
Production Editor: Louis C. Bruno Jr.
Senior Production Supervisor: Lisa McDowell
Executive Marketing Manager: Sandra McGuire
Copy Editor: Kathleen Smith
Senior Photo Editor: Christine Buese
Photo Researcher: Bruce Carson
Permissions Managers: Jennifer MacMillan and Kalina Ingham
Text Permissions Editor: Eve Lehmann
Senior Art Director: Anna Palchik
Cover Design: John Callahan
Cover Photo: Library of Congress, LC-DIG-cwpb-01666
Composition: Achorn International, Inc.
Printing and Binding: RR Donnelley and Sons

For information, write: Bedford/St. Martin's, 75 Arlington Street, Boston, MA 02116
  (617-399-4000)

ISBN 978-1-319-02966-1

Acknowledgments

Preface

From its inception, *America Firsthand* has proved to be a favorite among students and instructors alike. Its unique collection of personal views of how Americans lived, witnessed, and made history has resonated with students, while its breadth of coverage and blend of fresh and familiar primary sources have been welcomed by instructors. As a tool for student learning, *America Firsthand* is more vital today than ever before. For while the Internet and the ongoing digitization of the humanities have revolutionized access to historical documents, they have created fresh problems of quality, credibility, and contextualization. Instructors now have access to an unprecedented number of documents online, but many find selecting the most teachable sources to be a frustrating and time-consuming endeavor. Students surfing the Web can easily and quickly come across a series of "hits" on any given topic, but it is not so easy for students to judge the reliability of these sites, assess the accuracy of their information, and detect bias and point of view. Reading primary sources gathered on the Web, students lack the tools to test their veracity, question the perspective of the authors, and situate documents in their proper historical milieu. *America Firsthand* meets these challenges because it provides teachable and engaging documents that instructors can rely on, presented within an organization and pedagogy designed to help students develop their skills of historical analysis and draw their own conclusions.

We aim to offer students a broad array of carefully vetted documents and introduce them to the core skills of the historical profession—skills useful for students who choose a wide range of majors and careers. Our goal for instructors is to offer a dependable resource that fits easily into a range of classroom activities and teaching styles and in a format that guarantees students will succeed. We have merged documents from earlier editions with a robust collection of new ones to create a type of laboratory wherein students and professors alike can examine slices of the past, connect them to their cultural settings, and test how they affirm or challenge the mores and values of their day. When studied collectively, the documents arranged in *America Firsthand* reveal patterns of continuity and change throughout United States history and, when used in conjunction with the supporting pedagogical apparatus, evoke habits of inquiry and critical reflection that lie at the heart of historical analysis.

NEW AND ENDURING FEATURES IN THIS EDITION

This tenth edition continues *America Firsthand*'s emphasis on individuals making and living history, adding newly uncovered and rediscovered selections with more of the voices and topics that reviewers have asked for and that reflect enduring and new themes and topics that American history instructors teach today. We have added more on early nineteenth-century religion and gender, opposition to slavery, the Korean War, sexism in the workplace, and the intersection of race and the criminal justice system. With twenty percent new selections, the tenth edition supplies a rich diversity of perspectives for students to explore. In Volume One, students meet William Strachey, an Englishman who was shipwrecked on Bermuda on his journey from England to Virginia in 1609. They also hear from Major John Norton about his command experience in the War of 1812; they read two women's reflections on the consequences of following their religious faiths; they view contemporary sketches and cartoons portraying controversial issues such as the domestic slave trade and women's rights; they see the Civil War's toll on the American landscape; and they consider one Northerner's observations of his fellow countrymen at the end of the war. Among the new selections in Volume Two, students read the testimony of a craftsman who observed the ways in which industrialization had reduced the quality of manufactured products. They also learn about the fight against the "white slave trade," a thinly veiled attempt to keep white women away from foreign-born men; they discover how new technologies like helicopters and antibiotics enabled Mobile Army Surgical Hospital (MASH) doctors to save lives in Korea; they read a female scientist's account of inequality and discrimination in academia in the 1960s; they witness the destruction of the Berlin Wall that signaled the beginning of the end of the Cold War around the world; and they read about an African American man's experience of "walking while black" in America in the early twenty-first century.

The tenth edition retains the popular **Points of View** part-opening features that juxtapose readings on a specific event or topic, providing students with contrasting perspectives from the past. Critical thinking questions at the close of each Points of View set help students sift through the evidence, make connections, and analyze the readings. The tenth edition includes two new Points of View: one on the Great Depression, which combines letters to the Roosevelts with an image of Americans seeking food relief and Morey Skaret's account of his homelessness as a teenager in the 1930s; and one on the public debate surrounding Somali immigration to Lewiston, Maine, in the early 2000s that originally appeared in the seventh edition of *America Firsthand*.

This edition features more **stand-alone visual documents**, sources that are treated the same as the textual documents, with headnotes and questions to help students interpret these images as evidence. For example, Volume One gives students the opportunity to savor the rough-

and-tumble life of a gold miner through a period daguerreotype and analyze a Mathew Brady photo of a soldier in the trenches, and Volume Two features photographs of a Woolworth's sit-in and a gay rights demonstration in the 1960s as well as a photograph of a Guantanamo Bay detainee.

As in previous editions, carefully written **headnotes** preceding the selections prepare students for each reading and help to locate personalities in their times and places. **Questions to Consider** following the headnotes offer students points on which to reflect when reading and encourage in-depth analysis of the evidence.

To equip students with the tools for working with all the sources—visual as well as textual—in this collection, we have updated the **Introduction: Using Sources to Study the Past**. This edition also features checklists for analyzing written and visual sources on the inside of the back cover.

This revision of *America Firsthand* has afforded us a wonderful opportunity to rethink core ideas about American history and how to present them to our students. It has also strengthened our conviction that, in the current technological age, *America Firsthand* is an essential instrument aiding students and instructors alike to work through judiciously selected and annotated documents with the overall goal of improving the teaching and learning of history. Indeed, we hope that this edition will provide a rewarding intellectual space for students, one in which they can develop a personal interest in firsthand sources to deepen their own historical knowledge and ultimately bring it to bear in the classroom and in the world beyond.

ACKNOWLEDGMENTS

We would like to thank all the instructors who graciously provided helpful and constructive comments for improving *America Firsthand*: George Cooper, Lone Star College–Montgomery; Petra DeWitt, Missouri University of Science and Technology; Thomas Anthony Greene, Elmhurst College; Vance Kincade, Arcadia University; Ann K. Lupo, SUNY Buffalo State College; Philip M. Montesano, City College of San Francisco; Stanley Rose, Nashville State Community College; Michael Sokolow, Kingsborough Community College, CUNY; Paul Swendson, El Camino College; Sharon Vriend-Robinette, Davenport University; and Valdenia C. Winn, Kansas City Kansas Community College.

We are also grateful to the members of the Bedford/St. Martin's staff and their associates who have made this edition of *America Firsthand* the best that it can be. Thanks to photo researcher Bruce Carson for implementation of the book's visual program; to John Callahan for creating the wonderful new book covers; to Kalina Ingham for expertly coordinating the text permissions; and to Louis Bruno for turning the final manuscript into a book. We also thank Michael Rosenberg and William

Lombardo for their support, and Jane Knetzger, who oversaw editorial development. Finally, Jennifer Jovin deserves far more than a simple line of thanks for her leadership and guidance in all stages of our work together. Her thoughtful advice, punchy prose, and superb editorial eye improved every aspect of *American Firsthand*.

Anthony Marcus
John M. Giggie

Contents

Preface v

Introduction: Using Sources to Study the Past xvii

PART ONE
Indians and Europeans:
New World Encounters 1

POINTS OF VIEW

Contact and Conquest (1502–1521)

1. HERNANDO CORTÉS, Dispatches of the Conquest from the New World 3

   In a letter to King Charles V of Spain, Hernando Cortés recounts his recent conquest of Mexico.

2. A Nahua Account of the Conquest of Mexico 7

   An anonymous Nahua account of the conquest of Mexico describes the Spanish conquest and suggests possible reasons for the native people's defeat.

   FOR CRITICAL THINKING 12

3. BARTOLOMÉ DE LAS CASAS, Destruction of the Indies 13

   The Dominican friar Bartolomé de Las Casas describes the horrors of the Spanish conquest in a report that is often referred to as the "Black Legend."

4. JOHN SMITH, Description of Virginia 18

   Captain John Smith describes Virginia and the Powhatan Indians he encountered at Jamestown in 1607.

5. WILLIAM STRACHEY, Travel to the New World   21
    *An early settler of Jamestown recounts his harrowing trans-Atlantic voyage,
    including shipwrecking on the Bermuda Islands.*

6. FATHER PAUL LE JEUNE, Encounter with the Indians   28
    *The French Jesuit missionary Father Paul Le Jeune reports from Quebec in 1634,
    where he lived among North American Indians.*

7. PEDRO NARANJO AND JOSEPHE, Testimony of Pueblo Indians   34
    *Pedro Naranjo of the Queres Nation and Josephe, a Spanish-speaking Indian,
    explain why they drove invaders from their villages in the Pueblo Revolt of
    1680.*

8. New World Images   40
    European artists convey differing perspectives on Native Americans.

PART TWO
The Colonial Experience:
A Rapidly Changing Society   45

POINTS OF VIEW
Captured by Indians in Colonial America

9. MARY ROWLANDSON, Prisoner of War   47
    *Mary Rowlandson describes her captivity and experiences with the
    Wampanoag during King Philip's War.*

10. MARY JEMISON, Captivity in a Different Light   54
    *Mary Jemison, who was taken by the Seneca as a child and chose to stay
    with them, presents a contrasting view of the Native Americans.*

    FOR CRITICAL THINKING   63

11. OLAUDAH EQUIANO, The African Slave Trade   63
    *Olaudah Equiano, an Ibo prince supposedly kidnapped in the early 1760s,
    gives an eyewitness account of the African slave trade.*

12. GOTTLIEB MITTELBERGER, On the Misfortune of Indentured
    Servants   68
    *A young German recounts his arrival in Pennsylvania in 1750 and his sale
    as an indentured servant.*

13. Eliza Lucas Pinckney, Daughter, Wife, Mother, and Planter   72
Eliza Lucas Pinckney documents her experiences as the manager of her family's estates in her mid-eighteenth-century letterbook.

14. Benjamin Franklin, Defending Colonial Activities before Parliament   80
Benjamin Franklin explains colonial opposition to the Stamp Act in 1766.

PART THREE
Resistance and Revolution: Struggling for Liberty   87

POINTS OF VIEW
The Boston Massacre (1770)

15. Thomas Preston, A British Officer's Description   88
A British officer stationed in Boston before the American Revolution recalls why his soldiers fired on Americans.

16. George Robert Twelves Hewes, John Tudor, and the *Boston Gazette and Country Journal*, Colonial Accounts   92
A patriot shoemaker, a Boston merchant, and the Boston Gazette and Country Journal *relate this bloody event from the colonists' perspective.*

FOR CRITICAL THINKING   99

17. Patriot and Loyalist Propaganda   100
Examples of British and American visual propaganda illuminates the intensifying strains and lingering sympathies between Great Britain and its North American colonies prior to the outbreak of war.

18. Joseph Plumb Martin, A Soldier's View of the Revolutionary War   104
Joseph Plumb Martin, who joined the Revolutionary Army before his sixteenth birthday, writes about life as a common soldier.

19. Boston King, Choosing Sides   111
A South Carolina slave escapes to enlist in the British Army and is rewarded with freedom in Canada in 1783.

20. CATHERINE VAN CORTLANDT, Secret Correspondence of a Loyalist
     Wife   116
     *Catherine Van Cortlandt sends letters to her Tory husband behind British
     lines in 1776 and 1777.*

21. ABIGAIL ADAMS, Republican Motherhood   120
     *Abigail Adams dispenses love, wisdom, and advice in letters to her husband
     and son John Quincy Adams.*

22. GEORGE RICHARDS MINOT, Shays's Rebellion: Prelude to the
     Constitution   125
     Boston lawyer George Richards Minot describes Shays's Rebellion of 1786–1787.

PART FOUR
Defining America:
The Expanding Nation   133

POINTS OF VIEW
Religion in the New Nation (1770–1830)

23. JAMES MCGREADY, The Great Revival of 1800   135
     A passionate evangelical minister recounts camp meeting revivals in Kentucky.

24. RICHARD ALLEN, Early Steps toward Freedom   139
     *African American minister Richard Allen recalls his early struggles in the
     late eighteenth century to worship freely and to hasten slavery's demise.*

     FOR CRITICAL THINKING   142

25. MAJOR JOHN NORTON (TEYONINHOK ARAWEN), A Native American
     Commander in the War of 1812   143
     A Scots-Iroquois chief supports the British Army in the War of 1812.

26. MERIWETHER LEWIS AND WILLIAM CLARK, Crossing the Continent   150
     *Meriwether Lewis and William Clark chronicle their experiences with canoe
     accidents, native peoples, and the Rocky Mountains during their expedition
     to the American Northwest from 1804 to 1806.*

27. THOMAS SWANN WOODCOCK, The Erie Canal: Providing Passage for a
     Growing Nation   157
     *A recent English immigrant describes his trip along the Erie Canal in 1836
     and offers glimpses of changes afoot in American culture and commerce.*

28. John Ross, The Trail of Tears   162

John Ross, of mixed Cherokee and white ancestry, protests efforts by President Andrew Jackson and Congress to remove his tribe from Georgia to Oklahoma Territory in the 1830s.

29. Priscilla Merriman Evans, Pulling a Handcart to the Mormon Zion   168

An emigrant woman arrives in Salt Lake City, Utah, in 1856, after walking one thousand miles from Iowa City, Iowa.

30. Guadalupe Vallejo et al., Life in California before the Gold Discovery   174

Aging Californios *remember their lives in California before the 1846 "Bear Flag Revolt" and the 1849 gold rush brought thousands of Anglo settlers to the region.*

31. Daguerreotype by Joseph B. Starkweather, Miners during the California Gold Rush   180

Joseph B. Starkweather's photograph from 1852 provides a glimpse of the lives of Chinese and Anglo miners in the California gold fields.

PART FIVE
Reimagining Family, Community, and Society:
An Age of Reform   183

POINTS OF VIEW
The Prison Reform Movement in the Early Republic

32. Charles Dickens, Philadelphia and Its Solitary Prison   184

English novelist Charles Dickens tours the recently constructed Eastern State Penitentiary and critically assesses the prison's operations in this 1842 account.

33. Frederick Marryat, A Different View of Solitary Confinement   190

Englishman Frederick Marryat visits the Eastern State Penitentiary in 1837 and evaluates the institution's positive and negative aspects.

FOR CRITICAL THINKING   193

34. Harriet Hanson Robinson, The Lowell Textile Workers   194

Harriet Hanson Robinson, who toiled in the Lowell, Massachusetts, mills between 1834 and 1848, captures the harsh experience of female textile workers in this account written later in her life.

35. Rebecca Cox Jackson, Religion and the Power to Challenge Society 200

A free black woman from Philadelphia experiences a series of spiritual visions that lead her to leave her husband, preach against the will of her family and friends, and endure death threats from men angered by her actions.

36. Harriet Jacobs, The Life of a Female Slave 204

Writing under a pseudonym, Harriet Jacobs tells the story of her sexual exploitation under slavery beginning at the age of fifteen.

37. Hammatt Billings, The Auction Sale 211

A leading sketch artist of the nineteenth century pens a portrait of the domestic slave trade.

38. Mary Lois Walker, Marriage and Mormonism 212

After losing her husband at a young age, a young Mormon woman ponders her new fate as a member of a plural marriage.

39. Elizabeth Cady Stanton, Pioneering Women's Rights 216

Elizabeth Cady Stanton remembers the 1848 Seneca Falls Convention and its famous "Declaration of Sentiments."

40. John Leech, Bloomerism 223

In a commentary on the expanding social movement for woman's rights in America and Britain, cartoonist John Leech satirizes the new fashion of suffragists.

PART SIX
The Growing Sectional Controversy: Slavery and Its Discontents 227

POINTS OF VIEW
Nat Turner's Rebellion (1831)

41. Nat Turner, A Slave Insurrection 228

Nat Turner confesses to leading a slave uprising in Southampton County, Virginia, where at least fifty whites were killed.

42. William Lloyd Garrison, Who Is to Blame? 235

Abolitionist William Lloyd Garrison, editor of the Liberator, *analyzes the reasons for and the responses to Nat Turner's slave insurrection.*

43. James Henry Hammond, Defending Slavery 238

Proslavery politician James Henry Hammond, in an 1844 letter, sheds light on why many white Americans championed slavery and denounced abolitionists.

FOR CRITICAL THINKING 242

44. DAVID WALKER, An Appeal for Revolution   242

   A free black man living in Boston warns of the terrible consequences if
   America does not repent for its sin of slavery and emancipate its bonds
   people immediately.

45. FREDERICK LAW OLMSTED, A Northern View of the Slave
   States   247

   The father of landscape architecture and future designer of Central Park
   describes his visit to the slave states and comments on racial tensions
   and racism.

46. HENRY "BOX" BROWN, A Family Torn Apart by Slavery   251

   A respected member of Richmond, Virginia's slave community, Henry "Box"
   Brown describes how an unscrupulous master sold away Brown's wife and
   children in 1849.

47. Visualizing the Peculiar Institution   257

   Period photographs offer glimpses of slaves' experiences.

48. OSBORNE P. ANDERSON, An African American at Harpers Ferry   260

   A participant in John Brown's raid on the federal arsenal at Harpers Ferry,
   African American Osborne Anderson gives his views on the failed campaign
   and critiques its leader.

49. CARL SCHURZ, Free Labor, Free Men   270

   Antislavery activist Carl Schurz, in an 1860 speech, stresses that the slavery
   system threatens the success of "free labor."

PART SEVEN
Civil War and Reconstruction:
The Price of War   275

POINTS OF VIEW
The Gathering Storm (1860)

50. ROBERT TOOMBS, Immediate Secession   276

   Georgia slavery supporter and politician Robert Toombs, in a speech before
   the state legislature in November 1860, presses his home state to sever ties
   with the Union.

51. ALEXANDER H. STEPHENS, A Course of Moderation   282

   Alexander Stephens challenges Toombs by arguing that Georgia lawmakers
   should proceed with extreme caution and restraint on the question of secession.

FOR CRITICAL THINKING   288

52.   Ellen Leonard, Three Days of Terror: The New York City
      Draft Riots   288
      *Ellen Leonard describes getting caught up in the violence of the draft riots
      of 1863 during a visit to family in New York City.*

53.   Samuel and Rachel Cormany, The Battle of Gettysburg:
      On the Field and at Home   296
      *A young couple with a new baby record their hopes and fears on Civil War
      battle and home fronts in 1863.*

54.   Black Union Soldiers, Fighting for the Union   305
      *African American soldiers express their concerns and hopes in letters to
      the press recounting their experience of fighting for the North.*

55.   Henry William Ravenel, A Slave Owner's Journal at the
      End of the War   312
      *A Southern slaveholder describes the effects of emancipation in South Carolina
      after Lee's surrender at Appomattox in 1865.*

56.   George Templeton Strong, A Northerner's View of the
      Confederacy's End   319
      *A famous New York socialite, lawyer, and leader of the civilian relief effort
      for the Union Army recounts popular northern opinion of the South as the
      Civil War comes to a close and Lincoln is assassinated.*

57.   George N. Barnard and Mathew Brady, The Aftermath of the
      Civil War   323
      *Two photographers capture some of the devastation wrought by Sherman's
      march in Charleston and by Grant's defeat of the Confederate Army at Fort
      Mahone in April 1865.*

Introduction: Using Sources to Study the Past

The study of history offers us a way of knowing who we are, where we have come from, and where we are headed. Perhaps because we live in the present, it is sometimes easy to assume that people of the past were basically like us, only with different clothing and hairstyles, as in many Hollywood history movies in which the characters are also made appealing to contemporary audiences by evincing modern goals and desires. In such "historical dramas" people fight for their nation, even if neither it nor the very idea of a nation yet exists; they make great sacrifices for romantic love, even if this concept has not yet been invented; they struggle to protect the innocence of children, even if there is not yet a concept of childhood; and they demand personal freedom in societies where the greatest goal is to have a defined place in the social order. Such usage of dramatic license to place modern motivations and values into the past is called historical anachronism, and it usually leads to good movies but a rather poor understanding of how our ancestors made decisions and took actions. History is a systematic attempt to study the differences and similarities between the past and the present, in order to understand how we got from there to here and how we may craft our future.

How, then, do we, as students of history or historians, approach the study of our past? A first step is to pose a research question about the past. For example:

- What were social relations like between African Americans and white Americans in colonial Virginia?

Asking this type of question is important because so much of our vision of race relations before the civil rights movement of the 1940s–1960s is built on visions of the hardened institutionalized slavery of the mid-nineteenth century and the Jim Crow segregation that followed. Some historians, among them Edmund Morgan, have argued that relations between whites and blacks were more fluid and equal in the first century of the British colonization of North America, when slavery was not hereditary or restricted to African Americans, who, if they were male, could still testify in court, cohabit with white women, buy their own freedom, and even own slaves—all provided that they had converted to Christianity.

Knowing something about how the nineteenth-century horrors of industrial-scale slavery, laws against literacy among slaves, and finally segregation emerged from an earlier time can help us understand the nature of race relations in America and tell us something about the potential for changes in the future. Whatever our motivation for posing questions such as the one above, the first step in trying to address them is to find relevant sources that may provide answers. These come in two broad categories: *primary sources* and *secondary sources*.

PRIMARY SOURCES

Primary sources are documents and artifacts directly produced by the individuals and groups that participated in or witnessed the situation, event, or topic being researched. They are a lot like the evidence and testimony that lawyers use in a courtroom to present different versions of what happened and why. Often answering the "why" question is just as important as figuring out what actually happened. For example, if it is known that a defendant shoved his brother off a roof to his death, it matters to the judge, jury, and district attorney whether the action was self-defense or an accident or occurred in the heat of anger. If the court can establish that the killer had invited his brother to the roof two days after learning that the brother had named him as sole beneficiary in a life insurance policy, the results are likely to be very different than if the court discovers that the dead brother had set up the rooftop meeting and that neither sibling stood to benefit from the death.

All the sources included in *America Firsthand* are primary sources, but the foregoing is only one example of what is possible in primary source research. Indeed, the types of primary sources are as limitless as the imagination of the historian. Human records of all kinds leave useful information for scholars and students. From a drawing done by an eighteenth-century child showing what was taught to young elites, to DNA evidence suggesting that Thomas Jefferson had children with his African American slave Sally Hemings, to a colonial New York candlestick holder made by a Portuguese Jew with designs borrowed from Native Americans, to oral history interviews—every primary source leaves behind clues for the historian. The problem is often sorting out which clues are useful and which are not. This may change depending on what questions are being asked and what techniques are available at the time of research.

Not only do science and technology make many old primary sources newly important; social and political change also opens up new possibilities for asking different *kinds* of questions of the evidence. Consider, for example, that Thomas Jefferson's DNA had little value before modern advances in genetics—but also consider that until the study of slavery and black–white sexual relations had advanced to a certain stage of intellectual development, few historians would have dared to ask questions about Jefferson's potential fathering of children by a slave woman. Similarly, historian James Lockhart probably never would have crossed the globe to bring together Nahua descriptions of the conquest of Mexico (Volume One, Document 2) if, when Lockhart was in school in the 1960s and 1970s, there had not been an indigenous civil rights movement that drew attention to the native point of view. And certainly the political growth of the women's movement and feminism in the last decades of the twentieth century fueled scholarly and popular interest in the diaries of women like Rebecca Cox Jackson (Volume One, Document 35), who found in religion a power to slip social strictures of race and gender in the early 1800s. Sometimes, forgotten documents, like Manuel Gamio's interviews with Mexican migrants in the Midwest in the 1920s (Volume Two, Document 36), become newly relevant and can be read differently in the face of contemporary debates around immigration (Volume Two, Documents 55 and 56) and the politics of ethnicity (Volume Two, Document 63). The changes of the present prompt historians to revisit old sources with new perspectives and to search for undiscovered new sources on old questions.

With respect to our question about the social relations between African Americans and white Americans in colonial Virginia, the relationship between Sally Hemings and Thomas Jefferson might tell us something important. Although Hemings was born at the end of the colonial period, the world that she and Jefferson inhabited may have been as much like the seventeenth century as the nineteenth century. Now that, thanks to DNA testing, it is widely accepted that Hemings bore Jefferson a child, much of the controversy revolves around how equal, unequal, voluntary, or coerced the sexual relationship was between an aged former president and the teenage girl who was his legal property. For some analysts, the inequality of race and age and the fact that Jefferson owned Hemings are decisive proof that it was a highly coercive relationship. For others, who argue that men and women of every race had legally unequal marriages at that time, the fact that Hemings signed legal documents for Jefferson, traveled with him, and chose to remain with him—even though they lived for a time in France, where she was legally a free woman and may have had offers of marriage from eligible Frenchmen—is proof that this relationship was somewhat mutual.

What kind of evidence do you think would show that this relationship was coercive and unequal? What kind of evidence would show that Hemings was her own woman? Does the fact that she was the half-sister of Jefferson's deceased wife say anything about the mixing of races among colonial American elites? For some commentators, "the bottom line" is that Jefferson never married Hemings and could not do so, by law. However, the existence of such key primary sources as laws allows a variety of interpretations. The mere fact that courts started to pass miscegenation laws (laws addressing marriage between people of different racial backgrounds) in the eighteenth century is a good sign that (a) there were such interracial marriages, (b) blacks and whites were increasingly being allocated different positions in society, and (c) inequality was becoming increasingly fixed. The historian may find clues in primary sources as complex as philosophic essays and autobiographies and as simple as shopping lists, photographs, and Hemings's signature on Jefferson household payments for animal feed.

SECONDARY SOURCES

Secondary sources are books and articles in scholarly journals that bring together collections of evidence in order to interpret and build arguments around what happened. They offer answers to research questions and provide stories that link together all the evidence into coherent and interesting narratives. Secondary sources provide background about a particular subject, include important references to primary sources through footnotes and bibliographies, and raise questions, topics, and debates that form the foundation for additional research. To carry the courtroom analogy a step further, it is the lawyer's job, like the historian's, to take the evidence (primary sources) and build a case (secondary source). It is impossible to build a case, however, unless you have some idea of what the other lawyers are saying, what their evidence is, and how they plan to structure their case.

This is why courts have a "discovery" process that requires lawyers to share their evidence with opposing counsel before trial. And it is why history teachers assign students to read secondary sources before giving them the difficult task of going through birth records or ship manifests looking for fresh evidence, trying to rearrange the old evidence, or combining the two to create a new understanding of what happened. The exciting part of history is coming up with your own questions about the past and finding answers that create knowledge and spark new ways of understanding the past, the present, and even the future.

APPROACHING SOURCES CRITICALLY

In any courtroom trial, opposing lawyers try many ways to poke holes in each other's argument, but at the end of the day, the jury must decide what evidence is most relevant, whose testimony is most reliable, and which argument is most convincing. The same standard applies to historical sources. In investigating whether slavery was economically inefficient, do we trust the tax office's records or the plantation owner's financial records, his complaints to his congressman about how much tax he was paying, or his boastful letters to his sister about cheating on his taxes? Is there a good reason why some or all of these sources may be lying, stretching the truth, or simply misleading? Who is a more reliable witness to slavery, the slave or the slaveholder; the Northern abolitionist or the Southern politician; the poor white farmer who hates the slave-holders or the English gentleman visiting his Georgia cousins? Every person has a unique point of view, set of beliefs, and reason for giving testimony; and we must critically analyze and evaluate everything—and assume nothing.

These factors constitute the bias of the source. Because all sources are biased, it is important to develop a set of questions for interrogating documentary sources. Some useful questions to ask are:

- What is the historical context for the document? When was it produced, and how does it relate to important events of the pe-riod? (Note: The headnotes for the sources included in this book provide you with background information.)
- Who is the author? What can you tell about that person's back-ground, social status, and so on?
- What can you infer about the purpose of the document? Who was its intended audience?
- What do the document's style and tone tell you about the au-thor's purpose?
- What main points does the author seek to communicate or express?
- What does the document suggest about the author's point of view and biases? Consider whether the author misunderstood what he or she was relating or had reason to falsify the account.
- What can you infer about how typical for the period the views expressed in the document are?

Additional thought must be given to visual sources. When working with visual material, ask the following questions along with those above:

- How is the image framed or drawn? What does the image in-clude? What might the creator of the work have excluded? What do the creator's decisions regarding the content tell you about the event, person, or place you are analyzing?
- What medium (drawing, painting, photograph, or other) did the creator employ? What constraints did the medium impose on the creator? For example, photographic technology in the nineteenth century was very rudimentary and involved large, bulky cameras with very slow shutter speeds. This technological context tells us something about why people often posed stiffly and without a smile for early photographs. Likewise, although there are nu-merous Civil War battlefront photographs, most were posed or

created after battles because the camera's shutter speeds did not allow for action photography.

- Do you know if the work was expensive or cheap to produce? Where was the work intended to be displayed—in a museum, a courthouse, a private home, a grocery store, or elsewhere? What might these considerations suggest about the event, person, or place you are analyzing?

Historians strive not to use the standards of the present to make judgments about the past. When working with both primary and secondary sources, the question of historical context must always be considered. For example, the decision to drop atomic bombs on Hiroshima and Nagasaki is often said to have been made without the same taboos, sociopolitical fears, and ecological concerns that are today tied to nuclear energy and nuclear weapons. It was largely assumed, during the entire process of developing atomic weapons, that they would be used. At the time, there was little serious discussion of not using this new war technology to hasten the end of the conflict with Japan, beyond a few last-minute letters and petitions from the very atomic scientists who had spent years and vast sums of money working to develop these new tools of war. This was the historical context in which the decision to drop the atomic bomb was made. To bring in more modern concerns, such as nuclear proliferation and environmental impact, when analyzing evidence from the period would be moving beyond this decision's historical context.

In this example, one should be wary, however, of reducing history to "the way people viewed things back then"—and, consequently, wary of absolving those who made the bomb, gave the orders, and carried out the mission. It is difficult enough to figure out today's social contexts and popular world views; the past is even more challenging to sort out. Many respected and influential people during the pre–World War II years had argued passionately against the dropping of bombs (then a relatively new technology, originating in the late nineteenth century) on civilians. They claimed that such a drastic measure was ethically unforgivable and not a particularly useful or effective practice; they argued that bombing might in fact strengthen a civilian population's will to fight rather than soften up the people for conquest. These commentators might have had no true understanding of the potential devastation of atomic weapons, but in the context of the times in which they lived, they certainly would not have viewed the bombing of Hiroshima and Nagasaki as acceptable acts of warfare. Consider, too, that several international conventions attempted to eliminate the bombing of civilians from modern warfare, and thousands of journals, letters, autobiographies, movies, novels, and popular songs suggest that throughout the twentieth century, many politicians, generals, and bomber pilots were uncomfortable with this peculiarly abstract and violent form of warfare against civilians.

There are therefore no easy answers to the question, "How did people view things back then?" Like the present, the past contains a multitude of contested and contradictory norms, values, and perspectives held by a variety of people with different understandings of the context in which individuals and groups took action and made history. These are the most complicated aspects of historical inquiry and interpretation—staking evidence, finding the right context, and telling a story about the similarities and differences between past and present. Returning to the first question in this introduction, we cannot know whether blacks and whites were once equal in seventeenth-century Virginia unless we know something about the values, rules, and social expectations of that time.

What did it mean to be equal? If being a member of the Church of England was the key marker of belonging in seventeenth-century Virginia, it may be that African converts to Christianity had more rights than Irish, Jews, and Native Americans. Such a situation would suggest that a fully formed code of caste/color inequality had not yet developed, and we might look for clues later in colonial history.

Because all sources—both firsthand primary accounts and secondary works by historians—have unique points of view and reasons for presenting things as they do, it is essential to question and to critically analyze everything. Read all historical documents with skepticism; take into account the "fit" of their authors' perspectives into the context of the time, the voices of their contemporaries, and the way the authors might have imagined themselves being remembered historically. This last consideration, people's own sense of how they make history, has always been important. But it may have become even more so in the contemporary world that artist Andy Warhol characterized as providing everybody with "fifteen minutes of fame." Ultimately, the craft of history is as subjective as a trial verdict.

Whether inquiring into the historical past or probing the unfolding of a crime, we can never know for certain what actually happened. Whether dealing with historical sources or with criminal evidence, we can establish a fair trial, one with relevant evidence, good witnesses, sound procedures, and brilliant insights. This process will get us closer to the truth—but never fully beyond a shadow of a doubt. Fortunately, practitioners and students of history have the ability to reopen any "case" at any time and to work to overturn a "verdict" that does not sit right. It is just a matter of getting in there, studying or restudying the sources, and developing new interpretations that will be subject to future analysis and research—and so the process of doing history continues.

PART ONE

Indians and Europeans
New World Encounters

The contact between two worlds—one of them "new," the other "old"—permanently changed the way people on both sides of the Atlantic Ocean lived and thought about themselves. For Europeans, Christopher Columbus's so-called discovery of the New World afforded opportunities to amass fortunes in precious metals, exotic spices, and new intoxicants. More important, the emerging European nations of the North Atlantic would eventually reconfigure the entire world, shifting its center away from the great civilizations of the East toward a new Atlantic basin economy. There, global empires would be built through the discovery of silver and the exploitation of land and labor to produce high-yield New World crops such as maize, manioc, and potatoes. This age of discovery, exploration, and conquest would touch off a scientific and commercial revolution, making Western Europe the world's cosmopolitan center by attracting new ideas, technologies, and forms of wealth and redistributing them across the globe.

However, Columbus's discovery did not affect all of Europe in the same way. For the Spanish and Portuguese who arrived in the New World first, the wealth of the great civilizations of Mexico and South America had by the seventeenth century distorted their economies by enriching and empowering an unproductive agrarian nobility at the expense of more productive middle classes in the towns. When the commoners left in search of their own New World opportunities, Spain suffered economic decline.

For the English, French, and Dutch who came later and settled in the poorer and less densely populated North America, there were no quick riches. Their New World colonies were difficult to build; costly to defend; and required large amounts of planning, coordination, and logistical support. Moreover, incentives were needed to convince people to cross the ocean and settle in the new land. The Dutch established New Amsterdam, the capital of their

1

colony of New Netherland, on the site of present-day New York City and built a scattering of sparsely populated commercial settlements along the Hudson River and the mid-Atlantic coast from Maryland to Rhode Island.

The British, whose commitment to settling North America was greater, used their military to secure a fledgling agricultural settlement in Jamestown, Virginia, where Captain John Smith had his famous encounter with Pocahontas and her father, Powhatan. Other English citizens followed Smith, and some, like William Strachey, barely survived crossing the Atlantic. Strachey and his fellow passengers were shipwrecked on the Bermuda islands and remained there for nearly a year before making their way to Jamestown. As the British home market grew, so too did Great Britain's New World colonies. There were no great precious metal discoveries or massive pools of native labor in the British settlements. Instead, the British imported laborers, typically in the form of British prisoners and Irish and African forced labor. The British would eventually cover the entire Atlantic coast with the permanent settlements that made up the thirteen colonies that founded the United States.

The French, whose colonies were owned by the Crown but built on a mix of religious missionary work and mercantile enterprises—especially the fur trade—claimed vast territories throughout the North American interior. However, they established a significant and enduring presence only in Louisiana, the Caribbean, and Eastern Canada where Father Paul Le Jeune described his struggle to understand and work with Native Americans.

For the native peoples of what would come to be called the Americas, European contact and subsequent settlement proved catastrophic. Settlers, soldiers, and missionaries, along with mostly enslaved Africans, introduced new plants, animals, and technologies that disrupted and radically reoriented life in the New World. The brutal tactics of European conquest and the spread of Old World diseases such as smallpox, for which Native Americans lacked immunity, led to the death of some thirty million native people within fifty years of European contact.

Many Europeans struggled with the human dimensions of the catastrophe that had been unleashed. Dominican friar Bartolomé de Las Casas's report of the Spanish conquest of the West Indies captures the horrors of that early colonial encounter between Europeans and Native Americans. This pattern of brutality, violence, and subjugation of indigenous peoples would be repeated many times during the following five centuries. Yet as the Spanish *conquistador* Hernando Cortés shows in his tale of the conquest of Mexico, the campaign was one not merely of violence and enslavement but also of politics and persuasion. The New World images illustrate some of these conflicting and contradictory views that Europeans held about Native Americans.

Native peoples rarely left a written record of their own perspective on these early encounters. Few were literate, and Europeans were rarely concerned with chronicling the lives of those they were conquering. Pedro Naranjo's and Josephe's testimonies regarding the Pueblo revolt are available only because they were given in a Spanish royal court. The Nahua, who ruled Mexico before the conquest, were unique among native peoples in that they had a well-developed ancient written tradition. During the early days after the conquest, Juan de Zumárraga, the first bishop of New Spain, attempted to destroy the entire body of Nahua manuscripts, usually referred to as codices. Despite his efforts, some codices survived and others were reproduced from memory shortly afterward with the help of Spanish priests who shared Las Casas's indignation at what was occurring. The selection from the Florentine Codex included in this chapter is one of these Nahua texts that shows the native perspective on conquest. Partly on the basis of these codices, many scholars now argue that the early relationships between indigenous peoples and Europeans may have often been more open and mutual than those occurring later in North America, where segregated and unequal societies on both sides brought much bitterness and many prejudices to the encounter.

POINTS OF VIEW
Contact and Conquest (1502–1521)

1

HERNANDO CORTÉS

Dispatches of the Conquest from the New World

The discovery of the Americas by Christopher Columbus set off a speculative economic frenzy in Spain and Portugal. Merchants, military men, and adventurers rushed to equip ships and send soldiers in search of the gold, slaves, and spices promised by this vast new world. Twenty-five years after Columbus's discovery, however, the payoff remained elusive. The Spanish colonies in the New World were little more than a few Caribbean islands with sparse populations of settlers, African slaves, and captive Taino natives, who often died of European diseases for which they had no immunity. It was contact with and conquest of the Aztec empire on the mainland and the creation of New Spain (present-day Mexico and Guatemala) in 1521 that finally brought Europeans and natives some understanding of what they could expect from one another and how the future of this new world might look.

Hernando Cortés, who led the conquest of New Spain, was not unlike many of the adventurers and businessmen who crossed the Atlantic in the first century after

---

Anthony Pagden, ed. and trans., *Hernan Cortés: Letters from Mexico* (New Haven, CT: Yale University Press, 1986), 35–36, 84–85, 88, 105, 106, 132.

Columbus. In 1504, at the age of nineteen, Cortés traveled to Hispaniola (now the Dominican Republic and Haiti) on a convoy of merchant ships. Using his training as a lawyer and family connections, he became the colony notary and received a repartimiento, *a Spanish colonial land grant, which included forced native labor. In 1511, he helped conquer Cuba, becoming clerk of the royal treasury; mayor of Havana; and a wealthy owner of land, Indians, and cattle. In 1517 and 1518, two expeditions to the Yucatán brought back rumors of gold and a great inland empire, and Cortés was asked by colonial authorities to command an exploratory expedition to the mainland.*

When Cortés and his army of 508 soldiers arrived, they found an Aztec empire in deep crisis. Rapid expansion from the center of power at Tenochtitlán, the world's largest city at the time and now present-day Mexico City, had stretched the empire's rigid political structure and low technological development to the breaking point. Unable to fully integrate the vast agricultural hinterlands into the empire, the Aztecs had resorted to increasingly brutal ritualized terror, human sacrifice, and militarization to keep control. The first natives that Cortés and his men encountered at the margins of the empire fought initially but often quickly changed sides, preferring to take their chances with the Spanish invaders.

With the help of Malinche, a native woman who became Cortés's lover, adviser, and interpreter, Cortés and his men swept through town after town, defeating local armies, abolishing human sacrifice and tax collection, and carrying out mass conversions to Christianity. By the time the Spanish finally arrived in Tenochtitlán, Cortés and his mistress were feared and admired as mythical liberators. The conquest required two more years of political maneuvering and bloody battles before culminating in the siege of Tenochtitlán in 1521. Cortés's army, bolstered by as many as 200,000 natives, toppled the Aztec empire and declared the creation of a Christian New Spain.

As word of the conquest filtered back to Cuba, the Spanish royal bureaucracy feared that the upstart Cortés would take all the New World wealth for himself, perhaps even establishing himself as a king. Colonial officials used every political weapon they could find to sabotage Cortés, including officially relieving him of command, organizing mutinies, and seizing all his possessions in Cuba—all to no avail. Realizing that he could trust no one in Havana, and now having great status as a conquistador, *he wrote directly to King Charles V of Spain about the things he had seen and done in the New World. These passages are from the dispatches that Cortés wrote to his king in the heat of conquest.*

QUESTIONS TO CONSIDER

1. Consider Hernando Cortés's possible motivations for writing. In what ways did his audience—the king of Spain—affect Cortés's account of the conquest?
2. Why were Cortés and 508 men able to conquer an empire of millions?
3. Was Cortés a liberator or an oppressor of the natives? Explain.

They [the Aztecs] have a most horrid and abominable custom which truly ought to be punished and which until now we have seen in no other part, and this is that, whenever they wish to ask something of the idols, in order that their plea may find more acceptance, they take many girls and boys and even adults, and in the presence of the idols they open their chests while they are still alive and take out their hearts and entrails and burn them before the idols, offering the smoke as sacrifice. Some of us have seen this, and they say it is the most terrible and frightful thing they have ever witnessed.

This these Indians do so frequently that, as we have been informed, and, in part, have seen from our own experience during the short while we have been here, not one year passes in which they do not kill and sacrifice some fifty persons in each temple; and this is done and held as customary from the island of Cozumel to this land where we now have settled. Your Majesties [the King and Queen of Spain and the Roman Empire] may be most certain that, as this land seems to us to be very large, and to have many temples in it, not one year has passed, as far as we have been able to discover, in which three or four thousand souls have not been sacrificed in this manner. . . .

After we had crossed [a] bridge, Moctezuma[1] came to greet us and with him some two hundred lords, all barefoot and dressed in a different costume, but also very rich in their way and more so than the others. They came in two columns, pressed very close to the walls of the street, which is very wide and beautiful and so straight that you can see from one end to the other. It is two-thirds of a league long and had on both sides very good and big houses, both dwellings and temples.

Moctezuma came down the middle of this street with two chiefs, one on his right hand and the other on his left. One of these was that great chief who had come on a litter to speak with me, and the other was Moctezuma's brother, chief of the city of Yztapalapa, which I had left that day. And they were all dressed alike except that Moctezuma wore sandals whereas the others went barefoot; and they held his arm on either side. When we met I dismounted and stepped forward to embrace him, but the two lords who were with him stopped me with their hands so that I should not touch him; and they likewise all performed the ceremony of kissing the earth. When this was over Moctezuma requested his brother to remain with me and to take me by the arm while he went a little way ahead with the other; and after he had spoken to me all the others in the two columns came and spoke with me, one after another, and then each returned to his column.

When at last I came to speak to Moctezuma himself I took off a necklace of pearls and cut glass that I was wearing and placed it round his neck; after we had walked a little way up the street a servant of his came with two necklaces, wrapped in a cloth, made from red snails' shells, which they hold in great esteem; and from each necklace hung eight shrimps of refined gold almost a span in length. When they had been brought he turned to me and placed them about my neck, and then continued up the street in the manner already described until we reached a very large and beautiful house which had been very well prepared to accommodate us. . . .

Most Invincible Lord, six days having passed since we first entered this great city of Tenochtitlán, during which time I had seen something of it, though little compared with how much there is to see and record, I decided

---

1. **Moctezuma:** Or, Montezuma; ruler of the Aztecs.

from what I had seen that it would benefit Your Royal service and our safety if Moctezuma were in my power and not in complete liberty, in order that he should not retreat from the willingness he showed to serve Your Majesty; but chiefly because we Spaniards are rather obstinate and persistent, and should we annoy him he might, as he is so powerful, obliterate all memory of us. Furthermore, by having him with me, all those other lands which were subject to him would come more swiftly to the recognition and service of Your Majesty, as later happened. I resolved, therefore, to take him and keep him in the quarters where I was, which were very strong. . . .

There are, in all districts of this great city, many temples or houses for their idols. They are all very beautiful buildings, and in the important ones there are priests of their sect who live there permanently; and, in addition to the houses for the idols, they also have very good lodgings. . . .

The most important of these idols, and the ones in whom they have most faith, I had taken from their places and thrown down the steps; and I had those chapels where they were cleaned, for they were full of the blood of sacrifices; and I had images of Our Lady and of other saints put there, which caused Moctezuma and the other natives some sorrow. . . .

Moctezuma, who together with one of his sons and many other chiefs who had been captured previously [and] was still a prisoner, asked to be taken out onto the roof of the fortress where he might speak to the captains of his people and tell them to end the fighting. I had him taken out, and when he reached a breastwork which ran out beyond the fortress, and was about to speak to them, he received a blow on his head from a stone; and the injury was so serious that he died three days later. I told two of the Indians who were captive to carry him out on their shoulders to the people. What they did with him I do not know; only the war did not stop because of it, but grew more fierce and pitiless each day. . . .

We already knew that the Indians in the city [Tenochtitlán] were very scared, and we now learnt from two wretched creatures who had escaped from the city and come to our camp by night that they were dying of hunger and used to come out at night to fish in the canals between the houses, and wandered through the places we had won in search of firewood, and herbs and roots to eat. And because we had already filled in many of the canals, and leveled out many of the dangerous stretches, I resolved to enter the next morning shortly before dawn and do all the harm we could. The brigantines[2] departed before daylight, and I with twelve or fifteen horsemen and some foot soldiers and Indians entered suddenly and stationed several spies who, as soon as it was light, called us from where we lay in ambush, and we fell on a huge number of people. As these were some of the most wretched people and had come in search of food, they were nearly all unarmed, and women and children in the main. We did them so much harm through all the streets in the city that we could reach, that the dead and the prisoners numbered more than eight hundred; the brigantines also took many people and canoes which were out fishing, and the destruction was very great. When the captains and lords of

2. **brigantine:** A small ship, typically with two masts.

the city saw us attack at such an unaccustomed hour, they were as frightened as they had been by the recent ambush, and none of them dared come out and fight; so we returned with much booty and food for our allies. . . .

On leaving my camp, I had commanded Gonzalo de Sandoval to sail the brigantines in between the houses in the other quarter in which the Indians were resisting, so that we should have them surrounded, but not to attack until he saw that we were engaged. In this way they would be surrounded and so hard pressed that they would have no place to move save over the bodies of their dead or along the roof tops. They no longer had nor could find any arrows, javelins or stones with which to attack us; and our allies fighting with us were armed with swords and bucklers, and slaughtered so many of them on land and in the water that more than forty thousand were killed or taken that day. So loud was the wailing of the women and children that there was not one man amongst us whose heart did not bleed at the sound; and indeed we had more trouble in preventing our allies from killing with such cruelty than we had in fighting the enemy. For no race, however savage, has ever practiced such fierce and unnatural cruelty as the natives of these parts. Our allies also took many spoils that day, which we were unable to prevent, as they numbered more than 150,000 and we Spaniards were only some nine hundred. Neither our precautions nor our warnings could stop their looting, though we did all we could. One of the reasons why I had avoided entering the city in force during the past days was the fear that if we attempted to storm them they would throw all they possessed into the water, and, even if they did not, our allies would take all they could find. For this reason I was much afraid that Your Majesty would receive only a small part of the great wealth this city once had, in comparison with all that I once held for Your Highness. Because it was now late, we could no longer endure the stench of the dead bodies that had lain in those streets for many days, which was the most loathsome thing in all the world, we returned to our camps.

2

A Nahua Account of the Conquest of Mexico

*For centuries it had been a well-known part of the "Black Legend" of the horrors of the Spanish conquest that the first archbishop of Mexico, Juan de Zumárraga, collected thousands of Nahua manuscripts and burned them. (*Nahua *is the word for the people and the language of the Aztec empire.) However, some Nahua documents survived the archbishop's fires, and others were re-created through oral histories taken shortly after the conquest by sympathetic Spanish priests and Nahua natives trained*

James Lockhart, ed. and trans., *We People Here: Nahuatl Accounts of the Conquest of Mexico* (Berkeley: University of California Press, 1993), 90–104.

in anthropological and historical skills. These documents, usually known as codices (a codex is a simple form of book), lay unread and unappreciated for centuries in libraries and private collections across Mexico, Europe, and the United States. In the 1960s, a new generation of social and ethnohistorians compiled and published native voices from the conquest. These accounts, translated into English and Spanish, contribute to our understanding of how the two sides understood what happened when people from Europe and the New World first made contact.

The following document is drawn from the Florentine Codex, named for its home in the Laurentian Library in Florence, Italy. Probably the most famous of the Nahua descriptions of the conquest, it was first transcribed from Nahua hieroglyphs by native scholars trained and educated in Latin and Spanish by Fra Bernardino de Sahagún. A Franciscan priest known for his rigorous and respectful study of native custom and history, Sahagún supervised the production of the original bilingual Spanish/Nahua edition in the mid-sixteenth century. The Nahua assistants who translated the hieroglyphs, compiled the oral histories, and searched other sources to write this history remain unknown. Contemporary historians struggle with conflicting accounts, different versions of the same documents, and complex political motivations behind the many views of the conquest.

QUESTIONS TO CONSIDER

1. Some scholars argue that Nahua accounts of the conquest are filled with scapegoats and excuses for the defeat. Which of these can you spot in this document?
2. Does this document contradict or confirm the traditional notion that the Nahua believed the Spanish were gods? Why should it matter to historians whether the Nahua believed this?
3. How might accounts of the conquest written by Tlascalans, a group in the hinterlands who had been conquered by the empire, differ from those of the Tenochca, who were living in the center of the empire in the capital city of Tenochtitlán?

Tenth chapter, where it is said how the Spaniards landed uncontested and came on their way in this direction, and how Moteucçoma[1] left the great palace and went to his personal home.

Then Moteucçoma abandoned his patrimonial home, the great palace, and came back to his personal home.

When at last [the Spaniards] came, when they were coming along and moving this way, a certain person from Cempoallan,[2] whose name was Tlacochcalcatl, whom they had taken when they first came to see the land and

---

1. **Moteucçoma:** Moctezuma or Montezuma, ruler of the Aztecs.
2. **Cempoallan:** Aztec province in what is now Veracruz.

the various altepetl,[3] also came interpreting for them, planning their route, conducting them, showing them the way, leading and guiding them.

And when they reached Tecoac, which is in the land of the Tlaxcalans,[4] where their Otomis[5] lived, the Otomis met them with hostilities and war. But they annihilated the Otomis of Tecoac, who were destroyed completely. They lanced and stabbed them, they shot them with guns, iron bolts, crossbows. Not just a few but a huge number of them were destroyed.

After the great defeat at Tecoac, when the Tlaxcalans heard it and found out about it and it was reported to them, they became limp with fear, they were made faint; fear took hold of them. Then they assembled, and all of them, including the lords and rulers, took counsel among themselves, considering the reports.

They said, "How is it to be with us? Should we face them? For the Otomis are great and valiant warriors, yet they thought nothing of them, they regarded them as nothing; in a very short time, in the blink of an eyelid, they destroyed the people. Now let us just submit to them, let us make friends with them, let us be friends, for something must be done about the common people."

Thereupon the Tlaxcalan rulers went to meet them, taking along food: turkey hens, eggs, white tortillas, fine tortillas. They said to them, "Welcome, our lords." [The Spaniards] answered them back, "Where is your homeland? Where have you come from?" They said, "We are Tlaxcalans. Welcome, you have arrived, you have reached the land of Tlaxcala, which is your home."

(But in olden times it was called Texcallan and the people Texcalans.)

Eleventh chapter, where it is said how the Spaniards reached Tlaxcala, [also] called Texcallan.

[The Tlaxcalans] guided, accompanied, and led them until they brought them to their palace[s] and placed them there. They showed them great honors, they gave them what they needed and attended to them, and then they gave them their daughters.

Then [the Spaniards] asked them, "Where is Mexico?[6] What kind of a place is it? Is it still far?" They answered them, "It's not far now. Perhaps one can get there in three days. It is a very favored place, and [the Mexica] are very strong, great warriors, conquerors, who go about conquering everywhere."

Now before this there had been friction between the Tlaxcalans and the Cholulans.[7] They viewed each other with anger, fury, hate, and disgust; they could come together on nothing. Because of this they put [the Spaniards] up to killing them treacherously.

---

3. **altepetl:** Nahua word for city or town.
4. **Tlaxcalans:** Also, Tlascalans—a large native group that allied with Cortés against the Mexica.
5. **Otomis:** A native group that lived near Tlaxcala.
6. **Mexico:** The Aztec empire.
7. **Cholulans:** A native group that the Spaniards defeated in battle as part of their alli[i] with the Tlaxcalans.

They said to them, "The Cholulans are very evil; they are our enemies. They are as strong as the Mexica, and they are the Mexica's friends."

When the Spaniards heard this, they went to Cholula. The Tlaxcalans and Cempoallans went with them, outfitted for war. When they arrived, there was a general summons and cry that all the noblemen, rulers, subordinate leaders, warriors, and commoners should come, and everyone assembled in the temple courtyard. When they had all come together, [the Spaniards and their friends] blocked the entrances, all of the places where one entered. Thereupon people were stabbed, struck, and killed. No such thing was in the minds of the Cholulans; they did not meet the Spaniards with weapons of war. It just seemed that they were stealthily and treacherously killed, because the Tlaxcalans persuaded [the Spaniards] to do it.

And a report of everything that was happening was given and relayed to Moteucçoma. Some of the messengers would be arriving as others were leaving; they just turned around and ran back. There was no time when they weren't listening, when reports weren't being given. And all the common people went about in a state of excitement; there were frequent disturbances, as if the earth moved and [quaked], as if everything were spinning before one's eyes. People took fright.

And after the dying in Cholula, [the Spaniards] set off on their way to Mexico, coming gathered and bunched, raising dust. Their iron lances and halberds[8] seemed to sparkle, and their iron swords were curved like a stream of water. Their cuirasses[9] and iron helmets seemed to make a clattering sound. Some of them came wearing iron all over, turned into iron beings, gleaming, so that they aroused great fear and were generally seen with fear and dread. Their dogs came in front, coming ahead of them, keeping to the front, panting, with their spittle hanging down.

Twelfth chapter, where it is said how Moteucçoma sent a great nobleman along with many other noblemen to go to meet the Spaniards, and what their gifts of greeting were when they greeted the Captain between Iztactepetl and Popocatepetl.[10]

Thereupon Moteucçoma named and sent the noblemen and a great many other agents of his, with Tzihuacpopocatzin[11] as their leader, to go meet [Cortés] between Popocatepetl and Iztactepetl, at Quauhtechcac. They gave [the Spaniards] golden banners, banners of precious feathers, and golden necklaces.

And when they had given the things to them, they seemed to smile, to rejoice and be very happy. Like monkeys they grabbed the gold. It was as though their hearts were put to rest, brightened, freshened. For gold was what they greatly thirsted for; they were gluttonous for it, starved for it, piggishly wanting it. They came lifting up the golden banners, waving them

---

8. **halberd:** A weapon with an axe and a long spike set on a long pole.
9. **cuirass:** Type of armor.
10. **Iztactepetl and Popocatepetl:** Respectively, the third-highest mountain in Mexico and an active volcano, both visible from Mexico City.
11. **Tzihuacpopocatzin:** An envoy from Moctezuma.

from side to side, showing them to each other. They seemed to babble; what they said to each other was in a babbling tongue.

And when they saw Tzihuacpopocatzin, they said, "Is this one then Moteuccoma?" They said it to the Tlaxcalans and Cempoallans, their lookouts, who came among them, questioning them secretly. They said, "It is not that one, o our lords. This is Tzihuacpopocatzin, who is representing Moteuccoma."

[The Spaniards] said to him, "Are you then Moteuccoma?" He said, "I am your agent Moteuccoma."

Then they told him, "Go on with you! Why do you lie to us? What do you take us for? You can't lie to us, you can't fool us, [turn our heads], flatter us, [make faces at us], trick us, confuse our vision, distort things for us, blind us, dazzle us, throw mud in our eyes, put muddy hands on our faces. It is not you. Moteuccoma exists; he will not be able to hide from us, he will not be able to find refuge. Where will he go? Is he a bird, will he fly? Or will he take an underground route, will he go somewhere into a mountain that is hollow inside? We will see him, we will not fail to gaze on his face and hear his words from his lips."

Therefore they just scorned and disregarded him, and so another of their meetings and greetings came to naught. Then they went straight back the direct way [to Mexico].

Thirteenth chapter, where it is said how Moteuccoma sent other sorcerers to cast spells on the Spaniards, and what happened to them on the way.

Another group of messengers—rainmakers, witches, and priests—had also gone out for an encounter, but nowhere were they able to do anything or to get sight of [the Spaniards]; they did not hit their target, they did not find the people they were looking for, they were not sufficient.

They just came up against a drunk man in the road; they went to meet him and were dumbfounded at him. The way they saw him, he seemed to be dressed as a Chalcan,[12] feigning to be a Chalcan. He seemed to be drunk, feigning drunkenness. On his chest were tied eight grass ropes. He came quarreling with them, coming ahead of the Spaniards.

He ranted at them, saying to them, "What are you still doing here? What more do you want? What more is Moteuccoma trying to do? Did he come to his senses yesterday? Has he just now become a great coward? He has done wrong, he has [abandoned] the people, he has destroyed people, [he has hit himself on the head and wrapped himself up in relation to people], he has mocked people and deceived them."

When they had seen this and heard what he said, they made an effort to address him humbly; they quickly set up for him a place to attend to him, an earthen platform with a straw bed, but he absolutely would not look at it. In vain they had set out for him the earthen platform they had tried to make for him there.

[It was as though they entered his mouth]; he scolded them, greatly scolded them with angry words, saying to them, "What is the use of your coming here? Mexico will never exist again, it [is gone] forever. Go on with

12. **Chalcan:** A native group renowned among the Aztecs for their poetry.

you; it is no longer there. Do turn around and look at what is happening in Mexico, what is going on."

Then they looked back, they quickly looked back, and saw all the temples, the calpulli [buildings], the calmecacs,[13] and all the houses in Mexico burning, and it seemed as though there were fighting.

And when the rainmakers had seen that, their hearts seemed to fail them, they were silent, as though someone had forced something down their throats. They said, "What we have seen was needed to be seen not by us but by Moteucçoma, for that was not just anyone, but the youth Tezcatlipoca."[14]

Then he vanished, and they saw him no more. And after that the messengers did not go to encounter [the Spaniards], did not move in their direction, but the rainmakers and priests turned back there and came to tell Moteucçoma. They came together with those who had first gone with Tzihuacpopocatzin.

And when the messengers got there, they told Moteucçoma what had happened and what they had seen. When Moteucçoma heard it, he just hung his head and sat there, not saying a word. He sat like someone on the verge of death; for a long time it was as though he had lost awareness.

He answered them only by saying to them, "What can be done, o men of unique valor? We have come to the end. We are resigned. Should we climb up in the mountains? But should we run away? We are Mexica. Will the Mexica state flourish [in exile]? Look at the sad condition of the poor old men and women, and the little children who know nothing yet. Where would they be taken? What answer is there? What can be done, whatever can be done? Where are we to go? We are resigned to whatever we will see, of whatever nature."

FOR CRITICAL THINKING

1. In what ways did the Florentine Codex represent the native population differently from the way in which Hernando Cortés did?
2. Many Nahua documents agreed with Spanish accounts claiming that Moctezuma acted timidly and lost his empire because he believed that the Spanish were gods. Why might some native chroniclers have had an interest in perpetuating this theory? Why might Europeans have also wanted to perpetuate this idea?
3. What evidence in these documents suggests that the Nahua believed the Spanish were gods?

---

13. **calmecacs:** Religious schools for boys run by Aztec priests.
14. **Tezcatlipoca:** Aztec god of the night, beauty, war, and material things. He often tempted men to do wicked things as a means of rewarding those who could resist temptations and punishing those who succumbed.

3

BARTOLOMÉ DE LAS CASAS

Destruction of the Indies

Bartolomé de Las Casas (1474–1566), a Spanish colonist and later a Dominican friar, saw Christopher Columbus in 1493 when the explorer passed through Seville on his return to Spain after having discovered the Americas the previous year. Las Casas's father and two uncles sailed that year on Columbus's second voyage. As news spread throughout Europe about what was believed to be a western route to the East Indies, rumors of an abundance of gold, spices, and other valuables attracted adventurers and others in search of fortune.

The Spanish built small colonies on the island of Hispaniola (now the Dominican Republic and Haiti). In 1502, Las Casas himself traveled to the New World to serve as an officer of the king. In exchange for his services, he was given an encomienda, *an estate that included native people forced to labor for him. Several years later, he was moved by a sermon given by a Dominican priest denouncing the treatment of the Indians by the Spanish. Las Casas returned his laborers to the governor and became a priest.*

Las Casas spent the rest of his long life attempting to protect the Native Americans against the massacres, tortures, and forced labor imposed on them by their Spanish conquerors. In 1515, Las Casas returned to Spain and pleaded before King Ferdinand for more humane treatment of the native people. His passionate defense of the indigenous Americans influenced Pope Paul III to declare the natives of America rational beings with souls. Las Casas traveled throughout Spain's new colonies and in the 1540s became bishop of Chiapas (now southern Mexico).

His powerful writings were part of the basis for the "Black Legend" of the Spanish conquest. Most modern scholars accept the accuracy of Las Casas's shocking portraits of devastation, much of which he personally witnessed, such as the violent and bloody conquest of Cuba. Today, however, many view these horrors not as the outcome of some peculiar Spanish cruelty but as characteristic of the bloody "Columbian encounter" between Europeans and other cultures in the age of exploration and conquest. Las Casas wrote the following treatise in Seville in 1552.

QUESTIONS TO CONSIDER

1. Was Bartolomé de Las Casas's view of the Native Americans accurate? Why or why not?
2. Was his criticism of the Spanish empire fair and accurate?

Francis Augustus MacNutt, *Bartholomew de Las Casas: His Life, His Apostolate, and His Writings* (New York: G. P. Putnam's Sons, 1909), 314–21.

3. Throughout his life Las Casas remained fiercely loyal to both the Spanish monarch and the Catholic Church. How would you reconcile these feelings with his condemnation of the Spanish empire's actions in the New World?

SHORT REPORT OF THE DESTRUCTION OF THE WEST INDIES

1. The Indies were discovered in the year fourteen hundred and ninety-two. The year following, Spanish Christians went to inhabit them, so that it is since forty-nine years that numbers of Spaniards have gone there: and the first land, that they invaded to inhabit, was the large and most delightful Isle of Hispaniola, which has a circumference of six hundred leagues.

2. There are numberless other islands, and very large ones, all around on every side, that were all—and we have seen it—as inhabited and full of their native Indian peoples as any country in the world.

3. Of the continent, the nearest part of which is more than two hundred and fifty leagues distant from this Island, more than ten thousand leagues of maritime coast have been discovered, and more is discovered every day; all that has been discovered up to the year forty-nine is full of people, like a hive of bees, so that it seems as though God had placed all, or the greater part of the entire human race in these countries.

4. God has created all these numberless people to be quite the simplest, without malice or duplicity, most obedient, most faithful to their natural Lords, and to the Christians, whom they serve; the most humble, most patient, most peaceful, and calm, without strife nor tumults; not wrangling, nor querulous, as free from uproar, hate and desire of revenge, as any in the world.

5. They are likewise the most delicate people, weak and of feeble constitution, and less than any other can they bear fatigue, and they very easily die of whatsoever infirmity; so much so, that not even the sons of our Princes and of nobles, brought up in royal and gentle life, are more delicate than they; although there are among them such as are of the peasant class. They are also a very poor people, who of worldly goods possess little, nor wish to possess: and they are therefore neither proud, nor ambitious, nor avaricious.

6. Their food is so poor, that it would seem that of the Holy Fathers in the desert was not scantier nor less pleasing. Their way of dressing is usually to go naked, covering the private parts; and at most they cover themselves with a cotton cover, which would be about equal to one and a half or two ells square of cloth. Their beds are of matting, and they mostly sleep in certain things like hanging nets, called in the language of Hispaniola *hamacas*.

7. They are likewise of a clean, unspoiled, and vivacious intellect, very capable, and receptive to every good doctrine; most prompt to accept our Holy Catholic Faith, to be endowed with virtuous customs; and they have as little difficulty with such things as any people created by God in the world.

8. Once they have begun to learn of matters pertaining to faith, they are so importunate to know them, and in frequenting the sacraments and

divine service of the Church, that to tell the truth, the clergy have need to be endowed of God with the gift of pre-eminent patience to bear with them: and finally, I have heard many lay Spaniards frequently say many years ago, (unable to deny the goodness of those they saw) certainly these people were the most blessed of the earth, had they only knowledge of God.

9. Among these gentle sheep, gifted by their Maker with the above qualities, the Spaniards entered as soon as they knew them, like wolves, tigers, and lions which had been starving for many days, and since forty years they have done nothing else; nor do they otherwise at the present day, than outrage, slay, afflict, torment, and destroy them with strange and new, and divers kinds of cruelty, never before seen, nor heard of, nor read of, of which some few will be told below: to such extremes has this gone that, whereas there were more than three million souls, whom we saw in Hispaniola, there are to-day, not two hundred of the native population left.

10. The island of Cuba is almost as long as the distance from Valladolid[1] to Rome; it is now almost entirely deserted. The islands of San Juan [Puerto Rico], and Jamaica, very large and happy and pleasing islands, are both desolate. The Lucaya Isles lie near Hispaniola and Cuba to the north and number more than sixty, including those that are called the Giants, and other large and small Islands; the poorest of these, which is more fertile, and pleasing than the King's garden in Seville, is the healthiest country in the world, and contained more than five hundred thousand souls, but to-day there remains not even a single creature. All were killed in transporting them, to Hispaniola, because it was seen that the native population there was disappearing.

11. A ship went three years later to look for the people that had been left after the gathering in, because a good Christian was moved by compassion to convert and win those that were found to Christ; only eleven persons, whom I saw, were found.

12. More than thirty other islands, about the Isle of San Juan, are destroyed and depopulated, for the same reason. All these islands cover more than two thousand leagues of land, entirely depopulated and deserted.

13. We are assured that our Spaniards, with their cruelty and execrable works, have depopulated and made desolate the great continent, and that more than ten Kingdoms, larger than all Spain, counting Aragon[2] and Portugal, and twice as much territory as from Seville to Jerusalem (which is more than two thousand leagues), although formerly full of people, are now deserted.

14. We give as a real and true reckoning, that in the said forty years, more than twelve million persons, men, and women, and children, have perished unjustly and through tyranny, by the infernal deeds and tyranny of the Christians; and I truly believe, nor think I am deceived, that it is more than fifteen.

15. Two ordinary and principal methods have the self-styled Christians, who have gone there, employed in extirpating these miserable nations and removing them from the face of the earth. The one, by unjust, cruel and

1. **Valladolid:** A city in northwestern Spain.
2. **Aragon:** A kingdom in what is now northeastern Spain.

tyrannous wars. The other, by slaying all those, who might aspire to, or sigh for, or think of liberty, or to escape from the torments that they suffer, such as all the native Lords, and adult men; for generally, they leave none alive in the wars, except the young men and the women, whom they oppress with the hardest, most horrible, and roughest servitude, to which either man or beast, can ever be put. To these two ways of infernal tyranny, all the many and divers other ways, which are numberless, of exterminating these people, are reduced, resolved, or sub-ordered according to kind.

16. The reason why the Christians have killed and destroyed such infinite numbers of souls, is solely because they have made gold their ultimate aim, seeking to load themselves with riches in the shortest time and to mount by high steps, disproportioned to their condition: namely by their insatiable avarice and ambition, the greatest, that could be on the earth. These lands, being so happy and so rich, and the people so humble, so patient, and so easily subjugated, they have had no more respect, nor consideration nor have they taken more account of them (I speak with truth of what I have seen during all the aforementioned time) than,—I will not say of animals, for would to God they had considered and treated them as animals,—but as even less than the dung in the streets.

17. In this way have they cared for their lives—and for their souls: and therefore, all the millions above mentioned have died without faith, and without sacraments. And it is a publicly known truth, admitted, and confessed by all, even by the tyrants and homicides themselves, that the Indians throughout the Indies never did any harm to the Christians: they even esteemed them as coming from heaven, until they and their neighbours had suffered the same many evils, thefts, deaths, violence and visitations at their hands.

OF HISPANIOLA

1. In the island of Hispaniola—which was the first, as we have said, to be invaded by the Christians—the immense massacres and destruction of these people began. It was the first to be destroyed and made into a desert. The Christians began by taking the women and children, to use and to abuse them, and to eat of the substance of their toil and labour, instead of contenting themselves with what the Indians gave them spontaneously, according to the means of each. Such stores are always small; because they keep no more than they ordinarily need, which they acquire with little labour; but what is enough for three households, of ten persons each, for a month, a Christian eats and destroys in one day. From their using force, violence and other kinds of vexations, the Indians began to perceive that these men could not have come from heaven.

2. Some hid their provisions, others, their wives and children: others fled to the mountains to escape from people of such harsh and terrible intercourse. The Christians gave them blows in the face, beatings and cudgellings,

even laying hands on the lords of the land. They reached such recklessness and effrontery, that a Christian captain violated the lawful wife of the chief king and lord of all the island.

3. After this deed, the Indians consulted to devise means of driving the Christians from their country. They took up their weapons, which are poor enough and little fitted for attack, being of little force and not even good for defence. For this reason, all their wars are little more than games with sticks, such as children play in our countries.

4. The Christians, with their horses and swords and lances, began to slaughter and practise strange cruelty among them. They penetrated into the country and spared neither children nor the aged, nor pregnant women, nor those in child labour, all of whom they ran through the body and lacerated, as though they were assaulting so many lambs herded in their sheepfold.

5. They made bets as to who would slit a man in two, or cut off his head at one blow: or they opened up his bowels. They tore the babes from their mothers' breast by the feet, and dashed their heads against the rocks. Others they seized by the shoulders and threw into the rivers, laughing and joking, and when they fell into the water they exclaimed: "boil body of so and so!" They spitted the bodies of other babes, together with their mothers and all who were before them, on their swords.

6. They made a gallows just high enough for the feet to nearly touch the ground, and by thirteens, in honour and reverence of our Redeemer and the twelve Apostles, they put wood underneath and, with fire, they burned the Indians alive.

7. They wrapped the bodies of others entirely in dry straw, binding them in it and setting fire to it; and so they burned them. They cut off the hands of all they wished to take alive, made them carry them fastened on to them, and said: "Go and carry letters": that is; take the news to those who have fled to the mountains.

8. They generally killed the lords and nobles in the following way. They made wooden gridirons of stakes, bound them upon them, and made a slow fire beneath: thus the victims gave up the spirit by degrees, emitting cries of despair in their torture.

9. I once saw that they had four or five of the chief lords stretched on the gridirons to burn them, and I think also there were two or three pairs of gridirons, where they were burning others; and because they cried aloud and annoyed the captain or prevented him sleeping, he commanded that they should strangle them: the officer who was burning them was worse than a hangman and did not wish to suffocate them, but with his own hands he gagged them, so that they should not make themselves heard, and he stirred up the fire, until they roasted slowly, according to his pleasure. I know his name, and knew also his relations in Seville. I saw all the above things and numberless others.

4

JOHN SMITH

Description of Virginia

Before he became one of the original settlers of Jamestown in 1607, Captain John Smith (1580–1631) was already experienced as a soldier and diplomat, having fought the Spanish in the Netherlands and the Turks in Hungary. At Jamestown he took part in governing the colony—leading it from 1608 to 1609—and in managing relations with the Native Americans. His story, told years later, of being saved from death by the friendly intervention of Pocahontas, the daughter of Chief Powhatan, has a secure place in American legend. Historians and ethnographers disagree about whether the incident happened and, if it did, whether Smith correctly understood its meaning in the context of the native culture. Many suspect that it was part of a ritual inducting Smith into the tribe rather than a rescue.

Smith returned to England in 1609. His later years were given over to promoting both himself and the settlement of the New World he had helped to colonize. His descriptions in numerous writings both of British America and of its Native American inhabitants set patterns that continued for centuries.

QUESTIONS TO CONSIDER

1. How would you describe Smith's account of Native Americans? What adjectives does he use?
2. How would you describe the nature of the relationship between the English settlers and the Native Americans?
3. In what ways does Smith's account seem reliable? In what ways does it seem unreliable?

THE COMMODITIES IN VIRGINIA
OR THAT MAY BE HAD BY INDUSTRY

The mildness of the air, the fertility of the soil, and the situation of the rivers are so propitious to the nature and use of man as no place is more convenient for pleasure, profit, and man's sustenance. Under that latitude or climate, here will live any beasts, as horses, goats, sheep, asses, hens, etc. The waters, islands, and shoals are full of safe harbors for ships of war or merchandise, for boats of all sorts, for transportation or fishing, etc.

Edward Arber, ed., *Capt. John Smith, of Willoughby by Alford, Lincolnshire; President of Virginia, and Admiral of New England. Works. 1608–1631,* The English Scholar's Library 16 (Birmingham, 1884), 63–67. The text has been modernized by Elizabeth Marcus.

The Bay and rivers have much marketable fish and places fit for salt works, building of ships, making of iron, etc.

Muscovia and Polonia[1] yearly receive many thousands for pitch, tar, soap ashes, rosin, flax, cordage, sturgeon, masts, yards, wainscot, furs, glass, and suchlike; also Swethland[2] for iron and copper. France, in like manner, for wine, canvas, and salt, Spain as much for iron, steel, figs, raisins and sherry. Italy with silks and velvets, consumes our chief commodities. Holland maintains itself by fishing and trading at our own doors. All these temporize with others for necessities, but all as uncertain as to peace or war, and besides the charge, travel and danger in transporting them, by seas, lands, storms and pirates. Then how much has Virginia the prerogative of all those flourishing kingdoms for the benefit of our lands, when as within one hundred miles all those are to be had, either ready provided by nature or else to be prepared, were there but industrious men to labor. Only copper might be lacking, but there is good probability that both copper and better minerals are there to be had if they are worked for. Their countries have it. So then here is a place a nurse for soldiers, a practice for mariners, a trade for merchants, a reward for the good, and that which is most of all, a business (most acceptable to God) to bring such poor infidels to the true knowledge of God and his holy Gospel.

OF THE NATURAL INHABITANTS OF VIRGINIA

The land is not populous, for the men be few, their far greater number is of women and children. Within 60 miles of Jamestown there are about some 5,000 people, but of able men fit for their wars scarce 1,500. To nourish so many together they have yet no means, because they make so small a benefit of their land, be it never so fertile.

Six or seven hundred have been the most that have been seen together, when they gathered themselves to have surprised Captain Smyth at Pamaunke, having but 15 to withstand the worst of their fury. As small as the proportion of ground that has yet been discovered, is in comparison of that yet unknown. The people differ very much in stature, especially in language, as before is expressed.

Some being very great as the Sesquaesahamocks, others very little as the Wighcocomocoes:[3] but generally tall and straight, of a comely proportion, and of a color brown, when they are of any age, but they are born white. Their hair is generally black, but few have any beards. The men wear half their heads shaven, the other half long. For barbers they use their women, who with 2 shells will grate away the hair in any fashion they please. The women are cut in many fashions agreeable to their years, but ever some part remain long.

1. **Muscovia and Polonia:** Latin for Moscow and Poland.
2. **Swethland:** Sweden.
3. **Sesquaesahamocks . . . Wighcocomocoes:** Indigenous groups of the region.

They are very strong, of an able body and full of agility, able to endure, to lie in the woods under a tree by the fire, in the worst of winter, or in the weeds and grass, in ambush in the summer. They are inconstant in everything, but what fear constrains them to keep. Crafty, timorous, quick of apprehension and very ingenious. Some are of disposition fearful, some bold, most cautious, all savage. Generally covetous of copper, beads and such like trash. They are soon moved to anger, and so malicious, that they seldom forget an injury: they seldom steal from one another, lest their conjurors[4] should reveal it, and so they be pursued and punished. That they are thus feared is certain, but that any can reveal their offenses by conjuration I am doubtful. Their women are careful not to be suspected of dishonesty without leave of their husbands.

Each household knows their own lands and gardens, and most live off their own labors.

For their apparel, they are some time covered with the skins of wild beasts, which in winter are dressed with the hair but in summer without. The better sort use large mantles of deerskin not much different in fashion from the Irish mantles. Some embroidered them with beads, some with copper, others painted after their manner. But the common sort have scarce to cover their nakedness but with grass, the leaves of trees or suchlike. We have seen some use mantles that nothing could be discerned but the feathers, that was exceedingly warm and handsome. But the women are always covered about their middles with a skin and are ashamed to be seen bare.

They adorn themselves most with copper beads and paintings. Their women have their legs, hands, breasts and face cunningly embroidered with diverse works, as beasts, serpents, artificially wrought into their flesh with black spots. In each ear commonly they have three great holes, from which they hang chains, bracelets or copper. Some of their men wear in those holes a small green and yellow colored snake, near half a yard in length, which crawling and lapping herself around his neck oftentimes familiarly would kiss his lips. Others wear a dead rat tied by the tail. Some on their heads wear the wing of a bird or some large feather, with a rattle; those rattles are somewhat like the chape of a rapier, but less, which they take from the tails of a snake. Many have the whole skin of a hawk or some strange fowl, stuffed with the wings abroad. Others a broad piece of copper, and some the hand of their enemy dried. Their heads and shoulders are painted red with the root Pocone[5] pounded to a powder mixed with oil; this they hold in summer to preserve them from the heat and in winter from the cold. Many other forms of paintings they use, but he is the most gallant that is the most monstrous to behold.

Their buildings and habitations are for the most part by the rivers or not far distant from some fresh spring. Their houses are built like our arbors of small young springs bowed and tied, and so close covered with mats or the barks of trees very handsomely, that notwithstanding either wind, rain or weather, they are as warm as stoves, but very smokey; yet at the top of the house there is a hole made for the smoke to go into right over the fire.

4. **conjuror:** A ritual specialist who can discern what people are thinking.
5. **Pocone:** Bloodroot.

Against the fire they lie on little mounds of reeds covered with a mat, borne from the ground a foot and more by a mound of wood. On these round about the house, they lie heads and points one by the other against the fire, some covered with mats, some with skins, and some stark naked lie on the ground, from 6 to 20 in a house.

Their houses are in the midst of their fields or gardens; which are small plots of ground, some 20, some 40, some 100, some 200, some more, some less. Sometimes from 2 to 100 of these houses are together, or but a little separated by groves of trees. Near their habitations is a little small wood, or old trees on the ground, by reason of their burning of them for fire. So that a man may gallop a horse among these woods anyway, but where the creeks or rivers shall hinder.

Men, women and children have their several names according to the particular whim of their parents. Their women (they say) are easily delivered of child, yet do they love children dearly. To make them hardy, in the coldest mornings they wash them in the rivers, and by painting and ointments so tan their skins that after a year or two no weather will hurt them.

The men bestow their times in fishing, hunting, wars, and such manlike exercises, scorning to be seen in any woman like exercise, which is the cause that the women be very painful and the men often idle. The women and children do the rest of the work. They make mats, baskets, pots, mortars, pound their corn, make their bread, prepare their victuals, plant their corn, gather their corn, bear all kinds of burdens and suchlike.

5

WILLIAM STRACHEY

Travel to the New World

Like John Smith, William Strachey (1572–1621) was an Englishman who settled Jamestown, Virginia, and wrote an important history of its founding, Historie of Travaile into Virginia Britannia. *Strachey also authored an earlier account of the New World, which is less well known but no less notable than* Historie. *That chronicle was based on his harrowing expedition to Virginia in which nothing went right for him.*

Strachey's transatlantic crossing in 1609 from England to the new British colony nearly cost him his life. A terrible storm swallowed his ship, the Sea Venture, *and spit it out on the shores of the Bermuda Islands. For nearly a year, Strachey and fellow*

A True Reportory of the Wreck and Redemption of Sir Thomas Gates, Knight, upon and from the Islands of the Bermudas: His Coming to Virginia and the Estate of that Colony Then and After, under the Government of the Lord La Warr, July 15, 1610, written by William Strachey, Esquire. (1625) http://www.virtualjamestown.org/TR modern.doc *survivors eked out a living, slowly gaining the strength and courage to continue their voyage northward. They eventually built two new small vessels, aptly called* Patience *and* Deliverance, *and successfully piloted them to Jamestown.*

Strachey's ordeal inspired him to ink a long letter to an unnamed "Excellent Lady" living in England. Dated July 15, 1610, it was published posthumously in 1625, as A true repertory of the wracke, and redemption of SIR THOMAS GATES Knight. *The letter is a riveting mix of observations about the storm, the stress of survival, the cutthroat tactics of rival groups of travelers jockeying for control over each other, the flora and fauna of the islands, and the eventual migration to Virginia. Besides its colorful evocation of the daily life of the shipwrecked, Strachey's letter offers a rare glimpse into the mind of a seventeenth-century man desperate to see the hand of God in every twist of fate. Equally important, it allows us to see how Strachey understood his relationship to Bermuda and strove to legitimate the Crown's subjugation of it.*

QUESTIONS TO CONSIDER

1. What is the role of God in Strachey's account of the storm and the subsequent settlement of Bermuda?
2. How does Strachey describe the natural resources of Bermuda? How do these descriptions put him in a position of power and control over his new environment?
3. In what ways can we read Strachey's letter as the first step in the process through which the British would eventually colonize Bermuda?

For four-and-twenty hours, the storm in a restless tumult had blown so exceedingly as we could not apprehend in our imaginations any possibility of greater violence; yet did we still find it not only more terrible, but more constant, fury added to fury, and one storm urging a second more outrageous than the former, whether it so wrought upon our fears or indeed met with new forces. Sometimes shrieks in our ship amongst women and passengers not used to such hurly and discomforts made us look one upon the other with troubled hearts and panting bosoms, our clamors drowned in the winds, and the winds in thunder. Prayers might well be in the heart and lips, but drowned in the outcries of the officers. Nothing heard that could give comfort, nothing seen that might encourage hope. It is impossible for me, had I the voice of Stentor and expression of as many tongues as his throat of voices, to express the outcries and miseries; not languishing, but wasting his spirits, and art constant to his own principles, but not prevailing. . . .

It pleased God to bring a greater affliction yet upon us; for in the beginning of the storm we had received likewise a mighty leak. And the ship, in every joint almost, having spewed out her oakum before we were aware (a casualty more desperate than any other that a voyage by sea draweth with it), was grown five foot suddenly deep with water above her ballast, and we almost drowned within whilst we sat looking when to perish from above. This, imparting no less terror than danger, ran through the whole ship with much fright and amazement, startled and turned the blood, and took down the braves of the most hardy mariner of them all, insomuch as he that before happily felt not the sorrow of others, now began to sorrow for himself when he saw such a pond of water so suddenly broken in and which he knew could not (without present avoiding) but instantly sink him.

So as joining (only for his own sake, not yet worth the saving) in the public safety there might be seen master, master's mate, boatswain, quartermaster, coopers, carpenters, and who not, with candles in their hands, creeping along the ribs viewing the sides, searching every corner and listening in every place if they could hear the water run. Many a weeping leak was this way found and hastily stopped, and at length one in the gunner room made up with I know not how many pieces of beef. But all was to no purpose; the leak (if it were but one) which drunk in our greatest seas and took in our destruction fastest could not then be found, nor ever was, by any labor, counsel, or search. . . .

So as I may well say, every four hours we quitted one hundred tons of water, and from Tuesday noon till Friday noon we bailed and pumped two thousand ton; and yet, do what we could, when our ship held least in her (after Tuesday night second watch), she bore ten foot deep; at which stay our extreme working kept her one eight glasses, forbearance whereof had instantly sunk us. And it being now Friday, the fourth morning, it wanted little, but that there had been a general determination to have shut up hatches, and commending our sinful souls to God, committed the ship to the mercy of the sea. Surely that night we must have done it, and that night had we then perished, but see the goodness and sweet introduction of better hope by our merciful God given unto us: Sir George Somers, when no man dreamed of such happiness, had discovered and cried land.

Indeed the morning, now three quarters spent, had won a little clearness from the days before, and it being better surveyed, the very trees were seen to move with the wind upon the shore side; whereupon our governor commanded the helm-man to bear up. The boatswain, sounding at the first, found it thirteen fathom, and when we stood a little, in seven fathom; and presently, heaving his lead the third time, had ground at four fathom; and by this we had got her within a mile under the southeast point of the land, where we had somewhat smooth water. But having no hope to save her by coming to an anchor in the same, we were enforced to run her ashore as near the land as we could, which brought us within three quarters of a mile of shore; and by the mercy of God unto us, making out our boats, we had ere night brought all our men, women, and children, about the number of one hundred and fifty, safe into the island.

We found it to be the dangerous and dreaded island, or rather islands, of the Bermuda; whereof let me give Your Ladyship a brief description before I proceed to my narration. And that the rather because they be so terrible to all that ever touched on them, and such tempests, thunders, and other fearful objects are seen and heard about them, that they be called commonly the Devil's Islands and are feared and avoided of all sea travelers alive above any other place in the world. Yet it pleased our merciful God to make even this hideous and hated place both the place of our safety and means of our deliverance. . . .

The Bermudas be broken islands, five hundred of them in manner of an archipelago (at least if you may call them all islands that lie, how little so ever, into the sea and by themselves) of small compass, some larger yet than other, as time and the sea hath won from them and eaten his passage through; and all now lying in the figure of a croissant, within the circuit of six or seven leagues at the most, albeit at first it is said of them that they were thirteen or fourteen leagues, and more in longitude, as I have heard. For no greater distance is it from the northwest point to Gates' Bay, as by this map Your Ladyship may see, in which Sir George Somers, who coasted in his boat about them all, took great care to express the same exactly and full, and made his draft perfect for all good occasions and the benefit of such who either in distress might be brought upon them or make sail this way. . . .

The soil of the whole island is one and the same; the mold dark, red, sandy, dry and uncapable, I believe, of any of our commodities or fruits. Sir George Somers in the beginning of August squared out a garden by the quarter (the quarter being set down before a goodly bay, upon which our governor did first leap ashore and therefore called it, as afore said, Gates' Bay, which opened into the east and into which the sea did ebb and flow according to their tides) and sowed muskmelons, peas, onions, radish, lettuce, and many English seeds and kitchen herbs. All which in some ten days did appear above ground, but whether by the small birds, of which there be many kinds, or by flies (worms I never saw any, nor any venomous thing, as toad, or snake, or any creeping beast hurtful; only some spiders, which, as many affirm, are signs of great store of gold; but they were long- and slender-leg spiders, and whether venomous or no I know not — I believe not, since we should still find them amongst our linen in our chests and drinking-cans, but we never received any danger from them; a kind of melantha or black beetle there was, which bruised, gave a savor like many sweet and strong gums punned together), whether, I say, hindered by these or by the condition or vice of the soil, they came to no proof, nor thrived. . . .

Likewise there grow great store of palm trees, not the right Indian palms such as in San Juan, Puerto Rico, are called cocos and are there full of small fruits like almonds (of the bigness of the grains in pomegranates), nor of those kind of palms which bears dates, but a kind of simerons or wild palms, in growth, fashion, leaves, and branches resembling those true palms. For the tree is high and straight, sappy and spongious, unfirm for any use, no branches but in the uppermost part thereof; and in the top grow leaves about the head of it (the most inmost part whereof they call palmetto, and it is the heart and pith of the same trunk, so white and thin as it will peel off into pleats as smooth and delicate as white satin into twenty folds, in which a man may write as in paper), where they spread and fall downward about the tree like an overblown rose, or saffron flower, not early gathered. So broad are the leaves as an Italian umbrella, a man may well defend his whole body under one of them from the greatest storm rain that falls; for they being stiff and smooth, as if so many flags were knit together, the rain easily slideth off. We oftentimes found growing to these leaves many silkworms involved therein, like those small worms which Acosta writeth of,[1] which grew in the leaves of the tuna tree, of which, being dried, the Indians make their cochineal so precious and merchantable. With these leaves we thatched our cabins, and roasting the palmetto or soft top thereof, they had a taste like fried melons, and being sod, they eat like cabbages, but not so offensively thankful to the stomach. Many an ancient burgher was therefore heaved at and fell, not for his place, but for his head. For our common people, whose bellies never had ears, made no breach of charity in their hot bloods and tall stomachs to murder thousands of them. They bear a kind of berry, black and round, as big as a damson, which about December were ripe and luscious; being scalded whilst they are green, they eat like bullaces.[2] These trees shed their leaves in the winter months, as withered or burnt with the cold blasts of the north wind, especially those that grow to the seaward; and in March there burgeon new in their room, fresh and tender. . . .

The shore and bays round about, when we landed first, afforded great store of fish, and that of divers kinds and good, but it should seem that our fires, which we maintained on the shore's side, drave them from us, so as we were in some want until we had made a flat-bottom gondola of cedar, with which we put off farther into the sea, and then daily hooked great store of many kinds, as excellent angelfish, salmon peal, bonitos, sting ray, cabally, snappers, hogfish, sharks, dogfish, pilchards, mullets, and rockfish, of which be divers kinds. And of these our governor dried and salted, and barreling them up, brought to sea five hundred; for he had procured salt to be made with some brine, which happily was preserved, and once having made a little quantity, he kept three or four pots boiling and two or three men attending nothing else in an house (some little distance from his bay) set up on purpose for the same work.

Fowl there is great store: small birds, sparrows fat and plump like a bunting, bigger than ours, robins of divers colors, green and yellow, ordinary and familiar in our cabins, and other of less sort. White and gray heronshaws, bitterns, teal, snipes, crows, and hawks, of which in March we found divers aeries, goshawks and tassels, oxbirds, cormorants, bald coots, moor hens, owls, and bats in great store. And upon New Year's Day in the morning, our governor being walked forth with another gentleman, Master James Swift, each of them with their pieces killed a wild swan in a great seawater bay or pond in our island. . . .

During our time of abode upon these islands, we had daily every Sunday two sermons preached by our minister; besides every morning and evening

1. **Acosta:** Jose de Acosta (1539–1600) was a Spanish Jesuit missionary and naturalist who worked and lived in Latin America and authored the influential *Historia natural y moral de las Indias*, which offered detailed observations of the natural environment of the New World.
2. **Bullace:** A plum.

at the ringing of a bell we repaired all to public prayer, at what time the names of our whole company were called by bill, and such as were wanting were duly punished.

The contents (for the most part) of all our preacher's sermons were especially of thankfulness and unity, etc.

It pleased God also to give us opportunity to perform all the other offices and rites of our Christian profession in this island: as marriage, for the six-and-twentieth of November we had one of Sir George Somers' men, his cook, named Thomas Powell, who married a maidservant of one Mistress Horton, whose name was Elizabeth Persons. And upon Christmas Eve, as also once before, the first of October, our minister preached a godly sermon, which being ended, he celebrated a Communion, at the partaking whereof our governor was and the greatest part of our company. And the eleventh of February we had the child of one John Rofe christened, a daughter, to which Captain Newport and myself were witnesses and the aforesaid Mistress Horton, and we named it Bermuda. As also, the five-and-twentieth of March, the wife of one Edward Eason, being delivered the week before of a boy, had him then christened, to which Captain Newport and myself and Master James Swift were godfathers, and we named it Bermudas.

Likewise, we buried five of our company: Jeffery Briars, Richard Lewis, William Hitchman, and my goddaughter, Bermuda Rolfe, and one untimely Edward Samuel, a sailor, being villainously killed by the foresaid Robert Waters (a sailor likewise) with a shovel, who struck him therewith under the lift of the ear; for which he was apprehended and appointed to be hanged the next day (the fact being done in the twilight). But being bound fast to a tree all night with many ropes, and a guard of five or six to attend him, his fellow sailors (watching the advantage of the sentinels' sleeping), in despite and disdain that justice should be showed upon a sailor and that one of their crew should be an example to others, not taking into consideration the unmanliness of the murder nor the horror of the sin, they cut his bonds and conveyed him into the woods, where they fed him nightly and closely, who afterward by the mediation of Sir George Somers, upon many conditions, had his trial respited by our governor. . . .

We had brought our pinnace so forward by this time, as the eight-and-twentieth of August we having laid her keel, the six-and-twentieth of February we now began to caulk. Old cables we had preserved unto us, which afforded oakum enough; and one barrel of pitch and another of tar we likewise saved, which served our use some little way upon the bilge. We breamed her otherwise with lime made of whelk shells and an hard white stone, which we burned in a kiln, slaked with fresh water, and tempered with tortoises' oil. The thirtieth of March, being Friday, we towed her out in the morning spring tide from the wharf where she was built, buoying her with four casks in her run only, which opened into the northwest and into which, when the breeze stood north and by west with any stiff gale and upon the spring tides, the sea would increase with that violence, especially twice it did so, as at the first time (before our governor had caused a solid causeway of an hundred load of stone to be brought from the hills and neighbor rocks and round about her ribs from stem to stem, where it made a pointed balk, and thereby brake the violence of the flow and billow) it endangered her overthrow and ruin, being green, as it were, upon the stocks. With much difficulty, diligence, and labor, we saved her at the first, all her bases, shores, and piles which underset her being almost carried from her, which was the second of January, when her knees were not set to, nor one joint firm.

We launched her unrigged to carry her to a little round island lying west-northwest and close aboard to the back side of our island, both nearer the ponds and wells of some fresh water, as also from thence to make our way to the sea the better, the channel being then sufficient and deep enough to lead her forth when her masts, sails, and all her trim should be about her. She was forty foot by the keel and nineteen foot broad at the beam, six-foot floor; her rake forward was fourteen foot, her rake aft from the top of her post (which was twelve foot long) was three foot; she was eight foot deep under her beam; between her decks she was four foot and an half, with a rising of half a foot more under her forecastle, of purpose to scour the deck with small shot if at any time we should be boarded by the enemy. She had a fall of eighteen inches aft to make her steerage and her great cabin the more large; her steerage was five foot long and six foot high, with a close gallery right aft, with a window on each side and two right aft. The most part of her timber was cedar, which we found to be bad for shipping, for that it is won-drous false inward, and besides it is so spalled or brickle that it will make no good planks. Her beams were all oak of our ruined ship, and some planks in her bow of oak, and the rest as is aforesaid. When she began to swim (upon her launching) our governor called her the "Deliverance," and she might be some eighty tons of burden.

Before we quitted our old quarter and dislodged to the fresh water with our pinnace, our governor set up in Sir George Somers' garden a fair mnemo-synon[3] in figure of a cross, made of some of the timber of our ruined ship, which was screwed in with strong and great trunnels to a mighty cedar, which grew in the midst of the said garden and whose top and upper branches he caused to be lopped, that the violence of the wind and weather might have the less power over her. In the midst of the cross, our governor fastened the picture of His Majesty in a piece of silver of twelvepence, and on each side of the cross he set an inscription graven in copper in the Latin and English to this purpose:

> In memory of our great deliverance, both from a mighty storm and leak, we have set up this to the honor of God. It is the spoil of an English ship (of three hundred ton) called the "Sea Venture," bound with seven ships more (from which the storm divided us) to Virginia, or Nova Britannia, in America. In it were two knights, Sir Thomas Gates, Knight, governor of the English forces and colony there, and Sir George Somers, Knight,

3. **Mnemosynon:** A memorial or monument.

admiral of the seas. Her captain was Christopher Newport; passengers and mariners she had beside (which came all safe to land) one hundred and fifty. We were forced to run her ashore (by reason of her leak) under a point that bore southeast from the northern point of the island, which we discovered first the eight-and-twentieth of July, 1609.

About the last of April, Sir George Somers launched his pinnace and brought her from his building bay in the main island into the channel where ours did ride; and she was by the keel nine-and-twenty foot, at the beam fifteen foot and an half, at the luff fourteen, at the transom nine; and she was eight foot deep and drew six foot water, and he called her the "Patience."

6

FATHER PAUL LE JEUNE

Encounter with the Indians

In the sixteenth and seventeenth centuries, France's Society of Jesus of the Roman Catholic Church, more commonly known as the Jesuits, energetically proselytized in virtually every Portuguese, Spanish, and French colony. The first Jesuit missionaries arrived in French Canada in 1632. They were determined to bring Christianity to the Indians by living with them, learning their languages, educating their children, and demonstrating (sometimes at the cost of their lives) that they were as brave as the Native Americans, some of whom regarded themselves as warriors. The French, although haughty and arrogant at times, were less authoritarian than the Spanish were in dealing with natives—and often more successful. The Jesuits played a major role in cementing French alliances with many Native American groups across Canada and into the Ohio Valley. These relationships gave France a strategic position in the New World, hemming the colonies of British North America against the eastern seaboard until French power was destroyed in the mid-eighteenth century. The Jesuits in Canada sent regular reports back to their superiors in France. These reports form an important account of American Indian life and greatly influenced the European perception of the New World. (Regrettably, no Indian accounts of the French Jesuits survive.)

Paul Le Jeune (1591–1664), born in France, became a Jesuit in 1613. He had been a professor of rhetoric as well as superior of the Jesuit House at Dieppe before he radically changed his activities by going to French North America in 1632. Father Le Jeune found much to admire in the Native Americans, as well as much that he could neither

Reuben Gold Thwaites, ed., *The Jesuit Relations and Allied Documents: Travels and Explorations of the Jesuit Missionaries in New France* (Cleveland: Burrows Brothers, 1987).

understand nor accept. The report included here was written in Quebec in August 1634.
Le Jeune worked among the Indians until 1649. He died in Paris in 1664.

QUESTIONS TO CONSIDER

1. What were Father Le Jeune's impressions and assessment of Native American religion?
2. What did he consider the Indians' virtues?
3. What did he consider their main vices?

CHAPTER IV. ON THE BELIEF, SUPERSTITIONS, AND ERRORS OF THE MONTAGNAIS[1] SAVAGES

I have already reported that the Savages believe that a certain one named Atahocam had created the world, and that one named Messou had restored it. I have questioned upon this subject the famous Sorcerer and the old man with whom I passed the Winter; they answered that they did not know who was the first Author of the world,—that it was perhaps Atahocam, but that was not certain; that they only spoke of Atahocam as one speaks of a thing so far distant that nothing sure can be known about it. . . .

As to the Messou, they hold that he restored the world, which was destroyed in the flood; whence it appears that they have some tradition of that great universal deluge which happened in the time of Noë.[2] . . .

They also say that all animals, of every species, have an elder brother, who is, as it were, the source and origin of all individuals, and this elder brother is wonderfully great and powerful. . . . Now these elders of all the animals are the juniors of the Messou. Behold him well related, this worthy restorer of the Universe, he is elder brother to all beasts. If any one, when asleep, sees the elder or progenitor of some animals, he will have a fortunate chase; if he sees the elder of the Beavers, he will take Beavers; if he sees the elder of the Elks, he will take Elks, possessing the juniors through the favor of their senior whom he has seen in the dream. . . .

Their Religion, or rather their superstition, consists of little besides praying; but O, my God, what prayers they make! In the morning, when the little children come out from their Cabins, they shout, *Cacouakhi, Pakhais Amiscouakhi, Pakhais Mousouakhi, Pakhais,* "Come, Porcupines; come, Beavers; come, Elk;" and this is all of their prayers.

When the Savages sneeze, and sometimes even at other times, during the Winter, they cry out in a loud voice, *Etouctaian miraounam an Mirouscamikhi,* "I shall be very glad to see the Spring." At other times, I have heard them pray for the Spring, or for deliverance from evils and other similar things; and they

1. **Montagnais:** French name for three groups of indigenous peoples who inhabit a region stretching from northern Quebec to Labrador.
2. **Noë:** Alternate spelling of Noah, from the Old Testament story of the destruction of the world by flood.

express all these things in the form of desires, crying out as loudly as they can, "I would be very glad if this day would continue, if the wind would change," etc. I could not say to whom these wishes are addressed, for they themselves do not know, at least those whom I have asked have not been able to enlighten me. . . .

CHAPTER V. ON THE GOOD THINGS WHICH
ARE FOUND AMONG THE SAVAGES

If we begin with physical advantages, I will say that they possess these in abundance. They are tall, erect, strong, well proportioned, agile; and there is nothing effeminate in their appearance. Those little Fops that are seen elsewhere are only caricatures of men, compared with our Savages. I almost believed, heretofore, that the Pictures of the Roman Emperors represented the ideal of the painters rather than men who had ever existed, so strong and powerful are their heads; but I see here upon the shoulders of these people the heads of Julius Caesar, of Pompey, of Augustus, of Otho, and of others, that I have seen in France, drawn upon paper, or in relief on medallions.

As to the mind of the Savage, it is of good quality. I believe that souls are all made from the same stock, and that they do not materially differ; hence, these barbarians having well formed bodies, and organs well regulated and well arranged, their minds ought to work with ease. Education and instruction alone are lacking. Their soul is a soil which is naturally good, but loaded down with all the evils that a land abandoned since the birth of the world can produce. I naturally compare our Savages with certain villagers, because both are usually without education, though our Peasants are superior in this regard; and yet I have not seen any one thus far, of those who have come to this country, who does not confess and frankly admit that the Savages are more intelligent than our ordinary peasants.

Moreover, if it is a great blessing to be free from a great evil, our Savages are happy; for the two tyrants who provide hell and torture for many of our Europeans, do not reign in their great forests, —I mean ambition and avarice. As they have neither political organization, nor offices, nor dignities, nor any authority, for they only obey their Chief through good will toward him, therefore they never kill each other to acquire these honors. Also, as they are contented with a mere living, not one of them gives himself to the Devil to acquire wealth.

They make a pretence of never getting angry, not because of the beauty of this virtue, for which they have not even a name, but for their own contentment and happiness, I mean, to avoid the bitterness caused by anger. The Sorcerer said to me one day, speaking of one of our Frenchmen, "He has no sense, he gets angry; as for me, nothing can disturb me; let hunger oppress me, let my nearest relation pass to the other life, let the Hiroquois, our enemies, massacre our people, I never get angry." What he says is not an article of faith; for, as he is more haughty than any other Savage, so I have seen him oftener out of humor than any of them; it is true also that he often restrains and governs himself by force, especially when I expose his foolishness. I have only heard one Savage pronounce this word, *Ninichcatihin*, "I am angry," and he only said it once. But I noticed that they kept their eyes on him, for when these Barbarians are angry, they are dangerous and unrestrained.

Whoever professes not to get angry, ought also to make a profession of patience; the Savages surpass us to such an extent, in this respect, that we ought to be ashamed. I saw them, in their hardships and in their labors, suffer with cheerfulness. My host, wondering at the great number of people who I told him were in France, asked me if the men were good, if they did not become angry, if they were patient. I have never seen such patience as is shown by a sick Savage.

You may yell, storm, jump, dance, and he will scarcely ever complain. I found myself, with them, threatened with great suffering; they said to me, "We shall be sometimes two days, sometimes three, without eating, for lack of food; take courage, *Chihiné*, let thy soul be strong to endure suffering and hardship; keep thyself from being sad, otherwise thou wilt be sick; see how we do not cease to laugh, although we have little to eat." One thing alone casts them down,—it is when they see death, for they fear this beyond measure; take away this apprehension from the Savages, and they will endure all kinds of degradation and discomfort, and all kinds of trials and suffering very patiently. . . .

They are very much attached to each other, and agree admirably. You do not see any disputes, quarrels, enmities, or reproaches among them. Men leave the arrangement of the household to the women, without interfering with them; they cut, and decide, and give away as they please, without making the husband angry. . . .

CHAPTER VI. ON THEIR VICES AND THEIR IMPERFECTIONS

The Savages, being filled with errors, are also haughty and proud. Humility is born of truth, vanity of error and falsehood. They are void of the knowledge of truth, and are in consequence, mainly occupied with thought of themselves. They imagine that they ought by right of birth, to enjoy the liberty of Wild ass colts, rendering no homage to any one whomsoever, except when they like. They have reproached me a hundred times because we fear our Captains, while they laugh at and make sport of theirs. All the authority of their chief is in his tongue's end; for he is powerful in so far as he is eloquent; and, even if he kills himself talking and haranguing, he will not be obeyed unless he pleases the Savages. . . .

I have shown in my former letters how vindictive the Savages are toward their enemies, with what fury and cruelty they treat them, eating them after they have made them suffer all that an incarnate fiend could invent. This fury is common to the women as well as to the men, and they even surpass the latter in this respect. I have said that they eat the lice they find upon themselves, not that they like the taste of them, but because they want to bite those that bite them.

These people are very little moved by compassion. When any one is sick in their Cabins, they ordinarily do not cease to cry and storm, and make as much noise as if everybody were in good health. They do not know what it is to take care of a poor invalid, and to give him the food which is good for him; if he asks for something to drink, it is given to him, if he asks for something to eat, it is given to him, but otherwise he is neglected; to coax him with love and gentleness, is a language which they do not understand. As long as a patient can eat, they will carry or drag him with them; if he stops eating, they believe that it is all over with him and kill him, as much to free him from the sufferings that he is enduring, as to relieve themselves of the trouble of taking him with them when they go to some other place. I have both admired and pitied the patience of the invalids whom I have seen among them.

The Savages are slanderous beyond all belief; I say, also among themselves, for they do not even spare their nearest relations, and with it all they are deceitful. For, if one speaks ill of another, they all jeer with loud laughter; if the other appears upon the scene, the first one will show him as much affection and treat him with as much love, as if he had elevated him to the third heaven by his praise. The reason of this is, it seems to me, that their slanders and derision do not come from malicious hearts or from infected mouths, but from a mind which says what it thinks in order to give itself free scope, and which seeks gratification from everything, even from slander and mockery. Hence they are not troubled even if they are told that others are making sport of them, or have injured their reputation. All they usually answer to such talk is, *mama irinisiou*, "He has no sense, he does not know what he is talking about"; and at the first opportunity they will pay their slanderer in the same coin, returning him the like.

Lying is as natural to Savages as talking, not among themselves, but to strangers. Hence it can be said that fear and hope, in one word, interest, is the measure of their fidelity. I would not be willing to trust them, except as they would fear to be punished if they had failed in their duty, or hoped to be rewarded if they were faithful to it. They do not know what it is to keep a secret, to keep their word, and to love with constancy, — especially those who are not of their nation, for they are harmonious among themselves, and their slanders and raillery do not disturb their peace and friendly intercourse. . . .

CHAPTER XII. WHAT ONE MUST SUFFER IN WINTERING WITH THE SAVAGES

In order to have some conception of the beauty of this edifice, its construction must be described. I shall speak from knowledge, for I have often helped to build it. Now, when we arrived at the place where we were to camp, the women, armed with axes, went here and there in the great forests, cutting the framework of the hostelry where we were to lodge; meantime the men, having drawn the plan thereof, cleared away the snow with their snowshoes, or with shovels which they make and carry expressly for this purpose. Imagine now a great ring or square in the snow, two, three or four feet deep, according to the weather or the place where they encamp. This depth of snow makes a white wall for us, which surrounds us on all sides, except the end where it is broken through to form the door. The framework having been brought, which consists of twenty or thirty poles, more or less, according to the size of the cabin, it is planted, not upon the ground but upon the snow; then they throw upon these poles, which converge a little at the top, two or three rolls of bark sewed together, beginning at the bottom, and behold, the house is made. The ground inside, as well as the wall of snow which extends all around the cabin, is covered with little branches of fir; and, as a finishing touch, a wretched skin is fastened to two poles to serve as a door, the doorposts being the snow itself. . . .

You cannot stand upright in this house, as much on account of its low roof as the suffocating smoke; and consequently you must always lie down, or sit flat upon the ground, the usual posture of the Savages. When you go out, the cold, the snow, and the danger of getting lost in these great woods drive you in again more quickly than the wind, and keep you a prisoner in a dungeon which has neither lock nor key.

This prison, in addition to the uncomfortable position that one must occupy upon a bed of earth, has four other great discomforts,—cold, heat, smoke, and dogs. As to the cold, you have the snow at your head with only a pine branch between, often nothing but your hat, and the winds are free to enter in a thousand places. . . . When I lay down at night I could study through this opening both the Stars and the Moon as easily as if I had been in the open fields.

Nevertheless, the cold did not annoy me as much as the heat from the fire. A little place like their cabins is easily heated by a good fire, which sometimes roasted and broiled me on all sides, for the cabin was so narrow that I could not protect myself against the heat. You cannot move to right or left, for the Savages, your neighbors, are at your elbows; you cannot withdraw to the rear, for you encounter the wall of snow, or the bark of the cabin which shuts you in. I did not know what position to take. Had I stretched myself out, the place was so narrow that my legs would have been halfway in the fire; to roll myself up in a ball, and crouch down in their way, was a position I could not retain as long as they could; my clothes were all scorched and burned. You will ask me perhaps if the snow at our backs did not melt under so much heat. I answer, "no"; that if sometimes the heat softened it in the least, the cold immediately turned it into ice. I will say, however, that both the cold and the heat are endurable, and that some remedy may be found for these two evils.

But, as to the smoke, I confess to you that it is martyrdom. It almost killed me, and made me weep continually, although I had neither grief nor sadness in my heart. It sometimes grounded all of us who were in the cabin;

that is, it caused us to place our mouths against the earth in order to breathe. For, although the Savages were accustomed to this torment, yet occasionally it became so dense that they, as well as I, were compelled to prostrate themselves, and as it were to eat the earth, so as not to drink the smoke. I have sometimes remained several hours in this position, especially during the most severe cold and when it snowed; for it was then the smoke assailed us with the greatest fury, seizing us by the throat, nose, and eyes. . . .

As to the dogs, which I have mentioned as one of the discomforts of the Savages' houses, I do not know that I ought to blame them, for they have sometimes rendered me good service. . . . These poor beasts, not being able to live outdoors, came and lay down sometimes upon my shoulders, sometimes upon my feet, and as I only had one blanket to serve both as covering and mattress, I was not sorry for this protection, willingly restoring to them a part of the heat which I drew from them. It is true that, as they were large and numerous, they occasionally crowded and annoyed me so much, that in giving me a little heat they robbed me of my sleep, so that I very often drove them away. . . .

7

PEDRO NARANJO AND JOSEPHE
Testimony of Pueblo Indians

Once Cortés conquered Tenochtitlán in 1521, the Spanish quickly gained control over the empire of the Mexica. Indians accustomed to tribute and forced labor adapted to new masters. But as Spanish soldiers, settlers, and missionaries moved northward in search of precious metals and outposts to secure their empire from European and Indian enemies, they found that the methods that had worked farther south failed among the more independent tribes that had never been conquered by their Aztec predecessors. Franciscan and Jesuit missionaries struggled mightily to convert Native Americans as settlement inched northward; by 1670, about twenty-eight hundred Spaniards populated the valley of the Rio Grande.

The country was generally poor, punctuated only by an occasional silver mine; the population lived largely by farming and raising livestock. Needed supplies from Mexico arrived infrequently and at great cost. Governors and missionaries battled for preeminence, while settlers, there at the king's command, were disgruntled. The Indians, however sincere their conversion to Catholicism, were at the bottom of society and bore the

Charles Wilson Hackett, *Revolt of the Pueblo Indians of New Mexico and Otermín's Attempted Reconquest, 1680–1682* (Albuquerque: University of New Mexico Press, 1942), 238–42, 245–49.

brunt of these harsh circumstances. Nor were the old religions dead. The valley was a true frontier, with Apache, Hopi, and Navaho—all beyond Spanish power—threatening the Pueblo Indians while providing a powerful example of freedom.

The uprising of the Pueblo Indians in 1680 drove the Spanish out of Santa Fe and the surrounding settlements. Four hundred Spaniards died during the conflict, and the rest retreated south to El Paso. Efforts at reconquest in 1681 had only temporary success. Many of the converted Indians who made peace at La Isleta moved south for Spanish protection against their tribal enemies. But others remained independent and returned to the practice of their native religions. In the 1690s, a new Spanish commander, Don Diego de Vargas, brought most of the Pueblo tribes back under Spanish rule. Meanwhile, however, use of Spanish horses among the Indians had spread far northward. The combined use of horses and the rifle—which had been carried westward by English and French frontiersmen and traders—transformed native life in the West and gave birth to the "brave" who has long dominated the American imagination.

Pedro Naranjo and Josephe were captured by the Spanish during the Pueblo rebellion and brought before a royal court in 1681. While Pedro was quite contrite in his testimony to the court regarding his admitted role in the revolt, Josephe seized the opportunity to tell of the colonists' cruelty.

QUESTIONS TO CONSIDER

1. How did Pedro Naranjo explain the revolt? To what extent do you think he was tailoring his answer to his Spanish questioners?
2. How did Josephe explain the revolt? What differences are there between his account and Pedro Naranjo's?
3. According to Josephe, what were the strategic objectives of the revolt's leaders? How did they inspire the Pueblo Indians to revolt?

DECLARATION OF PEDRO NARANJO OF THE QUERES NATION

December 19, 1681

In the said plaza de armas on the said day, month, and year, for the prosecution of the judicial proceedings of this case his lordship caused to appear before him an Indian prisoner named Pedro Naranjo, a native of the pueblo of San Felipe, of the Queres nation, who was captured in the advance and attack upon the pueblo of La Isleta. He makes himself understood very well in the Castilian [Spanish] language and speaks his mother tongue and the Tegua. He took the oath in due legal form in the name of God, our Lord, and a sign of the cross. . . .

Asked whether he knows the reason or motives which the Indians of this kingdom had for rebelling, forsaking the law of God and obedience to his Majesty, and committing such grave and atrocious crimes, and who were the leaders and principal movers, and by whom and how it was ordered; and why they burned the images, temples, crosses, rosaries, and things of divine worship, committing such atrocities as killing priests, Spaniards, women, and children, and the rest that he might know touching the question, he said that since the government of Señor General Hernando Ugarte y la Concha they have planned to rebel on various occasions through conspiracies of the Indian sorcerers, and that although in some pueblos the messages were accepted, in other parts they would not agree to it; and that it is true that during the government of the said señor general seven or eight Indians were hanged for this same cause, whereupon the unrest subsided. Some time thereafter they [the conspirators] sent from the pueblo of Los Taos through the pueblos of the custodia two deerskins with some pictures on them signifying conspiracy after their manner, in order to convoke the people to a new rebellion, and the said deerskins passed to the province of Moqui, where they refused to accept them. The pact which they had been forming ceased for the time being, but they always kept in their hearts the desire to carry it out, so as to live as they are living to-day. Finally, in the past years, at the summons of an Indian named Popé, who is said to have communication with the devil, it happened that in an estufa [meeting room] of the pueblo of Los Taos there appeared to the said Popé three figures of Indians who never came out of the estufa. They gave the said Popé to understand that they were going underground to the lake of Copala.[1] He saw these figures emit fire from all the extremities of their bodies, and that one of them was called Caudi, another Tilini, and the other Tleume; and these three beings spoke to the said Popé, who was in hiding from the secretary, Francisco Xavier, who wished to punish him as a sorcerer. They told him to make a cord of maguey fiber and tie some knots in it which would signify the number of days that they must wait before the rebellion. He said that the cord was passed through all the pueblos of the kingdom so that the ones which agreed to it [the rebellion] might untie one knot in a sign of obedience, and by the other knots they would know the days which were lacking; and this was to be done on pain of death to those who refused to agree to it. As a sign of agreement and notice of having concurred in the treason and perfidy they were to send up smoke signals to that effect in each one of the pueblos singly. The said cord was taken from pueblo to pueblo by the swiftest youths under the penalty of death if they revealed the secret. Everything being thus arranged, two days before the time set for its execution, because his lordship had learned of it and had imprisoned two Indian accomplices from the pueblo of Tesuque, it was carried out prematurely that night, because it seemed to them that they were now discovered; and they killed religious, Spaniards, women, and children. This being done, it was proclaimed in all the pueblos that everyone in common should obey the commands of their father whom they did not know, which would be given through El Caydi[2] or El Popé. This was heard by Alonso Catití, who came to the pueblo of this declarant to say that everyone must unite to go to the villa to kill the governor and the Spaniards who had remained with him, and that he who did not obey would, on their return, be beheaded; and in fear of this they

1. **Copala:** A mystical site.
2. **El Caydi:** A local leader; variant of *caudillo*.

agreed to it. Finally the señor governor and those who were with him escaped from the siege, and later this declarant saw that as soon as the Spaniards had left the kingdom an order came from the said Indian, Popé, in which he commanded all the Indians to break the lands and enlarge their cultivated fields, saying that now they were as they had been in ancient times, free from the labor they had performed for the religious and the Spaniards, who could not now be alive. He said that this is the legitimate cause and the reason they had for rebelling, because they had always desired to live as they had when they came out of the lake of Copala. Thus he replies to the question.

Asked for what reason they so blindly burned the images, temples, crosses, and other things of divine worship, he stated that the said Indian, Popé, came down in person, and with him El Saca and El Chato from the pueblo of Los Taos, and other captains and leaders and many people who were in his train, and he ordered in all the pueblos through which he passed that they instantly break up and burn the images of the holy Christ, the Virgin Mary and the other saints, the crosses, and everything pertaining to Christianity, and that they burn the temples, break up the bells, and separate from the wives whom God had given them in marriage and take those whom they desired. In order to take away their baptismal names, the water, and the holy oils, they were to plunge into the rivers and wash themselves with amole, which is a root native to the country, washing even their clothing, with the understanding that there would thus be taken from them the character of the holy sacraments. They did this, and also many other things which he does not recall, given to understand that this mandate had come from the Caydi and the other two who emitted fire from their extremities in the said estufa of Taos, and that they thereby returned to the state of their antiquity, as when they came from the lake of Copala; that this was the better life and the one they desired, because the God of the Spaniards was worth nothing and theirs was very strong, the Spaniards' God being rotten wood. These things were observed and obeyed by all except some who, moved by the zeal of Christians, opposed it, and such persons the said Popé caused to be killed immediately. He saw to it that they at once erected and rebuilt their houses of idolatry which they call estufas, and made very ugly masks in imitation of the devil in order to dance the dance of the cacina; and he said likewise that the devil had given them to understand that living thus in accordance with the law of their ancestors, they would harvest a great deal of maize, many beans, a great abundance of cotton, calabashes [pumpkins], and very large watermelons and cantaloupes; and that they could erect their houses and enjoy abundant health and leisure. As he has said, the people were very much pleased, living at their ease in this life of their antiquity, which was the chief cause of their falling into such laxity. Following what has already been stated, in order to terrorize them further and cause them to observe the diabolical commands, there came to them a pronouncement from the three demons already described, and from El Popé, to the effect that he who might still keep in his heart a regard for the priests, the governor, and the Spaniards would be known from his unclean face and clothes, and would be punished. And he stated that the said four persons stopped at nothing to have their commands obeyed. Thus he replies to the question.

Asked what arrangements and plans they had made for the contingency of the Spaniards' return, he said that what he knows concerning the question is that they were always saying they would have to fight to the death, for they do not wish to live in any other way than they are living at present; and the demons in the estufa of Taos had given them to understand that as soon as the Spaniards began to move toward this kingdom they would warn them so that they might unite, and none of them would be caught. He having been questioned further and repeatedly touching the case, he said that he has nothing more to say. . . . His declaration being read to him, he affirmed and ratified all of it. He declared himself to be eighty years of age, and he signed it with his lordship and the interpreters and assisting witnesses. . . .

DECLARATION OF JOSEPHE, SPANISH-SPEAKING INDIAN

December 19, 1681

In this said place and plaza de armas of this army on the 19th day of the month of December, 1681, for the said judicial proceedings of this case, his lordship caused to appear before him an Indian prisoner named Josephe, able to speak the Castilian language, a servant of Sargento Mayor Sebastián de Herrera who fled from him and went among the apostates. . . . Being asked why he fled from his master, the said Sargento Mayor Sebastián de Herrera, and went to live with the treacherous Indian apostates of New Mexico, where he has been until he came among us on the present occasion, he said that the reason why he left was that he was suffering hunger in the plaza de armas of La Toma [del Río del Norte], and a companion of his named Domingo urged this declarant to go to New Mexico for a while, so as to find out how matters stood with the Indians and to give warning to the Spaniards of any treason. They did not come with the intention of remaining always with the apostate traitors and rebels, and after they arrived they [the Indians] killed the said Domingo, his companion, because of the Pecos Indians having seen him fighting in the villa along with the Spaniards. He said that because his comrade was gone he had remained until now, when he saw the Spaniards and came to them, warning them not to be careless with the horses, because he had heard the traitors say that although the Spaniards might conclude peace with them, they would come to attack them by night and take away the horses. Thus he responds to this question.

Asked what causes or motives the said Indian rebels had for renouncing the law of God and obedience to his Majesty, and for committing so many kinds of crimes, and who were the instigators of the rebellion, and what he had heard while he was among the apostates, he said that the prime movers of the rebellion were two Indians of San Juan, one named El Popé and the other El Taqu, and another from Taos named Saca, and another from San Ildefonso named Francisco. He knows that these were the principals, and the causes they gave were alleged ill treatment and injuries received from the present secretary, Francisco Xavier, and the maestre de campo, Alonso García, and from the sargentos mayores, Luis de Quintana and Diego López, because they beat them, took away what they had, and made them work without pay. Thus he replies.

Asked why, since the said rebels had been of different minds, some believing that they should give themselves up peacefully and others opposing it, when the Spaniards arrived at the sierra of La Cieneguilla de Cochití, where the leaders of the uprising and people from all the nations were assembled, they had not attempted to give themselves up and return to the holy faith and to obedience to his Majesty—for while they had made some signs, they had done nothing definite—he said that although it is true that as soon as the Spaniards arrived some said that it was better to give up peaceably than to have war, the young men were unwilling to agree, saying that they wished to fight. In particular one Spanish-speaking Indian or coyote named Francisco, commonly called El Ollita, said that no one should surrender in peace, that all must fight, and that although some of his brothers were coming with the Spaniards, if they fought on the side of the Spaniards he would kill them, and if they came over to the side of the Indians he would not harm them. Whereupon everyone was disturbed, and there having arrived at this juncture Don Luis Tupatú, governor of the pueblo of Los Pecuríes, while they were thus consulting, news came to the place where the junta [meeting] was being held from another Indian named Alonso Catití, a leader of the uprising, believed to be a coyote, in which he sent to notify the people that he had already planned to deceive the Spaniards with feigned peace.

He had arranged to send to the pueblo of Cochití all the prettiest, most pleasing, and neatest Indian women so that, under pretense of coming down to prepare food for the Spaniards, they could provoke them to lewdness, and that night while they were with them, the said coyote Catití would come down with all the men of the Queres and Jemez nations, only the said Catití attempting to speak with the said Spaniards, and at a shout from him they would all rush down to kill the said Spaniards; and he gave orders that all the rest who were in the other junta where the said Don Luis and El Ollita were present, should at the same time attack the horse drove, so as to finish that too. This declarant being present during all these proceedings, and feeling compassion because of the treason they were plotting, he determined to come to warn the Spaniards, as he did, whereupon they put themselves under arms and the said Indians again went up to the heights of the sierra, and the Spaniards withdrew. Thus he replies to the question. . . .

. . . He said that what he has stated in his declaration is the truth and what he knows, under charge of his oath, which he affirms and ratifies, this, his said declaration, being read to him. He did not sign because of not knowing how, nor does he know his age. Apparently he is about twenty years old. . . .

8

New World Images

Native Americans did not consider themselves collectively as one group of people or as a single nation before their encounter with Europeans and did not have a universal term for themselves. By the time they realized the necessity of adopting a common name to differentiate themselves from the new strangers in their midst, Native Americans may have had little choice but to choose one that the whites had applied to them. In the end both sides adopted the word Indian, based on Christopher Columbus's geographical error in supposing he had arrived in Asia rather than in a new world.

The next most common name used by Europeans was much less attractive. Medieval legend had depicted wild club-swinging men of the forest as hairy, naked links between humans and animals. Named in Latin silvaticus, "men of the woods," they became sauvage in French and salvage in English, a word that finally turned into savage.

These and other names bestowed on Native Americans by whites, such as wildmen and barbarian, reflected a belief among Europeans that Indians were essentially their opposites. Whites defined Indians as "the other" and viewed them as heathens who performed human sacrifices and were cannibals. They saw them as dirty, warlike, superstitious, sexually promiscuous, and brutal to their captives and to their women.

At the same time, Europeans, troubled by what they regarded as the decadence of their own society, recognized positive traits in the Indians that Europeans lacked. To many Europeans, especially those who never migrated to the New World, Indians seemed direct, innocent, hospitable, courteous, handsome, and courageous. Their independence, proud bearing, and stamina suggested a nobility that Europeans seemed to be losing. From this image came the composite ideal of the "noble savage."

The earliest attempt by a European to depict the domestic lives of Native Americans can be seen in the first image below, an anonymous German woodcut published around 1505 and based on explorer and geographer Amerigo Vespucci's account of his voyages between 1497 and 1504 to the New World. The inscription describes natives as "naked, handsome, brown, well shaped in body; . . . No one has anything, but all things are in common. And the men have as wives those who please them, be they mothers, sisters or friends. . . . They also fight with each other; and they eat each other. . . . They become a hundred and fifty years old and have no government."

The second image below is another domestic scene of Indian life, this time from a French source, François de Creux's Historia Canadensis, published in 1664. Note that both figures in this image are Indian women.

From a very different era, the third image below depicts a conference between Colonel Henry Bouquet and some of the Indians he defeated at the Battle of Bushy Run in 1763. Many tribes in the Ohio Valley, led by Pontiac, a chief of the Ottawas, rose up against the British in 1763, laying waste to white settlements in the valley. The engraving's central focus is the return of white captives taken during these raids. The theme of whites, and especially white women, captured by Indians greatly fascinated the colonists and their European counterparts, and captivity narratives were best sellers on both sides of the Atlantic.

QUESTIONS TO CONSIDER

1. What perceptions of the New World inhabitants do these images present? How might Europeans have reacted to these images?
2. How does each image define Native Americans as inferior to Europeans but also suggest a sense of dignity and nobility?
3. Viewing the images in chronological order, how does the idea of Indian–white relations change over time?
4. What attitude toward the Indians and what view of Indian–white relations are suggested by the image of the English captives?

Unknown German artist, "First European Attempt to Depict the Domestic Life of Native Americans," ca. 1505. *Spencer Collection, The New York Public Library / Art Resource, NY*

Unknown French artist, "Huron Woman," 1664. *From* Histo-riae Canadensis *by Father Francisco Creuxio, 1664 / De Agostini Picture Library / M. Seemuller / Bridgeman Images*

The Indians delivering up the English Captives to Colonel Bouquet near his Camp at the Forks of Muskingum in North America in Novr. 1764.

Unknown European artist, "Return of English Captives during a Conference between Colonel Henry Bouquet and Indians on the Muskingum River," 1764. *Library of Congress, Prints and Photographs Division, LC-USZ62-103*

PART TWO

The Colonial Experience
A Rapidly Changing Society

B y the end of the seventeenth century, Europeans had experienced more than two centuries of contact with the New World. After an initial uncertain period of discovery and experimentation, the social institutions and patterns of life for European settlers had become stronger and more stable as their colonies developed. In 1660, the entire settler population of British America would have fit into a baseball stadium, but by 1750 the colonists numbered more than one million. New France, which at its peak in 1763 was less populous but larger in area than British North America, had also developed longstanding and successful patterns of settlement and commerce to the north in Quebec and to the west, running from Louisiana up the middle of the continent to Canada. Meanwhile, the Spanish, who controlled Florida and parts of the Caribbean, typically concentrated their mapmaking efforts on their vast, heavily populated, and wealthy territories in Mexico and South America and their less developed smattering of settlements in California and what is now the southwestern United States.

News of opportunities in British North America brought an increasing number of immigrants from every corner of Europe and even parts of the Middle East. Germans like Gottlieb Mittelberger were among the largest groups to populate the middle colonies of the Atlantic seaboard. Most signed on as indentured servants to pay their passage, facing extremely harsh circumstances when they arrived. Yet some eventually prospered and remade themselves as Americans. Some newcomers, like Eliza Lucas Pinckney, who arrived from Antigua in the British West Indies at an early age and was the child of a British army officer, were prosperous enough to own land and slaves. However, by the time such newcomers as Mittelberger and Pinckney arrived in the mid-eighteenth century, founding father Benjamin Franklin's family had already been in British North America for a century.

45

By the mid-eighteenth century Europeans firmly controlled the eastern seaboard and much of the Gulf coast. Native Americans and Europeans continued to wage deadly wars, sometimes as allies and sometimes as enemies. However, as the threat that natives would push out settlers receded, what seemed to concern many settlers even more than attack was the contradictory place that their indigenous neighbors held within the thriving colonies. The relentless European hunger for land to support new settlers created nearly constant day-to-day conflict rather than full-scale war. Settlers widely recognized that the Indians had taught them to hunt, to farm, to fight wars, and ultimately to survive in the New World, but often the same settlers viewed Native Americans as ignorant and in need of reeducation, protection, or even elimination. And the native peoples' persistent and prior claim to the land presented legal and social problems that continue to this day.

Mary Rowlandson's best-selling account of her brief captivity among the Wampanoag illustrates Anglo-Americans' anxieties about their Native American neighbors. Her narrative was the first in a long tradition of popular tales of life among the Indians that represented them in an aura of romance and danger that often contrasted with surprisingly ordinary, everyday encounters. Mary Jemison's account presents a different view of the relations between settlers and Native Americans: Jemison was taken by the Seneca as a child during the French and Indian War and chose to stay with them.

While patterns of interaction between Europeans and native peoples were becoming increasingly settled and familiar during the colonial period, North American slavery was still in its infancy. The transatlantic slave trade would eventually remove some twenty million laborers from Africa and impoverish much of the continent. The roughly twelve million who survived the brutal trip across the ocean contributed enormously to the colonies' prosperity through vast amounts of unpaid labor. Olaudah Equiano graphically describes what would become the critical workforce for the sugar plantations of the West Indies and, in the eighteenth century, would enrich the economies of the middle colonies and New England. By 1720, African slaves in South Carolina outnumbered whites by about two to one, and colonists started to pass laws based on race. These enactments would come to distinguish and define black and white as fundamentally different categories of settler.

In this period of accelerating growth and change, Benjamin Franklin may have provided the best assessment of the seeds of this new nation in the making. Testifying before the British Parliament, he described a people who were still loyal to their king—but who were becoming too American to remain loyal on any terms but their own.

9

MARY ROWLANDSON
Prisoner of War

The Sovereignty and Goodness of God, by Mary Rowlandson (ca. 1637–ca. 1711), first published in 1682, is an English Puritan woman's account of her capture and temporary slavery among Indians during Metacom's (King Philip's) War (1675–1676) in southeastern New England. King Philip's War had begun in 1675 after decades of tension between land-hungry settlers and Massachusetts Indians. Wampanoag chief Metacom, known to settlers as King Philip, made a bloody attempt to turn back the incursion of settlers into native lands. This uprising, by the very same Indians who only a half-century earlier had participated in the first Thanksgiving dinner, plunged New England into a violent conflict and forced native peoples from across the region to make difficult choices in allegiance between their fellow Native Americans and longtime European friends, business associates, and relatives by marriage.

The first in what would become a best-selling genre of "captivity narratives," Rowlandson's account describes her eighty-day ordeal, which began on February 20, 1676, when King Philip's native army burned her home to the ground, shot her relatives, and took her and her children captive. Only after Puritan English neighbors finally purchased Rowlandson's freedom was she able to return to her husband, minister Joseph Rowlandson.

Scholars have speculated about what in Rowlandson's narrative is true and what represents the influence of the powerful Puritan elders who had supervised the writing and publication of the manuscript. The text has been variously viewed as an early feminist text about the difficulties of being a woman in colonial America; a titillating tale of hidden social and sexual race-mixing between a minister's wife and the native man to whom she was given as a squaw; an attempt to justify settler brutality against Indians during King Philip's War; and even a story of Europeans becoming American. Whatever else it is, Rowlandson's account reflects the experience of one of the many ordinary people on both sides whose lives were plunged into chaos by the conflict.

Mary Rowlandson, *The Sovereignty and Goodness of God*, ed. Neal Salisbury (Boston: Bedford/St. Martin's, 1997), 68–112.

QUESTIONS TO CONSIDER

1. Why was Rowlandson's narrative such popular reading?
2. Rowlandson called the Indians "ravenous Beasts" but claimed that none of them "ever offered me the least abuse of unchastity." Explain this seeming contradiction.
3. Why were some of the Indians willing to help Rowlandson escape?
4. Who was Rowlandson's intended audience, and how did that audience shape what she wrote?

On the tenth of February 1675, Came the *Indians* with great numbers upon *Lancaster* [in Massachusetts, about thirty miles west of Boston]: Their first coming was about Sun-rising; hearing the noise of some Guns, we looked out; several Houses were burning, and the Smoke ascending to Heaven. There were five persons taken in one house, the Father, and the Mother and a sucking Child, they knockt on the head; the other two they took and carried away alive. There were two others, who being out of their Garison upon some occasion were set upon; one was knockt on the head, the other escaped: Another there was who running along was shot and wounded, and fell down; he begged of them his life, promising them Money (as they told me) but they would not hearken to him but knockt him in head, and stript him naked, and split open his Bowels. Another seeing many of the *Indians* about his Barn, ventured and went out, but was quickly shot down. There were three others belonging to the same Garison who were killed; the *Indians* getting up upon the roof of the Barn, had advantage to shoot down upon them over their Fortification. Thus these murtherous wretches went on, burning, and destroying before them.

At length they came and beset our own house, and quickly it was the dolefullest day that ever mine eyes saw. The House stood upon the edge of a hill; some of the *Indians* got behind the hill, others into the Barn, and others behind any thing that could shelter them; from all which places they shot against the House, so that the Bullets seemed to fly like hail; and quickly they wounded one man among us, then another, and then a third. About two hours (according to my observation, in that amazing time) they had been about the house before they prevailed to fire it (which they did with Flax and Hemp, which they brought out of the Barn, and there being no defence about the House, only two Flankers[1] at two opposite corners, and one of them not finished) they fired it once and one ventured out and quenched it, but they quickly fired it again, and that took. Now is that dreadfull hour come, that I have often heard of (in time of War, as it was the case of others) but now mine eyes see it. Some in our house were fighting for their lives, others wallowing in their blood, the House on fire over our heads, and the bloody Heathen ready to knock us on the head, if we stirred out. Now might we hear Mothers & Children crying out for themselves, and one another,

1. **Flankers:** Lateral projecting fortifications or walls.

Lord, What shall we do? Then I took my Children (and one of my sisters, hers)[2] to go forth and leave the house: but as soon as we came to the door and appeared, the *Indians* shot so thick that the bullets rattled against the House, as if one had taken an handfull of stones and threw them, so that we were fain to give back. . . . But out we must go, the fire increasing, and coming along behind us, roaring, and the Indians gaping before us with their Guns, Spears and Hatchets to devour us. No sooner were we out of the House, but my Brother in Law (being before wounded, in defending the house, in or near the throat) fell down dead, whereat the *Indians* scorn-fully shouted, and hallowed, and were presently upon him, stripping off his cloaths, the bulletts flying thick, one went through my side, and the same (as would seem) through the bowels and hand of my dear Child in my arms.[3] One of my elder Sisters Children, named *William*, had then his Leg broken, which the *Indians* perceiving, they knockt him on head. Thus were we butchered by those merciless Heathen, standing amazed, with the blood running down to our heels. My eldest Sister being yet in the House, and seeing those wofull sights, the Infidels haling Mothers one way, and Children another, and some wallowing in their blood: and her elder Son telling her that her Son *William* was dead, and my self was wounded, she said, And, *Lord, let me dy with them;* which was no sooner said, but she was struck with a Bullet, and fell down dead over the threshold. I hope she is reaping the fruit of her good labours, being faithfull to the service of God in her place. . . . [T]he *Indians* laid hold of us, pulling me one way, and the Children another, and said, *Come go along with us;* I told them they would kill me: they answered, *If I were willing to go along with them, they would not hurt me.*

Oh the doleful sight that now was to behold at this House! *Come, behold the works of the Lord, what desolations he has made in the Earth.*[4] Of thirty seven persons who were in this one House, none escaped either present death, or a bitter captivity, save only one, who might say as he, *Job* 1. 15. *And I only am escaped alone to tell the News.* There were twelve killed, some shot, some stab'd with their Spears, some knock'd down with their Hatchets. When we are in prosperity, Oh the little that we think of such dreadfull sights, and to see our dear Friends, and Relations ly bleeding out their heart-blood upon the ground. There was one who was chopt into the head with a Hatchet, and stript naked, and yet was crawling up and down. It is a solemn sight to see so many Christians lying in their blood, some here, and some there, like a company of Sheep torn by Wolves. All of them stript naked by a company of hell-hounds, roaring, singing, ranting and insulting, as if they would have torn our very hearts out; yet the Lord by his Almighty power preserved a number of us from death, for there were twenty-four of us taken alive and carried captive.

---

2. **"my Children (and one of my sisters, hers)":** Rowlandson had three children: Joseph Jr., fourteen, Mary, ten, and Sarah, six. Two of her sisters and their families were among the thirty-seven people living in the Rowlandson garrison.
3. **"dear Child in my arms":** Rowlandson's youngest child, Sarah.
4. Psalm 46:8.

I had often before this said, that if the *Indians* should come, I should chuse rather to be killed by them than be taken alive but when it came to the tryal my mind changed; their glittering weapons so daunted my spirit, that I chose rather to go along with those (as I may say) ravenous Beasts, than that moment to end my dayes; and that I may the better declare what happened to me during that grievous Captivity, I shall particularly speak of the severall Removes we had up and down the Wilderness.

THE FIRST REMOVE

Now away we must go with those Barbarous Creatures, with our bodies wounded and bleeding, and our hearts no less than our bodies. About a mile we went that night, up upon a hill within sight of the Town, where they intended to lodge. There was hard by a vacant house (deserted by the English before, for fear of the *Indians*). I asked them whither I might not lodge in the house that night to which they answered, what will you love *English men* still? This was the dolefullest night that ever my eyes saw. Oh the roaring, and singing and danceing, and yelling of those black creatures in the night, which made the place a lively resemblance of hell. And as miserable was the waste that was there made, of Horses, Cattle, Sheep, Swine, Calves, Lambs, Roasting Pigs, and Fowls (which they had plundered in the Town) some roasting, some lying and burning, and some boyling to feed our merciless Enemies; who were joyfull enough though we were disconsolate. To add to the dolefulness of the former day, and the dismalness of the present night: my thoughts ran upon my losses and sad bereaved condition. All was gone, my Husband gone (at least separated from me, he being in the Bay;[5] and to add to my grief, the *Indians* told me they would kill him as he came homeward) my Children gone, my Relations and Friends gone, our House and home and all our comforts within door, and without, all was gone, (except my life) and I knew not but the next moment that might go too. There remained nothing to me but one poor wounded Babe, and it seemed at present worse than death that it was in such a pitiful condition, bespeaking Compassion, and I had no refreshing for it, nor suitable things to revive it.[6] . . .

THE SECOND REMOVE

But now, the next morning, I must turn my back upon the Town, and travel with them into the vast and desolate Wilderness, I knew not whither. It is not my tongue, or pen can express the sorrows of my heart, and bitterness of my spirit, that I had at this departure: but God was with me, in a wonderfull manner, carrying me along, and bearing up my spirit, that it did not quite fail. One of the *Indians* carried my poor wounded Babe upon a horse; it went

---

5. **the Bay:** In the eastern part of the colony, near the bay known as Massachusetts Bay.
6. English people in the seventeenth century referred to little children by the gender-neutral *it* rather than by *she* or *he*.

moaning all along, I shall dy, I shall dy. I went on foot after it, with sorrow that cannot be exprest. At length I took it off the horse, and carried it in my arms till my strength failed, and I fell down with it: Then they set me upon a horse with my wounded Child in my lap. . . .

After this it quickly began to snow, and when night came on, they stopt: and now down I must sit in the snow, by a little fire, and a few boughs behind me, with my sick Child in my lap; and calling much for water, being now (through the wound) fallen into a violent Fever. My own wound also growing so stiff, that I could scarce sit down or rise up; yet so it must be, that I must sit all this cold winter night upon the cold snowy ground, with my sick Child in my armes. . . .

THE THIRD REMOVE

The morning being come, they prepared to go on their way: One of the Indians *got up upon a horse, and they set me up behind him, with my poor sick Babe in my lap.* A very wearisome and tedious day I had of it; what with my own wound, and my Childs being so exceeding sick, and in a lamentable condition with her wound. It may be easily judged what a poor feeble condition we were in, there being not the least crumb of refreshing that came within either of our mouths, from *Wednesday* night to *Saturday* night, except only a little cold water. . . . I sat much alone with a poor wounded Child in my lap, which moaned night and day, having nothing to revive the body, or cheer the spirits of her, but in stead of that, sometimes one *Indian* would come and tell me in one hour, that your *Master* will knock your Child in the head, and then a second, and then a third, your *Master* will quickly knock your Child in the head.

. . . Thus nine dayes I sat upon my knees, with my Babe in my lap, till my flesh was raw again; my Child being even ready to depart this sorrowful world, they bade me carry it out to another Wigwam (I suppose because they would not be troubled with such spectacles) whither I went with a very heavy heart, and down I sat with the picture of death in my lap. About two houres in the night, my sweet Babe, like a lamb departed this life, on *Feb. 18. 1675*, It being about six *yeares*, and *five months* old. It was *nine dayes* from the first wounding, in this miserable condition, without any refreshing of one nature or other, except a little cold water . . . I went to take up my dead child in my arms to carry it with me, but they bid me let it alone: there was no resisting, but goe I must and leave it. When I had been at my masters *wigwam*, I took the first opportunity I could get, to go look after my dead child: when I came I askt them what they had done with it? then they told me it was upon the hill: then they went and shewed me where it was, where I saw the ground was newly digged, and there they told me they had buried it: *There I left that Child in the Wilderness, and must commit it, and my self also in the Wilderness-condition, to him who is above all.* God having taken away this dear Child, I went to see my daughter *Mary,* who was at this same *Indian Town,* at a *Wigwam* not very far off, though we had little liberty or opportunity to see one another: she was about ten years old, & taken from the door at first by a *Praying Indian* & afterward sold for a gun. When I came in sight, she would fall a weeping; at which they were provoked, and would not let me come near her, but bade me be gone; which was a heart-cutting word to me. I had one Child dead, another in the Wilderness, I knew not where, the third they would not let me come near to. . . .

Now the Indians began to talk of removing from this place, some one way, and some another. There were now besides my self nine *English* Captives in this place (all of them Children, except one Woman). I got an opportunity to go and take my leave of them; they being to go one way, and I another, *I asked them whether they were earnest with God for deliverance;* they told me, they did as they were able, and it was some comfort to me, that the Lord stirred up *Children to look to him.* . . .

THE EIGHTH REMOVE

. . . We travelled on till night; and in the morning, we must go over the River to *Philip's* crew. When I was in the Cannoo, I could not but be amazed at the numerous crew of Pagans that were on the Bank on the other side. When I came ashore, they gathered all about me, I sitting alone in the midst: I observed they asked one another questions, and laughed, and rejoyced over their Gains and Victories. Then my heart began to fail: and I fell a weeping which was the first time to my remembrance, that I wept before them. Although I had met with so much Affliction, and my heart was many times ready to break, yet could I not shed one tear in their sight: but rather had been all this while in a maze, and like one astonished: but now I may say as, Psal.137. 1. *By the rivers of* Babylon, *there we sat down: yea, we wept when we remembered Zion.* There one of them asked me, why I wept, I could hardly tell what to say: yet I answered, they would kill me: No, said he, none will hurt you. Then came one of them and gave me two spoonfulls of Meal to comfort me, and another gave me half a pint of Pease; which was more worth than many Bushels at another time. Then I went to see King *Philip,* he bade me come in and sit down, and asked me whether I would smoke (a usual Complement now adayes amongst Saints and Sinners) but this no way suited me. . . .

Now the *Indians* gather their Forces to go against *North-Hampton:* overnight one went about yelling and hooting to give notice of the design. Whereupon they fell to boyling of Ground-nuts, and parching of Corn (as many as had it) for their Provision: and in the morning away they went. *During my abode in this place,* Philip *spake to me to make a shirt for his boy, which* I *did, for which he gave me a shilling: I offered the money to my master, but he bade me keep it: and with it I bought a piece of Horse flesh.* Afterwards he asked me to make a Cap for his boy, for which he invited me to Dinner. I went, and he gave me a Pancake, about as big as two fingers; it was made of parched wheat, beaten, and fryed in Bears grease, but I thought I never tasted pleasanter meat in my life. There was a *Squaw* who spake to me to make a shirt for her *Sannup,*[7] for which she gave me a piece of Bear. Another asked me to knit a pair of Stockins, for which she gave me a quart of Pease: I boyled my Pease and Bear together, and invited my master and mistress to dinner. . . .

THE TWENTIETH REMOVE

. . . My master after he had had his drink, quickly came ranting into the *Wigwam* again, and called for Mr. *Hoar,*[8] drinking to him, and saying, *He was a good man:* and then again he would say, *Hang him, Rogue:* Being almost drunk, he would drink to him, and yet presently say he should be hanged. Then he called for me, I trembled to hear him, yet I was fain to go to him, and he drank to me, shewing no incivility. He was the first *Indian* I saw drunk all the while that I was amongst them. At last his *Squaw* ran out, and he after her, round the *Wigwam,* with his money jingling at his knees: But she escaped him: But having an old *Squaw* he ran to her: and so through the Lords mercy, we were no more troubled that night. *Yet I had not a comfortable nights rest: for I think I can say, I did not sleep for three nights together.* The night before the Letter came from the Council, I could not rest, I was so full of feares and troubles, God many times leaving us most in the dark, when deliverance is nearest: yea, at this time I could not rest, night nor day. The next night I was overjoyed, Mr. *Hoar* being come, and that with such good tidings. The third night I was even swallowed up with all thoughts of things, *viz.* that ever I should go home again; and that I must go, leaving my Children behind me in the *Wilderness;* so that sleep was now almost departed from mine eyes.

On *Tuesday morning* they called their *General Court* (as they call it) to consult and determine, whether I should go home or no: And they all as one man did seemingly consent to it, that I should go home; except *Philip,* who would not come among them. . . .

But to return again to my going home, where we may see a remarkable change of Providence: At first they were all against it, except my Husband would come for me; but afterwards they assented to it, and seemed much to rejoyce in it; some askt me to send them some Bread, others some Tobacco, others shaking me by the hand, offering me a Hood and Scarfe to ride in; not one moving hand or tongue against it. Thus hath the Lord answered my poor desire, and the many earnest requests of others put up unto God for me. . . . O the wonderfull power of God that I have seen, and the experience that I have had: *I have been in the midst of those roaring Lyons, and Salvage Bears, that feared neither God, nor Man, nor the Devil, by night and day, alone and in company: sleeping all sorts together, and yet not one of them ever offered me the least abuse of unchastity to me, in word or action.*[9] . . . So I took my leave of them, and in coming along my heart melted into tears, more than all the

---

7. **Sannup:** Married man, in this case her husband.
8. John Hoar was a lawyer from Concord, Massachusetts, whom Joseph Rowlandson enlisted to help free his wife.
9. Despite colonial fears of native sexuality, there is no record of sexual violation of captive women by indigenous peoples of eastern North America.

while I was with them, and I was almost swallowed up with the thoughts that ever I should go home again. . . .

I have seen the extrem vanity of this World: One hour I have been in health, and wealth, wanting nothing: But the next hour in sickness and wounds, and death, having nothing but sorrow and affliction.

10

MARY JEMISON

Captivity in a Different Light

Colonial captivity narratives fascinated Americans well into the twentieth century. The Narrative of the Life of Mrs. Mary Jemison, *published in 1824, was probably the most famous. Mary Jemison (1743–1833) was born on a ship heading from Ireland to America. After arriving in the New World, her parents worked on Iroquois land in central Pennsylvania. When the French and Indian War broke out in 1754, a young teenaged Mary and her whole family were taken hostage by a group of Frenchmen and Indians during an early morning raid. The narrative continues through her adult life, in which Mary is adopted by two sisters of the Seneca tribe, falls in love with an Indian and marries him, takes a second husband after he dies, bears several Seneca children, and eventually becomes a tribal elder known widely among whites and Indians.*

Although written in the first person, the narrative is not a true autobiography. Jemison was eighty years old in 1823—and illiterate—when Protestant minister James E. Seaver interviewed her and wrote the narrative that was published in the following year. Jemison died at age ninety among the Seneca. This selection begins with her capture.

QUESTIONS TO CONSIDER

1. Why might Mary Jemison have decided not to try to escape from the Seneca?
2. What are the key factors that enabled Mary Jemison to integrate herself into the Seneca? What would Mary Jemison likely say to modern commentators who believed that she was suffering from Stockholm syndrome and had been brainwashed by the Seneca?
3. Did Jemison regard whites as friends or enemies? Explain.

James Seaver, *A Narrative of the Life of Mary Jemison: De he wäh mis, the White Woman of the Genesee,* 6th ed. (New York: G. P. Putnam's Sons / Knickerbocker Press, 1898), 41–47, 49, 54, 68, 102–7, 130–31.

CHAPTER III

Breakfast was not yet ready, when we were alarmed by the discharge of a number of guns, that seemed to be near. Mother and the women . . . almost fainted at the report, and every one trembled with fear. On opening the door, the man and horse lay dead near the house, having just been shot by the Indians. . . .

The party that took us consisted of six Indians and four Frenchmen, who immediately commenced plundering, as I just observed, and took what they considered most valuable; consisting principally of bread, meal and meat. Having taken as much provision as they could carry, they set out with their prisoners in great haste, for fear of detection, and soon entered the woods. On our march that day, an Indian went behind us with a whip, with which he frequently lashed the children to make them keep up. In this manner we travelled till dark without a mouthful of food or a drop of water; although we had not eaten since the night before. Whenever the little children cried for water, the Indians would make them drink urine or go thirsty. At night they encamped in the woods without fire and without shelter, where we were watched with the greatest vigilance. Extremely fatigued, and very hungry, we were compelled to lie upon the ground supperless and without a drop of water to satisfy the cravings of our appetites. As in the day time, so the little ones were made to drink urine in the night if they cried for water. Fatigue alone brought us a little sleep for the refreshment of our weary limbs; and at the dawn of day we were again started on our march in the same order that we had proceeded on the day before. About sunrise we were halted, and the Indians gave us a full breakfast of provision that they had brought from my father's house. Each of us being very hungry, partook of this bounty of the Indians, except father, who was so much overcome with his situation—so much exhausted by anxiety and grief, that silent despair seemed fastened upon his countenance, and he could not be prevailed upon to refresh his sinking nature by the use of a morsel of food. Our repast being finished, we again resumed our march, and, before noon passed a small fort that I heard my father say was called Fort Canagojigge.

That was the only time that I heard him speak from the time we were taken till we were finally separated the following night.

Towards evening we arrived at the border of a dark and dismal swamp, which was covered with small hemlocks, or some other evergreen, and other bushes, into which we were conducted; and having gone a short distance we stopped to encamp for the night.

Here we had some bread and meat for supper: but the dreariness of our situation, together with the uncertainty under which we all labored, as to our future destiny, almost deprived us of the sense of hunger, and destroyed our relish for food.

Mother, from the time we were taken, had manifested a great degree of fortitude, and encouraged us to support our troubles without complaining; and by her conversation seemed to make the distance and time shorter, and the way more smooth. But father lost all his ambition in the beginning of our trouble, and continued apparently lost to every care—absorbed in melancholy. Here, as before, she insisted on the necessity of our eating; and we obeyed her, but it was done with heavy hearts.

As soon as I had finished my supper, an Indian took off my shoes and stockings and put a pair of moccasins on my feet, which my mother observed; and believing that they would spare my life, even if they should destroy the other captives, addressed me as near as I can remember in the following words:—

"My dear little Mary, I fear that the time has arrived when we must be parted forever. Your life, my child, I think will be spared; but we shall probably be tomahawked here in this lonesome place by the Indians. O! how can I part with you my darling? What will become of my sweet little Mary? Oh! how can I think of your being continued in captivity without a hope of your being rescued? O that death had snatched you from my embraces in your infancy; the pain of parting then would have been pleasing to what it now is; and I should have seen the end of your troubles!—Alas, my dear! my heart bleeds at the thoughts of what awaits you; but, if you leave us, remember my child your own name, and the name of your father and mother. Be careful and not forget your English tongue. If you shall have an opportunity to get away from the Indians, don't try to escape; for if you do they will find and destroy you. Don't forget, my little daughter, the prayers that I have learned you—say them often; be a good child, and God will bless you. May God bless you my child, and make you comfortable and happy."

During this time, the Indians stripped the shoes and stockings from the little boy that belonged to the woman who was taken with us, and put moccasins on his feet, as they had done before on mine. I was crying. An Indian took the little boy and myself by the hand, to lead us off from the company, when my mother exclaimed, "Don't cry Mary—don't cry my child. God will bless you! Farewell—farewell!"

The Indian led us some distance into the bushes, or woods, and there lay down with us to spend the night. The recollection of parting with my tender mother kept me awake, while the tears constantly flowed from my eyes. A number of times in the night the little boy begged of me earnestly to run away with him and get clear of the Indians; but remembering the advice I had so lately received, and knowing the dangers to which we should be exposed, in travelling without a path and without a guide, through a wilderness unknown to us, I told him that I would not go, and persuaded him to lie still till morning.

Early the next morning the Indians and Frenchmen that we had left the night before, came to us; but our friends were left behind. It is impossible for any one to form a correct idea of what my feelings were at the sight of those savages, whom I supposed had murdered my parents and brothers, sister, and friends, and left them in the swamp to be devoured by wild beasts! But what could I do? A poor little defenceless girl; without the power or means of escaping; without a home to go to, even if I could be liberated; without a knowledge of the direction or distance to my former place of residence; and without a living friend to whom to fly for protection, I felt a kind of horror, anxiety, and dread, that, to me, seemed insupportable. I durst not cry—I durst not complain; and to inquire of them the fate of my friends (even if I could have mustered resolution) was beyond my ability, as I could not speak their language, nor they understand mine. My only relief was in silent stifled sobs.

My suspicions as to the fate of my parents proved too true; for soon after I left them they were killed and scalped, together with Robert, Matthew, Betsey, and the woman and her two children, and mangled in the most shocking manner. . . .

In the course of the night they made me to understand that they should not have killed the family if the whites had not pursued them. . . .

At night we arrived at a small Seneca Indian town, at the mouth of a small river, that was called by the Indians, in the Seneca language, She-nan-jee, where the two Squaws to whom I belonged resided. There we landed, and the Indians went on; which was the last I ever saw of them.

Having made fast to the shore, the Squaws left me in the canoe while they went to their wigwam or house in the town, and returned with a suit of Indian clothing, all new, and very clean and nice. My clothes, though whole and good when I was taken, were now torn in pieces, so that I was almost naked. They first undressed me and threw my rags into the river; then washed me clean and dressed me in the new suit they had just brought, in complete Indian style; and then led me home and seated me in the center of their wigwam.

I had been in that situation but a few minutes before all the Squaws in the town came in to see me. I was soon surrounded by them, and they immediately set up a most dismal howling, crying bitterly, and wringing their hands in all the agonies of grief for a deceased relative.

Their tears flowed freely, and they exhibited all the signs of real mourning. At the commencement of this scene, one of their number began, in a voice somewhat between speaking and singing, to recite some words to the following purport, and continued the recitation till the ceremony was ended; the company at the same time varying the appearance of their countenances, gestures and tone of voice, so as to correspond with the sentiments expressed by their leader:

"Oh our brother! Alas! He is dead—he has gone; he will never return! Friendless he died on the field of the slain, where his bones are yet lying unburied! Oh, who will not mourn his sad fate? No tears dropped around him; oh, no! No tears of his sisters were there! He fell in his prime, when his arm was most needed to keep us from danger! Alas! he has gone! and left us in sorrow, his loss to bewail: Oh where is his spirit? His spirit went naked, and hungry it wanders, and thirsty and wounded it groans to return! Oh helpless and wretched, our brother has gone! . . . Though he fell on the field of the slain, with glory he fell, and his spirit went up to the land of his fathers in war! Then why do we mourn? With transports of joy they received him, and fed him, and clothed him, and welcomed him there! Oh friends, he is happy; then dry up your tears! His spirit has seen our distress, and sent us a helper whom with pleasure we greet. Dickewamis has come: then let us receive her with joy! She is handsome and pleasant! Oh! she is our sister, and gladly we welcome her here. In the place of our brother she stands in our tribe. With care we will guard her from trouble; and may she be happy till her spirit shall leave us."

In the course of that ceremony, from mourning they became serene— joy sparkled in their countenances, and they seemed to rejoice over me as over a long lost child. I was made welcome amongst them as a sister to the two Squaws before mentioned, and was called Dickewamis; which being interpreted, signifies a pretty girl, a handsome girl, or a pleasant, good thing. That is the name by which I have ever since been called by the Indians.

I afterwards learned that the ceremony I at that time passed through, was that of adoption. The two squaws had lost a brother in Washington's war, sometime in the year before and in consequence of his death went up to Fort Pitt, on the day on which I arrived there, in order to receive a prisoner or an enemy's scalp, to supply their loss.

It is a custom of the Indians, when one of their number is slain or taken prisoner in battle, to give to the nearest relative to the dead or absent, a prisoner, if they have chanced to take one, and if not, to give him the scalp of an enemy. On the return of the Indians from conquest, which is always announced by peculiar shoutings, demonstrations of joy, and the exhibition of some trophy of victory, the mourners come forward and make their claims. If they receive a prisoner, it is at their option either to satiate their vengeance by taking his life in the most cruel manner they can conceive of; or, to receive and adopt him into the family, in the place of him whom they have lost. All the prisoners that are taken in battle and carried to the encampment or town by the Indians, are given to the bereaved families, till their number is made good.

And unless the mourners have but just received the news of their bereavement, and are under the operation of a paroxysm of grief, anger and revenge; or, unless the prisoner is very old, sickly, or homely, they generally save him, and treat him kindly. But if their mental wound is fresh, their loss so great that they deem it irreparable, or if their prisoner or prisoners do not meet their approbation, no torture, let it be ever so cruel, seems sufficient to make them satisfaction. It is family, and not national, sacrifices amongst the Indians, that has given them an indelible stamp as barbarians, and identified their character with the idea which is generally formed of unfeeling ferocity, and the most abandoned cruelty.

It was my happy lot to be accepted for adoption; and at the time of the ceremony I was received by the two squaws, to supply the place of their brother in the family; and I was ever considered and treated by them as a real sister, the same as though I had been born of their mother.

During my adoption, I sat motionless, nearly terrified to death at the appearance and actions of the company, expecting every moment to feel their vengeance, and suffer death on the spot. I was, however, happily disappointed, when at the close of the ceremony the company retired, and my sisters went about employing every means for my consolation and comfort.

Being now settled and provided with a home, I was employed in nursing the children, and doing light work about the house. Occasionally I was sent out with the Indian hunters, when they went but a short distance, to help them carry their game.

My situation was easy; I had no particular hardships to endure. But still, the recollection of my parents, my brothers and sisters, my home, and my own captivity, destroyed my happiness, and made me constantly solitary, lonesome and gloomy.

My sisters would not allow me to speak English in their hearing; but remembering the charge that my dear mother gave me at the time I left her, whenever I chanced to be alone I made a business of repeating my prayer, catechism, or something I had learned in order that I might not forget my own language. By practising in that way I retained it till I came to Genesee flats, where I soon became acquainted with English people with whom I have been almost daily in the habit of conversing.

My sisters were diligent in teaching me their language; and to their great satisfaction I soon learned so that I could understand it readily, and speak it fluently. I was very fortunate in falling into their hands; for they were kind good natured women; peaceable and mild in their dispositions; temperate and decent in their habits, and very tender and gentle towards me. I have great reason to respect them, though they have been dead a great number of years. . . .

Not long after the Delawares came to live with us, at Wiishto, my sisters told me that I must go and live with one of them, whose name was Sheninjee. Not daring to cross them, or disobey their commands, with a great degree of reluctance I went; and Sheninjee and I were married according to Indian custom.

Sheninjee was a noble man; large in stature; elegant in his appearance; generous in his conduct; courageous in war; a friend to peace, and a great lover of justice. He supported a degree of dignity far above his rank, and merited and received the confidence and friendship of all the tribes with whom he was acquainted. Yet, Sheninjee was an Indian. The idea of spending my days with him, at first seemed perfectly irreconcilable to my feelings: but his good nature, generosity, tenderness, and friendship towards me, soon gained my affection; and, strange as it may seem, I loved him!—To me he was ever kind in sickness, and always treated me with gentleness; in fact, he was an agreeable husband, and a comfortable companion.

We lived happily together till the time of our final separation, which happened two or three years after our marriage, as I shall presently relate.

In the second summer of my living at Wiishto, I had a child at the time that the kernels of corn first appeared on the cob. When I was taken sick, Sheninjee was absent, and I was sent to a small shed, on the bank of the river, which was made of boughs, where I was obliged to stay till my husband returned. My two sisters, who were my only companions, attended me, and on the second day of my confinement my child was born but it lived only two days. It was a girl: and notwithstanding the shortness of the time that I possessed it, it was a great grief to me to lose it.

After the birth of my child, I was very sick, but was not allowed to go into the house for two weeks; when, to my great joy, Sheninjee returned, and I was taken in and as comfortably provided for as our situation would admit of. . . . I continued to gain my health, and in the fall was able to go to our winter quarters, on the Sciota, with the Indians.

From that time, nothing remarkable occurred to me till the fourth winter of my captivity, when I had a son born, while I was at Sciota: I had a quick recovery, and my child was healthy. To commemorate the name of my much lamented father, I called my son Thomas Jemison.

CHAPTER V

. . . I spent the winter comfortably, and as agreeably as I could have expected to, in the absence of my kind husband. Spring at length appeared, but Sheninjee was yet away; summer came on, but my husband had not found me. Fearful forebodings haunted my imagination; yet I felt confident that his affection for me was so great that if he was alive he would follow me and I should again see him. In the course of the summer, however, I received intelligence that soon after he left me at Yiskahwana he was taken sick and died at Wiishto. This was a heavy and an unexpected blow. I was now in my youthful days left a widow, with one son, and entirely dependent on myself for his and my support. My mother and her family gave me all the consolation in their power, and in a few months nay grief wore off and I became contented.

In a year or two after this, according to my best recollection of the time, the King of England offered a bounty to those who would bring in the prisoners that had been taken in the war, to some military post where they might be redeemed and set at liberty.

John Van Sice, a Dutchman, who had frequently been at our place, and was well acquainted with every prisoner at Genishau, resolved to take me to Niagara, that I might there receive my liberty and he the offered bounty. I was notified of his intention; but as I was fully determined not to be redeemed at that time, especially with his assistance, I carefully watched his movements in order to avoid falling into his hands. It so happened, however, that he saw me alone at work in a corn-field, and thinking probably that he could secure me easily, ran towards me in great haste. I espied him at some distance, and well knowing the amount of his errand, run from him with all the speed I was mistress of, and never once stopped till I reached Gardow. He gave up the chase, and returned: but I, fearing that he might be lying in wait for me, stayed three days and three nights in an old cabin at Gardow, and then went back trembling at every step for fear of being apprehended. I got home without difficulty; and soon after, the chiefs in council having learned the cause of my elopement, gave orders that I should not be taken to any military post without my consent; and that as it was my choice to stay, I should live amongst them quietly and undisturbed. But, notwithstanding the will of the chiefs, it was but a few days before the old king of our tribe told one of my Indian brothers that I should be redeemed, and he would take me to Niagara himself. In reply to the old king, my brother said that I should not be given up; but that, as it was my wish, I should stay with the tribe as long as I was pleased to. Upon this a serious quarrel ensued between them, in which my brother frankly told him that sooner than I should be taken by force, he would kill me with his own hands!—Highly enraged at the old king; my brother came to my sister's house, where I resided, and informed her of all that had passed respecting me; and that, if the old king should attempt to take me, as he firmly believed he would, he would immediately take my life, and hazard the consequences. He returned to the old king. As soon as I came in, my sister told me what she had just heard, and what she expected without doubt would befal me. Full of pity, and anxious for my preservation, she then directed me to take my child and go into some high weeds at no great distance from the house, and there hide myself and lay still till all was silent in the house, for my brother, she said, would return at evening and let her know the final conclusion of the matter, of which she promised to inform me in the following manner: If I was to be killed, she said she would bake a small cake and lay it at the door, on the outside, in a place that she then pointed out to me. When all was silent in the house, I was to creep softly to the door, and if the cake could not be found in the place specified, I was to go in: but if the cake was there, I was to take my child and, go as fast as I possibly could to a large spring on the south side of Samp's Creek, (a place that I had often seen,) and there wait till I should by some means hear from her.

Alarmed for my own safety, I instantly followed her advice, and went into the weeds, where I lay in a state of the greatest anxiety, till all was silent in the house, when I crept to the door, and there found, to my great distress, the little cake! I knew my fate was fixed, unless I could keep secreted till the storm was over, and accordingly crept back to the weeds, where my little Thomas lay, took him on my back, and laid my course for the spring as fast as my legs would carry me. Thomas was nearly three years old, and very large and heavy. I got to the spring early in the morning, almost overcome with fatigue, and at the same time fearing that I might be pursued and taken, I felt my life an almost insupportable burthen. I sat down with my child at the spring, and he and I made a breakfast of the little cake, and water of the spring, which I dipped and supped with the only implement which I possessed, my hand.

In the morning after I fled, as was expected, the old King came to our house in search of me, and to take me off; but, as I was not to be found, he gave me up, and went to Niagara with the prisoners he had already got into his possession.

As soon as the old King was fairly out of the way, my sister told my brother where he could find me. He immediately set out for the spring, and found me about noon. The first sight of him made me tremble with the fear of death; but when he came near, so that I could discover his countenance, tears of joy flowed down my cheeks, and I felt such a kind of instant relief as no one can possibly experience, unless when under the absolute sentence of death he receives an unlimited pardon. We were both rejoiced at the event of the old King's project; and after staying at the spring through the night, set out together for home early in the morning. When we got to a cornfield near the town, my brother secreted me till he could go and ascertain how my case stood; and finding that the old King was absent, and that all was peaceable, he returned to me, and I went home joyfully.

Not long after this, my mother went to Johnstown, on the Mohawk river, with five prisoners, who were redeemed by Sir William Johnson, and set at liberty.

When my son Thomas was three or four years old, I was married to an Indian, whose name was Hiokatoo, commonly called Gardow, by whom I had four daughters and two sons. . . .

CHAPTER IX

Soon after the close of the revolutionary war, my Indian brother, Kau-jises-tau-ge-au . . . offered me my liberty, and told me that if it was my choice I might go to my friends.

My son, Thomas, was anxious that I should go; and offered to go with me and assist me on the journey, by taking care of the younger children, and providing food as we travelled through the wilderness. But the Chiefs of our tribe, suspecting from his appearance, actions, and a few warlike exploits, that Thomas would be a great warrior, or a good counsellor, refused to let him leave them on any account whatever.

To go myself, and leave him, was more than I felt able to do; for he had been kind to me, and was one on whom I placed great dependence. The Chiefs refusing to let him go, was one reason for my resolving to stay; but another, more powerful, if possible, was, that I had got a large family of Indian children, that I must take with me; and that if I should be so fortunate as to find my relatives, they would despise them, if not myself; and treat us as enemies; or, at least with a degree of cold indifference, which I thought I could not endure.

Accordingly, after I had duly considered the matter, I told my brother that it was my choice to stay and spend the remainder of my days with my Indian friends, and live with my family as I had heretofore done. He appeared well pleased with my resolution, and informed me, that as that was my choice, I should have a piece of land that I could call my own, where I could live unmolested, and have something at my decease to leave for the benefit of my children.

FOR CRITICAL THINKING

1. Consider the differences between Mary Jemison's and Mary Rowlandson's lives before they were taken captive. How might these differences have affected their experiences with "Indian captivity"?
2. In what ways were their experiences with the Indians similar?
3. Rowlandson's narrative was published in 1682, during the early days
   of English colonization, while Jemison's was published in 1824, two
   generations after colonialization ended. How did the different peri-
   ods in which the two women lived influence their narratives and the
   way they were received?

11

OLAUDAH EQUIANO

The African Slave Trade

The Life of Olaudah Equiano, or Gustavus Vassa, the African, Written by Himself
*(1789) is one of the most important eyewitness accounts of the African slave trade.
While scholars have long agreed on the horrors of the trade, they have argued for more
than a century over how many people were involved. Estimates range from about nine-
and-a-half million to nearly fifteen million Africans imported into the Western Hemisphere. These numbers do not include those who were killed while resisting capture or
who died during passage.*

*Equiano's book is also the pioneering African American narrative of the journey
from slavery to freedom. It established many of the conventions for the more than six
thousand subsequent interviews, essays, and books by which former slaves told their
dramatic stories.*

*According to his own account, Equiano (ca. 1750–1797), an Ibo prince kidnapped
into slavery when he was eleven years old, was first brought to Barbados and then sent
to Virginia. After service in the British navy, he was at last sold to a Quaker merchant
who allowed Equiano to purchase his freedom in 1766. In later years he worked to advance the Church of England, his adopted religion, and to abolish the slave trade. Recent
scholarship suggests that Equiano may have been born in South Carolina, and this*

Olaudah Equiano, *The Life of Olaudah Equiano, or Gustavus Vassa, the African, Written by Himself* (New York: Isaac Knapp, 1837), 41–52.

work throws into question the reliability of his details of eighteenth-century life in West Africa. Despite this ongoing controversy, Equiano's narrative continues to fascinate and inform.

QUESTIONS TO CONSIDER

1. How does the narrative describe the treatment of slaves in the slave trade?
2. What were Olaudah Equiano's greatest fears during passage?
3. Equiano asked, "Learned you this from your God, who says unto you, Do unto all men as you would men should do unto you?" How might a slave trader have answered his question?

The first object which saluted my eyes when I arrived on the [Western Africa] coast, was the sea, and a slave ship, which was then riding at anchor, and waiting for its cargo. These filled me with astonishment, which was soon converted into terror, when I was carried on board. I was immediately handled, and tossed up to see if I were sound, by some of the crew; and I was now persuaded that I had gotten into a world of bad spirits, and that they were going to kill me. Their complexions, too, differing so much from ours, their long hair, and the language they spoke, (which was very different from any I had ever heard) united to confirm me in this belief. Indeed, such were the horrors of my views and fears at the moment, that, if ten thousand worlds had been my own, I would have freely parted with them all to have exchanged my condition with that of the meanest slave in my own country. When I looked round the ship too, and saw a large furnace of copper boiling, and a multitude of black people of every description chained together, every one of their countenances expressing dejection and sorrow, I no longer doubted of my fate; and, quite overpowered with horror and anguish, I fell motionless on the deck and fainted. When I recovered a little, I found some black people about me, who I believed were some of those who had brought me on board, and had been receiving their pay; they talked to me in order to cheer me, but all in vain. I asked them if we were not to be eaten by those white men with horrible looks, red faces, and long hair. They told me I was not: and one of the crew brought me a small portion of spirituous liquor in a wine glass, but, being afraid of him, I would not take it out of his hand. One of the blacks, therefore, took it from him and gave it to me, and I took a little down my palate, which, instead of reviving me, as they thought it would, threw me into the greatest consternation at the strange feeling it produced, having never tasted any such liquor before. Soon after this, the blacks who brought me on board went off, and left me abandoned to despair.

I now saw myself deprived of all chance of returning to my native country, or even the least glimpse of hope of gaining the shore, which I now considered as friendly; and I even wished for my former slavery in preference to my present situation, which was filled with horrors of every kind, still heightened by my ignorance of what I was to undergo. I was not long suffered to indulge my grief; I was soon put down under the decks, and there I received such a salutation in my nostrils as I had never experienced in my life: so that, with the loathsomeness of the stench, and crying together, I became so sick and low that I was not able to eat, nor had I the least desire to taste any thing. I now wished for the last friend, death, to relieve me; but soon, to my grief, two of the white men offered me eatables; and, on my refusing to eat, one of them held me fast by the hands, and laid me across, I think the windlass, and tied my feet, while the other flogged me severely.

I had never experienced any thing of this kind before, and although not being used to the water, I naturally feared that element the first time I saw it, yet, nevertheless, could I have got over the nettings, I would have jumped over the side, but I could not; and besides, the crew used to watch us very closely who were not chained down to the decks, lest we should leap into the water; and I have seen some of these poor African prisoners most severely cut, for attempting to do so, and hourly whipped for not eating. This indeed was often the case with myself. In a little time after, amongst the poor chained men, I found some of my own nation, which in a small degree gave ease to my mind. I inquired of these what was to be done with us? they gave me to understand, we were to be carried to these white people's country to work for them. I then was a little revived, and thought, if it were no worse than working, my situation was not so desperate; but still I feared I should be put to death, the white people looked and acted, as I thought, in so savage a manner; for I had never seen among any people such instances of brutal cruelty; and this not only shown towards us blacks, but also to some of the whites themselves. One white man in particular I saw, when we were permitted to be on deck, flogged so unmercifully with a large rope near the foremast, that he died in consequence of it; and they tossed him over the side as they would have done a brute. This made me fear these people the more; and I expected nothing less than to be treated in the same manner. I could not help expressing my fears and apprehensions to some of my countrymen; I asked them if these people had no country, but lived in this hollow place? (the ship) they told me they did not, but came from a distant one. "Then," said I, "how comes it in all our country we never heard of them?" They told me because they lived so very far off. I then asked where were their women? Had they any like themselves? I was told they had. "And why," said I, "do we not see them?" They answered, because they were left behind. I asked how the vessel could go? They told me they could not tell; but that there was cloth put upon the masts by the help of the ropes I saw, and then the vessel went on; and the white men had some spell or magic they put in the water when they liked, in order to stop the vessel. I was exceedingly amazed at this account, and really thought they were spirits. I therefore wished much to be from amongst them, for I expected they would sacrifice me; but my wishes were vain—for we were so quartered that it was impossible for any of us to make our escape. . . .

At last, when the ship we were in, had got in all her cargo, they made ready with many fearful noises, and we were all put under deck, so that we could not see how they managed the vessel. But this disappointment was the least of my sorrow. The stench of the hold while we were on the coast was so intolerably loathsome, that it was dangerous to remain there for any time, and some of us had been permitted to stay on the deck for the fresh air; but now that the whole ship's cargo were confined together, it became absolutely pestilential. The closeness of the place, and the heat of the climate, added to the number in the ship, which was so crowded that each had scarcely room to turn himself, almost suffocated us. This produced copious perspirations, so that the air soon became unfit for respiration, from a variety of loathsome smells, and brought on a sickness among the slaves, of which many died—thus falling victims to the improvident avarice, as I may call it, of their purchasers. This wretched situation was again aggravated by the galling of the chains, now became insupportable; and the filth of the necessary tubs, into which the children often fell, and were almost suffocated. The shrieks of the women, and the groans of the dying, rendered the whole a scene of horror almost inconceivable. Happily perhaps, for myself, I was soon reduced so low here that it was thought necessary to keep me almost always on deck; and from my extreme youth I was not put in fetters. In this situation I expected every hour to share the fate of my companions, some of whom were almost daily brought upon deck at the point of death, which I began to hope would soon put an end to my miseries. Often did I think many of the inhabitants of the deep much more happy than myself. I envied them the freedom they enjoyed, and as often wished I could change my condition for theirs. Every circumstance I met with, served only to render my state more painful, and heightened my apprehensions, and my opinion of the cruelty of the whites.

One day they had taken a number of fishes; and when they had killed and satisfied themselves with as many as they thought fit, to our astonishment who were on deck, rather than give any of them to us to eat, as we expected, they tossed the remaining fish into the sea again, although we begged and prayed for some as well as we could, but in vain; and some of my countrymen, being pressed by hunger, took an opportunity, when they thought no one saw them, of trying to get a little privately; but they were discovered, and the attempt procured them some very severe floggings. One day, when we had a smooth sea and moderate wind, two of my wearied countrymen who were chained together, (I was near them at the time,) preferring death to such a life of misery, somehow made through the nettings and jumped into the sea: immediately, another quite dejected fellow, who, on account of his illness, was suffered to be out of irons, also followed their example. . . .

During our passage, I first saw flying fishes, which surprised me very much; they used frequently to fly across the ship, and many of them fell on the deck. I also now first saw the use of the quadrant; I had often with astonishment seen the mariners make observations with it, and I could not think what it meant.

They at last took notice of my surprise; and one of them, willing to increase it, as well as to gratify my curiosity, made me one day look through it. The clouds appeared to me to be land, which disappeared as they passed along. This heightened my wonder; and I was now more persuaded than ever, that I was in another world, and that every thing about me was magic. At last, we came in sight of the island of Barbados, at which the whites on board gave a great shout, and made many signs of joy to us. We did not know what to think of this; but as the vessel drew nearer, we plainly saw the harbor, and other ships of different kinds and sizes, and we soon anchored amongst them, off Bridgetown. Many merchants and planters now came on board, though it was in the evening. They put us in separate parcels, and examined us attentively. They also made us jump, and pointed to the land, signifying we were to go there. We thought by this, we should be eaten by these ugly men, as they appeared to us; and, when soon after we were all put down under the deck again, there was much dread and trembling among us, and nothing but bitter cries to be heard all the night from these apprehensions, insomuch, that at last the white people got some old slaves from the land to pacify us. They told us we were not to be eaten, but to work, and were soon to go on land, where we should see many of our country people. This report eased us much. And sure enough, soon after we were landed, there came to us Africans of all languages.

We were conducted immediately to the merchant's yard, where we were all pent up together, like so many sheep in a fold, without regard to sex or age. As every object was new to me, every thing I saw filled me with surprise. What struck me first, was, that the houses were built with bricks and stories, and in every other respect different from those I had seen in Africa; but I was still more astonished on seeing people on horseback. I did not know what this could mean; and, indeed, I thought these people were full of nothing but magical arts. While I was in this astonishment, one of my fellow-prisoners spoke to a countryman of his, about the horses, who said they were the same kind they had in their country. I understood them, though they were from a distant part of Africa; and I thought it odd I had not seen any horses there; but afterwards, when I came to converse with different Africans, I found they had many horses amongst them, and much larger than those I then saw.

We were not many days in the merchant's custody before we were sold after their usual manner, which is this:—On a signal given, (as the beat of a drum,) the buyers rush at once into the yard where the slaves are confined, and make choice of that parcel they like best. The noise and clamor with which this is attended, and the eagerness visible in the countenances of the buyers, serve not a little to increase the apprehension of terrified Africans, who may well be supposed to consider them as the ministers of that destruction to which they think themselves devoted. In this manner, without scruple, are relations and friends separated, most of them never to see each other again. I remember, in the vessel in which I was brought over, in the men's apartment, there were several brothers, who, in the sale, were sold in different lots; and it was very moving on this occasion, to see and hear their cries at parting. O, ye nominal Christians! might not an African ask you—Learned you this from your God, who says unto you, Do unto all men as you would men should do unto you? Is it not enough that we are torn from our country and friends, to toil for your luxury and lust of gain? Must every tender feeling be likewise sacrificed to your avarice? Are the dearest friends and relations, now rendered more dear by their separation from their kindred, still to be parted from each other, and thus prevented from cheering the gloom of slavery, with the small comfort of being together, and mingling their sufferings and sorrows? Why are parents to lose their children, brothers their sisters, or husbands their wives? Surely, this is a new refinement in cruelty, which, while it has no advantage to atone for it, thus aggravates distress, and adds fresh horrors even to the wretchedness of slavery.

12

GOTTLIEB MITTELBERGER
On the Misfortune of Indentured Servants

Indentured, or bonded, servants were an important source of labor in seventeenth- and eighteenth-century America. The term indentured *generally refers to immigrants who, in return for passage from Europe to America, bound themselves to work in America for a specified number of years, after which time they would become completely free. The practice was closely related to the tradition of apprenticeship, in which a youth was assigned to work for a master in a trade for a certain number of years and in return was taught the skills of that trade. Convicts were another important source of colonial labor; thousands of English criminals were sentenced to labor in the colonies for a specified period, after which they were freed.*

Many indentured servants had valuable skills that they hoped to make better use of in the New World than they had been able to do at home. Some in fact did just that, while others, as Gottlieb Mittelberger describes, did not fare well. Mittelberger migrated to Pennsylvania from Germany in 1750. His own fortunes were not so bleak as those of his shipmates. He served as a schoolmaster and organist in Philadelphia for three years and then returned to Germany in 1754.

QUESTIONS TO CONSIDER

1. How did the treatment of indentured servants, as described by Gottlieb Mittelberger, compare to the treatment of slaves in the slave trade described in the preceding reading?

Gottlieb Mittelberger, *Journey to Pennsylvania in the Year 1750 and Return to Germany in the Year 1754*, trans. Carl Theo (Philadelphia: John Joseph McVey, 1898), 19–29.

2. What happened to children whose parents died during the journey?
3. Why did Mittelberger return to Germany?

Both in Rotterdam and in Amsterdam the people are packed densely, like herrings so to say, in the large sea-vessels. One person receives a place of scarcely 2 feet width and 6 feet length in the bedstead, while many a ship carries four to six hundred souls; not to mention the innumerable implements, tools, provisions, water-barrels and other things which likewise occupy much space.

On account of contrary winds it takes the ships sometimes 2, 3 and 4 weeks to make the trip from Holland to . . . England. But when the wind is good, they get there in 8 days or even sooner. Everything is examined there and the custom-duties paid, whence it comes that the ships ride there 8, 10 to 14 days and even longer at anchor, till they have taken in their full cargoes. During that time every one is compelled to spend his last remaining money and to consume his little stock of provisions which had been reserved for the sea; so that most passengers, finding themselves on the ocean where they would be in greater need of them, must greatly suffer from hunger and want. Many suffer want already on the water between Holland and Old England.

When the ships have for the last time weighed their anchors near the city of Kaupp [Cowes] in Old England, the real misery begins with the long voyage.

For from there the ships, unless they have good wind, must often sail 8, 9, 10 to 12 weeks before they reach Philadelphia. But even with the best wind the voyage lasts 7 weeks.

But during the voyage there is on board these ships terrible misery, stench, fumes, horror, vomiting, many kinds of sea-sickness, fever, dysentery, headache, heat, constipation, boils, scurvy, cancer, mouth-rot, and the like, all of which come from old and sharply salted food and meat, also from very bad and foul water, so that many die miserably.

Add to this want of provisions, hunger, thirst, frost, heat, dampness, anxiety, want, afflictions and lamentations, together with other trouble, as . . . the lice abound so frightfully, especially on sick people, that they can be scraped off the body. The misery reaches the climax when a gale rages for 2 or 3 nights and days, so that every one believes that the ship will go to the bottom with all human beings on board. In such a visitation the people cry and pray most piteously.

When in such a gale the sea rages and surges, so that the waves rise often like high mountains one above the other, and often tumble over the ship, so that one fears to go down with the ship; when the ship is constantly tossed from side to side by the storm and waves, so that no one can either walk, or sit, or lie, and the closely packed people in the berths are thereby tumbled over each other, both the sick and the well—it will be readily understood that many of these people, none of whom had been prepared for hardships, suffer so terribly from them that they do not survive it.

I myself had to pass through a severe illness at sea, and I best know how I felt at the time. These poor people often long for consolation, and I often entertained and comforted them with singing, praying and exhorting; and whenever it was possible and the winds and waves permitted it, I kept daily prayer-meetings with them on deck. Besides, I baptized five children in distress, because we had no ordained minister on board. I also held divine service every Sunday by reading sermons to the people; and when the dead were sunk in the water, I commended them and our souls to the mercy of God.

Among the healthy, impatience sometimes grows so great and cruel that one curses the other, or himself and the day of his birth, and sometimes come near killing each other. Misery and malice join each other, so that they cheat and rob one another. One always reproaches the other with having persuaded him to undertake the journey. Frequently children cry out against their parents, husbands against their wives and wives against their husbands, brothers and sisters, friends and acquaintances against each other. But most against the soultraffickers.

Many sigh and cry: "Oh, that I were at home again, and if I had to lie in my pig-sty!" Or they say: "O God, if I only had a piece of good bread, or a good fresh drop of water." Many people whimper, sigh and cry piteously for their homes; most of them get home-sick. Many hundred people necessarily die and perish in such misery, and must be cast into the sea, which drives their relatives, or those who persuaded them to undertake the journey, to such despair that it is almost impossible to pacify and console them. . . .

No one can have an idea of the sufferings which women in confinement have to bear with their innocent children on board these ships. Few of this class escape with their lives; many a mother is cast into the water with her child as soon as she is dead. One day, just as we had a heavy gale, a woman in our ship, who was to give birth and could not give birth under the circumstances, was pushed through a loop-hole [port-hole] in the ship and dropped into the sea, because she was far in the rear of the ship and could not be brought forward.

Children from 1 to 7 years rarely survive the voyage. I witnessed . . . misery in no less than 32 children in our ship, all of whom were thrown into the sea. The parents grieve all the more since their children find no resting-place in the earth, but are devoured by the monsters of the sea.

That most of the people get sick is not surprising, because, in addition to all other trials and hardships, warm food is served only three times a week, the rations being very poor and very little. Such meals can hardly be eaten, on account of being so unclean. The water which is served out on the ships is often very black, thick and full of worms, so that one cannot drink it without loathing, even with the greatest thirst. Toward the end we were compelled to eat the ship's biscuit which had been spoiled long ago; though in a whole biscuit there was scarcely a piece the size of a dollar that had not been full of red worms and spiders' nests. . . .

At length, when, after a long and tedious voyage, the ships come in sight of land, so that the promontories can be seen, which the people were so eager and anxious to see, all creep from below on deck to see the land from afar, and they weep for joy, and pray and sing, thanking and praising God. The sight of the land makes the people on board the ship, especially the sick and the half dead, alive again, so that their hearts leap within them; they shout and rejoice, and are content to bear their misery in patience, in the hope that they may soon reach the land in safety. But alas!

When the ships have landed at Philadelphia after their long voyage, no one is permitted to leave them except those who pay for their passage or can give good security; the others, who cannot pay, must remain on board the ships till they are purchased, and are released from the ships by their purchasers. The sick always fare the worst, for the healthy are naturally preferred and purchased first; and so the sick and wretched must often remain on board in front of the city for 2 or 3 weeks, and frequently die, whereas many a one, if he could pay his debt and were permitted to leave the ship immediately, might recover and remain alive.

The sale of human beings in the market on board the ship is carried on thus: Every day Englishmen, Dutchmen, and High-German people[1] come from the city of Philadelphia and other places, in part from a great distance, say 20, 30, or 40 hours away, and go on board the newly arrived ship that has brought and offers for sale passengers from Europe, and select among the healthy persons such as they deem suitable for their business, and bargain with them how long they will serve for their passage money, which most of them are still in debt for. When they have come to an agreement, it happens that adult persons bind themselves in writing to serve 3, 4, 5, or 6 years for the amount due by them, according to their age and strength. But very young people, from 10 to 15 years, must serve till they are 21 years old.

Many parents must sell and trade away their children like so many head of cattle; for if their children take the debt upon themselves, the parents can leave the ship free and unrestrained; but as the parents often do not know where and to what people their children are going, it often happens that such parents and children, after leaving the ship, do not see each other again for many years, perhaps no more in all their lives.

It often happens that whole families, husband, wife, and children, are separated by being sold to different purchasers, especially when they have not paid any part of their passage money.

When a husband or wife has died at sea, when the ship has made more than half of her trip, the survivor must pay or serve not only for himself or herself, but also for the deceased.

When both parents have died over half-way at sea, their children, especially when they are young and have nothing to pawn or to pay, must stand

---

1. **High-German people:** People who had emigrated from central or southern Germany.

for their own and their parents' passage, and serve till they are 21 years old. When one has served his or her term, he or she is entitled to a new suit of clothes at parting; and if it has been so stipulated, a man gets in addition a horse, a woman, a cow.

When a serf has an opportunity to marry in this country, he or she must pay for each year which he or she would have yet to serve, 5 to 6 pounds. But many a one who has thus purchased and paid for his bride, has subsequently repented his bargain, so that he would gladly have returned his exorbitantly dear ware, and lost the money besides.

If some one in this country runs away from his master, who has treated him harshly, he cannot get far. Good provision has been made for such cases, so that a runaway is soon recovered. He who detains or returns a deserter receives a good reward.

If such a runaway has been away from his master one day, he must serve for it as a punishment a week, for a week a month, and for a month half a year.

13

ELIZA LUCAS PINCKNEY

Daughter, Wife, Mother, and Planter

Born on the island of Antigua in the British West Indies, Eliza Lucas (1722–1793) moved at age fifteen to South Carolina, where her father owned three plantations. Two years later, her father, who was a British military officer, was called back to the Caribbean because of conflict with the Spanish. Lucas, who had excelled in botany while a student in London, took over the family estates at the age of seventeen and began a variety of experiments that would make her a famous early American agronomist. She pioneered the cultivation of several new crops, most notably indigo, a source of the dye that became a keystone of the economy of the Carolinas. In 1744 she married Charles Pinckney, a prominent lawyer, political leader, and planter, and had three children by him. After her husband died of malaria in 1758, Eliza Lucas Pinckney returned to managing the now much larger family estates.

Her two sons, Charles Cotesworth Pinckney and Thomas Pinckney, both rose to the rank of general in the Revolutionary War, signed the Constitution, and held major offices in the new federal government. Pinckney herself became famous as a landowner, agricultural innovator, and patriot. When she died in 1793, President George Washington

Walter Muir Whitehall, ed., *The Letterbook of Eliza Lucas Pinckney, 1739–1762* (Chapel Hill: University of North Carolina Press, 1972), 5–8, 15–17, 22, 34–35, 96–97, 146–49, 164–65.

insisted on being one of the casket bearers. The following selections come from Eliza Lucas Pinckney's letterbook, in which she kept copies of all her outgoing mail, and memos to herself.

QUESTIONS TO CONSIDER

1. Eliza Lucas Pinckney was one of the most successful women in colonial America. From her letters, what do you think were the reasons for her success?
2. Describe Pinckney's relationships with the men in her life. Contrast her experiences of colonial life with those of the other settlers in Part Two.
3. Based on her mention of "negroes" in her letterbook, describe her relationship with African Americans.

[To Colonel Lucas]
Hond. Sir

Your letter by way of Philadelphia which I duly received was an additional proof of that paternal tenderness which I have always Experienced from the most Indulgent of Parents from my Cradle to this time, and the subject of it is of the utmost importance to my peace and happiness.

As you propose Mr. L. to me I am sorry I can't have Sentiments favourable enough of him to take time to think on the Subject, as your Indulgence to me will ever add weight to the duty that obliges me to consult what best pleases you, for so much Generosity on your part claims all my Obedience, but as I know tis my happiness you consult [I] must beg the favour of you to pay my thanks to the old Gentleman for his Generosity and favourable sentiments of me and let him know my thoughts on the affair in such civil terms as you know much better than any I can dictate; and beg leave to say to you that the riches of Peru and Chili if he had them put together could not purchase a sufficient Esteem for him to make him my husband.

As to the other Gentleman you mention, Mr. Walsh, you know, Sir, I have so slight a knowledge of him I can form no judgment of him, and a Case of such consiquence requires the Nicest distinction of humours and Sentiments. But give me leave to assure you, my dear Sir, that a single life is my only Choice and if it were not as I am yet but Eighteen, hope you will [put] aside the thoughts of my marrying yet these 2 or 3 years at least.

You are so good to say you have too great an Opinion of my prudence to think I would entertain an indiscreet passion for any one, and I hope heaven will always direct me that I may never disappoint you; and what indeed could induce me to make a secret of my Inclination to my best friend, as I am well aware you would not disapprove it to make me a Sacrifice to Wealth, and I am as certain I would indulge no passion that had not your aprobation, as I truly am

Dr. Sir, Your most dutiful and affecte. Daughter
E. Lucas

May the 2nd [1740]

To my good friend Mrs. Boddicott[1]
Dear Madam,

I flatter myself it will be a satisfaction to you to hear I like this part of the world, as my lott has fallen here—which I really do. I prefer England to it, 'tis true, but think Carolina greatly preferable to the West Indias, and was my Papa here I should be very happy.

We have a very good acquaintance from whom we have received much friendship and Civility. Charles Town, the principal one in this province, is a polite, agreeable place. The people live very Gentile and very much in the English taste. The Country is in General fertile and abounds with Venison and wild fowl; the Venison is much higher flavoured than in England but 'tis seldom fatt.

My Papa and Mama's great indulgence to me leaves it to me to chose our place of residence either in town or Country, but I think it more prudent as well as most agreeable to my Mama and self to be in the Country during my Father's absence. We are 17 mile by land and 6 by water from Charles Town—where we have about 6 agreeable families around us with whom we live in great harmony.

I have a little library well furnished (for my papa has left me most of his books) in which I spend part of my time. My Musick and the Garden, which I am very fond of, take up the rest of my time that is not imployed in business, of which my father has left me a pretty good share—and indeed, 'twas inavoidable as my Mama's bad state of health prevents her going through any fatigue.

I have the business of 3 plantations to transact, which requires much writing and more business and fatigue of other sorts than you can imagine. But least you should imagine it too burthensom to a girl at my early time of life, give me leave to answer you: I assure you I think myself happy that I can be useful to so good a father, and by rising very early I find I can go through much business. But least you should think I shall be quite moaped with this way of life I am to inform you there is two worthy Ladies in Charles Town, Mrs. Pinckney and Mrs. Cleland, who are partial enough to me to be always pleased to have me with them, and insist upon my making their houses my home when in town and press me to relax a little much oftener than 'tis in my honor to accept of their obliging intreaties. But I some times am with one or the other for 3 weeks or a month at a time, and then enjoy all the pleasures Charles Town affords, but nothing gives me more than subscribing my self

---

1. **Mrs. Boddicott:** Guardian of the Lucas children.

Dear Madam,
Yr. most affectionet and
most obliged humble Servt.
Eliza. Lucas

Pray remember me in the best manner to my worthy friend Mr. Boddicott.

July [1740]

Wrote my Father a very long letter on his plantation affairs and on his change of commissions with Major Heron; On the Augustine Expedition;[2] On the pains I had taken to bring the Indigo, Ginger, Cotton and Lucerne [alfalfa] and Casada [cassava] to perfection, and had greater hopes from the Indigo (if I could have the seed earlier next year from the West India's) than any of the rest of the things I had tryd.

June the 4th, 1741

To my Father,
Hon'd Sir

Never were letters more welcome than yours of Feb. 19th and 20th and March the 15th and 21st, which came almost together. It was near 6 months since we had the pleasure of a line from you. Our fears increased apace and we dreaded some fatal accident befallen, but hearing of your recovery from a dangerous fitt of Illness has more than equaled, great as it was, our former Anxiety. Nor shall we ever think ourselves sufficiently thankful to Almighty God for the continuance of so great a blessing.

I simpathize most sincerely with the Inhabitance of Antigua in so great a Calamity as the scarcity of provisions and the want of the Necessarys of life to the poorer sort. We shall send all we can get of all sorts of provisions particularly what you write for. I wrote this day to Starrat for a barrel [of] butter.

We expect the boat dayly from Garden Hill when I shall be able to give you an account of affairs there. The Cotton, Guiney corn, and most of the Ginger planted here was cutt off by a frost. I wrote you in [a] former letter we had a fine Crop of Indigo Seed upon the ground, and since informed you the frost took it before it was dry. I picked out the best of it and had it planted, but there is not more than a hundred bushes of it come up—which proves the more unluckey as you have sent a man to make it. I make no doubt Indigo will prove a very valuable Commodity in time if we could have the seed from the west Indias [in] time enough to plant the latter end of March, that the seed might be dry enough to gather before our frost. I am sorry we lost this season. . . .

2. **Augustine expedition:** Reference to a British attack on the Spanish city of St. Augustine in Florida in May 1740.

The death of my Grandmama was, as you imagine, very shocking and grievous to my Mama, but I hope the considerations of the misery's that attend so advanced an age will help time to wear it off.

I am very much obliged to you for the present you were so good to send me of the fifty pound bill of Exchange which I duely received. . . .

Mama tenders you her affections and Polly joyns in duty with

> My Dr. Papa
> Y. m. obt. and ever D[evoted] D[aughter]
> E. Lucas

September 20, 1741. Wrote to my father on plantation business and concerning a planter's importing Negroes for his own use. Colo. Pinckney thinks not, but thinks it was proposed in the Assembly and rejected. [He] promised to look over the Act and let me know. Also informed my father of the alteration 'tis soposed there will be in the value of our money—occasioned by a late Act of Parliment that Extends to all America—which is to disolve all private banks, I think by the 30th of last month, or be liable to lose their Estates, and put themselves out of the King's protection. Informed him of the Tyranical Government at Georgia.

October 14th, 1741. Wrote to my father informing him we made 20 w[eight] of Indigo and expected 10 more. 'Tis not quite dry or I should have sent him some. Now desire he will send us a hundred weight of seed to plant in the spring.

[To Miss Bartlett]
Dr. Miss B

. . . Why, my dear Miss B, will you so often repeat your desire to know how I triffle away my time in our retirement in my fathers absence. Could it afford you advantage or pleasure I should not have hesitated, but as you can expect neither from it I would have been excused; however, to show you my readiness in obeying your commands, here it is.

In general then I rise at five o'Clock in the morning, read till Seven, then take a walk in the garden or field, see that the Servants are at their respective business, then to breakfast. The first hour after breakfast is spent at my musick, the next is constantly employed in recolecting something I have learned least for want of practise it should be quite lost, such as French and short hand. After that I devote the rest of the time till I dress for dinner to our little Polly and two black girls who I teach to read, and if I have my papa's approbation (my Mamas I have got) I intend [them] for school mistres's for the rest of the Negroe children—another scheme you see. But to proceed, the first hour after dinner as the first after breakfast at musick, the rest of the afternoon in Needle work till candle light, and from that time to bed time read or write. 'Tis the fashion here to carry our work abroad with us so that having company, without they are great strangers, is no interruption to that affair; but I have particular matters for particular days, which is an interruption to mine. Mondays my musick Master is here. Tuesdays my friend Mrs. Chardon (about 3 mile distant) and I are constantly engaged to each other, she at our house one Tuesday—I at hers the next and this is one of the happiest days I spend at Woppoe. Thursday the whole day except what the necessary affairs of the family take up is spent in writing, either on the business of the plantations, or letters to my friends. Every other Fryday, if no company, we go a vizeting so that I go abroad once a week and no oftener. . . .

O! I had like to forgot the last thing I have done a great while. I have planted a large figg orchard with design to dry and export them. I have reckoned my expence and the prophets to arise from these figgs, but was I to tell you how great an Estate I am to make this way, and how 'tis to be laid out you would think me far gone in romance. Your good Uncle I know has long thought I have a fertile brain at schemeing. I only confirm him in his opinion; but I own I love the vegitable world extremly. I think it an innocent and useful amusement. Pray tell him, if he laughs much at my project, I never intend to have my hand in a silver mine and he will understand as well as you what I mean.

Our best respects wait on him and Mrs. Pinckney. . . .

Y m o s
E. Lucas

[In July 1758 Eliza Lucas Pinckney's husband, Charles Pinckney, died of malaria. The following letter was sent in August to the headmaster of the Camberwell School in England, where her two sons, Charles (twelve) and Thomas (eight), were studying. She included a letter that she had written directly to her sons, but left it to the headmaster to determine how to inform them of their father's death.]

To Mr. Gerrard
Sir

This informs you of the greatest misfortune that could have happened to me and my dear children on this side Eternity! I am to tell you, hard as the task is, that my dear, dear Mr. Pinckney, the best of men, of husbands and of fathers, is no more! Comfort, good Sir, Comfort the tender hearts of my dear children. God Almighty bless them, and if he has any more blessings for me in this world may He give it me in them and their sister.

The inclosed for the dear boys be so good to give them when you think it a proper time. What anguish do I and shall I feel for my poor Infants when they hear the most afflicting sound that could ever reach them!

I remember poor Tommy, upon the first talk of our coming to Carolina early one morning as he lay abed, and I alone with him, without any discourse leading to it, told me he had a favour to beg of me, which was: If we went to Carolina and his dear papa should dye there that he might never know it, and that he would ask his papa the same favour if I dyed there. I think my poor dear Charles has expressed something of the same sentiment, and I am sure he has not less filial affection and sensibility than his brother. I therefore submit it to you and Mrs. Evance[3] whether to let them know it now, or not—for I am not capable to think for my self.

I know your humanity will induce you to a greater care and tenderness of them, if 'tis possible, than ever when you consider them in their present meloncholy circumstances as poor little fatherless children.

I have beged the favour of my friend Mrs. Evance to pay the childrens bills punctually: but my debt of gratitude will always be due. My return to them is at present uncertain, but my heart is with them; and as soon as I can consistent with there interest they may be sure I shall, by the Divine permission, see them. . . .

March 15th, [17]60

[To Mrs. Evance]

With how much pleasure I receive your letters, My Dear friend, I wont attempt to say, and the comfort I have at hearing my dear children are well your own maternal heart can better conceive than I express. So far I can with great truth affirm that 'tis the greatest felicity I have upon Earth. In consiquence of this tender attachment I am under very frequent apprehensions for my dear, dear little Tomm from the tenderness of his constitution. Pray God Almighty bless and restore him. . . . You make me very happy by the account you give me of my dear Charles. . . .

A great cloud seems at present to hang over this province. We are continually insulted by the Indians on our back settlements, and a violent kind of small pox rages in Charles Town that almost puts a stop to all business. Several of those I have to transact business with are fled into the Country, but by the Divine blessing I hope a month or two will change the prospect. We expect shortly troops from Gen. Amherst, which I trust will be able to manage these savage Enemies. And the small pox, as it does not spread in the Country, must be soon over for want of subjects.

I am now at Belmont to keep my people out of the way of the violent distemper for the poor blacks have died very fast even by inocculation. But the people in Charles Town were inocculation mad, I think I may call it, and

3. **Mrs. Evance:** Guardian of Charles and Thomas in England.

rushed into it with such presipitation that I think it impossible they could have had either a proper preparation or attendance had there been 10 Doctors in town to one. . . .

I absolutely aprove what you and my other friends have done in removing my children, if there were no other reason in the world for it but the air's not agreeing with Tommy. I always thought my self very much obliged to Mr. G for his care and tenderness to them and really think him too reasonable a man to wish them to continue when the circumstance of health is in the case. I would inlarge but the ships are so near sailing, and I must write a line to my dear boys, that I can only say I am

Your truely obliged and affecte.
E. Pinckney

April 13th, 1761

To the Honble. Mrs. King
Dr. Madm.

I cant resist the temptation of paying you my respects when a fleet sails though I did my self the honor To write you by the Man of War in Feb.—which letter with the Seeds for Mr. King I hope are safe arrived by this time.

Our hopes and Expectations are a good deal raised by the great fleet we are told that is bound from England for America this spring. We flatter our selves they will take The Mississippi in their way, which if they succeed inn must put an end to all our Indian Warrs, as they could never molest us if the French from thence did not supply them with arms and Ammunition. Our army has marched for the Cheerokee nation. They consist of regular troops and provincials. 'Tis a disagreeable Service but they have this to comfort them, that whether they are successful or other ways they may be pretty sure of gathering Laurels from the bounty of the English news writers; for after the incomiums opon the last Cheerokee expedition, there surely can nothing be done there that dont merit praise.

If the 50 Mohocks arrive safe that we expect from Genl. Amherst, I hope we shall be able to quel those Barbarians; for the Mohocks are very fine men—five of them are now here—and they are looked upon by the rest of the Indians with both dread and respect for they think them the greatest warriors in the world.

Many thanks to good Mr. King for my beer, which came in very good order and is extreamly good, though it had a long voyage and went first to Lisbon. . . .

I am with great gratitude and affection.

Dr. Madm.
Your most obliged and most obedt.
Servant
E. Pinckney

14

BENJAMIN FRANKLIN

Defending Colonial Activities before Parliament

Benjamin Franklin, more than any other founding father, exemplifies the Enlightenment in America. A scientist, journalist, moral philosopher, and political reformer, Franklin believed in the power of human reason to understand nature and improve the lot of humankind. Among his many accomplishments were the inventions of bifocal glasses, the glass harmonica, improved navigational instruments and ships' lanterns, the lightning rod, and, of course, the Franklin stove. A best-selling author and the publisher of America's first bilingual newspaper (in English and German), Franklin had the added distinction of being the only man to sign all three fundamental U.S. documents: the Declaration of Independence, the Constitution, and the Bill of Rights. He served as chief negotiator of the Treaty of Paris, which ended America's war for independence; governor of Pennsylvania; and president of the Pennsylvania Abolition Society.

In 1764 he traveled to London to petition King George to convert Pennsylvania from a proprietary Penn family holding to a publicly administered royal colony. While Franklin was in London, the British Parliament passed the Stamp Act of 1765 to fund the militarization of the western frontier of British North America, which was facing threats from Native Americans and the French Crown. Franklin at first supported the Stamp Act, but after discovering how deeply hated it was in Pennsylvania, soon argued against "taxation without representation."

The following exchange was first published in London in 1766 as a pamphlet titled "The Examination of Doctor Franklin." Owing to the secrecy of the session of Parliament, the pamphlet gave no hint about who had printed the piece or where the examination had taken place, but later editions described it as having transpired "before an august assembly," understood to be the British Parliament. The pamphlet was reprinted in 1766 in Philadelphia, New York, Boston, New London, and other American cities and was much in demand across the colonies.

QUESTIONS TO CONSIDER

1. How representative of American colonial opinion was Benjamin Franklin when he said that Americans will "wear their old cloaths over again, till they can make new ones"?
2. What did Franklin mean when he described trade with Indians as "not an American interest"?

William Jennings Bryan, ed., *The World's Famous Orations*, vol. 2 (New York: Funk & Wagnalls, 1906), 248–54.

3. Why did Franklin say that Americans "consider themselves as a part of the British empire"?

Q: Are not the Colonies, from their circumstances, very able to pay the stamp duty?

A: In my opinion, there is not gold and silver enough in the Colonies to pay the stamp duty for one year.

Q: Don't you know that the money arising from the stamps was all to be laid out in America?

A: I know it is appropriated by the act to the American service; but it will be spent in the conquered Colonies, where the soldiers are, not in the Colonies that pay it. . . .

Q: Do you think it right that America should be protected by this country, and pay no part of the expence?

A: That is not the case. The Colonies raised, cloathed and paid, during the last war [French and Indian War], near 25000 men, and spent many millions.

Q: Were you not reimbursed by parliament?

A: We were only reimbursed what, in your opinion, we had advanced beyond our proportion, or beyond what might reasonably be expected from us; and it was a very small part of what we spent. Pennsylvania, in particular, disbursed about 500,000 Pounds, and the reimbursements, in the whole, did not exceed 60,000 Pounds. . . .

Q: Do not you think the people of America would submit to pay the stamp duty, if it was moderated?

A: No, never, unless compelled by force of arms. . . .

Q: What was the temper of America towards Great-Britain before the year 1763?

A: The best in the world. They submitted willingly to the government of the Crown, and paid, in all their courts, obedience to acts of parliament. Numerous as the people are in the several old provinces, they cost you nothing in forts, citadels, garrisons or armies, to keep them in subjection. They were governed by this country at the expence only of a little pen, ink and paper. They were led by a thread. They had not only a respect, but an affection, for Great-Britain, for its laws, its customs and manners, and even a fondness for its fashions, that greatly increased the commerce. Natives of Britain were always treated with particular regard; to be an old England-man was, of itself, a character of some respect, and gave a kind of rank among us.

Q: And what is their temper now?

A: O, very much altered.

Q: Did you ever hear the authority of parliament to make laws for America questioned till lately?

A: The authority of parliament was allowed to be valid in all laws, except such as should lay internal taxes. It was never disputed in laying duties to regulate commerce. . . .

Q: In what light did the people of America use to consider the parliament of Great-Britain?

A: They considered the parliament as the great bulwark and security of their liberties and privileges, and always spoke of it with the utmost respect and veneration. Arbitrary ministers, they thought, might possibly, at times, attempt to oppress them; but they relied on it, that the parliament, on application, would always give redress. They remembered, with gratitude, a strong instance of this, when a bill was brought into parliament, with a clause to make royal instructions laws in the Colonies, which the house of commons would not pass, and it was thrown out.

Q: And have they not still the same respect for parliament?

A: No; it is greatly lessened.

Q: To what causes is that owing?

A: To a concurrence of causes; the restraints lately laid on their trade, by which the bringing of foreign gold and silver into the Colonies was prevented; the prohibition of making paper money among themselves; and then demanding a new and heavy tax by stamps; taking away, at the same time, trials by juries, and refusing to receive and hear their humble petitions.

Q: Don't you think they would submit to the stamp-act, if it was modified, the obnoxious parts taken out, and the duty reduced to some particulars, of small moment?

A: No; they will never submit to it. . . .

Q: Was it an opinion in America before 1763, that the parliament had no right to lay taxes and duties there?

A: I never heard any objection to the right of laying duties to regulate commerce; but a right to lay internal taxes was never supposed to be in parliament, as we are not represented there.

Q: On what do you found your opinion, that the people in America made any such distinction?

A: I know that whenever the subject has occurred in conversation where I have been present, it has appeared to be the opinion of every one, that we could not be taxed in a parliament where we were not represented. But the payment of duties laid by act of parliament, as regulations of commerce, was never disputed.

Q: But can you name any act of assembly, or public act of any of your governments, that made such distinction?

A: I do not know that there was any; I think there was never an occasion to make any such act, till now that you have attempted to tax us; that has occasioned resolutions of assembly, declaring the distinction, in which I think every assembly on the continent, and every member in every assembly, have been unanimous. . . .

Q: You say the Colonies have always submitted to external taxes, and object to the right of parliament only in laying internal taxes; now can you shew that there is any kind of difference between the two taxes to the Colony on which they may be laid?

A: I think the difference is very great. An external tax is a duty laid on commodities imported; that duty is added to the first cost, and other charges on the commodity, and when it is offered to sale, makes a part of the price.

If the people do not like it at that price, they refuse it; they are not obliged to pay it. But an internal tax is forced from the people without their consent, if not laid by their own representatives. The stamp-act says, we shall have no commerce, make no exchange of property with each other, neither purchase nor grant, nor recover debts; we shall neither marry, nor make our wills, unless we pay such and such sums, and thus it is intended to extort our money from us, or ruin us by the consequences of refusing to pay it.

Q: But supposing the external tax or duty to be laid on the necessaries of life imported into your Colony, will not that be the same thing in its effects as an internal tax?

A: I do not know a single article imported into the Northern Colonies, but what they can either do without, or make themselves.

Q: Don't you think cloth from England absolutely necessary to them?

A: No, by no means absolutely necessary; with industry and good management, they may very well supply themselves with all they want.

Q: Will it not take a long time to establish that manufacture among them? And must they not in the mean while suffer greatly?

A: I think not. They have made a surprising progress already. And I am of opinion, that before their old clothes are worn out, they will have new ones of their own making.

Q: Can they possibly find wool enough in North-America?

A: They have taken steps to increase the wool. They entered into general combinations to eat no more lamb, and very few lambs were killed last year. This course persisted in, will soon make a prodigious difference in the quantity of wool. And the establishing of great manufactories, like those in the clothing towns here, is not necessary, as it is where the business is to be carried on for the purposes of trade. The people will all spin, and work for themselves, in their own houses. . . .

Q: Considering the resolutions of parliament, as to the right, do you think, if the stamp-act is repealed, that the North Americans will be satisfied?

A: I believe they will.

Q: Why do you think so?

A: I think the resolutions of right will give them very little concern, if they are never attempted to be carried into practice. The Colonies will probably consider themselves in the same situation, in that respect, with Ireland; they know you claim the same right with regard to Ireland, but you never exercise it. And they may believe you never will exercise it in the Colonies, any more than in Ireland, unless on some very extraordinary occasion.

Q: But who are to be the judges of that extraordinary occasion? Is it not the parliament?

A: Though the parliament may judge of the occasion, the people will think it can never exercise such right, till representatives from the Colonies are admitted into parliament, and that whenever the occasion arises, representatives will be ordered. . . .

Q: Can any thing less than a military force carry the stamp-act into execution?

A: I do not see how a military force can be applied to that purpose.

Q: Why may it not?

A: Suppose a military force [is] sent into America, they will find nobody in arms; what are they then to do? They cannot force a man to take stamps who chooses to do without them. They will not find a rebellion; they may indeed make one.

Q: If the act is not repealed, what do you think will be the consequences?

A: A total loss of the respect and affection the people of America bear to this country, and of all the commerce that depends on that respect and affection.

Q: How can the commerce be affected?

A: You will find, that if the act is not repealed, they will take very little of your manufactures in a short time.

Q: Is it in their power to do without them?

A: I think they may very well do without them.

Q: Is it their interest not to take them?

A: The goods they take from Britain are either necessaries, mere conveniences, or superfluities. The first, as cloth, &c. with a little industry they can make at home; the second they can do without, till they are able to provide them among themselves; and the last, which are much the greatest part, they will strike off immediately. They are mere articles of fashion, purchased and consumed, because the fashion in a respected country, but will now be detested and rejected. The people have already struck off, by general agreement, the use of all goods fashionable in mournings, and many thousand pounds worth are sent back as unsaleable. . . .

Q: Then no regulation with a tax would be submitted to?

A: Their opinion is, that when aids to the Crown are wanted, they are to be asked of the several assemblies, according to the old established usage, who will, as they always have done, grant them freely. And that their money ought not to be given away without their consent, by persons at a distance, unacquainted with their circumstances and abilities. The granting aids to the Crown, is the only means they have of recommending themselves to their sovereign, and they think it extremely hard and unjust, that a body of men, in which they have no representatives, should make a merit to itself of giving and granting what is not its own, but theirs, and deprive them of a right they esteem of the utmost value and importance, as it is the security of all their other rights. . . .

Q: Supposing the stamp-act continued, and enforced, do you imagine that ill humour will induce the Americans to give as much for worse manufactures of their own, and use them, preferably to better of ours?

A: Yes, I think so. People will pay as freely to gratify one passion as another, their resentment as their pride. . . .

Q: If the stamp act should be repealed, would not the Americans think they could oblige the parliament to repeal every external tax law now in force?

A: It is hard to answer questions of what people at such a distance will think.

Q: But what do you imagine they will think were the motives of repealing the act?

A: I suppose they will think that it was repealed from a conviction of its inexpediency; and they will rely upon it, that while the same inexpediency subsists, you will never attempt to make such another.

Q: What do you mean by its inexpediency?

A: I mean its inexpediency on several accounts; the poverty and inability of those who were to pay the tax; the general discontent it has occasioned; and the impracticability of enforcing it. . . .

Q: But if the legislature should think fit to ascertain its right to lay taxes, by any act laying a small tax, contrary to their opinion, would they submit to pay the tax?

A: The proceedings of the people in America have been considered too much together. The proceedings of the assemblies have been very different from those of the mobs, and should be distinguished, as having no connection with each other. The assemblies have only peaceably resolved what they take to be their rights; they have taken no measures for opposition by force; they have not built a fort, raised a man, or provided a grain of ammunition, in order to such opposition. The ringleaders of riots they think ought to be punished; they would punish them themselves, if they could. Every sober sensible man would wish to see rioters punished; as otherwise peaceable people have no security of person or estate. But as to any internal tax, how small soever, laid by the legislature here on the people there, while they have no representatives in this legislature, I think it will never be submitted to. They will oppose it to the last. They do not consider it as at all necessary for you to raise money on them by your taxes, because they are, and always have been, ready to raise money by taxes among themselves, and to grant large sums, equal to their abilities, upon requisition from the Crown. They have not only granted equal to their abilities, but, during all the last war,[1] they granted far beyond their abilities, and beyond their proportion with this country, you yourselves being judges, to the amount of many hundred thousand pounds, and this they did freely and readily, only on a sort of promise from the secretary of state, that it should be recommended to parliament to make them compensation. It was accordingly recommended to parliament, in the most honourable manner, for them. America has been greatly misrepresented and abused here, in papers, and pamphlets, and speeches, as ungrateful, and unreasonable, and unjust, in having put this nation to immense expence for their defence, and refusing to bear any part of that expence. The Colonies raised, paid and clothed, near 25000 men during the last war, a number equal to those sent from Britain, and far beyond their proportion; they went deeply into debt in doing this, and all their taxes and estates are mortgaged, for many years to come, for discharging that debt. . . .

Q: But suppose Great-Britain should be engaged in a war in Europe, would North-America contribute to the support of it?

---

1. **last war:** The Seven Years' War, known in North America as the French and Indian War.

A: I do think they would, as far as their circumstances would permit. They consider themselves as a part of the British empire, and as having one common interest with it; they may be looked on here as foreigners, but they do not consider themselves as such. They are zealous for the honour and prosperity of this nation, and, while they are well used, will always be ready to support it, as far as their little power goes. In 1739 they were called upon to assist in the expedition against Carthagena,[2] and they sent 3000 men to join your army. It is true Carthagena is in America, but as remote from the Northern Colonies, as if it had been in Europe. They make no distinction of wars, as to their duty of assisting in them. I know the last war is commonly spoke of here as entered into for the defence, or for the sake of the people of America. I think it is quite misunderstood. It began about the limits between Canada and Nova-Scotia, about territories to which the Crown indeed laid claim, but were not claimed by any British Colony; none of the lands had been granted to any Colonist; we had therefore no particular concern or interest in that dispute. As to the Ohio, the contest there began about your right of trading in the Indian country, a right you had by the treaty of Utrecht,[3] which the French infringed; they seized the traders and their goods, which were your manufactures; they took a fort which a company of your merchants, and their factors and correspondents, had erected there, to secure that trade. Braddock[4] was sent with an army to re-take that fort (which was looked on here as another incroachment on the King's territory) and to protect your trade. It was not till after his defeat that the Colonies were attacked. They were before in perfect peace with both French and Indians; the troops were not therefore sent for their defence. The trade with the Indians, though carried on in America, is not an American interest. The people of America are chiefly farmers and planters; scarce any thing that they raise or produce is an article of commerce with the Indians. The Indian trade is a British interest; it is carried on with British manufactures, for the profit of British merchants and manufacturers; therefore the war, as it commenced for the defence of territories of the Crown, the property of no American, and for the defence of a trade purely British, was really a British war — and yet the people of America made no scruple of contributing their utmost towards carrying it on, and bringing it to a happy conclusion. . . .

Q: What used to be the pride of the Americans?

A: To indulge in the fashions and manufactures of Great-Britain.

Q: What is now their pride?

A: To wear their old cloaths over again, till they can make new ones.

---

2. **Carthagena:** The most important battle in the War of Jenkins' Ear between Spain and Great Britain, 1739–1748.
3. **Utrecht:** The 1713 treaty that ended the Spanish War of Succession.
4. **Braddock:** General Edward Braddock, commander-in-chief for the British side in North America during the beginning of the French and Indian War.

PART THREE

Resistance and Revolution
Struggling for Liberty

The generation that guided the colonies through the revolutionary era was welded together, despite remarkable differences among the colonies and their peoples, by a growing commitment to American nationality. That nationality was defined by birth in the new continent or the ordeal of migration and settlement and also by a long-standing British political heritage.

When, after 1763, the English developed restrictive colonial policies to raise revenues for the administration of an enlarged empire, colonists like Benjamin Franklin quickly perceived threats to their traditional liberties (see Document 14). Newspapers like the *Boston Gazette and Country Journal* and political leaders and pamphleteers like John Adams directly challenged Great Britain's right to legislate for the colonies. So did the growing army of Republican political cartoonists, who openly attacked their loyalist counterparts in the popular press. Many radicals on the other side of the Atlantic also criticized their country's governance of its North American colonies, as is evidenced by the brisk market in England for Paul Revere's engraving of the Boston Massacre. Leaders such as Captain Thomas Preston discovered how the rules of order had changed. Plain people like shoemaker George R. T. Hewes, who took part in both the Boston Massacre and the Boston Tea Party; Joseph Plumb Martin, who fought throughout the long war; and Boston merchant John Tudor developed new visions of their position in society.

To other colonists, commitment to the British tradition meant adherence to Britain. Many Americans remained loyal to the king, often at great personal cost, as Philip and Catherine Van Cortlandt's experience illustrates.

For many slaves and Native Americans, patriot success portended crushed expectations or even disaster. Slaves took desperate risks seeking freedom, often suffering when their gamble failed. Some, like Boston King, did gain their freedom by going over to the British side, but they encountered uncertainty and hardship after the war. Most Native American nations found their strength undermined by the long war and its freeing of the colonists from British restrictions.

The American Revolution challenged long-held convictions that denied the capacity of human beings to use their reason in creating a new form of government. Women like Abigail Adams reflected this new spirit as vividly as any founding father. And many colonists saw an opportunity to participate in political life in a way that government based on heredity, nobility, and tradition did not allow. Such were the high stakes in the argument raging throughout the colonies over Shays's Rebellion (1786), which offered a prelude to the debates over ratification of the Constitution of the United States. At issue in both the uprising and those debates was a vision of the American Revolution as one of the climactic events of human history—a demonstration that people of virtue and reason can deliberately establish order and justice.

POINTS OF VIEW
The Boston Massacre (1770)

15

THOMAS PRESTON

A British Officer's Description

Some historians in recent years have stressed the important role of the "crowd"—of anonymous colonists who took to the streets—in the coming of the American Revolution. Firsthand accounts by such participants, however, do not necessarily make it easy to determine precisely what occurred. In early 1770 British troops were quartered in Boston. Many townspeople resented their presence, and on March 5 a mob of about sixty attacked a small group of soldiers. Some soldiers, without orders, fired on the mob, killing five people and wounding eight. The incident was taken up by anti-British radicals—the "patriots"—in Boston, who called it the "Boston Massacre."

This selection is the account of the British officer who was tried for murder along with several of his men. John Adams and Josiah Quincy Jr., convinced that anyone

Merrill Jensen, ed., *English Historical Documents*, vol. 9 (London: Eyre and Spottiswoode, 1955), 750–53.

accused of a crime should have legal counsel, defended the men. Two of the soldiers were convicted of manslaughter, and the others, including Preston, were acquitted; however, the "massacre" inflamed anti-British sentiment throughout the colonies.

QUESTIONS TO CONSIDER

1. What was Captain Preston's view of the Boston crowd?
2. Were his soldiers justified in using violence? Explain.
3. Was the outcome of the trial fair? Why or why not?

CAPTAIN THOMAS PRESTON'S ACCOUNT OF THE BOSTON MASSACRE (MARCH 13, 1770)

It is [a] matter of too great notoriety to need any proofs that the arrival of his Majesty's troops in Boston was extremely obnoxious to its inhabitants. They have ever used all means in their power to weaken the regiments, and to bring them into contempt by promoting and aiding desertions, and with impunity, even where there has been the clearest evidence of the fact, and by grossly and falsely propagating untruths concerning them. On the arrival of the 64th and 65th [regiments] their ardour seemingly began to abate; it being too expensive to buy off so many, and attempts of that kind rendered too dangerous from the numbers.

And [conflict in the streets of Boston] has ever since their departure been breaking out with greater violence after their embarkation. One of their justices, most thoroughly acquainted with the people and their intentions, on the trial of a man of the 14th Regiment, openly and publicly in the hearing of great numbers of people and from the seat of justice, declared "that the soldiers must now take care of themselves, *nor trust too much to their arms,* for they were but a handful; that the inhabitants carried weapons concealed under their clothes, and would destroy them in a moment, *if they pleased.*" This, considering the malicious temper of the people, was an alarming circumstance to the soldiery. Since which several disputes have happened between the townspeople and the soldiers of both regiments, the former being encouraged thereto by the countenance of even some of the magistrates, and by the protection of all the party against government. In general such disputes have been kept too secret from the officers. On the 2d instant [day of March] two of the 29th [regiment] going through one Gray's ropewalk, the rope-makers insultingly asked them if they would empty a vault. This unfortunately had the desired effect by provoking the soldiers, and from words they went to blows. Both parties suffered in this affray, and finally the soldiers retired to their quarters. The officers, on the first knowledge of this transaction, took every precaution in their power to prevent any ill consequence. Notwithstanding which, single quarrels could not be prevented, the inhabitants constantly provoking and abusing the soldiery. The insolence as well as utter hatred of the inhabitants to the troops increased daily, insomuch that Monday and Tuesday, the 5th and 6th instant [day of March], were privately agreed on for a general engagement, in consequence of which several of the militia came from the country armed to join their friends, menacing to destroy any who should oppose them. This plan has since been discovered.

On Monday night about 8 o'clock two soldiers were attacked and beat. But the party of the townspeople in order to carry matters to the utmost length, broke into two meeting houses and rang the alarm bells, which I supposed was for fire as usual, but was soon undeceived. About 9 some of the guard came to and informed me the town inhabitants were assembling to attack the troops, and that the bells were ringing as the signal for that purpose and not for fire, and the beacon intended to be fired to bring in the distant people of the country. This, as I was captain of the day, occasioned my repairing immediately to the main guard. On my way there I saw the people in great commotion, and heard them use the most cruel and horrid threats against the troops. In a few minutes after I reached the guard, about 100 people passed it and went towards the custom house where the king's money is lodged. They immediately surrounded the sentry posted there, and with clubs and other weapons threatened to execute their vengeance on him. I was soon informed by a townsman their intention was to carry off the soldier from his post and probably murder him. On which I desired him to return for further intelligence, and he soon came back and assured me he heard the mob declare they would murder him. This I feared might be a prelude to their plundering the king's chest. I immediately sent a non-commissioned officer and 12 men to protect both the sentry and the king's money, and very soon followed myself to prevent, if possible, all disorder, fearing lest the officer and soldiers, by the insults and provocations of the rioters, should be thrown off their guard and commit some rash act. They soon rushed through the people, and by charging their bayonets in half-circles, kept them at a little distance. Nay, so far was I from intending the death of any person that I suffered the troops to go to the spot where the unhappy affair took place without any loading in their pieces; nor did I ever give orders for loading them. This remiss conduct in me perhaps merits censure; yet it is evidence, resulting from the nature of things, which is the best and surest that can be offered, that my intention was not to act offensively, but the contrary part, and that not without compulsion. The mob still increased and were more outrageous, striking their clubs or bludgeons one against another, and calling out, come on you rascals, you bloody backs, you lobster scoundrels, fire if you dare, G—d damn you, fire and be damned, we know you dare not, and much more such language was used. At this time I was between the soldiers and the mob, parleying with, and endeavouring all in my power to persuade them to retire peaceably, but to no purpose. They advanced to the points of the bayonets, struck some of them and even the muzzles of the pieces, and seemed to be endeavoring to close with the soldiers. On which some well behaved persons asked me if the guns were charged. I replied yes. They then asked me if I intended to order the men to fire. I answered no, by no means, observing to them that I was advanced before the muzzles of the men's pieces, and must fall a sacrifice if they fired; that the soldiers were upon the half cock and charged bayonets, and my giving the word fire under those circumstances would prove me to be no officer. While I was thus speaking, one of the soldiers having received a severe blow with a stick, stepped a little on one side and instantly fired, on which turning to and asking him why he fired without orders, I was struck with a club on my arm, which for some time deprived me of the use of it, which blow had it been placed on my head, most probably would have destroyed me. On this a general attack was made on the men by a great number of heavy clubs and snowballs being thrown at them, by which all our lives were in imminent danger, some persons at the same time from behind calling out, damn your bloods—why don't you fire. Instantly three or four of the soldiers fired, one after another, and directly after three more in the same confusion and hurry. The mob then ran away, except three unhappy men who instantly expired, in which number was Mr. Gray at whose rope-walk the prior quarrels took place; one more is since dead, three others are dangerously, and four slightly wounded. The whole of this melancholy affair was transacted in almost 20 minutes. On my asking the soldiers why they fired without orders, they said they heard the word fire and supposed it came from me. This might be the case as many of the mob called out fire, fire, but I assured the men that I gave no such order; that my words were, don't fire, stop your firing. In short, it was scarcely possible for the soldiers to know who said fire, or don't fire, or stop your firing. . . .

[All was uproar and confusion, but somehow the regiment managed to retire to its barracks without immediate further incident.]

A Council was immediately called, on the breaking up of which three justices met and issued a warrant to apprehend me and eight soldiers. On hearing of this procedure I instantly went to the sheriff and surrendered myself, though for the space of 4 hours I had it in my power to have made my escape, which I most undoubtedly should have attempted and could have easily executed, had I been the least conscious of any guilt. On the examination before the justices, two witnesses swore that I gave the men orders to fire. The one testified he was within two feet of me; the other that I swore at the men for not firing at the first word. Others swore they heard me use the word "fire," but whether do or do not fire, they could not say; others that they heard the word fire, but could not say if it came from me. The next day they got 5 or 6 more to swear I gave the word to fire. So bitter and inveterate are many of the malcontents here that they are industriously using every method to fish out evidence to prove it was a concerted scheme to murder the inhabitants. Others are infusing the utmost malice and revenge into the minds of the people who are to be my jurors by false publications, votes of towns, and all other artifices. That so from a settled rancour against the officers and troops in general, the suddenness of my trial after the affair while the people's minds are all greatly inflamed, I am, though perfectly innocent, under most unhappy circumstances, having nothing in reason to expect but the loss of life in a very ignominious manner, without the interposition of his Majesty's royal goodness.

16

GEORGE ROBERT TWELVES HEWES, JOHN TUDOR, AND THE *BOSTON GAZETTE AND COUNTRY JOURNAL*

Colonial Accounts

George Robert Twelves Hewes (1742–1840) was in his nineties in 1833 when he told publisher James Hawkes the story of his experiences in revolutionary Boston. Careful checking by the distinguished labor historian Alfred F. Young has authenticated much of Hewes's account. Hewes's story provides a rare opportunity to see an ordinary citizen taking a direct part in a great historical event. Hewes also participated in the Boston Tea Party of December 16, 1773, dressing as an Indian and pitching casks of tea into the harbor. These experiences had a profound personal effect on Hewes. In the 1760s he had been an awkward young cobbler nervously deferring to his aristocratic customers. A decade later, he would risk his employment—and perhaps even a beating—for his refusal to take off his hat "for any man." For Hewes, the American Revolution meant that the poor and the ordinary no longer owed the rich and powerful what in the eighteenth century was called "deference."

Boston merchant John Tudor (1709–1795), in his diary, gives a simpler account of the Boston Massacre than does Hewes. Tudor's version captures some of the sentiment following the deaths of the colonists.

The Boston Gazette and Country Journal *was one of several struggling Boston journals. Ever since being threatened with taxation under the Stamp Act of 1763, colonial newspapers, particularly those in Boston, had tended to support the patriot perspective. Journalism was not yet a profession, as most newspapers were produced by printers or postmasters, and the tradition of impartial reporting would not be established for many decades.*

QUESTIONS TO CONSIDER

1. According to Hewes, what sparked the Boston Massacre?
2. What role did Hewes play in the event and the subsequent trial?

James Hawkes [supposed author], *A Retrospect of the Boston Tea-Party, with a Memoir of George R. T. Hewes, a Survivor of the Little Band of Patriots Who Drowned the Tea in Boston Harbour in 1773, by a Citizen of New York* (New York, 1834), 27–33, 36–41; John Tudor, *Deacon Tudor's diary; or, "Memorandums from 1709"* (Boston: Press of W. Spooner, 1896), 1, vi, 110, [vii]–xxxvii, [7]; *Boston Gazette and Country Journal*, March 12, 1770, reprinted in Merrill Jensen, ed., *English Historical Documents*, vol. 9 (London: Eyre and Spottiswoode, 1955), 745–49.

3. Tudor wrote his account at the time of the event, whereas Hewes related his story to Hawkes six decades later. To what extent might this time gap explain their different perspectives?

4. What political points does the *Boston Gazette and Country Journal* make about the Boston Massacre?

ACCOUNT OF GEORGE ROBERT TWELVES HEWES AS TOLD TO JAMES HAWKES

On my inquiring of Hewes what knowledge he had of that event [the Boston Massacre], he replied, that he knew nothing from history, as he had never read any thing relating to it from any publication whatever, and can therefore only give the information which I derived from the event of the day upon which the catastrophe happened. On that day, one of the British officers applied to a barber, to be shaved and dressed; the master of the shop, whose name was Pemont, told his apprentice boy he might serve him, and receive the pay to himself, while Pemont left the shop. The boy accordingly served him, but the officer, for some reason unknown to me, went away from the shop without paying him for his service. After the officer had been gone some time, the boy went to the house where he was, with his account, to demand payment of his bill, but the sentinel, who was before the door, would not give him admittance, nor permit him to see the officer; and as some angry words were interchanged between the sentinel and the boy, a considerable number of the people from the vicinity, soon gathered at the place where they were, which was in King street, and I was soon on the ground among them. The violent agitation of the citizens, not only on account of the abuse offered to the boy, but other causes of excitement, then fresh in the recollection, was such that the sentinel began to be apprehensive of danger, and knocked at the door of the house, where the officers were, and told the servant who came to the door, that he was afraid of his life, and would quit his post unless he was protected. The officers in the house then sent a messenger to the guard-house, to require Captain Preston to come with a sufficient number of his soldiers to defend them from the threatened violence of the people. On receiving the message, he came immediately with a small guard of grenadiers, and paraded them before the custom-house, where the British officers were shut up. Captain Preston then ordered the people to disperse, but they said they would not, they were in the king's highway, and had as good a right to be there as he had. The captain of the guard then said to them, if you do not disperse, I will fire upon you, and then gave orders to his men to make ready, and immediately after gave them orders to fire. Three of our citizens fell dead on the spot, and two, who were wounded, died the next day; and nine others were also wounded. The persons who were killed I well recollect, said Hewes; they were, Gray, a rope maker, Marverick, a young man, Colwell, who was the mate of Captain Colton, Attuck[s], a mulatto, and Carr, who was an Irishman. Captain Preston then immediately fled with his grenadiers back to the guardhouse. The people who were assembled on that occasion, then immediately chose a committee to report to the governor the result of Captain Preston's conduct, and to demand of him satisfaction. The governor told the committee, that if the people would be quiet that night he would give them satisfaction, so far as was in his power; the next morning Captain Preston, and those of his guard who were concerned in the massacre, were, accordingly, by order of the governor, given up, and taken into custody the next morning, and committed to prison.

It is not recollected that the offence given to the barber's boy is mentioned by the historians of the revolution; yet there can be no doubt of its correctness. The account of this single one of the exciting causes of the massacre, related by Hewes, at this time, was in answer to the question of his personal knowledge of that event.

A knowledge of the spirit of those times will easily lead us to conceive, that the manner of the British officers application to the barber, was a little too strongly tinctured with the dictatorial hauteur [haughtiness], to conciliate the views of equality, which at that period were supremely predominant in the minds of those of the whig party [supporters of the revolution], even in his humble occupation; and that the disrespectful notice of his loyal customer, in consigning him to the attention of his apprentice boy, and abruptly leaving his shop, was intended to be treated by the officer with contempt, by so underrating the services of his apprentice, as to deem any reward for them beneath his attention. The boy too, may be supposed to have imbibed so much of the spirit which distinguished that period of our history, that he was willing to improve any occasion to contribute his share to the public excitement; to add an additional spark to the fire of political dissention which was enkindling.

When Hewes arrived at the spot where the massacre happened, it appears his attention was principally engaged by the clamours of those who were disposed to aid the boy in avenging the insult offered to him by the British officer, and probably heard nothing, at that time, of any other of the many exciting causes which led to that disastrous event, though it appeared from his general conversation, his knowledge of them was extensive and accurate.

But to pursue the destiny of Captain Preston, and the guard who fired on the citizens; in about a fortnight after, said Hewes, they were brought to trial and indicted for the crime of murder.

The soldiers were tried first, and acquitted, on the ground, that in firing upon the citizens of Boston, they only acted in proper obedience to the captain's orders. When Preston, their captain, was tried, I was called as one of the witnesses, on the part of the government, and testified, that I believed it was the same man, Captain Preston, that ordered his soldiers to make ready, who also ordered them to fire. Mr. John Adams, former president of the United States, was advocate for the prisoners, and denied the fact, that Captain Preston gave orders to his men to fire; and on his cross examination of me asked whether my position was such, that I could see the captain's lips in motion when the order to fire was given; to which I answered, that I could not. Although the evidence of Preston's having given orders to the soldiers to fire, was thought by the jury sufficient to acquit them, it was not thought to be of weight enough to convict him of a capital offence; he also was acquitted.

Although the excitement which had been occasioned by the wanton massacre of our citizens, had in some measure abated, it was never extinguished until open hostilities commenced, and we had declared our independence. The citizens of Boston continued inflexible in their demand, that every British soldier should be withdrawn from the town, and within four days after the massacre, the whole army decamped. But the measures of the British parliament, which led the American colonies to a separation from that government, were not abandoned.

JOHN TUDOR DESCRIBES THE MASSACRE IN HIS DIARY[1]

On Monday Evening the 5th current, a few minutes after 9 O'Clock a most horrid murder was committed in King Street before the Customhouse Door by eight or nine Soldiers under the Command of Captain Thomas Preston drawn of from the Main Guard on the South side of the Townhouse.

This unhappy affair began by Some Boys and young fellows throwing Snow Balls at the sentry placed at the Customhouse Door. On which eight or nine Soldiers Came to his assistance. Soon after a Number of people collected, when the Captain commanded the Soldiers to fire, which they did and three Men were Kil'd on the Spot and several Mortally Wounded, one of which died next morning. The Captain soon drew off his Soldiers up to the Main Guard, or the Consequences might have been terrible, for on the Guns firing the people were alarmed and set the Bells a Ringing as if for Fire, which drew Multitudes to the place of action. Lieutenant Governor Hutchinson, who was commander in Chief, was sent for and Came to the Council Chamber, where some of the Magistrates attended. The Governor desired the Multitude about 10 O'Clock to separate and go home peaceable and he would do all in his power that Justice should be done &c. The 29 Regiment being ten under Arms on the south side of the Townhouse, but the people insisted that the Soldiers should be ordered to their Barracks first before they would separate, Which being done the people separated about 1 O'Clock.—Captain Preston was taken up by a warrant given to the high Sheriff by Justice Dania and Tudor and came under Examination about 2 O'Clock and we sent him to Gaol soon after 3, having Evidence sufficient, to commit him, on his ordering the soldiers to fire: So about 4 O'clock the Town became quiet. The next forenoon the 8 Soldiers that fired on the inhabitants was also sent to Gaol. Tuesday A.M. the inhabitants met at Faneuil Hall and after some pertinent speeches, chose a Committee of 15 Gentlemen to wait on the Lieutenant Governor in Council to request the immediate removal of the Troops. . . .

1. Spelling and punctuation have been modernized.

(Thursday) Agreeable to a general request of the Inhabitants, were follow'd to the Grave (for they were all Buried in one) in succession the four Bodies of Messer's Samuel Gray, Samuel Maverick, James Caldwell, and Crispus Attucks, the unhappy victims who fell in the Bloody Massacre. On this sorrowful Occasion most of the shops and stores in Town were shut, all the Bells were order'd to toll a solemn peal in Boston, Charlesto[w]n, Cambridge, and Roxb[u]ry. The several Hearses forming a junction in King Street, the Theatre of that inhuman Tragedy, proceeded from thence thro' the main street, lengthened by an immense Concourse of people, So numerous as to be obliged to follow in Ranks of 4 and 6 abreast and brought up by a long Train of Carriages. The sorrow Visible in the Countenances, together with the peculiar solemnity, Surpass description, it was suppos'd that the Spectators and those that follow'd the corps amounted to 15,000, some supposed 20,000. Note Captain Preston was tried for his Life on the affair of the above October 24, 1770. The Trial lasted five Days, but the Jury brought him in not Guilty.

ACCOUNT IN THE *BOSTON GAZETTE AND COUNTRY JOURNAL*

March 12, 1770

The town of Boston affords a recent and melancholy demonstration of the destructive consequences of quartering troops among citizens in a time of peace, under a pretence of supporting the laws and aiding civil authority; every considerate and unprejudiced person among us was deeply impressed with the apprehension of these consequences when it was known that a number of regiments were ordered to this town under such a pretext, but in reality to enforce oppressive measures; to awe and control the legislative as well as executive power of the province, and to quell a spirit of liberty, which however it may have been basely opposed and even ridiculed by some, would do honour to any age or country. A few persons amongst us had determined to use all their influence to procure so destructive a measure with a view to their securely enjoying the profits of an American revenue, and unhappily both for Britain and this country they found means to effect it.

It is to Governor Bernard, the commissioners, their confidants and coadjutors, that we are indebted as the procuring cause of a military power in this capital. The Boston Journal of Occurrences, as printed in Mr. Holt's *New York Gazette,* from time to time, afforded many striking instances of the distresses brought upon the inhabitants by this measure; and since those Journals have been discontinued, our troubles from that quarter have been growing upon us. We have known a party of soldiers in the face of day fire off a loaded musket upon the inhabitants, others have been pricked with bayonets, and even our magistrates assaulted and put in danger of their lives, when offenders brought before them have been rescued; and why those and other bold and base criminals have as yet escaped the punishment due to their crimes may be soon matter of enquiry by the representative body of this people. It is natural to suppose that when the inhabitants of this town saw those laws which had been enacted for their security, and which they were ambitious of holding up to the soldiery, eluded, they should more commonly resent for themselves; and accordingly it has so happened. Many have been the squabbles between them and the soldiery; but it seems their being often worsted by our youth in those encounters, has only served to irritate the former. What passed at Mr. Gray's rope-walk has already been given the public and may be said to have led the way to the late catastrophe. That the rope-walk lads, when attacked by superior numbers, should defend themselves with so much spirit and success in the club-way, was too mortifying, and perhaps it may hereafter appear that even some of their officers were unhappily affected with this circumstance. Divers stories were propagated among the soldiery that served to agitate their spirits; particularly on the Sabbath that one Chambers, a sergeant, represented as a sober man, had been missing the preceding day and must therefore have been murdered by the townsmen. An officer of distinction so far credited this report that he entered Mr. Gray's rope-walk that Sabbath; and when required of by that gentleman as soon as he could meet him, the occasion of his so doing, the officer replied that it was to look if the sergeant said to be murdered had not been hid there. This sober sergeant was found on the Monday unhurt in a house of pleasure. The evidences already collected show that many threatenings had been thrown out by the soldiery, but we do not pretend to say that there was any preconcerted plan. When the evidences are published, the world will judge. We may, however, venture to declare that it appears too probable from their conduct that some of the soldiery aimed to draw and provoke the townsmen into squabbles, and that they then intended to make use of other weapons than canes, clubs, or bludgeons.

On the evening of Monday, being the fifth current, several soldiers of the 29th Regiment were seen parading the streets with their drawn cutlasses and bayonets, abusing and wounding numbers of the inhabitants.

A few minutes after nine o'clock four youths, named Edward Archbald, William Merchant, Francis Archbald, and John Leech, jun., came down Cornhill together, and separating at Doctor Loring's corner, the two former were passing the narrow alley leading to Murray's barrack in which was a soldier brandishing a broad sword of an uncommon size against the walls, out of which he struck fire plentifully. A person of mean countenance armed with a large cudgel bore him company. Edward Archbald admonished Mr. Merchant to take care of the sword, on which the soldier turned round and struck Archbald on the arm, then pushed at Merchant and pierced through his clothes inside the arm close to the armpit and grazed the skin. Merchant then struck the soldier with a short stick he had; and the other person ran to the barrack and brought with him two soldiers, one armed with a pair of tongs, the other with a shovel. He with the tongs pursued Archbald back through the alley, collared and laid him over the head with the tongs. The noise brought people together; and John Hicks, a young lad, coming up, knocked the soldier down but let him get up again; and more lads gathering, drove them back to the barrack where the boys stood some time as it were to keep them in. In less than a minute ten or twelve of them came out with drawn cutlasses, clubs, and bayonets and set upon the unarmed boys and young folk who stood them a little while but, finding the inequality of their equipment, dispersed. On hearing the noise, one Samuel Atwood came up to see what was the matter; and entering the alley from dock square, heard the latter part of the combat; and when the boys had dispersed he met the ten or twelve soldiers aforesaid rushing down the alley towards the square and asked them if they intended to murder people? They answered Yes, by G—d, root and branch! With that one of them struck Mr. Atwood with a club which was repeated by another; and being unarmed, he turned to go off and received a wound on the left shoulder which reached the bone and gave him much pain. Retreating a few steps, Mr. Atwood met two officers and said, gentlemen, what is the matter? They answered, you'll see by and by. Immediately after, those heroes appeared in the square, asking where were the boogers? where were the cowards? But notwithstanding their fierceness to naked men, one of them advanced towards a youth who had a split of a raw stave in his hand and said, damn them, here is one of them. But the young man seeing a person near him with a drawn sword and good cane ready to support him, held up his stave in defiance; and they quietly passed by him up the little alley by Mr Silsby's to King Street where they attacked single and unarmed persons till they raised much clamour, and then turned down Cornhill Street, insulting all they met in like manner and pursuing some to their very doors. Thirty or forty persons, mostly lads, being by this means gathered in King Street, Capt. Preston with a party of men with charged bayonets, came from the main guard to the commissioner's house, the soldiers pushing their bayonets, crying, make way!

They took place by the custom house and, continuing to push to drive the people off, pricked some in several places, on which they were clamorous and, it is said, threw snow balls. On this, the Captain commanded them to fire; and more snow balls coming, he again said, damn you, fire, be the consequence what it will! One soldier then fired, and a townsman with a cudgel struck him over the hands with such force that he dropped his firelock; and, rushing forward, aimed a blow at the Captain's head which grazed his hat and fell pretty heavy upon his arm. However, the soldiers continued the fire successively till seven or eight or, as some say, eleven guns were discharged.

By this fatal maneuver three men were laid dead on the spot and two more struggling for life; but what showed a degree of cruelty unknown to British troops, at least since the house of Hanover has directed their operations, was an attempt to fire upon or push with their bayonets the persons who undertook to remove the slain and wounded!

Mr. Benjamin Leigh, now undertaker in the Delph manufactory, came up; and after some conversation with Capt. Preston relative to his conduct in this affair, advised him to draw off his men, with which he complied.

The dead are Mr. Samuel Gray, killed on the spot, the ball entering his head and beating off a large portion of his skull.

A mulatto man named Crispus Attucks, who was born in Framingham, but lately belonged to New-Providence and was here in order to go for North

Carolina, also killed instantly, two balls entering his breast, one of them in special goring the right lobe of the lungs and a great part of the liver most horribly.

Mr. James Caldwell, mate of Capt. Morton's vessel, in like manner killed by two balls entering his back.

Mr. Samuel Maverick, a promising youth of seventeen years of age, son of the widow Maverick, and an apprentice to Mr. Greenwood, ivory-turner, mortally wounded; a ball went through his belly and was cut out at his back. He died the next morning.

A lad named Christopher Monk, about seventeen years of age, an apprentice to Mr. Walker, shipwright, wounded; a ball entered his back about four inches above the left kidney near the spine and was cut out of the breast on the same side. Apprehended he will die.

A lad named John Clark, about seventeen years of age, whose parents live at Medford, and an apprentice to Capt. Samuel Howard of this town, wounded; a ball entered just above his groin and came out at his hip on the opposite side. Apprehended he will die.

Mr. Edward Payne of this town, merchant, standing at his entry door received a ball in his arm which shattered some of the bones.

Mr. John Green, tailor, coming up Leverett's Lane, received a ball just under his hip and lodged in the under part of his thigh, which was extracted.

Mr. Robert Patterson, a seafaring man, who was the person that had his trousers shot through in Richardson's affair, wounded; a ball went through his right arm, and he suffered a great loss of blood.

Mr. Patrick Carr, about thirty years of age, who worked with Mr. Field, leather breeches-maker in Queen Street, wounded; a ball entered near his hip and went out at his side.

A lad named David Parker, an apprentice to Mr. Eddy, the wheelwright, wounded; a ball entered in his thigh.

The people were immediately alarmed with the report of this horrid massacre, the bells were set a-ringing, and great numbers soon assembled at the place where this tragical scene had been acted. Their feelings may be better conceived than expressed; and while some were taking care of the dead and wounded, the rest were in consultation what to do in those dreadful circumstances.

But so little intimidated were they, notwithstanding their being within a few yards of the main guard and seeing the 29th Regiment under arms and drawn up in King Street, that they kept their station and appeared, as an officer of rank expressed it, ready to run upon the very muzzles of their muskets.

FOR CRITICAL THINKING

1. How does the account of the riot as reported in the *Boston Gazette and Country Journal* differ from Hewes's version? How do these accounts differ from Captain Preston's? How might the differences among these accounts be explained?

2. If you were John Adams, determined to prove that British officers and soldiers could receive a fair trial in Boston, what strategy would you use to defend Captain Preston?
3. What verdict would you have favored if you had been deciding the trial? Why?

17

Patriot and Loyalist Propaganda

Propaganda has always been a crucial part of waging war, shoring up support for the cause, and portraying the enemy as unjust, corrupt, and dangerous. The American Revolution was fought in picture and print as well as on land and sea.

"The Bloody Massacre," Paul Revere's woodblock print of 1770, depicts a conflict in the streets of Boston in that same year that led to the death of five civilians at the hands of British troops. Though it might not have seemed terribly bloody to many people of the time, the incident will always be remembered as the Boston Massacre, thanks in part to Revere's print. In a world in which many people never learned to read, such mass-produced political drawings were the medium by which many received their news and political commentary, and colonial politicians knew how to exploit it.

In 1754, Benjamin Franklin first published the woodblock print "Join, or Die" in the Pennsylvania Gazette, and he is reputed to be the image's creator. The snake, believed capable of reconstituting itself from pieces, served as a call on the diffuse, disparate, and often mutually antagonistic British colonies along the eastern seaboard to unite against the French and their indigenous allies in the French and Indian War of 1754–1763. Although Franklin did not know it at the time, this was a remarkable first step toward revolution and independence from Britain. It is probably the first popular depiction of the idea of a united British North America, encompassing the colonies of New England, New York, New Jersey, Pennsylvania, Maryland, Virginia, North Carolina, and South Carolina. A decade later, when opponents of the Stamp Act of 1765 recycled the cartoon, Franklin disavowed his snake because it was being used against the British Crown. Later, during the run-up to the American Revolution, the snake returned as an image of unity and resistance to the British monarchy. Patriot Benjamin Franklin now welcomed back his American snake.

Nearly two decades later, the Boston Tea Party of December 1773 excited passions on both sides of the Atlantic and spawned sympathetic actions across the colonies. The Provincial Deputies of North Carolina resolved to boycott all British tea and cloth received after September 10, 1774. The women of Edenton, North Carolina, displayed their self-conscious sense of being American when they ardently supported the boycott resolution. The women signed an agreement stating that they were "determined to give memorable proof of their patriotism" and could not be "indifferent on any occasion that appears nearly to affect the peace and happiness of our country." Shortly afterward, in October 1774, Mrs. Penelope Barker organized the Edenton Tea Party, bringing together fifty-one North Carolina women to fight against "taxation without representation."

News of the Edenton Tea Party, a political movement led by women, shocked loyalists on both sides of the Atlantic. It provoked denunciations, sarcastic commentary, and public ridicule of the type exemplified by the third image below, which was published in London in March 1775. For many conservative British, Penelope Barker became a symbol of what was wrong with the colonies.

QUESTIONS TO CONSIDER

1. How does Revere depict the British as bloodthirsty and merciless?
2. Why is the "snake" image so easily used both to support and oppose the Crown?
3. In "The Edenton Tea Party," how is gender used to criticize the patriots?
4. How is visual propaganda today different from or similar to these images? How have political cartoons changed?

"The Bloody Massacre," engraving by Paul Revere, 1770. © *Massachusetts Historical Society, Boston, Massachusetts, USA / Bridgeman Images.*

"Join, or Die," 1754. *Library of Congress, Prints and Photographs Division, LC-USZ62-9701.*

The Edenton Tea Party, 1775. *Granger NYC—All rights reserved.*

18

JOSEPH PLUMB MARTIN

A Soldier's View of the Revolutionary War

Joseph Plumb Martin, born in western Massachusetts in 1760, became a soldier in the Revolution before his sixteenth birthday. After serving with Connecticut troops in 1776, he enlisted as a regular in the Continental Army in April 1777 and persevered until the army was demobilized in 1783. During this period he fought with the Light Infantry as well as in the Corps of Sappers and Miners, who built fortifications and dug trenches. One of the few soldiers to serve for virtually the entire war, he repeatedly risked health and life: in the defense of New York City in 1776, at the Battle of Germantown in Pennsylvania in 1777, at Valley Forge in the winter of 1777–1778, at the Battle of Monmouth in New Jersey in 1778, and at the climactic siege of Yorktown in 1781.

Published in Maine in 1830, Martin's A Narrative of Some of the Adventures, Dangers, and Sufferings of a Revolutionary Soldier *is a usually good-humored, unvarnished picture of an ordinary soldier whose major concern is often his next meal or keeping warm through a cold night. Yet he expresses sharply the widely shared resentment among common soldiers toward civilian patriots "sitting still and expecting the army to do notable things while fainting from sheer starvation." And he fundamentally objects to the way his generation remembered the history of the war: "great men get great praise, little men, nothing. But it always was so and always will be." In fact, historians in the present age have at last devoted energy to recapturing the contributions of men like Joseph Plumb Martin, whose narrative offers the only detailed account historians have discovered of the wartime experience of a common Revolutionary War soldier.*

QUESTIONS TO CONSIDER

1. Why did Joseph Plumb Martin begin with an apology for writing his memoirs? How did he justify writing them?
2. How well did the civilian population seem to support the soldiers of the Continental Army?
3. If conditions were as bad as Martin describes them, why didn't he desert the army?

James Kirby Martin, ed., *Ordinary Courage: The Revolutionary War Adventures of Joseph Plumb Martin*, rev. ed. (St. James, N.Y.: Brandywine Press, 1999), 1–2, 15–17, 29, 34–35, 61–64.

PREFACE

. . . I shall . . . by way of preface, inform the reader that my intention is to give a succinct account of some of my adventures, dangers, and sufferings during my several campaigns in the Revolutionary army. My readers . . . must not expect any great transactions to be exhibited to their notice. "No alpine wonders thunder through my tale," but they are here, once for all, requested to bear it in mind, that they are not the achievements of an officer of high grade which they are perusing, but the common transactions of one of the lowest in station in an army, a private soldier.

Should the reader chance to ask himself this question . . . how could any man of common sense ever spend his precious time in writing such a rhapsody of nonsense? To satisfy his inquiring mind, I would inform him, that, as the adage says, "every crow thinks her own young the whitest," so every private soldier in an army thinks his particular services as essential to carry on the war he is engaged in, as the services of the most influential general: And why not? What could officers do without such men? Nothing at all. Alexander[1] never could have conquered the world without private soldiers.

But, says the reader, this is low; the author gives us nothing but everyday occurrences; I could tell as good a story myself. Very true, Mr. Reader, everyone can tell what he has done in his lifetime, but everyone has not been a soldier, and consequently can know but little or nothing of the sufferings and fatigues incident to an army. All know everyday occurrences, but few know the hardships of the "tented field." I wish to have a better opinion of my readers, whoever they may be, than even to think that any of them would wish me to stretch the truth to furnish them with wonders that I never saw, or acts or deeds I never performed. I can give them no more than I have to give, and if they are dissatisfied after all, I must say I am sorry for them and myself too; for them, that they expect more than I can do, and myself, that I am so unlucky as not to have it in my power to please them. . . .

The critical grammarian may find enough to feed his spleen upon if he peruses the following pages; but . . . if the common readers can understand [my account], it is all I desire; and to give them an idea, though but a faint one, of what the army suffered that gained and secured our independence, is all I wish. . . .

A note of interrogation: Why we were made to suffer so much in so good and just a cause; and a note of admiration to all the world, that an army voluntarily engaged to serve their country, when starved, and naked, and suffering everything short of death (and thousands even that), should be able to persevere through an eight years war, and come off conquerors at last! But lest I should make my preface longer than my story, I will here bring it to a close.

---

1. **Alexander:** Alexander the Great, the ancient Macedonian king who conquered territories from Greece to Egypt to India and beyond.

CAMPAIGN OF 1776

I remained in New York two or three months, in which time several things occurred, but so trifling that I shall not mention them; when, sometime in the latter part of the month of August, I was ordered upon a fatigue party. We had scarcely reached the grand parade when I saw our sergeant major directing his course up Broadway toward us in rather an unusual step for him. He soon arrived and informed us, and then the commanding officer of the party, that he had orders to take off all belonging to our regiment and march us to our quarters, as the regiment was ordered to Long Island, the British having landed in force there. Although this was not unexpected to me, yet it gave me rather a disagreeable feeling, as I was pretty well assured I should have to sniff a little gunpowder. However, I kept my cogitations to myself, went to my quarters, packed up my clothes, and got myself in readiness for the expedition as soon as possible. I then went to the top of the house where I had a full view of that part of the Island; I distinctly saw the smoke of the field artillery, but the distance and the unfavorableness of the wind prevented my hearing their report, at least but faintly. The horrors of battle then presented themselves to my mind in all their hideousness; I must come to it now, thought I. Well, I will endeavor to do my duty as well as I am able and leave the event with Providence.

We were soon ordered to our regimental parade, from which, as soon as the regiment was formed, we were marched off for the ferry. At the lower end of the street were placed several casks of sea bread, . . . nearly hard enough for musket flints; the casks were unheaded and each man was allowed to take as many as he could as he marched by. As my good luck would have it, there was a momentary halt made; I improved the opportunity thus offered me, as every good soldier should upon all important occasions, to get as many of the biscuits as I possibly could; no one said anything to me, and I filled my bosom and took as many as I could hold in my hand, a dozen or more in all, and when we arrived at the ferry stairs I stowed them away in my knapsack. We quickly embarked on board the boats. As each boat started, three cheers were given by those on board, which was returned by the numerous spectators who thronged the wharves; they all wished us good luck, apparently, although it was with most of them perhaps nothing more than ceremony.

We soon landed at Brooklyn, upon the Island, marched up the ascent from the ferry to the plain. We now began to meet the wounded men, another sight I was unacquainted with, some with broken arms, some with broken legs, and some with broken heads. The sight of these a little daunted me, and made me think of home, but the sight and thought vanished together. We marched a short distance, when we halted to refresh ourselves. Whether we had any other victuals besides the hard bread I do not remember, but I remember my gnawing at them; they were hard enough to break the teeth of a rat. One of the soldiers complaining of thirst to his officer, "Look at that man," said he, pointing to me, "he is not thirsty, I will warrant it." I felt a little elevated to be styled a man.

While resting here, which was not more than 20 minutes or half an hour, the Americans and British were warmly engaged within sight of us. What were the feelings of most or all the young soldiers at this time, I know not, but I know what were mine. But let mine or theirs be what they might, I saw a lieutenant who appeared to have feelings not very enviable; whether he was actuated by fear or the canteen I cannot determine now. I thought it fear at the time, for he ran round among the men of his company, sniveling and blubbering, praying each one if he had aught against him, or if *he* had injured anyone that they would forgive him, declaring at the same time that he, from his heart, forgave them if they had offended him, and I gave him full credit for his assertion; for had he been at the gallows with a halter about his neck, he could not have shown more fear or penitence. A fine soldier you are, I thought, a fine officer, an exemplary man for young soldiers! I would have then suffered anything short of death rather than have made such an exhibition of myself. . . .

. . . A number of our sick were sent off to Norwalk in Connecticut to recruit [rest]. I was sent with them as a nurse. We were billeted [housed] among the inhabitants. I had in my ward seven or eight *sick soldiers,* who were (at least soon after their arrival there) as well in health as I was. All they wanted was a cook and something for a cook to exercise his functions upon. The inhabitants here were almost entirely what were in those days termed tories. An old lady, of whom I often procured milk, used always when I went to her house to give me a lecture on my opposition to our good King George. She had always said (she told me) that the regulars would make us fly like pigeons. . . .

Our surgeon came among us soon after this and packed us all off to camp, save two or three who were discharged. I arrived at camp with the rest, where we remained, moving from place to place as occasion required, undergoing hunger, cold, and fatigue until the 25th day of December, 1776, when I was discharged (my term of service having expired) at Philipse Manor, in the state of New York near Hudson's River.

Here ends my first campaign. I had learned something of a soldier's life, enough I thought to keep me at home for the future. Indeed, I was then fully determined to rest easy with the knowledge I had acquired in the affairs of the army. But the reader will find . . . that the ease of a winter spent at home caused me to alter my mind. I had several *kind* invitations to enlist into the standing army then about to be raised, especially a very pressing one to engage in a regiment of horse, but I concluded to try a short journey on foot first. Accordingly, I set off for my good old grandsire's, where I arrived, I think, on the 27th, two days after my discharge, and found my friends all alive and well. They appeared to be glad to see me, and I am sure I was *really* glad to see them.

CAMPAIGN OF 1777

. . . [W]e joined the grand army near Philadelphia, and the heavy baggage being sent back to the rear of the army, we were obliged to put us up huts by laying up poles and covering them with leaves, a capital shelter from winter storms. Here we continued to fast; indeed we kept a continual Lent as faithfully as ever any of the most rigorous of the Roman Catholics did. But there was this exception; we had no fish or eggs or any other substitute for our commons. Ours was a real fast and, depend upon it, we were sufficiently mortified.[2]

About this time the whole British army left the city, came out, and encamped, or rather lay, on Chestnut Hill in our immediate neighborhood. We hourly expected an attack from them; we had a commanding position and were very sensible of it. We were kept constantly on the alert, and wished nothing more than to have them engage us, for we were sure of giving them a drubbing, being in excellent fighting trim, as we were starved and as cross and ill-natured as curs. The British, however, thought better of the matter, and, after several days maneuvering on the hill, very civilly walked off into Philadelphia again. . . .

Soon after the British had quit their position on Chestnut Hill, we left this place, and after marching and countermarching back and forward some days, we crossed the Schuylkill on a cold, rainy, and snowy night upon a bridge of wagons set end to end and joined together by boards and planks. And after a few days more maneuvering we at last settled down at a place called "the Gulf" (so named on account of a remarkable chasm in the hills); and here we encamped some time, and here we had liked to have encamped forever—for starvation here *rioted* in its glory. . . .

While we lay here, there was a Continental thanksgiving ordered by Congress; and as the army had all the cause in the world to be particularly thankful, if not for being well off, at least that it was no worse, we were ordered to participate in it. We had nothing to eat for two or three days previous, except what the trees of the fields and forests afforded us. But we must now have what Congress said—a sumptuous thanksgiving to close the year of high living we had now nearly seen brought to a close. Well, to add something extraordinary to our present stock of provisions, our country, ever mindful of its suffering army, opened her sympathizing heart so wide upon this occasion as to give us something to make the world stare. And what do you think it was, reader? Guess. You cannot guess, be you as much of a Yankee as you will. I will tell you: It gave each and every man *half* a *gill* of rice [about 2 ounces] and a *tablespoonful* of vinegar!!

After we had made sure of this extraordinary superabundant donation, we were ordered out to attend a meeting and hear a sermon delivered upon the happy occasion. We accordingly went, for we could not help it. . . . I

---

2. A humorous reference to the Catholic tradition of fasting by eating fish and eggs in place of meat.

remember the text, like an attentive lad at church. I can *still* remember that it was this, "And the soldiers said unto him, And what shall we do? And he said unto them, Do violence to no man, nor accuse anyone falsely." The preacher ought to have added the remainder of the sentence to have made it complete: "And be content with your wages." But that would not do, it would be too apropos; however, he heard it as soon as the service was over, it was shouted from a hundred tongues. . . .

The army was now not only starved but naked. The greatest part were not only shirtless and barefoot but destitute of all other clothing, especially blankets. I procured a small piece of raw cowhide and made myself a pair of moccasins, which kept my feet (while they lasted) from the frozen ground, although as I well remember the hard edges so galled my ankles while on a march that it was with much difficulty and pain that I could wear them afterwards; but the only alternative I had was to endure this inconvenience or to go barefoot, as hundreds of my companions had to, till they might be tracked by their blood upon the rough frozen ground. But hunger, naked-ness, and sore shins were not the only difficulties we had at that time to encounter; we had hard duty to perform and little or no strength to perform it with.

The army continued at and near the Gulf for some days, after which we marched for the Valley Forge in order to take up our winter quarters. We were now in a truly forlorn condition—no clothing, no provisions, and as dis-heartened as need be. We arrived, however, at our destination a few days be-fore Christmas. Our prospect was indeed dreary. In our miserable condition, to go into the wild woods and build us habitations to *stay* (not to *live*) in, in such a weak, starved, and naked condition, was appalling in the highest de-gree, especially to New Englanders, unaccustomed to such kind of hardships at home. However, there was no remedy, no alternative but this or dispersion; but dispersion, I believe, was not thought of—at least I did not think of it. We had engaged in the defense of our injured country and were willing, nay, we were determined to persevere as long as such hardships were not altogether intolerable. I had experienced what I thought sufficient of the hardships of a military life the year before (although nothing in comparison to what I had suffered the present campaign) . . .; but we were now absolutely in danger of perishing, and that too in the midst of a plentiful country. We then had but little and often nothing to eat for days together; but now we had nothing and saw no likelihood of any betterment of our condition. Had there fallen deep snows (and it was the time of year to expect them) or even heavy and long rainstorms, the whole army must inevitably have perished. Or had the enemy, strong and well provided as he then was, thought fit to pursue us, our poor emaciated carcasses must have "strewed the plain." But a kind and holy Providence took more notice and better care of us than did the country in whose service we were wearing away our lives by piecemeal.

We arrived at the Valley Forge in the evening. It was dark; there was no water to be found, and I was perishing with thirst. . . . [T]wo soldiers whom I did not know passed by; they had some water in their canteens which they told me they had found a good distance off, but could not direct me to the place as it was very dark. I tried to beg a draught of water from them, but they were as rigid as Arabs. At length I persuaded them to sell me a drink for three pence, Pennsylvania currency, which was every cent of property I could then call my own, so great was the necessity I was then reduced to.

I lay here two nights and one day and had not a morsel of anything to eat all the time, save half of a small pumpkin, which I cooked by placing it upon a rock, the skin side uppermost, and making a fire upon it. By the time it was heat[ed] through I devoured it with as keen an appetite as I should a pie made of it at some other time.

The second evening after our arrival here I was warned to be ready for a two days command. I never heard a summons to duty with so much disgust before or since as I did that; how I could endure two days more fatigue without nourishment of some sort I could not tell. . . . However, in the morning . . . I went to the parade where I found a considerable number ordered upon the same business, whatever it was. We were ordered to go to the quartermaster general and receive from him our final orders. We accordingly repaired to his quarters, which was about three miles from camp; here we understood that our destiny was to go into the country on a foraging expedition, which was nothing more nor less than to procure provisions from the inhabitants for the men in the army and forage for the poor perishing cattle belonging to it, at the point of the bayonet. We stayed at the quartermaster general's quarters till sometime in the afternoon, during which time a beef creature was butchered for us. I well remember what fine stuff it was. . . .

We were then divided into several parties and sent off upon our expedition. . . . We marched till night when we halted, and . . . this day we arrived at Milltown, or Downingstown, a small village halfway between Philadelphia and Lancaster, which was to be our quarters for the winter. . . . There was a commissary and a wagonmaster general stationed here, the commissary to take into custody the provisions and forage that we collected, and the wagonmaster general to regulate the conduct of the wagoners and direct their motions. The next day after our arrival at this place we were put into a small house in which was only one room, in the center of the village. We were immediately furnished with rations of good and wholesome beef and flour, built us up some berths to sleep in, and filled them with straw, and felt as happy as any other pigs that were no better off than ourselves. And now having got into winter quarters and ready to commence our foraging business, I shall here end my account of my second campaign.

19

BOSTON KING

Choosing Sides

For many British North American colonists, especially those who were uneducated or lived in the hinterlands, the decision over which side to support often hinged on such pedestrian concerns as which side of a river they lived on, who shared their property line, and where they were when war broke out. Boston King faced a more difficult choice. His decision was daunting because he was a black slave.

Both loyalists and patriots recognized blacks' importance to the war effort. Most free blacks supported the revolutionaries, and northern states such as Connecticut and Rhode Island, with little plantation slavery, raised all-black regiments and made widespread use of blacks in their militias. But southern states such as Virginia, South Carolina, and Georgia were more circumspect about allowing blacks to serve in the military, fearing that their involvement might undermine slavery.

Early in the war, the British actively encouraged slaves to desert revolutionary masters in order to expand the loyalist forces and to weaken the rebel economy. In 1775, the British governor of Virginia, Lord Dunmore, issued a proclamation promising freedom to any slave who escaped a rebel master and took up arms for the king. Many slaves heeded this call despite the dangers of escape and the terrifying threats of punishment against family and friends of runaways. In 1778, the Continental Army responded with its own policy of freeing loyalist slaves, although in practice slaves of captured masters were often resold for profit. Boston King was one of the thousands of slaves who responded to the promises of freedom by escaping to the British lines and fighting for the crown.

Born on a plantation near Charles Town (now Charleston), South Carolina, around 1760, King had been raised as a "privileged" house slave. Learning to read and write and apprenticing to a carpenter as an adolescent, he had valuable skills and a freedom of movement that was rare for slaves. His fear of severe punishment after a misdeed prompted his flight to the British in his late teens. In 1782, after serving in the British army and twice escaping reenslavement, King found himself in New York, the last British stronghold, among thousands of loyalist refugees awaiting repatriation to Canada, West Florida, and Jamaica.

Ultimately, it was decided that all blacks who had come to the British lines before the signing of the provisional peace treaty of 1782 would be free, and all others would be returned to their masters. Boston and his wife, Violet King, also an escaped slave,

---

Boston King, "Memoirs of the Life of Boston King, a Black Preacher, Written by Himself, during His Residence at Kingswood-School," <http://collections.ic.gc.ca/blackloyalists /documents/diaries/king-memoirs.htm> (1 Dec. 2002); originally published in *Arminian [or the Methodist] Magazine* XXI (March, April, May, June, 1798): 105–11, 157–61, 209–13, 261–65.

were repatriated to Birchtown, Nova Scotia, where they joined the nucleus of Canada's first black community. Ten years later, they moved to Sierra Leone with nearly twelve hundred of their neighbors, where King started a school for natives, became a Methodist minister, and worked on his memoirs, published in 1798.

QUESTIONS TO CONSIDER

1. If you had been a slave during the American Revolution, which side would you have supported? Why?
2. What obstacles did Boston King face in his escape from slavery?
3. Why did King go to such lengths to explain that his decision to escape was based on his fear of severe punishment? Would he have attempted escape anyway? Why or why not?

I was born in the Province of South Carolina, 28 miles from Charles Town. My father was stolen away from Africa when he was young. . . . My mother was employed chiefly in attending upon those that were sick, having some knowledge of the virtue of herbs, which she learned from the Indians. She likewise had the care of making the people's clothes, and on these accounts was indulged with many privileges which the rest of the slaves were not. . . .

. . . When 16 years old, I was bound apprentice to a trade. After being in the shop about two years, I had the charge of my master's[1] tools, which being very good, were often used by the men, if I happened to be out of the way: When this was the case, or any of them were lost, or misplaced, my master beat me severely, striking me upon my head, or any other part without mercy. . . . About eight months after, we were employed in building a storehouse, and nails were very dear at that time, it being in the American war, so that the workmen had their nails weighed out to them; on this account they made the younger apprentices watch the nails while they were at dinner. It being my lot one day to take care of them, which I did till an apprentice returned to his work, and then I went to dine. In the mean time he took away all the nails belonging to one of the journeymen, and he being of very violent temper, accused me to the master with stealing of them. For this offense I was beat and tortured most cruelly, and was laid up three weeks before I was able to do any work. My proprietor,[2] hearing of the bad usage I received, came to town, and severely reprimanded my master for beating me in such a manner, threatening him, that if he ever heard the like again, he would take me away and put me to another master to finish my time, and make him pay for it. This had a good effect and he behaved much better to me, the two succeeding years, and I began to acquire a proper knowledge of my trade.

My master being apprehensive that Charles Town was in danger on account of the war, removed into the country, about 38 miles off. Here we built

---

1. The master of his apprenticeship, who was paid by King's owner to teach him carpentry.
2. King's owner.

a large house for Mr. Waters, during which time the English took Charles Town. Having obtained leave one day to see my parents, who had lived about 12 miles off, and it being late before I could go, I was obliged to borrow one of Mr. Waters's horses; but a servant of my master's took the horse from me to go [on] a little journey, and stayed two or three days longer than he ought. This involved me in the greatest perplexity, and I expected the severest punishment, because the gentleman to who the horse belonged was a very bad man, and knew not how to show mercy. To escape his cruelty, I determined to go [to] Charles Town, and throw myself into the hands of the English. They received me readily, and I began to feel the happiness, liberty, of which I knew nothing before, altho' I was grieved at first, to be obliged to leave my friends, and among strangers.

In this situation I was seized with the smallpox and suffered great hardships; for all the Blacks affected with that disease, were ordered to be carried a mile from the camp, lest the soldiers should be infected, and disabled from marching. This was a grievous circumstance to me and many others. We lay sometimes a whole day without any thing to eat or drink; but Providence sent a man, who belonged to the York volunteers whom I was acquainted with, to my relief. He brought me such things as I stood in need of; and by the blessing of the Lord I began to recover. . . .

[King continues his stint in the British army in the service of a Captain Grey.]

I tarried with Captain Grey about a year, and then left him, and came to Nelson's ferry. Here I entered into the service of the commanding officer of that place. But our situation was very precarious; and we expected to be made prisoners every day; for the Americans had 1,600 men, not far off; whereas our whole number amounted only to 250: But here were 1,200 English about 30 miles off; only we knew not how to inform them of our danger, as the Americans were in possession of the country. Our commander at length determined to send me with a letter, promising me great rewards, if I was successful in the business, I refused going on horseback, and set off on foot about 3 o'clock in the afternoon; I expected every moment to fall in with the enemy, whom I well knew would show me no mercy. I went on without interruption, till I got within six miles of my journey's end, and then was alarmed with a great noise a little before me. But I stepped out of the road, and fell flat upon my face till they were gone by. I then arose, and praised the Name of the Lord for his great mercy, and again pursued my journey, till I came to Mums-corner tavern. I knocked at the door, but they blew out the candle. I knocked again, and entreated the master to open the door. At last he came with a frightful countenance, and said "I thought it was the Americans; for they were here about an hour ago, and I thought they were returned again." I asked, how many were there? He answered, "about one hundred." I desired him to saddle his horse for me, which he did, and went with me himself. When we had gone about two miles, we were stopped by the picket-guard, till the Captain came out with 30 men: As soon as he knew that I had brought an express from Nelson's ferry, he received me with great kindness, and expressed his approbation of my courage and conduct in this danger-ous business. Next morning, Colonel Small . . . sent 600 men to relieve the troops at Nelson's ferry.

Soon after I went to Charles Town, and entered on board a [man] of war. As we were going to Chesapeake Bay, we were at the taking of a rich prize. We stayed in the bay two days, and they sailed for New-York, where I went on shore. Here I endeavoured to follow my trade, but for want of tools was obliged to relinquish it, and enter into service. But the wages were so low that I was not able to keep myself in clothes, so that I was under the ne-cessity of leaving my master and going to another. I stayed with him four months, but he never paid me, and I was obliged to leave him also, and work about the town until I was married.

A year after I was taken very ill, but the Lord raised me up again in about five weeks. I then went out in a pilotboat. We were at sea eight days, and had only provisions for five, so that we were in danger of starving. On the 9th day we were taken by an American whaleboat. I went on board them with a cheerful countenance, and asked for bread and water, and made very free with them. They carried me to Brunswick, and used me well. Notwithstand-ing which, my mind was fairly distressed at the thought of being again re-duced to slavery, and separated from my wife and family; and at the same time it was exceeding difficult to escape from my bondage, because the river at Amboy was above a mile over, and likewise another to cross at Staten-Island.

I called to remembrance the many great deliverances the Lord had wrought for me, and besought him to save me this once, and I would serve him all the days of my life. While my mind was thus exercised, I went into the jail to see a lad whom I was acquainted with at New-York. He had been taken prisoner, and attempted to make his escape, but was caught 12 miles off: They tied him to the tail of a horse, and in this manner brought him back to Brunswick. When I saw him, his feet were fastened in the stocks, and at night both his hands. This was a terrifying sight to me, as I expected to meet with the same kind of treatment, if taken in the act of attempting to re-gain my liberty. I was thankful that I was not confined in a jail, and my mas-ter used me as well as I could expect; and indeed the slaves about Baltimore, Philadelphia, and New-York, have as good victuals as many of the English; for they have meat once a day, and milk for breakfast and supper; and what is better than all, many of the masters send their slaves to school at night, that they may learn to read the Scriptures. This is a privilege indeed. But alas, all these enjoyments could not satisfy me without liberty! Sometimes I thought, if it was the will of God that I should be a slave, I was ready to resign myself to his will; but at other times I could not find the least desire to con-tent myself in slavery.

Being permitted to walk about when my work was done, I used to go to the ferry, and observed, that when it was low water the people waded across the river; tho' at the same time I saw there were guards posted at the place to prevent the escape of prisoners and slaves. As I was at prayer on Sun-day evening, I thought the Lord heard me, and would mercifully deliver me.

Therefore putting my confidence in him, about one o'clock in the morning I went down to the river side, and found the guards were either asleep or in the tavern. I instantly entered into the river, but when I was a little distance from the opposite shore, I heard the sentinels disputing among themselves: One said "I am sure I saw a man cross the river." Another replied, "There is no such thing." It seems they were afraid to fire at me, or make an alarm, lest they should be punished for their negligence. When I had got a little distance from the shore, I fell down upon my knees, and thanked God for the deliverance. I traveled till about five in the morning, and then concealed myself till seven o'clock at night, when I proceeded forward, thro' bushes and marshes, near the road, for fear of being discovered. When I came to the river, opposite Staten-Island, I found a boat; and altho' it was very near a whaleboat, yet I ventured into it, and cutting the rope, got safe over. The commanding officer, when informed of my case, gave me a passport, and I proceeded to New-York.

When I arrived at New-York, my friends rejoiced to see me once more restored to liberty, and joined me in praising the Lord for his mercy and goodness. But notwithstanding this great deliverance, and the promises I had made to serve God, yet my good resolutions soon vanished away like the morning dew: The love of this world extinguished my good desires, and stole away my heart from God, so that I rested in a mere form of religion for near three years. About which time, (in 1783) the horrors and devastation of war happily terminated and peace was restored between America and Great Britain, which diffused universal joy among all parties; except us, who had escaped from slavery and taken refuge in the English army; for a report prevailed at New-York, that all the slaves, in number 2000, were to be delivered up to their masters altho' some of them had been three or four years among the English. This dreadful rumour filled us all with inexpressible anguish and terror, especially when we saw our old masters coming from Virginia, North Carolina, and other parts, and seizing upon their slaves in the streets of New-York, or even dragging them out of their beds. Many of the slaves had very cruel masters, so that the thoughts of returning home with them embittered life to us. For some days we lost our appetite for food, and sleep departed from our eyes.

The English had compassion upon us in the day of distress, and issued out a Proclamation, importing, That all slaves should be free, who had taken refuge in the British lines, and claimed the sanction and privileges of the Proclamations respecting the security and protection of Negroes. In consequence of this, each of us received a certificate from the commanding officer at New-York, which dispelled all our fears, and filled us with joy and gratitude. Soon after, ships were fitted out, and furnished with every necessary for conveying us to Nova Scotia. We arrived at Birch Town in the month of August, where we all safely landed. Every family had a lot of land, and we exerted all our strength in order to build comfortable huts before the cold weather set in.

20

CATHERINE VAN CORTLANDT

Secret Correspondence of a Loyalist Wife

The Revolution was also a civil war. While most white Americans favored the patriot cause, loyalists were strong in many locations and among many groups. The areas surrounding New York City and along the Hudson River were predominantly Tory, as were the eastern shore of Maryland and much of what was then the western frontier, particularly the Carolinas and Georgia. Old loyalties died hard. Benjamin Franklin's son William, as governor of New Jersey, was a prominent loyalist. George Washington, already commanding the Continental Army, still drank to the king's health daily until January 1776, when Thomas Paine's Common Sense *convinced him that the day of monarchy had passed.*

Philip Van Cortlandt of Hanover, New Jersey, retained his allegiance to the king. He escaped arrest by a patriot party in December 1776 and entered military service on the British side, receiving his commission from William Franklin. In letters sent to him by secret messenger from the patriot stronghold in which she was living, his wife, Catherine Van Cortlandt, described the family's plight. Finally, George Washington took pity on the family and gave them a pass to join Van Cortlandt in New York. The Van Cortlandts never returned to New Jersey. Like many loyalists, they migrated first to Nova Scotia and then to England.

QUESTIONS TO CONSIDER

1. Did Revolutionary War soldiers have the right to seize Catherine Van Cortlandt's provisions and destroy her property? Why or why not?
2. Why did George Washington give the family a pass to rejoin Van Cortlandt in New York?

December 15, 1776, Hanover, New Jersey

My dearest love,

You had not left us ten minutes last Sunday when a party of Light Horsemen, headed by Joseph Morris, came to our once peaceful mansion all armed, who said they had positive orders to take you, my dear Philly, prisoner to Easton, and your favourite horse Sampson to be carried to Morristown for the use of

---

H. O. H. Vernon-Jackson, ed., "A Loyalist's Wife: Letters of Mrs. Philip Van Cortlandt, December 1776–February 1777," *History Today* 14 (1964): 574–80.

General Lee from whom these cruel mandates were issued. What were my emotions on seeing these wretches alight and without ceremony enter the doors you can only conceive, you who know their base characters and how their present errand must be received by your beloved family. When these bloody-minded men came into the dining room our little flock gathered around me and with anxious eyes watched my looks, whilst I was answering questions. . . . One of them (flourishing his sword) swore bitterly that, if you was to be found alive on earth, he would take you or have your heart's blood. This was too much. They fled into their nursery, bursting into tears; screams out, "Oh my dear Pappa, they will kill him, they will kill him." One of the inhuman men seemed touched and endeavoured an excuse by saying they were sent by their General and therefore were obliged to do their duty, even though against a person they formerly much esteemed, but had been represented to General Lee as one too dangerous to be permitted to stay in the country. Finding you was certainly gone . . . they went off and left me in a situation . . . scarce to be described. My first care was the nursery to comfort those innocent pledges of our mutual love. . . . Their sobbing and crying had almost overcome them; and they would not be persuaded from a belief that the wretches were gone to murder their dear Pappa. . . .

. . . The house is surrounded by eighteen or twenty armed men every night in expectation of intercepting you, as they observed that you was too much attached to your family to be long absent. Our dear children are again taken from school in consequence of the cruel insults they daily receive for the principles of their parents.

I now write in fear and trembling and venture this by an honest Dutch farmer who says he will deliver it into your hands.

January 20, 1777, Hanover, New Jersey

My beloved Philly,

. . . The arrival of the Rebel Troops in this neighbourhood has been severely felt by us. Parties continually passing this way were always directed by officious people to stop at our house to breakfast, dine, or stay the night; the horses from the teams were put into our barns to feed, without even the ceremony of asking liberty. During the stay of the officers of the hospital we had some protection. But immediately on their removal, several field officers from the New England line and a company of privates took possession. . . . They were the most disorderly of their species and their officers were from the dregs of the people. Indeed, two lieutenants messed and slept in the kitchen altogether, and would not be prevailed upon to leave their quarters. . . . A French general has also come on the hill at Dashwood, and daily draws his supply for his numerous cavalry from our granary and barrack.

Many of our female neighbours have been here, but I find their visits are only to gratify curiosity and to add insult to our unremitted distress. One of them who lives across the river, whose family we took so much pleasure in relieving when friendless . . . said that formerly she always respected you and loved the ground over which you walked, but now could with plea-sure see your blood run down the road. . . . The pious, devout and Reverend Mr. Green is very industrious in promoting your ruin by declaring you an en-emy to their cause. The farmers are forbid to sell me provisions, and the mill-ers to grind our grain. Our woods are cut down for the use of their army, and that which you bought and left corded near the river my servants are forbid to touch, though we are in the greatest distress for the want of it. . . . Our dear children have been six weeks without any other covering to their tender feet but woollen rags sewed round them to keep them from freezing.

A few days ago, the colonel and other officers quartered here told me they expected some of their brother officers to dine and spend the evening with them. This I understood as a hint to provide accordingly, which I was determined to do to the utmost of my powers, *though from necessity.* . . . Af-ter removal of the cloth, I took the earliest opportunity . . . to absent myself; and then they set in for a drinking match, every few minutes calling aloud upon the *landlady* to replenish the decanters which were kept continually going. . . . At length, one of them [the children] observed that the Gentle-men who used to dine with Papa never did so; and if these were not his friends, why did Mamma treat them so well. . . .

A Servant came down and said the Gentlemen desired my company, as they were going to dance. This confounded me. . . . Though I was much distressed, my resolution supported me whilst I told him that the present situation of myself and children would sufficiently apologize for my refus-ing to partake of any scenes of mirth where my husband could not attend me. . . . Near ten o'clock . . . he returned and entreated me to honour the Company for a few minutes as a Spectator. . . . The Officers were dancing Reels with some tawdry dressed females I had never seen. . . .

February 12, 1777, Hanover, New Jersey

. . . The narrow escape of your last was something remarkable. I was sitting about the dusk of evening in my room, very disconsolate with our dear chil-dren around me, reflecting on our deplorable situation and the gloomy pros-pects before me, when I heard a sudden rap at the street door. . . . I went myself to see who it was, and lucky I did. A tall, thin man presented himself, and on my stooping to unbolt the door whispered, he had a letter for me. My heart fluttered. The sentry was walking before the door, and two of the Officers were coming towards me. I recollected myself and *"desired the good man to walk into my room until I could give him a little wine for the sick woman."* He took the hint, and as soon as he came to my fireside gave me a letter, the outside of which I just looked at and threw it under the head of my bed and immediately set about getting him some wine for his wife to prevent suspi-cion. . . . The honest man after taking a dram went away, being followed out of doors and questioned by the Officers, who had been venting, cursing, and swearing against the sentry for permitting anyone to approach the house or speak to me without their first being acquainted with it. . . . The frequent frolics of the Officers in the house, the Soldiers in the Nursery, and Cattle constantly fed here has reduced our late Stock of plenty to a miserable pittance. The other day was almost too much for me. We had been several days without bread and were subsisting upon a half bushel of Indian meal which had been given me by a Dutch farmer I did not know, who said he had heard of our situation and would take no pay. . . . Our stock of meal had been expended five days and the Soldiers not being about, our little Sally immediately went into the Nursery, and picking up a piece of dirty bread which had been trod under their feet came running up to me, wiping it with her frock, and with joy sparkling in her eyes presented it to me crying out, "Do eat it, Mamma. 'Tis good. 'Tis charming good bread. Indeed it is. I have tasted it." This was too much.

The next day Doctor Bond . . . came to the house, and passing me suddenly went into the back room and taking from under his coat a loaf of bread he gave it to the children and before I could thank him he ran past me with his handkerchief and hat before his face. . . .

A few days after, Doctor Bond came here and with a faltering voice told me he was sent by General Washington to inform me that it was his positive orders that our house should be taken as an Hospital to innoculate his Army with the smallpox, and if I chose he would innoculate my family at the same time. . . . He . . . promised to use his influence with the General to obtain the only favour I had now to ask of him; which was, to go to my husband with my children, servants, and such effects as I could take with me. . . .

February 19, 1777, Hoboken Ferry
My beloved husband,

Doctor Bond succeeded and with orders for my removal brought me General Washington's pass which I now enclose.

To describe the scene at parting with our few though sincere friends, the destruction of our property, the insulting looks and behaviour of those who had been accessory to our ruin . . . is more than I dare attempt. At four in the afternoon, a cold, disagreeable day, we bid adieu to our home to make room for the sick of General Washington's Army and, after an unpleasant and fatiguing journey, arrived at twelve o'clock at night at the Fork of the Rivers Rockaway, Pompton and Haakinsack. A Young Woman, whose father and brother were both in the Rebel service, was much affected with my situation and endeavoured to remove me into another room. The next evening, after a most distressing ride through snow and rain . . . we arrived at Campbell's Tavern at Haakinsack, the mistress of which refused me admittance when she was informed whose family it was, alleging as an excuse that she expected a number of Officers. . . .

The town was filled with Soldiers and the night advancing . . . a person came up to me, looked me in the face, and asked me to accompany him to his Uncle's house with my whole family. On entering a room with a large fire, it had an effect on the children, whose stomachs had been empty the greatest part of the day, that caused instant puking, and was near proving fatal to them.

The next morning early, we again set off in a most uncomfortable sleet and snow. . . . Our youngest children could not pass a farm yard where they were milking cows without wishing for some. My little Willing was almost in agonies, springing in my Arms and calling for milk. I therefore rode up and requested the good man to let me have some from one of his pails. . . . The man stopped, asked who we were, and . . . swore bitterly he would not give a drop to any Tory Bitch. I offered him money, my children screamed; and, as I could not prevail, I drove on.

. . . [T]he servants . . . had been obliged to leave me soon after setting off from Haakinsack, on account of the baggage and the badness of the roads. About two hours ago, they came in and inform[ed] me that, crossing the river on the ice at the ferry, they were stopped and fired upon by a party of armed Rebels, nearly killing several of them. . . . Upon being shewn a copy of General Washington's pass, . . . they damned the General "for giving the mistress a pass" and said they were sorry they had not come a little sooner as they would have stopped the whole . . . and immediately fell to plundering chests, trunks, boxes, etc., throwing the heavy Articles into a hole in the ice, and breaking a barrel of old fashioned China into a thousand pieces. . . .

. . . [B]e not surprised, my dear Pappa, if you see your Kitty altered. Indeed, I am much altered. But I know your heart, you will not love me less, but heal with redoubled affection and tenderness the wounds received in your behalf for those principles of loyalty which alone induced you to leave to the mercy of Rebels nine innocent children and your fond and ever affectionate Wife,

C.V.C.

21

ABIGAIL ADAMS

Republican Motherhood

Abigail Adams exemplified the ideal of the "Republican mother," a woman who took an active role in public affairs within the narrow bounds allowed by eighteenth-century marriage while inculcating the love of virtue and country in her children.

Born Abigail Smith in Weymouth, Massachusetts, in 1744, Adams, like most young women of the era, was educated at home by her parents and relatives. John Adams, a

Charles Francis Adams, ed., *Letters of Mrs. Adams, the Wife of John Adams* (Boston: Wilkins, Carter, 1848), 94–96, 152–55; Charles Francis Adams, ed., *Familiar Letters of John Adams and His Wife Abigail Adams, during the Revolution* (Boston: Houghton, Mifflin, 1875), 148–50.

serious young lawyer, began courting her in 1761, and three years later they wed. The couple had five children, four of whom survived into adulthood.

Abigail Adams's letters to her husband and her son John Quincy Adams, who spent much of his childhood on overseas diplomatic missions with his father, illustrate the power of her personality and the sense of authority—different from the authority accorded eighteenth-century men—that she created from the role of wife and mother. Never forgetting the sharp distinction that society made between men's responsibilities and women's, she nonetheless took clear stands on the moral and political issues of her day and molded her son into a man of virtue and patriotism according to her definitions of those traits.

QUESTIONS TO CONSIDER

1. What standards did Abigail Adams set for her son?
2. What lessons did Adams expect her son to learn from the American Revolution?
3. Compare the tone of Adams's letter to her son with that of the letter to her husband.
4. What does this famous letter ask of John Adams?

LETTERS TO JOHN QUINCY ADAMS

June, 1778

My Dear Son,

'Tis almost four months since you left your native land, and embarked upon the mighty waters, in quest of a foreign country. Although I have not particularly written to you since, yet you may be assured you have constantly been upon my heart and mind.

It is a very difficult task, my dear son, for a tender parent to bring her mind to part with a child of your years going to a distant land; nor could I have acquiesced in such a separation under any other care than that of the most excellent parent and guardian who accompanied you. You have arrived at years capable of improving under the advantages you will be likely to have, if you do but properly attend to them. They are talents put into your hands, of which an account will be required of you hereafter; and being possessed of one, two, or four, see to it that you double your numbers.

The most amiable and most useful disposition in a young mind is diffidence of itself; and this should lead you to seek advice and instruction from him, who is your natural guardian, and will always counsel and direct you in the best manner, both for your present and future happiness. You are in possession of a natural good understanding, and of spirits unbroken by adversity and untamed with care. Improve your understanding by acquiring useful knowledge and virtue, such as will render you an ornament to society, an honor to your country, and a blessing to your parents. Great learning and superior abilities, should you ever possess them, will be of little value and small estimation, unless virtue, honor, truth, and integrity are added to them. Adhere to those religious sentiments and principles which were early instilled into your mind, and remember that you are accountable to your Maker for all your words and actions.

You have entered early in life upon the great theatre of the world, which is full of temptations and vice of every kind. You are not wholly unacquainted with history, in which you have read of crimes which your inexperienced mind could scarcely believe credible. You have been taught to think of them with horror, and to view vice as

a monster of so frightful mien,
That, to be hated, needs but to be seen.

Yet you must keep a strict guard upon yourself, or the odious monster will soon lose its terror by becoming familiar to you. The modern history of our own times, furnishes as black a list of crimes, as can be paralleled in ancient times, even if we go back to Nero, Caligula,[1] or Cæsar Borgia.[2] Young as you are, the cruel war, into which we have been compelled by the haughty tyrant of Britain and the bloody emissaries of his vengeance, may stamp upon your mind this certain truth, that the welfare and prosperity of all countries, communities, and, I may add, individuals, depend upon their morals.

That nation to which we were once united, as it has departed from justice, eluded and subverted the wise laws which formerly governed it, and suffered the worst of crimes to go unpunished, has lost its valor, wisdom and humanity, and, from being the dread and terror of Europe, has sunk into derision and infamy.

Be assured I am most affectionately yours,

————.

12 January, 1780

My Dear Son,

... These are times in which a genius would wish to live. It is not in the still calm of life, or the repose of a pacific station, that great characters are formed. Would Cicero[3] have shone so distinguished an orator if he had not been roused, kindled, and inflamed by the tyranny of Catiline, Verres, and Mark Anthony?[4] The habits of a vigorous mind are formed in contending

1. **Nero, Caligula:** Two corrupt, depraved Roman emperors.
2. **Cæsar Borgia:** An Italian Renaissance aristocrat infamous for his conniving and cruelty.
3. **Cicero:** A famous Roman orator.
4. **Catiline, Verres, and Mark Anthony:** A reference to the conspiracies and tyrannies instituted by Rome's strongmen.

with difficulties. All history will convince you of this, and that wisdom and penetration are the fruit of experience, not the lessons of retirement and leisure. Great necessities call out great virtues. When a mind is raised and animated by scenes that engage the heart, then those qualities, which would otherwise lie dormant, wake into life and form the character of the hero and the statesman. War, tyranny, and desolation are the scourges of the Almighty, and ought no doubt to be deprecated. Yet it is your lot, my son, to be an eyewitness of these calamities in your own native land, and, at the same time, to owe your existence among a people who have made a glorious defence of their invaded liberties, and who, aided by a generous and powerful ally, with the blessing of Heaven, will transmit this inheritance to ages yet unborn.

Nor ought it to be one of the least of your incitements towards exerting every power and faculty of your mind, that you have a parent who has taken so large and active a share in this contest, and discharged the trust reposed in him with so much satisfaction as to be honored with the important embassy which at present calls him abroad.

The strict and inviolable regard you have ever paid to truth, gives me pleasing hopes that you will not swerve from her dictates, but add justice, fortitude, and every manly virtue which can adorn a good citizen, do honor to your country, and render your parents supremely happy, particularly your ever affectionate mother,

A. A.

Braintree, 26 December, 1783

My Dear Son,

The early age at which you went abroad gave you not an opportunity of becoming acquainted with your own country. Yet the revolution, in which we were engaged, held it up in so striking and important a light, that you could not avoid being in some measure irradiated with the view. The characters with which you were connected, and the conversation you continually heard, must have impressed your mind with a sense of the laws, the liberties, and the glorious privileges, which distinguish the free, sovereign, independent States of America.

Let your observations and comparisons produce in your mind an abhorrence of domination and power, the parent of slavery, ignorance, and barbarism, which places man upon a level with his fellow tenants of the woods;

A day, an hour, of virtuous liberty
Is worth a whole eternity of bondage.

You have seen power in its various forms,—a benign deity, when exercised in the suppression of fraud, injustice, and tyranny, but a demon, when nited with unbounded ambition,—a wide-wasting fury, who has destroyed her thousands. Not an age of the world but has produced characters, to which whole human hecatombs[5] have been sacrificed.

What is the history of mighty kingdoms and nations, but a detail of the ravages and cruelties of the powerful over the weak? Yet it is instructive to trace the various causes, which produced the strength of one nation, and the decline and weakness of another; to learn by what arts one man has been able to subjugate millions of his fellow creatures, the motives which have put him upon action, and the causes of his success;—sometimes driven by ambition and a lust of power; at other times, swallowed up by religious enthusiasm, blind bigotry, and ignorant zeal; sometimes enervated with luxury and debauched by pleasure, until the most powerful nations have become a prey and been subdued by these Sirens, when neither the number of their enemies, nor the prowess of their arms, could conquer them. . . .

The history of your own country and the late revolution are striking and recent instances of the mighty things achieved by a brave, enlightened, and hardy people, determined to be free; the very yeomanry of which, in many instances, have shown themselves superior to corruption, as Britain well knows, on more occasions than the loss of her André.[6] Glory, my son, in a country which has given birth to characters, both in the civil and military departments, which may vie with the wisdom and valor of antiquity. As an immediate descendant of one of those characters, may you be led to an imitation of that disinterested patriotism and that noble love of your country, which will teach you to despise wealth, titles, pomp, and equipage, as mere external advantages, which cannot add to the internal excellence of your mind, or compensate for the want of integrity and virtue.

May your mind be thoroughly impressed with the absolute necessity of universal virtue and goodness, as the only sure road to happiness, and may you walk therein with undeviating steps,—is the sincere and most affectionate wish of

Your mother,
A. Adams

LETTER TO JOHN ADAMS

Braintree, 31 March, 1776

I wish you would ever write me a letter half as long as I write you, and tell me, if you may, where your fleet are gone; what sort of defense Virginia can make against our common enemy; whether it is so situated as to make an able defense.

---

5. **human hecatombs:** The ancient Greek tradition of sacrificing 100 cattle to the gods.
6. **André:** Major John André, a British officer hanged as a spy for traveling under a false identity as part of a loyalist conspiracy involving Benedict Arnold.

Are not the gentry lords, and the common people vassals? Are they not like the uncivilized vassals Britain represents us to be? I hope their riflemen, who have shown themselves very savage and even blood-thirsty, are not a specimen of the generality of the people. I am willing to allow the colony great merit for having produced a Washington; but they have been shamefully duped by a Dunmore [British commander].

I have sometimes been ready to think that the passion for liberty cannot be equally strong in the breasts of those who have been accustomed to deprive their fellow-creatures of theirs. Of this I am certain, that it is not founded upon that generous and Christian principle of doing to others as we would that others should do unto us.

I long to hear that you have declared an independency. And, by the way, in the new code of laws which I suppose it will be necessary for you to make, I desire you would remember the ladies and be more generous and favorable to them than your ancestors. Do not put such unlimited power into the hands of the husbands. Remember, all men would be tyrants if they could. If particular care and attention is not paid to the ladies, we are determined to foment a rebellion, and will not hold ourselves bound by any laws in which we have no voice or representation.

That your sex are naturally tyrannical is a truth so thoroughly established as to admit of no dispute; but such of you as wish to be happy willingly give up the harsh title of master for the more tender and endearing one of friend. Why, then, not put it out of the power of the vicious and the lawless to use us with cruelty and indignity with impunity? Men of sense in all ages abhor those customs which treat us only as the vassals of your sex; regard us then as beings placed by Providence under your protection, and in imitation of the Supreme Being make use of that power only for our happiness.

22

GEORGE RICHARDS MINOT

Shays's Rebellion: Prelude to the Constitution

During the 1780s, political conflict splintered much of the country. For relief from the postwar economic hardships, farmers looked to local and state government to pass and enforce laws that favored debtors over creditors. Wealthier townspeople wanted strong government that would ensure sound money, promote trade, pay the public debt, and keep order.

George Richards Minot, *The History of the Insurrections in Massachusetts, in the Year Seventeen Hundred and Eighty Six, and the Rebellion Consequent Thereon,* 2d ed. (Boston: Books for Libraries Press, 1810), 108–25.

Nowhere was this battle waged more fiercely than in Massachusetts. Poor harvests made it difficult for farmers to pay their debts to merchants and to meet the high taxes levied by the state to discharge its Revolutionary War obligations. Soon creditors and the state were dispossessing farmers of their land and livestock, and some farmers were thrown into jail for nonpayment of debt. To improve their situation, farmers demanded lower taxes, the issuance of paper money to make debt repayment easier, and "stay laws" to postpone payment to creditors. When these efforts failed, the farmers took more dramatic action, forming paramilitary units. Their main target was the courts where creditors and tax collectors gathered to collect what they were owed. In a plainly illegal manner, they surrounded courthouses and stopped proceedings. They had few recognized leaders, but the former Revolutionary War officers among them, like Daniel Shays of Pelham, drilled the men and became at least their nominal leaders.

Perhaps speaking for the many merchants, professionals, and government leaders who were horrified by the court closings, Boston lawyer George Richards Minot (1758–1802) shouted for "Daniel Shays's decapitation." In just a year, however, when Minot wrote the account excerpted here, he clearly had moderated his opinion. Governor James Bowdoin called for "the most vigorous measures . . . to enforce obedience to the law," and the state legislature responded as Massachusetts organized an army under Revolutionary War general Benjamin Lincoln.

The Shaysite armies harassed merchants and tried to capture the federal arsenal at Springfield. In the end, though, General Lincoln's army of militiamen easily defeated them. By the following year the economy had swung upward, and the Massachusetts government eased the credit squeeze by a limited issuance of paper money.

The rebellion had alarmed political leaders throughout the colonies and greatly strengthened the position of those who advocated a stronger central government to control such uprisings. Shays's Rebellion was extensively debated as the Constitution was drafted and approved. The arguments over ratification in Massachusetts followed quite closely the political divisions expressed in the insurrection. Only their superior organization enabled the Federalists to achieve victory in this pivotal state by the close vote of 187 to 168.

QUESTIONS TO CONSIDER

1. What position on Shays's Rebellion did George Richards Minot take in his account?
2. What strategy did the Shaysites pursue? How aggressive do they seem? How determined were they to bring the issue to actual combat?
3. What strategy did General Benjamin Lincoln, who led the state's army, pursue? How aggressive does he seem? How determined was he to bring the issue to actual combat?
4. Why did Shays's Rebellion become an important issue throughout the colonies?

. . . General Shepard, about 4 o'clock in the afternoon of the 25th, perceived Shays advancing on the Boston road, towards the arsenal where the militia were posted, with his troops in open column. Possessed of the importance of that moment, in which the first blood should be drawn in the contest, the General sent one of his aids with two other gentlemen, several times, to know the intention of the enemy, and to warn them of their danger. The purport of their answer was, that they would have possession of the barracks; and they immediately marched onwards to within 250 yards of the arsenal. A message was again sent to inform them, that the militia were posted there by order of the Governour, and of Congress, and that if they approached nearer, they would be fired upon. To this, one of their leaders replied, that *that* was all they wanted; and they advanced one hundred yards further. Necessity now compelled General Shepard to fire, but his humanity did not desert him. He ordered the two first shots to be directed over their heads; this however, instead of retarding, quickened their approach; and the artillery was at last pointed at the centre of their column. This measure was not without its effect. A cry of murder arose from the rear of the insurgents, and their whole body was thrown into the utmost confusion. Shays attempted to display his column, but it was in vain. His troops retreated with precipitation to Ludlow, about ten miles from the place of action, leaving three of their men dead, and one wounded on the field.

The advantages which the militia had in their power, both from the disorder of this retreat, which was as injudicious as the mode of attack, and from the nature of the ground, would have enabled them to have killed the greater part of the insurgents, had a pursuit taken place. But, the object of the commander was rather to terrify, than to destroy the deluded fugitives. . . . Notwithstanding the fatigue of a march, performed in an uncommonly severe winter, the army were ordered under arms at half past three o'clock, the same day on which they arrived. Four regiments, with four pieces of artillery, and the horse, crossed the river upon the ice, while the Hampshire troops, under the command of General Shepard, moved up the river, as well to prevent a junction of the party under Shays, who were on the east side, with those under Day, on the west, as to cut off the retreat of the latter. It was also a great object by this manoeuvre [maneuver], to encircle Day, with a force so evidently superior, as to prevent his people from firing, and thereby to avoid the shedding of blood. Upon the appearance of the army on the river, the guard at the ferry house turned out, but forsook the pass; and after a small shew of opposition, near the meeting house, retired in the utmost confusion. This was attended with the flight of all Day's party, who escaped to Northampton, with the loss of a very small number, that were overtaken by the light horse. The insurgent forces under Shays, made no greater opposition, on the day following. When the army approached him, he immediately began a retreat, through South-Hadley to Amherst, supplying the hunger of his men by plunder. . . .

The appearance of things was exceedingly changed by the flight of the insurgents from Springfield. . . . The apprehensions of the inhabitants had been . . . greatly raised, from the various reports of the numbers and objects of the insurgents; and more than all, from the aid which they affected to rely on, from secret, but influential characters within the state, and the discontented of neighbouring governments. . . .

The pursuit of Shays and his party, which commenced at two o'clock in the morning, was continued till the army reached Amherst, through which place, however, he passed before their arrival, on his way to Pelham, with the main body of his men. General Lincoln, finding the enemy out of his reach, directed his march to Hadley, the nearest place which could be found to afford a cover for his troops. Upon an examination of the houses at Amherst, it was discovered, that most of the male inhabitants had quitted them to follow the insurgents; and that ten sleigh loads of provisions had gone forward from the county of Berkshire for their use. Under such appearances, a strict prohibition was laid upon the remaining inhabitants, against affording any supplies to their deluded neighbours.

The morning after the arrival of the army at Hadley, information was received that a small number of General Shepard's men had been captured at Southampton, and that the enemy's party still continued there. The Brookfield volunteers, consisting of fifty men, and commanded by Colonel Baldwin, were sent in sleighs, with 100 horse, under the command of Colonel Crafts, to pursue them. They were soon found to consist of eighty men with ten sleighs, and at twelve o'clock the same night were overtaken at Middlefield. They had quartered themselves in separate places; and about one half of them, with one Luddington their captain, being lodged in a house together, were first surrounded. It was a singular circumstance, that among the government's volunteers, happened to be General Tupper, who had lately commanded a continental regiment, in which Luddington had served as a Corporal. The General, ignorant of the character of his enemy, summoned the party to surrender. How astonished was the Corporal at receiving the summons, in a voice to which he had never dared to refuse obedience!

A momentary explanation took place, which but heightened the General's commands. Resistance was no longer made, the doors were opened, and a surrender was agreed to. By this time, the rest of the party had paraded under arms, at the distance of 200 yards, where they were met by a number of men prepared for their reception. Both sides were on the point of firing, but, upon an artful representation of the strength of the government's troops, the insurgents laid down their arms, and fifty-nine prisoners, with nine sleigh loads of provisions, fell into the hands of the conquerors, who returned to the army on the day following.

The whole force of the insurgents having taken post on two high hills in Pelham, called east and west hills, which were rendered difficult of access by the depth of the snow around them, General Lincoln, on the 30th of January, sent a letter directed to Captain Shays, and the officers commanding the men in arms against the government of the Commonwealth, as follows:

> Whether you are convinced or not of your error in flying to arms, I am fully persuaded that before this hour, you must have the fullest

conviction upon your own minds, that you are not able to execute your original purposes.

Your resources are few, your force is inconsiderable, and hourly decreasing from the disaffection of your men; you are in a post where you have neither cover nor supplies, and in a situation in which you can neither give aid to your friends, nor discomfort to the supporters of good order and government.—Under these circumstances, you cannot hesitate a moment to disband your deluded followers. If you should not, I must approach, and apprehend the most influential characters among you. Should you attempt to fire upon the troops of government, the consequences must be fatal to many of your men, the least guilty. To prevent bloodshed, you will communicate to your privates, that if they will instantly lay down their arms, surrender themselves to government, and take and subscribe the oath of allegiance to this Commonwealth, they shall be recommended to the General Court for mercy. If you should either withhold this information from them, or suffer your people to fire upon our approach, you must be answerable for all the ills which may exist in consequence thereof.

To this letter the following Answer was received.

Pelham, January 30th, 1787

To General Lincoln, commanding the government troops at Hadley.

Sir,

The people assembled in arms from the counties of Middlesex, Worcester, Hampshire and Berkshire, taking into serious consideration the purport of the flag just received, return for answer, that however unjustifiable the measures may be which the people have adopted, in having recourse to arms, various circumstances have induced them thereto. We are sensible of the embarrassments the people are under; but that virtue which truly characterizes the citizens of a republican government, hath hitherto marked our paths with a degree of innocence; and we wish and trust it will still be the case. At the same time, the people are willing to lay down their arms, on the condition of a general pardon, and return to their respective homes, as they are unwilling to stain the land, which we in the late war purchased at so dear a rate, with the blood of our brethren and neighbours. Therefore, we pray that hostilities may cease, on your part, until our united prayers may be presented to the General Court, and we receive an answer, as a person is gone for that purpose. If this request may be complied with, government shall meet with no interruption from the people, but let each army occupy the post where they now are.

DANIEL SHAYS, *Captain*

On the next day, three of the insurgent leaders came to Head Quarters with the following letter.

The Honourable General Lincoln.

Sir,

As the officers of the people, now convened in defence of their rights and privileges, have sent a petition to the General Court, for the sole purpose of accommodating our present unhappy affairs, we justly expect that hostilities may cease on both sides, until we have a return from our legislature.

Your Honour will therefore be pleased to give us an answer.

Per order of the committee for reconciliation.

FRANCIS STONE, *Chairman*
DANIEL SHAYS, *Captain*
ADAM WHEELER

Pelham, January 31, 1787

To this the following Answer was sent.

Hadley, January 31st, 1787

Gentlemen,

Your request is totally inadmissible, as no powers are delegated to me which would justify a delay of my operations. Hostilities I have not commenced.

I have again to warn the people in arms against government, immediately to disband, as they would avoid the ill consequences which may ensue, should they be inattentive to this caution.

B. LINCOLN

To FRANCIS STONE,
DANIEL SHAYS,
ADAM WHEELER

During these negotiations between the army and the insurgents, the time arrived for the assembling of the legislature. . . . The Court then acquainted the Governour, that they were prepared to receive his communications, and he addressed them by a speech from the chair, which contained a retrospective account of the malcontents, as to their views and proceedings, and of the measures which the government had adopted to oppose them. Vigour and energy were strongly recommended, as the proper means of crushing so unprovoked an insurrection, while a want of them might draw on the evils of a civil war. . . .

Affairs had been brought to such a crisis, that there was no room left for the legislature to waver in their opinions, or to delay their measures. The whole community were in an alarm, and the appeal to the sword was actually made. One army or the other was to be supported, and there could be no hesitation in the mind of any reasonable man, which it ought to be. On the next day, therefore, a declaration of Rebellion was unanimously passed in the Senate, and concurred by the lower House. This however was accompanied by a resolve, approving of General Lincoln's offer of clemency to the privates among the insurgents, and empowering the Governour in the name of the General Court to promise a pardon, under such disqualifications, as should afterwards be provided, to all privates and noncommissioned officers, that were in arms against the Commonwealth [of Massachusetts], unless excepted by the general officer commanding the troops, upon condition of their surrendering their arms, and taking and subscribing the oath of allegiance, within a time to be prescribed by the Governour.

On the same day, an answer was also sent to the Governour's speech. In this the Court informed his Excellency of their entire satisfaction, in the measures which he had been pleased to take for subduing a turbulent spirit, that had too long insulted the Government of the Commonwealth; and congratulated him on the success which had attended them. They earnestly intreated him still to continue them, with such further constitutional measures, as he might think necessary, to extirpate the spirit of rebellion; for the better enabling of him to do which, they thought it necessary to declare that a rebellion existed. . . . They subjoined that they would vigorously pursue every measure, which would be calculated to support the constitution, and would continue to redress any real grievances, if such should be found to exist.

PART FOUR

Defining America
The Expanding Nation

When the turmoil resulting from the American Revolution and the ratification of the Constitution finally subsided in the 1790s, thirteen colonies had been forged into a new nation. Covering more than a thousand miles of the Atlantic coast, from Maine to Georgia, the United States of America already was populated by millions of people who spoke more than a dozen European languages and countless Native American tongues. Although the country was divided between the mercantile, agricultural-industrial North and the plantation South, a powerful bond seemed to unite its peoples: a shared desire for land and the opportunity for a better life.

For almost two hundred years, American society had been confined to the corridor between the Atlantic Ocean and the Appalachian Mountains. The continuing Native American presence and conflict among European powers had discouraged settlers from pushing westward. Then, after about 1795, with many Native Americans having been defeated or assimilated during the Revolution and the price of good eastern land climbing, a sizable white westward migration began. Thomas Jefferson's purchase of the vast Louisiana Territory in 1803 and his sponsorship of the expedition by Meriwether Lewis and William Clark quickened this movement, as did rising world prices for agricultural products. American westward expansion was also aided by the outcome of the War of 1812, in which the U.S. Army minimized the threat of military aggression from Native American tribes and leaders like John Norton.

A transportation revolution further encouraged the migration. Turnpikes replaced stump-filled rutted paths; steamboats overtook sailing ships and river rafts; and man-made waterways like the Erie Canal became the great engines of growth and development during the first half of the nineteenth century. These advances in transport provided the first economical means of moving bulky products from western farms to the markets of the eastern states and gave the fledgling national government experience at administrating people, places, and things on a grand scale. First opened for use in 1825, the Erie Canal would eventually fade in favor of the railroad, the great catalyst of growth in the second half of the nineteenth century. Thomas Woodcock's journey along the canal provides a glimpse of the ways in which economic development fired change and controversy across the countryside. In 1828, construction began on the first westward railroad, the Baltimore and Ohio; four decades later, in 1869, the last spike was hammered into the transcontinental railroad at Promontory, Utah.

By the 1840s, the land seemed to have tilted permanently, shaking its human burden westward in a long, rough tumble toward the Pacific. But the improved life people sought in the West was far more than one of simple economic gain: evangelical preachers such as James McGready, father of the camp meeting, crisscrossed the Western territories spreading their message, while believers such as Priscilla Merriman Evans and her husband trekked heroically to reach their Mormon Zion in the wilderness. Yet the quest for a better life did not always take people westward. African Americans like Reverend Richard Allen of Philadelphia preached a message of racial liberation along the seaboard of the Middle Atlantic states.

For the new Westerners, the land they moved onto was far from empty. Indeed, before the arrival of these newcomers, Native Americans had been forced westward for generations by white settlement. Then in 1838 the U.S. Army drove more than fifteen thousand Cherokee Indians in an agonizing march from Georgia to Oklahoma. John Ross's letter presents a Native American's view of these events. The relocation of the Cherokee put them into competition with groups already living in the West, including other Native Americans in the Western territories and the Spanish and their heirs, the *Mexicanos*, *Californios*, and *Tejanos*, who owned much of the land and resources in those territories.

When Mexico and the United States went to war over Texas and the Southwest in 1846, it was not a surprise to most Mexicans in the West. Like Guadalupe Vallejo, Prudencia Higuera, and Amalia Sibrian, whose recollections are featured in this chapter, they had seen a steady stream of land-hungry settlers permanently changing the sleepy world of *Alta California* and other parts of the northern Mexican frontier. In fact, the conflicts with Mexico determined the future of nearly a million square miles of what is now Texas, New Mexico, Arizona, Nevada, California, Utah, and parts of Colorado, Wyoming, Kansas, and Oklahoma. The discovery of gold in California in 1848 sealed the fate of the West as part of the United States. California was fast-tracked to statehood in 1850 as a rush of miners and entrepreneurs from China, South America, Europe, and the eastern states accelerated settlement. Controversial decisions about the future of these new territories would soon lead to the Civil War.

23

JAMES McGREADY

The Great Revival of 1800

Evangelicalism, the highly emotional proselytizing religion so characteristic of American Protestantism, began in the 1730s and 1740s with the English preacher George White-field's visits to the colonies. Whitefield's public meetings triggered what became known as the Great Awakening. Thousands responded to the dynamic preaching of Whitefield and the ministers he inspired with dramatic accounts of religious conversion. After a lull, revivalism once again burst forth at the turn of the nineteenth century, giving rise to a religious movement still vibrant in the United States today. The new inspiration came from the settlements that were farthest west, in Kentucky.

Kentucky's Presbyterian and Methodist ministers revolted against the "formality and deadness" of their churches and encouraged direct, emotional displays of religious fervor. The curious came, and many became converts. When the numbers of worshippers exceeded the seating capacity of the church, services were held outdoors. The most enthusiastic participants camped out for several days. In this way the camp meeting was born. In 1800, a meeting was announced for August 6 at Cane Ridge, Kentucky. Word flew about the hollows and cabins, and a crowd estimated at more than twenty thousand people (nearly 10 percent of the state's population) gathered for the largest religious service ever experienced up to that time in the United States.

Western evangelists traveled almost endlessly across sparsely settled territory during the first decades of the nineteenth century, preaching their highly emotional and individualistic religion. Their creeds emphasized personal morality, civic virtue, and education. In this reading you will see the revivals through the eyes of Kentucky Presbyterian minister James McGready (1760–1817), writing to a friend. McGready was widely credited with being the father of camp meetings.

QUESTIONS TO CONSIDER

1. What similarities and differences are there between camp meetings and contemporary religious gatherings?
2. Why did whole families travel great distances to attend these events?

Rev. James Smith, ed., *Posthumous Works of the Reverend and Pious James M'Gready, Minister of the Gospel, in Henderson, Kentucky*, 2 vols. (Louisville, Ky.: W. W. Worsley, 1831).

3. How might more traditional religious leaders have viewed camp meetings? Why do you think the "Rev. J. B." came and "involved our infant churches in confusion, disputation, &c."?

Logan County, Kentucky, October 23, 1801.

But I promised to give you a short statement of our blessed revival; on which you will at once say, the Lord has done great things for us in the wilderness, and the solitary place has been made glad: the desert has rejoiced and blossomed as the rose. . . .

A woman, who had been a professor,[1] in full communion with the church, found her old hope false and delusive—she was struck with deep conviction, and in a few days was filled with joy and peace in believing. She immediately visited her friends and relatives, from house to house, and warned them of their danger in a most solemn, faithful manner, and plead with them to repent and seek religion. This, as a mean, was accompanied with the divine blessing to the awakening of many. About this time the ears of all in that congregation seemed to be open to receive the word preached, and almost every sermon was accompanied with the power of God, to the awakening of sinners. During the summer about ten persons in the congregation were brought to Christ. In the fall of the year a general deadness seemed to creep on apace. Conviction and conversion work, in a great measure, ceased; and no visible alteration for the better took place, until the summer of 1798, at the administration of the sacrament[2] of the supper, which was in July. On Monday the Lord graciously poured out his *Spirit*; a very general awakening took place—perhaps but few families in the congregation could be found who, less or more, were not struck with an awful sense of their lost estate.[3] During the week following but few persons attended to worldly business, their attention to the business of their souls was so great. On the first Sabbath of September, the sacrament was administered at Muddy River (one of my congregations). At this meeting the Lord graciously poured forth his spirit, to the awakening of many careless sinners. Through these two congregations already mentioned, and through Red River, my other congregation, awakening work went on with power under every sermon. The people seemed to hear, as for eternity. In every house, and almost in every company, the whole conversation with people, was about the state of their souls. About this time the Rev. J. B. came here, and found a Mr. R. to join him. In a little time he involved our infant churches in confusion, disputation, &c. Opposed the doctrines preached here; ridiculed the whole work of the revival; formed a considerable party, &c. &c. In a few weeks this seemed to have put a final stop to the whole work, and our infant congregation remained in a state of deadness and darkness from the fall, through the winter,

1. **professor:** One who professes or declares a particular faith.
2. **sacrament:** Sacred rite or ritual.
3. **lost estate:** Sinful condition.

and until the month of July, 1799, at the administration of the sacrament at Red River. This was a very solemn time throughout. On Monday the power of God seemed to fill the congregation; the boldest, daring sinners in the country covered their faces and wept bitterly. After the congregation was dismissed, a large number of people stayed about the doors, unwilling to go away. Some of the ministers proposed to me to collect the people in the meeting-house again, and perform prayer with them; accordingly we went in, and joined in prayer and exhortation. The mighty power of God came amongst us like a shower from the everlasting hills—God's people were quickened and comforted; yea, some of them were filled with joy unspeakable, and full of glory. Sinners were powerfully alarmed, and some precious souls were brought to feel the pardoning love of Jesus.

At Gasper river (at this time under the care of Mr. Rankin, a precious instrument in the hand of God) the sacrament was administered in August. This was one of the days of the Son of Man, indeed, especially on Monday. I preached a plain gospel sermon on Heb. 11 and 16. The better country. A great solemnity continued during the sermon. After sermon Mr. Rankin gave a solemn exhortation—the congregation was then dismissed; but the people all kept their seats for a considerable space, whilst awful solemnity appeared in the countenances of a large majority. Presently several persons under deep convictions broke forth into a loud outcry—many fell to the ground, lay powerless, groaning, praying and crying for mercy. As I passed through the multitude, a woman, lying in awful distress, called me to her. Said she, "I lived in your congregation in Carolina; I was a professor, and often went to the communion; but I was deceived; I have no religion; I am going to hell." In another place an old, gray-headed man lay in an agony of distress, addressing his weeping wife and children in such language as this: "We are all going to hell together; we have lived prayerless, ungodly lives; the work of our souls is yet to begin; we must get religion, or we will all be damned." . . .

. . . But the year 1800 exceeds all that my eyes ever beheld upon earth. All that I have related is only, as it were, an introduction. Although many souls in these congregations, during the three preceding years, have been savingly converted, and now give living evidences of their union to Christ; yet all that work is only like a few drops before a mighty rain, when compared with the wonders of Almighty Grace, that took place in the year 1800.

In June the sacrament was administered at Red River. This was the greatest time we had ever seen before. On Monday multitudes were struck down under awful conviction; the cries of the distressed filled the whole house. There you might see profane swearers, and sabbath-breakers pricked to the heart, and crying out, "what shall we do to be saved?" There frolickers and dancers crying for mercy. There you might see little children of 10, 11 and 12 years of age, praying and crying for redemption, in the blood of Jesus, in agonies of distress. During this sacrament, and until the Tuesday following, ten persons, we believe, were savingly brought home to Christ.

In July the sacrament was administered in Gasper River Congregation. Here multitudes crowded from all parts of the country to see a strange work, from the distance of forty, fifty, and even a hundred miles; whole families came in their wagons; between twenty and thirty wagons were brought to the place, loaded with people, and their provisions, in order to encamp at the meetinghouse. On Friday nothing more appeared, during the day, than a decent solemnity. On Saturday matters continued in the same way, until in the evening. Two pious women were sitting together, conversing about their exercises; which conversation seemed to affect some of the by-standers; instantly the divine flame spread through the whole multitude. Presently you might have seen sinners lying powerless in every part of the house, praying and crying for mercy. Ministers and private Christians were kept busy during the night conversing with the distressed. This night a goodly number of awakened souls were delivered by sweet believing views of the glory, fulness, and sufficiency of Christ, to save to the uttermost. Amongst these were some little children—a striking proof of the religion of Jesus. Of many instances to which I have been an eyewitness, I shall only mention one, viz. A little girl. I stood by her whilst she lay across her mother's lap almost in despair. I was conversing with her when the first gleam of light broke in upon her mind—She started to her feet, and in an ecstacy of joy, she cried out, "O he is willing, he is willing—he is come, he is come—O what a sweet Christ he is—O what a precious Christ he is—O what a fulness I see in him—O what a beauty I see in him—O why was it that I never could believe! That I never could come to Christ before, when Christ was so willing to save me?" . . . Then turning round, she addressed sinners, and told them of the glory, willingness and preciousness of Christ, and plead with them to repent; and all this in language so heavenly, and, at the same time, so rational and scriptural, that I was filled with astonishment. But were I to write you every particular of this kind that I have been an eye and ear witness to, during the two past years, it would fill many sheets of paper.

At this sacrament a great many people from Cumberland, particularly from *Shiloh* Congregation, came with great curiosity to see the work, yet prepossessed with strong prejudices against it; about five of whom, I trust, were savingly and powerfully converted before they left the place. A circumstance worthy of observation, they were sober professors in full communion. It was truly affecting to see them lying powerless, crying for mercy, and speaking to their friends and relations, in such language as this: "O, we despised the work that we heard of in *Logan*; but, O, we were deceived—I have no religion; I know now there is a reality in these things: three days ago I would have despised any person that would have behaved as I am doing now; but, O, I feel the very pains of hell in my soul." This was the language of a precious soul, just before the hour of deliverance came. When they went home, their conversation to their friends and neighbors, was the means of commencing a glorious work that has overspread all the Cumberland settlements to the conversion of hundreds of precious souls. The work continued night and day at this sacrament, whilst the vast multitude continued upon the ground until Tuesday morning. According to the best computation, we believe that forty-five souls were brought to Christ on this occasion.

Muddy River Sacrament, in all its circumstances, was equal, and in some respects superior, to that at Gasper River. This sacrament was in August. We believe about fifty persons, at this time, obtained religion.

At Ridge Sacrament, in Cumberland, the second Sabbath in September, about forty-five souls, we believe, obtained religion. At Shiloh Sacrament, the third Sabbath in September, about seventy persons. At Mr. Craighead's Sacrament, in October, about forty persons. At the Clay-Lick Sacrament, *congregation*, in Logan County, in October, eight persons. At Little Muddy-Creek Sacrament, in November, about twelve. At Montgomery's Meeting-house, in Cumberland, about forty. At Hopewell Sacrament, in Cumberland, in November, about twenty persons. To mention the circumstances of more private occasions, common-days preaching, and societies, would swell a letter to a volume.

The present year has been a blessed season likewise; yet not equal to last year in conversion work. I shall just give you a list of our Sacraments, and the number, we believe, experienced religion at each, during the present year, 1801.

[McGready went on to mention several different sacraments, held at different places, and the number that he hoped obtained true religion, amounting to 144 persons in total. He then went on to finish the letter.]

I would just remark that, among the great numbers in our country that professed to obtain religion, I scarcely know an instance of any that gave a comfortable ground of hope to the people of God, that they had religion, and have been admitted to the privileges of the church, that have, in any degree, disgraced their profession, or given us any ground to doubt their religion.

The original is signed, JAMES M'GREADY.

24

RICHARD ALLEN

Early Steps toward Freedom

Richard Allen (1760–1831) was an early leader in the movement among free blacks to form their own churches. Born a slave in Philadelphia, he was sold at age seven with his family to a new master in Dover, Delaware. There he learned the blacksmith's trade and eventually converted to Christianity, joining the Methodists. He purchased his freedom

Richard Allen, *The Life, Experience, and Gospel Labours of the Rt. Rev. Richard Allen. To Which Is Annexed the Rise and Progress of the African Methodist Episcopal Church in the United States of America. Containing a Narrative of the Yellow Fever in the Year of Our Lord 1793: With an Address to the People of Colour in the United States. Written by Himself and Published by His Request* (Philadelphia: Martin & Boden, Printers, 1833), 14–16.

in 1781 and soon began to spread the Gospel among slaves and freed people alike. His talents were considerable and quickly noticed.

Ordained as a Methodist preacher in 1784, Allen began traveling with bishops who had called on him to visit unchurched blacks and win their souls for the Methodist cause. However, he soon demanded that he and fellow African Methodists be allowed to worship alone and on their own terms. Failing to earn the blessing of his superiors, Allen formed the Free African Society in 1787 and, seven years later, a black Methodist Church, Mother Bethel, in Philadelphia. Allen united Bethel with sixteen other black congregations across the mid-Atlantic and northern states in 1816 to form the African Methodist Episcopal Church, over which he presided as bishop until his death.

The Life, Experience, and Gospel Labours of the Rt. Rev. Richard Allen *was published two years after Allen's death. It chronicles his struggles to worship freely and promote the end of slavery and offers a rare glimpse at black institution building during the late eighteenth century. Its account of the refusal of Allen and his fellow worshippers to sit in the "black" section of St. George Methodist Church in Philadelphia in 1786, and of their subsequent dismissal from the church, stands as an early example of blacks' demands for religious liberty.*

QUESTIONS TO CONSIDER

1. Why did Allen refuse to accompany Bishop Asbury on his travels?
2. What gave Allen the confidence to leave St. George Church and start his own church?
3. How did Allen's view of the Gospel differ from the views of his white Methodist peers?

In 1785 the Rev. Richard Watcoat was appointed on Baltimore circuit. He was, I believe, a man of God. I found great strength in travelling with him — a father in Israel. In his advice he was fatherly and friendly. He was of a mild and serene disposition. . . . Rev. Bishop Asberry[1] sent for me to meet him at Henry Gaff's. I did so. He told me he wished me to travel with him. He told me that in the slave countries, Carolina and other places, I must not intermix with the slaves, and I would frequently have to sleep in his carriage, and he would allow me my victuals and clothes. I told him I would not travel with him on these conditions. He asked me my reason. I told him if I was taken sick, who was to support me? and that I thought people ought to lay up something while they were able, to support themselves in time of sickness or old age. He said that was as much as he got, his victuals and clothes. I told him he would be taken care of, let his afflictions be as they were, or let him be taken sick where he would, he would be taken care of; but I doubted whether it would be the case with myself. He smiled, and told me he would give me from then until he returned from the eastward to make up my mind, which would be

---

1. **Bishop Asberry:** Bishop Francis Asbury (1745–1816) was one of the founding bishops of the Methodist Episcopal Church in America.

about three months. But I made up my mind that I would not accept of his proposals. Shortly after I left Hartford Circuit, and came to Pennsylvania, on Lancaster Circuit. I travelled several months on Lancaster Circuit with the Rev. Peter Morratte and Irie Ellis. They were very kind and affectionate to me, in building me up; for I had many trials to pass through, and I received nothing from the Methodist connexion. My usual method was, when I would get bare of clothes, to stop travelling and go to work, so that no man could say I was chargeable to the connexion. My hands administered to my necessities.

Preaching was given out for me at five o'clock in the morning at St. George's Church. I strove to preach as well as I could, but it was a great cross to me; but the Lord was with me. We had a good time, and several souls were awakened, and were earnestly seeking redemption in the blood of Christ. I thought I would stop in Philadelphia a week or two. I preached at different places in the city. My labour was much blessed. I soon saw a large field open in seeking and instructing my African brethren, who had been a long forgotten people and few of them attended public worship. I preached in the commons, in Southwark, Northern Liberties, and wherever I could find an opening. I frequently preached twice a day, at 5 o'clock in the morning and in the evening, and it was not uncommon for me to preach from four to five times a day. I established prayer meetings; I raised a society in 1786 of forty-two members. I saw the necessity of erecting a place of worship for the coloured people. I proposed it to the most respectable people of colour in this city; but here I met with opposition. I had but three coloured brethren that united with me in erecting a place of worship—the Rev. Absalom Jones, William White, and Dorus Ginnings.

We all belonging to St. George's church—Rev. Absalom Jones, William White and Dorus Ginnings. We felt ourselves much cramped; but my dear Lord was with us, and we believed, if it was his will, the work would go on, and that we would be able to succeed in building the house of the Lord. We established prayer meetings and meetings of exhortation, and the Lord blessed our endeavours, and many souls were awakened; but the elder soon forbid us holding any such meetings; but we viewed the forlorn state of our coloured brethren, and that they were destitute of a place of worship. They were considered as a nuisance.

A number of us usually attended St. George's Church in Fourth street; and when the coloured people began to get numerous in attending the church, they moved us from the seats we usually sat on, and placed us around the wall, and on Sabbath morning we went to church and the sexton stood at the door, and told us to go in the gallery. He told us to go, and we would see where to sit. We expected to take the seats over the ones we formerly occupied below, not knowing any better. We took those seats. Meeting had begun, and they were nearly done singing, and just as we got to the seats, the elder said, "let us pray." We had not been long upon our knees before I heard considerable scuffling and low talking. I raised my head up and saw one of the trustees, H—— M——, having hold of the Rev. Absalom Jones, pulling him up off of his knees, and saying, "You must get up—you must not kneel here."

Mr. Jones replied, "wait until prayer is over." Mr. H—— M—— said "no, you must get up now, or I will call for aid and I force you away." Mr. Jones said, "wait until prayer is over, and I will get up and trouble you no more." With that he beckoned to one of the other trustees, Mr. L—— S——, to come to his assistance. He came, and went to William White to pull him up. By this time prayer was over, and we all went out of the church in a body, and they were no more plagued with us in the church.

Here was the beginning and rise of the first African church in America. But the elder of the Methodist church still pursued us. Mr. J—— M—— called upon us and told us if we did not erase our names from the subscription paper,[2] and give up the paper, we would be publicly turned out of meeting. We asked him if we had violated any rules of discipline by so doing. He replied, "I have the charge given to me by the Conference, and unless you submit I will read you publicly out of meeting." We told him we were willing to abide by the discipline of the Methodist church; "and if you will show us where we have violated any law of discipline of the Methodist church, we will submit; and if there is no rule violated in the discipline, we will proceed on." He replied, "we will read you all out." We told him if he turned us out contrary to rule of discipline, we should seek further redress. We told him we were dragged off of our knees in St. George's church, and treated worse than heathens; and we were determined to seek out for ourselves, the Lord being our helper. He told us we were not Methodists, and left us. Finding we would go on in raising money to build the church, he called upon us again, and wished to see us all together. We met him. He told us that he wished us well, and that he was a friend to us, and used many arguments to convince us that we were wrong in building a church. We told him we had no place of worship; and we did not mean to go to St. George's church any more, as we were so scandalously treated in the presence of all the congregation present; "and if you deny us your name, you cannot seal up the scriptures from us, and deny us a name in heaven. We believe heaven is free for all who worship in spirit and truth." And he said, "so you are determined to go on." We told him—"yes, God being our helper." He then replied, "we will disown you all from the Methodist connexion." We believed if we put our trust in the Lord, he would stand by us. This was a trial that I never had to pass through before. I was confident that the great head of the church would support us. My dear Lord was with us. We went out with our subscription paper, and met with great success. We had no reason to complain of the liberality of the citizens. The first day the Rev. Absalom Jones and myself went out we collected three hundred and sixty dollars.

FOR CRITICAL THINKING

1. How did the different audiences for whom these two authors were writing affect their thoughts on the meaning of religion in America?

2. **subscription paper:** Deed.

2. In these two accounts, how does religion both encourage and retard political change?

3. Are the social goals articulated by each author similar to ones expressed by contemporary religious leaders—or are they simply quaint artifacts of the past? Explain.

25

MAJOR JOHN NORTON (TEYONINHOKARAWEN)

A Native American Commander in the War of 1812

Major John Norton, or Teyoninhokarawen, was a Mohawk chief who led Native Americans living in the U.S.–Canadian border region into the War of 1812 on the side of the British. His warriors made a key contribution to the military defeat of the U.S. Army at Queenston Heights, Stoney Creek, and, most famously, the Siege of Detroit.

Probably born in Scotland in the 1760s to a Cherokee who had served in the British Army and a Scottish mother, Norton himself joined the British Army as a young man, serving in Ireland and later Canada in the 1780s. While in Canada he rediscovered his native roots, teaching and trading among the Five Nations Iroquois, marrying an Iroquois woman, and learning the Iroquois language and customs.

He began his Native American political career when he was adopted as nephew by Indian leader Joseph Brant (Thayendanegea), perhaps the most famous Native American of his time, who had distinguished himself on the side of the British during the American Revolution. Norton used his connections to Brant to become a chief, and after Brant's death he was drawn back into military service in Tecumseh's war against the Americans at the Battle of Tippecanoe in 1811. When the War of 1812 broke out the following year, Norton traveled among his adopted people, trying to recruit them to fight on the side of the British.

The Five Nations had been split by the outcome of the American Revolution, with many remaining on the American side and some moving across the border to Canada. Sitting along the U.S.–Canadian border, the Five Nations struggled with a difficult neutrality in the War of 1812. They hoped that the white men would fight one another to the death and leave them in peace, but they also feared that as the war dragged on, the two powers might force them onto opposite sides of the conflict. Norton rejected this attempt to steer a path between the two powers and argued that the biggest danger native

The Journal of Major John Norton, 1816, The Publications of the Champlain Society (Toronto: The Champlain Society, 1970), 289–95.

peoples faced was in not *getting into the war at the beginning and proving necessary to one power.*

The following passages, taken from Norton's journal, describe his failed attempts to rally the Five Nations of the Iroquois Confederacy to the side of the British king and the delicate discussions about how Native Americans could avoid the danger of being dragged into fighting one another on opposite sides of the conflict. Norton did recruit many Native American warriors to his military command, which, along with those serving under Joseph Brant's son John, fought several successful battles against the Americans, including the Siege of Detroit, described in this passage, in which British general Isaac Brock led a dramatic victory over American general William Hull.

QUESTIONS TO CONSIDER

1. Were the Native Americans living in the border region between Canada and the United States right to remain neutral during the War of 1812?
2. How representative was John Norton's view among Native Americans that it was better to fight for the British crown than for the Americans?
3. What factors went into Native American decisions about which side to take in the War of 1812?

. . . In June 1812,—a Deputation of the Younger Chiefs from the Ondowaga, Onondague and Cayugwas living within the American Boundary, came to the council fire at the Grand River;—they avowed their Motive was to commune with their Brethren, that they might avoid involving themselves in the difficulties attendant on War. The Chiefs and Warriors of the Grand River assembled,—and on the first day the Ondowaga, opening the Council after the usual salutations,—Billy, as speaker for the Deputation, arose and spoke to this purport,—"Brother,—We have come from our homes to warn you, that you may preserve yourselves and families from distress. We discover that the British and the Americans are on the Eve of a War,—they are in dispute respecting some rights on the Sea, with which we are unacquainted;—should it end in a Contest, let us keep aloof:—Why should we again fight, and call upon ourselves the resentment of the Conquerors? We know that neither of these powers have any regard for us. In the former War, we espoused the cause of the King, We thought it the most honourable,—all our former Treaties having been made with his Representatives. After contending seven years without ever listening to the pacific overtures sent from the Enemy,—we found,—that Peace was concluded across the Sea, and that our Enemy claimed our Territory in consequence of the Boundary Line then acceded to. We found none to assist us to obtain Justice; We were compelled to rely on ourselves, & make the best of it. Experience has convinced us of their neglect, except when they want us. Why then should we endanger the comfort, even the existence of our families, to enjoy their smiles only for the Day in which they need us?

"The American Agent, who lives in our Neighbourhood, has told us, that the United States do not require our assistance, — that their number is endless and adequate to every emergency of War: — this entirely meets our sentiments, — We are in their power, but we do not wish to join them in War.

"Brother, — We entreat that you also sit still in your habitations, regardless of the Tempest of Battle, — you may thus escape unhurt & unobserved by the enraged Combatants.

"Let us now pledge ourselves to each other to observe a strict neutrality. We may then meet again with our hearts unclouded by disagreable circumstances — when the storm of War shall have blown over, & left the sky clear, — without a threatening Cloud. We hope our Words may penetrate your hearts, — take this Wampum, — in token of our sincerity."

Taking the Wampum, the People of the Grand River withdrew to deliberate. At this time, there was a party among the Mohawks strongly inclined to pursue the Line of conduct recommended by the Deputation from the other side, and ambitious to inculcate similar sentiments into the minds of all the people of the Grand River; — this called forth more strongly the Exertions of the firm and loyal, to render steady such as wavered from the apprehension of the great number and power of the Americans, — so strongly vaunted by themselves, and in the various Rumours circulating through Upper Canada.

It took up two days before an answer could be made for the Senecas, — in that time two of their most respectable Chiefs calling upon me, entered into conversation to this effect: "Friend, — We view you with apprehension & suspicion: — We think you so zealously disposed to serve the King that you are inclined to draw after you all these people without considering the difficulties in which you may thereby involve them. Perhaps you also imagine that we come here entirely under the Influence of the American Agent, only prepared to rehearse the Lesson he may have given us. We may both be mistaken. To convince you that we act from a disinterested Love to our people, and to ensure their welfare and preservation, — We shall lay before you the reasons which induce us to recommend a neutrality. The gloomy Day, foretold by our ancients, has at last arrived; — the Independance and Glory of the Five Nations has departed from us; — We find ourselves in the hands of two powerful Nations, who can crush us when they please. They are the same in every respect, although they are now preparing to contend. We are ignorant of the real motives which urge them to arm, but we are well assured that we have no interest therein, and that neither one nor other have any affection towards us. We know that our Blood shed in their Battles will not even ensure their compassion to our Widows and Orphans, — nor respect to our Tribes weakened in their Contests. Has not our Nation partaken in ev'ry War in which the English have been engaged, — since they first joined hands, (for then the English & Americans were one). In Standing between them and the French, many a Valiant Warrior has fallen. But although we have thus been weakened, & deprived of our Independance, it has not been by the Victories of a Conqueror; — it has been the neglect or Unkindness of our Friends. Seeing therefore, that no good can be derived from War, we think we should only seek the surest means of averting its attendant Evils;—We are of opinion that we should follow the example of some of their people,[1] who never bear arms in war, & deprecate the principle of hostility."

I answered, "What you have now said is certainly applicable to you who remain on the other side. The Americans have gained possession of all your Country, excepting the small part which you have reserved. They have enveloped you:—it is out of your power to assist us,—because in doing so,—you would hazard the Destruction of your families. You can however have no motive to assist them;—The King does not want to take your Lands nor to injure you, and the Americans will not give you more for assisting them. Even should your actions or courage merit a glorious report,—they will hardly allow you that which they bargain for themselves. It is therefore both your Interest and your Duty to remain peaceable at home.

"Our Situation is very different. You know that the preferring to live under the protection of the King, rather than fall under the power or influence of the Americans,—induced us to fix our habitations at this place. If the King is attacked, we must support him, we are sure that such conduct is honourable;—but how profitable it might be to submit to these Mighty Men without resistance, we can, by no means ascertain;—We know that We would feel it highly disgraceful, and we remember what has been the fate of those who have thought that a passive inoffensive Demeanour would be a sufficient protection. Witness the peaceable People of Conestogue butchered at Lancaster,—the harmless Moravian Delawares, murdered at their own Village on Muskingum,—and many other instances that clearly demonstrate a manly resistance to be the strongest security against armed enemies like them, who invade us with their host of new made soldiers, only confident of awing by the pomp of military parade & numbers. We know them to have always been the Enemies of the Aboriginal Nations. Last autumn, they commenced their grand Military atchievements, & marched against the Village of Tippicanoe,—astonished at the resistance of a few Warriors whom they found there, they returned home, to meditate on a more easy method of conquering."

These men spoke openly their minds. There were others, who, I discovered, had been spreading dreadful alarms of the immense preparations of the Americans,—that they would cross the Line with a great force from Detroit,—from Presqu'ile to Long Point,—from Black Rock to Fort Erie,—& that another army would invade Lower Canada, whilst the Country People in many places would espouse the Cause of the Enemy. These reports alarmed the Women, & indeed seemed to cause many others to waver: an apparent Majority however unanimously determined to give the following answer,—whilst the wavering retired.

"Brothers,—we thank you for this further proof of your affection, which you have now shewn us, in coming to forewarn us of impending danger. We

---

1. The Quakers. [Note provided by original editor of the document.]

lament with you the Situation in which we are now placed, by being separated. You have fallen under the power of those who were once our Enemies, and are likely to become so again;—they have encompassed you, and as we cannot extricate you from the Difficulties in which you are involved,—we recommend to you peace, & request that you restrain all your young Men from becoming subservient to the Americans;—We would be ashamed of our Tribes, should any be found among the Common Enemy of our race. They have said—that they require no assistance,—keep them to their word. In the former War they held the same Language to the Oniadas,—but when they had them in their power, they insisted on their joining,—& you know we found them in arms combined with our Enemies, and many of them have fallen by our hands.

"Brothers,—Our Forefathers, when they first took the English by the hand,—agreed to risk with them. When those who had surrounded our Villages under the name of brothers, raised their arm against our Father the King,—we all joined him because he was our father;—at the peace, we removed here to live under his protection, & if he is now attacked, we will risk with him:—We are not alarmed at the boasted numbers of the Americans,—for it is he who dwells above that will decide on our fate. We cannot lie down at ease when our Father is threatened, he has not yet given us the Hatchet,[2] but should the Enemy invade us suddenly,—we hope to find something wherewith to Strike. Brothers,—We will never consider you as belonging to them. We will caution all our Western Brethren not to hurt you, in striking at the Americans who dwell around you. May the great Spirit preserve you in peace!"

Many of these people expressed the most earnest desire that the peace might continue without interruption:—they appeared very sensible of the awkward situation in which they were placed, and notwithstanding the pacific Language of the Americans, they apprehended that they might entice some of their thoughtless young Men to join them.

A few days after the Departure of these people,—we gained notice of the Declaration of War. It was then all Bustle throughout the Country,—calling together the Militia, and making every preparation to meet the Attack expected.

The People of the grand River met again in council, although I had supposed that already they had decided on the part they would take. A small Party only repaired to Niagara, & many of these not the most steady men. General Brock however received me with that pleasing affability so natural to him, & appeared as well satisfied as if there had been with me a thousand Men. He asked me, "Can you confide in the People of the Grand River,—Do you think that they will be faithful to you, tell me without reserve:" I replied, "They are unfortunately divided into parties, and there are some plausible

2. Implying that they had not yet been called upon to take up arms. [Note provided by original editor of the document.]

men, who succeed in retarding their coming forth,—but when they engage, I have no doubts they are not so depraved as to be faithless. It will be necessary however, in order to render them steady & permanently serviceable to allow them a regular stipend for their support,—otherwise want will oblige them to return to their usual occupations for the Support of their families,— their present Situation being now very different from what it was; when they possessed an extensive Country,—abounding in Game,—Wide ranges for Cattle,—& were protected from the sudden assaults of the Enemy by a desert frontier." He answered that he saw clearly the propriety of my remark, at the same time adding that he thought Goods might answer the purpose better than money.

From what passed within our observation on the opposite side of the River, it appeared that the Enemy had not as yet collected any considerable force there. With us, the Militia of the Adjacent Country had assembled & made a formidable appearance: a proportion of them, called the flank companies, were retained to do duty with the Troops, and the main body was permitted to return home, that the agriculture might not be too much neglected.

At this time, the Commander on the American side, wrote a Letter to General Brock, intimating that some Chiefs of the Ondowaga desiring to communicate with their Brethren on the Canadian Shore, had required him to ask permission for them to come over to meet them:—he acceded to their proposition and requested me to meet them, with some Chiefs, at Queenstown, as it would not be prudent to admit them into the Country, where they might have ascertained the Quality and Quantity of our force.

At Queenstown we met the Senecas or Ondowaga. The principal Man is named Arosa,—(one of his Ancestors of the same name was a celebrated Warrior in the French War, remarkable for his fidelity to the English, by whom he was called *Silver Heels*). They were saluted with much cordiality;—they seemed strongly impressed with the importance of their Mission, and after having been seated for a few minutes, Arosa stood forth, holding some Wampum in his hand,—he thus began,—"Brothers,—feeling that tender anxiety for your Welfare which should always influence people of the same blood and kindred,—we have come to you to explain the sentiments of our hearts. It was our intention to have abode with you some days, to gratify our Eyes with a Sight of our Brethren, but the gathering Clouds of War, covering the Earth with the Gloom of darkness, forbid us passing this place:—We, shall therefore deliver immediately what moves within our Breasts.

"Brothers,—our hearts overflow with Tenderness when we look upon you. We lament that you are on the Eve of being plunged into the Miseries of War, and we beseech you to avert them by remaining peaceably at home, unmindful of the Din of arms. We know that War is destructive;—its conclusion may be ruinous, & it is well ascertained that misery is its constant attendant.

"Brothers,—the People of the great King are our old friends, & the Americans are our Neighbours. We grieve to see them prepare to imbrue their hands in the blood of each other. We have determined not to interfere, for how could we spill the Blood of the English or of our Brethren? We entreat you therefore to imitate our Determination;—for, remember, we are in the power of the Americans, & perhaps when you shall have spread Destruction through their Ranks, they will change their Language, and insist upon us to join them:—they may compel our young Men to fight against their kindred,—and like devoted animals,—we shall be brought to destroy each other."

After deliberating a few minutes, an Onondaga Chief arose,—& as speaker for the people of the Grand River, answered in their behalf: "Brothers,—we have heard your Words with pleasure, because we know they proceed from the Goodness of your heart. We regret that we are separated, for if we had been living together, we would have been of one mind.

"Brothers,—you know that we removed from the Country of our ancestors when overhung by the power of the Americans,—in order to place ourselves under the protection of the King. He does not desire to invade the Americans, but if they follow us here to attack our Father, we cannot be passive Spectators,—we must share the same fate with him. We shall participate in the Shout of Victory,—or in the Grave,—whichever He who rules may allot us. Brothers, we commend your resolution not to join in the approaching contest,—you can have no Interest therein;—but we regret that we shall be separated. May He to whom we look for aid protect you!"

Arosa stood forth again, and spoke thus: "Brothers,—We see our Words have no Effect,—but we are easy,—We have done what we judged our Duty, & we perceive you have made your Election. Therefore we shall yet further exhort you;—As you will join with Europeans in their Wars, imitate their Example, in humanely treating your Prisoners:—Let the Warriors rage only be felt in combat, by his armed opponents;—Let the unoffending cultivator of the Ground, and his helpless family, never be alarmed by your onset, nor injured by your depredation: And you,—Teyoninhoharawen[3]—we exhort you, that, as the Five Nations listen to your Words, you will help them, & endeavour to make them happy in the favour of the Great King, and should you pass thro' the Chance of War, be to them a protector. May he who dwells above the Clouds avert ev'ry Evil from your heads, & lead you by the Hand!"

He ended,—bidding us Adieu in a Manner truly affecting, while every feature expressed the Sensibility of his heart, & they recrossed the River. . . .

---

3. Spellings were often inconsistent in the eighteenth and nineteenth centuries, and different versions of the same name were not uncommon, especially with unfamiliar Indian names, hence "Teyoninhoharawen" here instead of "Teyoninhokarawen."

26

MERIWETHER LEWIS AND WILLIAM CLARK

Crossing the Continent

The most famous expedition in American history was the brainchild of Thomas Jefferson. For years Jefferson had dreamed that a party of explorers could search out a passage to the Pacific; win the allegiance of the native inhabitants to the new republic; and study the geography, plants, and minerals of a vast and unknown territory.

Meriwether Lewis (1774–1809) and William Clark (1770–1838) were two young men willing to follow Jefferson's dream. Their expedition from St. Louis to the mouth of the Columbia River and back is one of the great adventure stories of U.S. history. The journals and notebooks that members of the party kept have been invaluable to historians, geographers, anthropologists, botanists, and zoologists.

The selections here begin with Lewis and Clark's accounts of an episode in May 1805, in which one of the expedition's interpreters, French Canadian trapper Toussaint de Charbonneau (husband of Lewis and Clark's guide, Sacajawea), nearly capsizes a canoe carrying valuable materials. A few months later, the expedition crosses the Great Divide—the peak of the Rocky Mountains where the rivers flow either to the east or to the west—in one of the most difficult parts of their journey. There, the expedition meets up with a party of Shoshone, Sacajawea's native nation from which she was separated as a small child, led by her long-lost brother Cameahwait. The reader can see the explorers' careful search for information about the best route west and their close observation of Native American ways.

QUESTIONS TO CONSIDER

1. What happened with the near-capsizing of the perogue (canoe)? What can we glean about Charbonneau and Sacajawea from Lewis and Clark's accounts of this incident?
2. Imagine that you were Cameahwait, one of the chiefs about whom Meriwether Lewis wrote. How would you have described the historic meeting with U.S. government representatives in Washington, D.C.?
3. What was Lewis's strategy for gaining the chiefs' support?
4. Why was Lewis writing about the sexual mores of the Shoshone? How were they different from the practices he was used to?
5. Why did Lewis write about the Spanish?

Bernard DeVoto, ed., *The Journals of Lewis and Clark* (Boston: Houghton Mifflin, 1953), 202–6, 207–11, 213–14.

MERIWETHER LEWIS

Tuesday May 14th 1805

. . . we had been halted by an occurrence, which I have now to recappitu-late, and which altho' happily passed without ruinous injury, I cannot rec-ollect but with the utmost trepidation and horror; this is the upseting and narrow escape of the white perogue. It happened unfortunately for us this evening that Charbono [Charbonneau] was at the helm of this Perogue, in stead of Drewyer, who had previously steered her; Charbono cannot swim and is perhaps the most timid waterman in the world; perhaps it was equally unluckey that Capt. C. [Clark] and myself were both on shore at that mo-ment, a circumstance which rarely happened; and tho' we were on the shore opposite to the perogue, were too far distant to be heard or to do more than remain spectators of her fate; in this perogue [blank with apparent erasures] were embarked, our papers, Instruments, books[,] medicine, a great part of our merchandize and in short almost every article indispensibly necessary to further the views, or insure the success of the enterprise in which we are now launched to the distance of 2200 miles. surfice it to say, that the Perogue was under sail when a sudon squawl of wind struck her obliquely, and turned her considerably, the steersman allarmed, in stead of puting her before the wind, lufted her up into it, the wind was so violent that it drew the brace of the squarsail out of the hand of the man who was attending it, and instantly upset the perogue and would have turned her completely topsaturva [topsy-turvy], had it not have been from the resistance mad by the oarning against the water; in this situation Capt. C and myself both fired our guns to attract the attention if possible of the crew and ordered the halyards to be cut and the sail hawled in, but they did not hear us; such was their confusion and consternation at this moment, that they suffered the perogue to lye on her side for half a minute before they took the sail in, the perogue then wrighted but had filled within an inch of the gunw-als; Charbono still crying to his god for mercy, had not yet recollected the rudder, nor could the repeated orders of the Bowsman, Cruzat, bring him to his recollection untill he threatend to shoot him instantly if he did not take hold of the rudder and do his duty, the waves by this time were runing very high, but the fortitude resolution and good conduct of Cruzat saved her; he ordered 2 of the men to throw out the water with some kettles that fortunately were convenient, while himself and two others rowed her as[h]ore, where she arrived scarcely above the water; we now took every ar-ticle out of her and lay them to drane as well as we could for the evening, baled out the canoe and secured her; there were two other men beside Char-bono on board who could not swim, and who of course must also have perished had the perogue gone to the bottom. . . . After having all matters ar-ranged for the evening as well as the nature of circumstances would permit, we thought it a proper occasion to console ourselves and cheer the sperits of our men and accordingly took a drink of grog and gave each man a gill of sperits.

WILLIAM CLARK

14th of May Tuesday 1805

A verry Clear Cold morning a white frost & some fog on the river the Thermomtr Stood at 32 above 0, wind from the S.W. we proceeded on verry well untill about 6 oClock a Squawl of wind Struck our Sale broad Side and turned the perogue nearly over, and in this Situation the Perogue remained untill the Sale was Cut down in which time She nearly filed with water—the articles which floated out was nearly all caught by the Squar who was in the rear. This accident had like to have cost us deerly; for in this perogue were embarked our papers, Instruments, books, medicine, a great proportion of our merchandize, and in short almost every article indispensibly necessary to further the views, or insure the success of the enterprize in which, we are now launched to the distance of 2,200 miles. it happened unfortunately that Capt. Lewis and myself were both on shore at the time of this occurrence, a circumstance which seldom took place; and tho' we were on the shore opposit to the perogue were too far distant to be heard or do more than remain spectators of her fate; we discharged our guns with the hope of attracting the attention of the crew and ordered the sail to be taken in but such was their consternation and confusion at the instant that they did not hear us. when however they at length took in the sail and the perogue wrighted; the bowsman Cruzatte by repeated threats so far brought Charbono the Sternman to his recollection that he did his duty while two hands bailed the perogue and Cruzatte and two others rowed her on shore were she arrived scarcely above the water. we owe the preservation of the perogue to the resolution and fortitude of Cruzatte. . . .

MERIWETHER LEWIS

Thursday May 16th

The morning was fair and the day proved favorable to our operations; by 4 oClock in the evening our Instruments, Medicine, merchandize provision &c, were perfectly dryed, repacked and put on board the perogue. the loss we sustained was not so great as we had at first apprehended; our medicine sustained the greatest injury, several articles of which were intirely spoiled, and many others considerably injured; the ballance of our losses consisted of some gardin seeds, a small quantity of gunpowder, and a few culinary articles which fell overboard and sunk, the Indian woman [Sacajawea] to whom I ascribe equal fortitude and resolution, with any person onboard at the time of the accedent, caught and preserved most of the light articles which were washed overboard all matters being now arranged for our departure we lost no time in seting out; proceeded on tolerably well about seven miles and encamped on the Stard. side. . . .

MERIWETHER LEWIS

Saturday August 17th 1805.

we made them [the Indians] sensible of their dependance on the will of our government for every species of merchandize as well for their defence & comfort; and apprized them of the strength of our government and it's friendly dispositions towards them. we also gave them as a reason why we wished to pe[ne]trate the country as far as the ocean to the west of them was to examine and find out a more direct way to bring merchandize to them. that as no trade could by carryed on with them before our return to our homes that it was mutually advantageous to them as well as to ourselves that they should render us such aids as they had in their power to furnish in order to haisten our voyage and of course our return home. that such were their horses to transport our baggage without which we could not subsist, and that a pilot to conduct us through the mountains was also necessary if we could not decend the river by water. but that we did not ask either their horses or their services without giving a satisfactory compensation in return. that at present we wished them to collect as many horses as were necessary to transport our baggage to their village on the Columbia where we would then trade with them at our leasure for such horses as they could spare us.

the chief thanked us for friendship towards himself and nation & declared his wish to serve us in every rispect. that he was sorry to find that it must yet be some time before they could be furnished with firearms but said they could live as they had done heretofore until we brought them as we had promised. he said they had not horses enough with them at present to remove our baggage to their village over the mountain, but that he would return tomorrow and encourage his people to come over with their horses and that he would bring his own and assist us. this was complying with all we wished at present.

we next enquired who were chiefs among them. Cameahwait pointed out two others whom he said were Chiefs. we gave him a medal of the small size with the likeness of Mr. Jefferson the President of the U' States in releif on one side and clasp hands with a pipe and tomahawk in the other, to the other Chiefs we gave each a small medal which were struck in the Presidency of George Washing[ton] Esqr. we also gave small medals of the last discription two young men whom the 1st Chief informed us were good young men and much rispected among them. we gave the 1st Chief an uniform coat shirt a pair of scarlet legings a carrot of tobacco and some small articles to each of the others we gave a shi[r]t leging[s] handkerchief a knife some tobacco and a few small articles we also distributed a good quantity paint mockerson awles

knives beads looking-glasses &c among the other Indians and gave them a
plentifull meal of lyed corn which was the first they had ever eaten in their
lives. they were much pleased with it. every article about us appeared to excite astonishment in there minds; the appearance of the men, their arms, the
canoes, our manner of working them, the b[l]ack man york and the sagacity
of my dog were equally objects of admiration. I also shot my air-gun which
was so perfectly incomprehensible that they immediately denominated it the
great medicine.

Capt. Clark and myself now concerted measures for our future operations, and it was mutually agreed that he should set out tomorrow morning
with eleven men furnished with axes and other necessary tools for making
canoes, their arms accoutrements and as much of their baggage as they could
carry. also to take the indians, C[h]arbono and the indian woman with him;
that on his arrival at the Shoshone camp he was to leave Charbono and the
Indian woman to haisten the return of the Indians with their horses to this
place, and to proceede himself with the eleven men down the Columbia in
order to examine the river and if he found it navigable and could obtain timber to set about making canoes immediately. In the mean time I was to bring
the party and baggage to the Shoshone Camp, calculating that by the time
I should reach that place that he would have sufficiently informed himself
with rispect to the state of the river &c. as to determine us whether to pros-
icute our journey from thence by land or water. in the former case we should
want all the horses which we could perchase, and in the latter only to hire the
Indians to transport our baggage to the place at which we made the canoes.

Monday August 19th 1805.

The Shoshonees may be estimated at about 100 warriors, and about three
times that number of women and children[1] they have more children among
them than I expected to have seen among a people who procure subsistence
with such difficulty. there are but few very old persons, nor did they appear to treat those with much tenderness or rispect. The man is the sole pro-
pryetor of his wives and daughters, and can barter or dispose of either as he
thinks proper. a plurality of wives is common among them, but these are not
generally sisters as with the Minnitares & Mandans but are purchased of different fathers. The father frequently disposes of his infant daughters in marriage to men who are grown or to men who have sons for whom they think
proper to provide wives. the compensation given in such cases usually consists of horses or mules which the father receives at the time of contract and
converts to his own uce. the girl remains with her parents untill she is conceived to have obtained the age of puberty which with them is considered to
be about the age of 13 or 14 years. the female at this age is surrendered to her
soveriegn lord and husband agreeably to contract, and with her is frequently

1. Lewis's figures refer to this band only.

restored by the father quite as much as he received in the first instance in payment for his daughter; but this is discretionary with the father. Sah-car-gar-we-ah had been thus disposed of before she was taken by the Minnetares, or had arrived to the years of puberty. the husband was yet living with this band. he was more than double her age and had two other wives. he claimed her as his wife but said that as she had had a child by another man, who was Charbono, that he did not want her.

They seldom correct their children particularly the boys who soon become masters of their own acts. they give as a reason that it cows and breaks the sperit of the boy to whip him, and that he never recovers his independence of mind after he is grown. They treat their women but with little rispect, and compel them to perform every species of drudgery. they collect the wild fruits and roots, attend to the horses or assist in that duty, cook, dress the skins and make all their apparel, collect wood and make their fires, arrange and form their lodges, and when they travel pack the horses and take charge of all the baggage; in short the man dose little else except attend his horses hunt and fish. the man considers himself degraded if he is compelled to walk any distance; and if he is so unfortunately poor as only to possess two horses he rides the best himself and leavs the woman or women if he has more than one, to transport their baggage and children on the other, and to walk if the horse is unable to carry the additional weight of their persons. the chastity of their women is not held in high estimation, and the husband will for a trifle barter the companion of his bead for a night or longer if he conceives the reward adiquate; tho' they are not so importunate that we should caress their women as the siouxs were. and some of their women appear to be held more sacred than in any nation we have seen.

I have requested the men to give them no cause of jealousy by having connection with their women without their knowledge, which with them, strange as it may seem is considered as disgracefull to the husband as clandestine connections of a similar kind are among civilized nations. to prevent this mutual exchange of good officies altogether I know it impossible to effect, particularly on the part of our young men whom some months abstanence have made very polite to those tawney damsels. no evil has yet resulted and I hope will not from these connections.

notwithstanding the late loss of horses which this people sustained by the Minnetares the stock of the band may be very safely estimated at seven hundred of which they are perhaps about 40 coalts and half that number of mules. their arms offensive and defensive consist in the bow and arrows shield, some lances, and a weapon called by the Cippeways [Chippewas] who formerly used it, the pog-gar'- mag-gon' [war club]. in fishing they employ wairs, gigs, and fishing hooks. the salmon is the principal object of their pursuit. they snair wolves and foxes.

I was anxious to learn whether these people had the venerial, and made the enquiry through the interpreter and his wife; the information was that they sometimes had it but I could not learn their remedy; they most usually die with it's effects. this seems a strong proof that these disorders bothe ganaraehah and Louis Venerae[2] are native disorders of America. tho' these people have suffered much by the small pox which is known to be imported and perhaps those other disorders might have been contracted from other indian tribes who by a round of communications might have obtained from the Europeans since it was introduced into that quarter of the globe. but so much detached on the other ha[n]d from all communication with the whites that I think it most probable that those disorders are original with them. . . .

I spend the day smoking with them and acquiring what information I could with respect to their country. they informed me that they could pass to the Spaniards by the way of the yellowstone river in 10 days. I can discover that these people are by no means friendly to the Spaniards. their complaint is, that the Spaniards will not let them have fire arms and ammunition, that they put them off by telling them that if they suffer them to have guns they will kill each other, thus leaving them defenceless and an easy prey to their bloodthirsty neighbours to the East of them, who being in possession of fire arms hunt them up and murder them without rispect to sex or age and plunder them of their horses on all occasions. they told me that to avoid their enemies who were eternally harrassing them that they were obliged to remain in the interior of these mountains at least two thirds of the year where the[y] suffered as we then saw great heardships for the want of food sometimes living for weeks without meat and only a little fish roots and berries. but this added Câmeahwait, with his ferce eyes and lank jaws grown meager for the want of food, would not be the case if we had guns, we could then live in the country of buffaloe and eat as our enimies do and not be compelled to hide ourselves in these mountains and live on roots and berries as the bear do. we do not fear our enimies when placed on an equal footing with them. I told them that the Minnetares Mandans . . . had promised us to desist from making war on them & that we would indevour to find the means of making the Minnetares of fort d[e] Prarie or as they call them Pahkees desist from waging war against them also. that after our finally returning to our homes towards the rising sun whitemen would come to them with an abundance of guns and every other article necessary to their defence and comfort, and that they would be enabled to supply themselves with these articles on reasonable terms in exchange for the skins of the beaver Otter and Ermin so abundant in their country. they expressed great pleasure at this information and said they had been long anxious to see the whitemen that traded guns; and that we might rest assured of their friendship and that they would do whatever we wished them.

---

2. **ganaraehah and Louis Venerae:** Gonorrhea and syphilis.

27

THOMAS SWANN WOODCOCK

The Erie Canal: Providing Passage for a Growing Nation

The most expensive infrastructure project in American history, the Erie Canal was ridiculed by opponents as "Clinton's big ditch"—a reference to New York governor De Witt Clinton, who had shepherded the project through the state legislature in 1817. Completed in 1825 at a cost of $7 million, the canal wound 363 miles through the Mohawk Valley from Albany to Buffalo on Lake Erie. Along the way, eighty-three locks lifted boats up and down the 650-foot elevation, while eighteen stone aqueducts carried the canal over rivers and streams. Horses pulled barges along the route—an excruciatingly slow but economically very profitable method of transport.

Most significantly for the nation's economic development, the cost of hauling grain across the Appalachian foothills to New York City had, before the canal, been more expensive than importing it from overseas. Suddenly, the cost of transporting these goods to the city diminished as hundred-ton barges, loaded with wheat and a diverse array of America's products, moved along Clinton's ditch toward the growing markets of the Atlantic basin.

Ultimately, the Erie, along with smaller and less successful canals in other states, would open economic development of the western states and dominate domestic transportation, communication, and freight shipment until later in the century, when the railroad would overtake the canal as the preferred vehicle of commerce. Towns along the Erie's route, from Albany to Buffalo and farther west to Cleveland and Chicago, would prosper and grow.

Thomas Woodcock, whose diary entry follows, was an English-born engraver who migrated to the United States in 1830. In 1836 Woodcock bought a guidebook written by Captain Basil Hall and joined millions of tourists, travel writers, merchants, and laborers in taking the route from New York to Niagara Falls. His writings offer a window onto the shifting world of commerce and culture during the early nineteenth century.

QUESTIONS TO CONSIDER

1. In what ways is Woodcock's portrait of the canal positive? In what ways is it negative?
2. Based on Woodcock's account of the trip, who might have been opposed to the canal, and who might have supported it?

Deoch Fulton, ed., *New York to Niagara, 1836: The Journal of Thomas S. Woodcock* (New York: New York Public Library, 1938), 5–7, 10–16, 19–20, 22.

3. In what ways does Buffalo's booming economy seem similar to economic conditions in the present?

SOME ACCOUNT OF A TRIP TO THE "FALLS OF NIAGARA"

Performed in the Month of May 1836 by Thos. S. Woodcock

May 24th. Left New York in the Steam Boat Albany at 7 O Clock A. M. for the City of Albany the Distance is 145 Miles and the fare is $3 Meals extra. there are two lines of Boats up the River, one being a day and the other a Night line. the night line leaves at 5 O Clock and is fitted up with elegant Berths for sleeping and is certainly the most convenient way of travelling, unless as in my case the Traveller has not previously been up the river, and is desirous of seeing, its highly picturesque scenery. Our Boat though not the swiftest and most elegant of the line, is still a very handsome affair. she is upwards of 200 feet long, and has an Engine of 200 horse power. she has boilers on both sides of her, the quantity of *Wood* consumed in a trip is enormous, and being pine, seems to burn as fast as it can be put in. unlike the steam Boats in the Irish channel, her Machinery is all on deck, and ascending a flight of steps, there is another deck called the promenade Deck. it is supported by pillars, and has an awning spread over it to keep of[f] the rays of the Sun. as she has her Machinery on Deck, it allows her to have a cabin the whole of her length, for though some of her Machinery must unavoidably come through it is so boxed up as to be no detriment to her appearance. in the forward part, is a bar room where Gentlemen can obtain refreshments, and lounge on the settees, as it is against the rules of the Boat to lounge in the Dining Cabin. the Cabin immediately aft is the Ladies Saloon or retiring room. next is the Ladies Cabin, in which Gentlemen in Company with Ladies, may enjoy their society. the Dining Cabin which is very large fills the rest of the space. this is well fitted up. Between the windows in this Cabin are some large and very respectable oil pictures, by Native Artists. contrary to the custom prevailing in Europe the helmsman is forward instead of aft, which enables him to have a better lookout. he has a small room elevated above the Deck and entirely seperate from the passengers. the helmsman or Pilot has *three* assistants the wheel being double and requiring two men to each wheel. . . .

Newburgh . . . is the first landing after passing through the high lands, and as none other is practicable it must be the Depot for the Country produce. the impossibility of a competetor rising up, is on account of the formidable barrier presented by Nature. it is situated on the declivity of a hill, sloping gradually to the shore. I could perceive many new buildings springing up. opposite to this place is Fishkill Landing and up the Creek is the *Matteawan Factory*. After passing Many Villages, we arrive at Catskill, behind which is the celebrated Mountains, one of the Peaks of which is elevated about 3,000 feet above the River. there is an Hotel upon it and it is a place of resort during the Summer Months. the landing is 112 Miles from New York.

about 6 Miles further up is the City of Hudson. b[e]hind this City, *"Marshalls"* of Manchester have a large Calico printing Establishment. this is the highest point to which *Ships* can go. a Whaling Compy fits out Ships from this place. after passing here, the River becomes thickly studded with small islands, which though very picturesque render the navigation difficult. . . .

At 8 O Clock P. M. we arrived at Albany. it was now quite dark, consequently we could not judge of its appearance, particularly as there are no lamps in the Streets. our passage it will be perceived was about 13 hours, a long one, as it has frequently been done in 10 hours. Albany is the Capital of the State. The State House or Capitol occupies a very elevated and commanding situation. the assembly were in session but we had not time to listen to their discussions. the City is built on a declivity but with the exception of the public Buildings there is nothing particular to admire.

May 25th. Left Albany at 9 O Clock by the Railway for Schenectady, a distance of 17 Miles, for which 62½ cents is charged. we were drawn by Horses about 2 Miles, being a steep ascent. we then found a Steam Engine waiting for us . . . the road is then quite level for 14 Miles through the poorest Country I ever saw. . . . we at length stop to have our carriages attached to a stationary Engine which lets us down an [inclined] plane, from the top of which we have a fine view of Schenectady. . . . we arrived at this place at half past 10. from the cars we proceeded to enter our names for the Packet Boat. . . . We arrived in Utica [via the packet boat] at about half 8 O'Clock AM. I had resolved to stay at this place and visit Trenton Falls, but owing to the unfavourable state of the Weather I concluded to proceed, our Boat went close alongside the Packet for Rochester, so we had only to step out of one onto the other, which as soon as we had done she immediately sailed. we paid $6.50 each the distance being 160 Miles. our living was first rate. . . . We at length arrived at Rochester at Eleven O Clock P. M. and went immediately to the Clinton Hotel where we staid for the Night. this City is elevated 500 feet above the Hudson River, from which place it is distant 270 Miles. it was first settled in 1812, and in 1827 contained 10,818 Inhabitants. the Genesee River runs through the City, the Canal being carried over by means of an aquaduct. it consists of ten arches of stone. the water rushes under with fearful rapidity, so much as to force itself up the battlements of the bridge. . . . Everything here is *new* but the Forests, log houses of all grades from the Whitewashed, neatly fenced in, to the black looking, mud-surrounded hovel. the roads are of the kind called corderoy consisting of logs of Wood rolled together. . . . The trees of former Generations lie in vast heaps in all the stages of decomposition. you may observe the prostrate trunk of some deceased Monarch that is apparantly sound, but if you but step upon it, it crumbles to dust. the rays of the sun cannot penetrate these recesses, consequently there is no grass or underwood. it is only in the thinly wooded country that cattle can find pasture. still when this land is cleared, it yields enormous crops. . . . Returned to Rochester in the Afternoon, took a survey of the flour Mills, which are fine stone Building of an immense size. at 5 O Clock went on board the Canal Boat. the distance to Buffaloe is 93 Miles, 63 of which is on a level. the fare was $3.50 but owing to opposition is now reduced to $1.50. night soon coming on prevented me from seeing much of the Country. the next morning we found ourselves in the Neighbourhood of Lockport. at this place there are five double locks of excellent workmanship which elevate us 60 feet. we are therefore 560 above the Hudson and have attained the same elevation as the "falls" from which place we are only distant about 12 Miles. The following inscription I copied from the stone work on entering the lock. *Erie Canal*—"Let posterity be excited to perpetuate our free Institutions, and to make still greater efforts, than their Ancestors, to promote *Public Prosperity* by the recollection that these works of Internal Improvement were achieved by the spirit and perseverance of Republican Freemen." after going through the deep cutting immediately following the locks we arrive at Pendleton, the Entrance to the Tonawanda creek, . . . and obtain the first glimpse of Canada and the Niagara River which now is only seperated from the Canal by an embankment. we here only see one half of the River, Grand Island being in the centre. this Island is about 12 Miles long and is covered with Oak timber. a Boston Company have Steam Saw Mills erected for the purpose of sawing it up into plank. two Ships have just been built here, the first that have been built for the Lake Trade. . . . We next arrive at Black Rock, from which place we can distinctly see the buildings on the Canada Side. one large Building had written upon it in large letters "Cloth Establishment". the reason is obvious. John Bull can sell Cloth to his Brother Jonathan Free of duty. consequently he crosses the river for his clothes. Jonathan in turn accomodates John by letting him have his tea duty free. at ½ past 2 O Clock we arrived at Buffaloe, and proceeded to the Mansion House where we put up. Buffaloe is a lake Port. Steam Boats run from here to the far West. a few years ago and this was considered as such, but now nothing short of the Pacific Ocean can be considered such. from the description I had read of this place by Capt. Basil Hall, I had expected to find it a thriving though a small place, and the buildings to be chiefly of wood, but instead of this I found Main Street to be entirely of brick and the Stores really splendid. fine brick buildings were springing up in all directions. at the foot of Main Street there was 17 Brick Stores nearly finished and I was told that they were all ready rented at $700 a year. how these rents are to be paid I really cannot tell as the Port must be closed 5 Months in the year. the streets were most abominably muddy, they not being paved, a circumstance not to be Wondered at when we find that they cannot speculate in paving stones. I observed that Gentlemen wore their Pantaloons inside their boots to protect them from the mud. this is the place for speculation. the people are all going mad. in the bar rooms of the Hotels plans of intended Towns are stuck up in the same style that play bills are stuck up in Manchester. these plans look very pretty indeed. the lots are laid out quite regular, and every thing cut and dried. a parcel of these lots are put up at Auction, terms so much per cent. say 10 at the day of sale 30 per cent in 2 Months the rest on Bond and Mor[t]gage. the buyer gets a title. they are then puffed off in the newspapers and the individuals go round peddling them. sells them for an advance, pockets the difference and speculates again. sensible men agree that these places will not be settled upon during the present Generation but it serves to speculate upon and for all usefull purposes land in the Moon would do just as well. in this way Chicago has been got up, but they have managed to build some houses there. it is 1,000 Miles from Buffaloe, and lots sell for from $70 to 250 dollars a foot. that is, if a lot of Ground is 25 feet by 100 or so it would be called 25 feet. now this Buffalo is a most corrupt place as regards money matters. the whole of these fine buildings being build upon Credit, should an alteration in the value of money take place, and it most assuredly will, then these men cannot pay their Mortgages. the Banks will then claim them and as I firmly believe the Banks cannot redeem their paper now how will it be then? there is a person here by the name of Rathbun who they say has built up the place. he is the greatest builder, the Greatest Stage Contractor in fact he is at the head of everything and I see by the papers has lately offered Niagara Falls for sale for Manufacturing purposes. now this man is admitted on all hands to be unable to pay his debts and yet his notes pass current for money, the people declaring that they dare not let him break as it would ruin the whole place. . . . Here I also found great numbers of emigrants ready to embark for the West. great numbers of poor Germans and also many Wealthy Yankees who having sold excellent farms to the Eastward were going into a Wilderness because the *land* was so very rich. . . .

Monday May 30th: Left Buffaloe for the "Falls" on board the steam boat Victory. the distance is about 20 Miles and the fare 75 cents this includes the Stage from Chipewa to the falls. we passed on the American side of Grand Island. on going down the River the Rapidity of the current evidently increased. when we got to the end of the island we made for the American Side and landed some of our passengers. we then crossed over to the British side. . . . I cannot find words to describe the appearance of this awe inspiring spectacle. I shall therefore not attempt to do so, and so exclaim with Fanny Kemble "Oh! God, it is indescribable.". . .

Returned to Buffaloe. . . . And on the Morning of the 2nd of June I left Buffalo, and arrived in New York safe and sound—taking the same route that I came.

28

JOHN ROSS

The Trail of Tears

John Ross (1790–1866), of mixed Cherokee and European ancestry, epitomized the "civilized," literate, and prosperous Native American gentleman farmer of the antebellum South. He fought as an officer under Andrew Jackson against the Creek Indians at Horseshoe Bend and owned a three-hundred-acre plantation and more than twenty slaves. In the years after the War of 1812, the prosperous and rapidly expanding Georgia settler society came into conflict about land with an equally prosperous and growing Cherokee nation. The Cherokee were considered a "civilized tribe." They had developed a representative democratic government based on the U.S. Constitution; built their own schools, roads, and churches; and created an alphabet for use in the fledgling Cherokee press.

Young, educated, and diplomatically astute, Ross was pushed forward by older chiefs to represent the growing Cherokee nation to the leaders in Washington. In 1818 Ross was named president of the Cherokee National Committee. In 1827, upon the death of his mentor, Pathkiller, Ross became the Principal Chief of the United Cherokee Nation, a position to which he would be elected ten times during the following forty years.

In 1828 the state of Georgia subjected the Cherokee to direct control, in the hopes of precipitating their removal to less-productive lands in the West. Ross led a legal battle against Georgia and its ally, President Andrew Jackson. He brought his case to Congress and the Supreme Court, but in 1835, a few hundred Cherokee, who had lost faith in Ross's tactics, signed a treaty authorizing removal behind the backs of the roughly 17,000 Cherokee who had elected Ross to represent them. Ratification of the removal act passed in the Senate by one vote, and the U.S. Army general responsible resigned his commission in protest, but the removal proceeded according to Andrew Jackson's will.

In 1838 the U.S. Army began what would be called the Trail of Tears, the forced march of the Cherokee to Oklahoma. Thousands died from winter cold and the army's brutal indifference. In response, Ross convinced the government to allow him to manage his people's journey west. His own wife, Quatie, a full-blooded Cherokee, died during the journey.

QUESTIONS TO CONSIDER

1. How did John Ross argue the case against the Cherokee removal in the Memorial and Petition submitted to the Senate and House of Representatives? What were his key points? How persuasive is his argument?

Gary E. Moulton, ed., *The Papers of Chief John Ross*, vol. 1, *1807–1839* (Tulsa: University of Oklahoma Press, 1985), 470–74, 704–05.

2. Based on Ross's letter to Brigadier General Matthew Arbuckle, what were the main problems Ross faced in carrying out the removal of his people to the West?

TO THE SENATE AND HOUSE OF REPRESENTATIVES

Washington City February 22nd 1837

The memorial and petition of the undersigned, a delegation appointed by the Cherokee nation in full council respectfully showeth:

That the Cherokee Nation deeply sensible of the evils under which they are now laboring and the still more frightful miseries which they have too much reason to apprehend, have in the most formal and solemn manner known to them, assembled in General Council to deliberate upon their existing relations with the Government of the United States, and to lay their case with respectful deference before your honorable bodies.

Invested with full powers to conclude an arrangement upon all the matters which interest them we have arrived at the seat of Government, and, in accordance with our usual forms of proceeding have notified the Honorable the Secretary of War [Benjamin F. Butler] that we had reached this place and, through him, solicited an interview with the Executive [Andrew Jackson]. This request has not yet been granted, nor has it to this day received an official answer, but we have reason to apprehend from circumstances which have reached us that we shall be denied this application, and are thus compelled in the discharge of our duty to our constituents, to submit to your Honorable bodies the memorial of which we are the bearers.

On former occasions we have in much detail laid before you the prominent facts of our case. We have reminded you of our long and intimate connexion with the United States, of the scenes of peril and difficulty which we have shared in common; of the friendship which had so long been generously proffered and affectionately and gratefully accepted; of the aids which were supplied us in promoting our advancement in the arts of civilized life, of the political principles which we had imbibed, of the religious faith we have been taught.

We have called your attention to the progress which under your auspices we have made, of the improvements which have marked our social and individual states; our lands brought into cultivation, our natural resources developed, our farms, workshops and factories, approximating in character and value to those of our brethren whose example we had diligently imitated.

A smooth and beautiful prospect of future advancement was opened before us. Our people had abandoned the pursuits, the habits and the tastes of the savage, and had put on the vestments of civilization, of intelligence and of a pure religion. The progress we had made furnished us with the most assured hopes of continued improvement, and we indulged in the anticipation that the time was not far distant when we should be recognised, on the footing of equality by the brethren from whom we had received all which we were now taught to prize.

This promise of golden sunshine is now overspread. Clouds and darkness have obscured its brilliancy. The winds are beginning to mutter their awful forebodings, the tempest is gathering thick and heavy over our heads, and threatens to burst upon us with terrific energy and overwhelming ruin.

In this season of calamity, where can we turn with hope or confidence? On all former occasions of peril or of doubt the Government of the United States spread over us its broad and paternal shield. It invited us to seek an asylum and a protection under its mighty arm. It assisted us with its encouragement and advice, it soothed us with its consoling assurances, it inspired us with hope and gave us a feeling of confidence and security.

But alas! this our long-cherished friend seems now to be alienated from us: this our father has raised his arm to inflict the hostile blow; this strength so long our protection is now exerted against us, and on the wide scene of existence no human aid is left us. Unless you avert your arm we are destroyed. Unless your feelings of affection and compassion are once more awakened towards your destitute and despairing children our annihilation is complete.

It is a natural inquiry among all who commiserate our situation what are the causes which have led to this disastrous revolution, to this entire change of relations? By what agency have such results been accomplished?

We have asked, and we reiterate the question how have we offended? Show us in what manner we have, however unwittingly, inflicted upon you a wrong, you shall yourselves be the judges of the extent and manner of compensation. Show us the offence which has awakened your feelings of justice against us and we will submit to that measure of punishment which you shall tell us we have merited. We cannot bring to our recollections anything we have done or anything we have omitted calculated to awaken your resentment against us.

But we are told a treaty has been made and all that is required at our hands is to comply with its stipulations. Will the faithful historian, who shall hereafter record our lamentable fate, say—the Cherokee Nation executed a treaty by which they freely and absolutely ceded the country in which they were born and educated, the property they had been industriously accumulating and improving, and, abandoning the high road to which they had been advancing from savagism had precipitated themselves into worse than their pristine degradation, will not the reader of such a narrative require the most ample proof before he will credit such a story? Will he not inquire where was the kind and parental guardian who had heretofore aided the weak, assisted the forlorn, instructed the ignorant and elevated the depressed? Where was the Government of the United States with its vigilant care over the Indian when such a bargain was made? How will he be surprised at hearing that the United States was a party to the transaction—that the authority of that Government, and the representatives of that people, which had for years been employed in leading the Cherokees from ignorance to light, from barbarism to civilization, from paganism to christianity, who had taught them new habits and new hopes was the very party which was about to appropriate to itself the fruits of the Indian's industry, the birth places of his children and the graves of his ancestors.

If such a recital could command credence must it not be on the ground that experience had shown the utter failure of all the efforts and the disappointment of all the hopes of the philanthropist and the Christian? That the natives of this favored spot of God's creation were incapable of improvement and unsusceptible of education and that they in wilful blindness, spurning the blessings which had been proffered and urged upon them would pertinaciously prefer the degradation from which it had been attempted to lead them and the barbarism from which it had been sought to elevate them?

How will his astonishment be augmented when he learns that the Cherokee people almost to a man denied the existence and the obligation of the alleged compact—that they proclaimed it to have been based in fraud and concocted in perfidy—that no authority was ever given to those who undertook in their names and on their behalf to negotiate it; that it was repudiated with unexampled unanimity when it was brought to their knowledge; that they denied that it conferred any rights or imposed any obligations.

Yet such must be the story which the faithful historian must record. In the name of the whole Cherokee people we protest against this unhallowed and unauthorized and unacknowledged compact. We deny its binding force. We recognise none of its stipulations. If contrary to every principle of justice it is to be enforced upon us, we shall at least be free from the disgrace of self humiliation. We hold the solemn disavowal of its provisions by eighteen thousand of our people.

We, the regularly commissioned delegation of the Cherokee Nation in the face of Heaven and appealing to the Searcher of all hearts for the truth of our statements ask you to listen to our remonstrances. We implore you to examine into the truth of our allegations. We refer you to your own records, to your own agents, to men deservedly enjoying your esteem and confidence as our witnesses, and we proffer ourselves ready if you will direct the inquiry to establish the truth of what we aver. If we fail to substantiate our statements overwhelm us with ignominy and disgrace. Cast us off from you forever. If however on the other hand every allegation we make shall be sustained by the most convincing and abundant proof, need we make further or stronger appeals than the simple facts of the case will themselves furnish, to secure your friendship, your sympathy and your justice.

We will not and we cannot believe after the long connexion that has subsisted between us, after all that has been done and all that has been promised that our whole nation will be forcibly ejected from their native land and from their social hearths without the pretence of crime, without charge, without evidence, without trial: that we shall be exiled from all that we hold dear and venerable and sacred, and driven into a remote, a strange and a sterile region, without even the imputation of guilt. We will not believe that this will be done by our ancient allies, our friends, our brethren. Yet between this and the abrogation to the pretended treaty there is no medium. Such an instrument so obtained, so contaminated cannot cover the real nature of the acts which it is invoked to sanction. If power is to be exerted let it come unveiled. We shall but submit and die. . . .

> Jno Ross [and members of the delegations from the Eastern Cherokees and the Western Cherokees]

TO MATTHEW ARBUCKLE[1]

Illinois [Cherokee Nation] Apl 23rd 1839

Sir

From the many complaints which are daily made to me by Cherokees who have been recently removed into this country, of their sufferings, from the want of being properly subsisted with provisions, I am constrained to address you this hasty letter. It is reported that, apart from the scantiness of the ration allowed under the contract made on the part of the United States Government with [James] Glasgow & [James] Harrison, many inconveniences have been experienced by the Cherokee people, from the irregularity of proceedings on the part of those employed for carrying out the contract.

It has also been stated that the contractors were only required to furnish "one pound of fresh beef, three half pints of corn & four qts. of salt to every 100 lbs. of beef—or, if they (the contractors) choose they might furnish in lieu of the beef, 3/4 lb. salt pork or bacon provided the Indians will receive it." The beef being poor & not considered wholesome this season of the year, the Cherokees have generally objected to and refused receiving it and have insisted on being furnished with Salt Pork or Bacon in lieu of the beef, but it seems that the contractors do not choose and have refused to comply with the demand; saying that they were only bound to furnish Beef rations. Yet they would commute the ration by paying in money one dollar pr. month for the same. Thus the Cherokees are placed in a situation by compulsion to accept of either the beef or the money offered or to go unsupplied altogether. Here I must beg leave to remark, that previous to the removal of the Cherokees from the East to the West, the subject of providing subsistence for them after their arrival in this country was fully discussed with Major Genl. [Winfield] Scott who communicated with the War Deptmt.[2] in reference to it. And we were afterwards informed by that distinguished officer that the Hon. Secry. of War [Joel R. Poinsett] had decided that the Cherokees should at least for a time be subsisted with provisions in kind, until they could provide for themselves, and then such an arrangement as would be most satisfactory to

1. **Matthew Arbuckle:** Brigadier General Arbuckle was area commander in the Indian Territory.
2. **War Deptmt.:** The Department of War, the federal office in charge of the nation's defense; forerunner to the Department of Defense.

them should be made with them through Capt. Collins. Now Sir, it is evident from the exorbitant prices of meat and bread stuffs in this country that the Cherokees who have thus been forced to receive commutation in money from the contractors at the rate stated will soon be found in a starving condition—instead of being provided with subsistence as was anticipated and promised them. If the articles of agreement entered into with the contractors are to be construed so as to leave it wholly optional with them whether to furnish Salt Pork or Bacon in lieu of Beef, then it is obvious that there were no practical advantage for the interest of the Cherokees to have inserted any clause in that instrument in regard to Salt Pork or Bacon—for its effect has only been and will continue to be to mislead the mind of the people. And how it can be reconciled with the obligations imposed by the contract for the contractors to adopt the mode of commuting the subsistence rations they have engaged to furnish the Cherokees with and that too by a rate fixed by themselves, is a mystery which the Cherokees cannot understand—for it is not pretended that such a right or discretion has ever been given to them by the contract with the agents or the U.S. Govt. for subsisting the Cherokees. Nor can the sacred principle of justice sanction such a course under existing circumstances. Confiding however in the fair intentions of the Government towards them on this subject, the Cherokees still believe that the Hon. Secry. of War will when deemed expedient commute their rations at a rate at least equal to any sum fully ample to purchase provisions with for their comfortable subsistence—and that no sum less will be offered than what others would engage to supply the same for. I beg leave herewith to lay before you copies of sundry letters which I have just received from several leading men on behalf of the Cherokees on this very unpleasant subject. And in conclusion will further remark, that the health and existence of the whole Cherokee people who have recently been removed to this distant country demands a speedy remedy for the inconveniences and evils complained of, & unless a change of the quantity and the kind of rations as well as of the mode of issuing the same, be made from that which has heretofore been granted and observed, the Cherokees must inevitably suffer. Therefore to avoid hunger & starvation they are reduced to the necessity of calling upon you and other officers as the proper representatives of the U.S. Govt. in this matter, to take immediate steps as will ensure the immediate subsistence of the Cherokees who have recently been removed here, with ample and wholesome provisions, until such other arrangements, as may be most satisfactory to them, can be made for subsisting themselves &c. When every thing in reference to the late removal of the Cherokee nation from the East to the West is considered, and seen that it has been consummated through the military authority of the U.S. Govt. I trust you will pardon me for addressing this communication to you, especially when you are assured that the Cherokee people have been taught to expect that justice and protection would be extended to them through the Commanding General in this Hemisphere.

Jno Ross

29

PRISCILLA MERRIMAN EVANS

Pulling a Handcart to the Mormon Zion

Many of the men and women who settled the Far West endured extraordinary physical hardships and dangers to reach their destinations. The Mormon pioneers who walked from Iowa City, Iowa, to Salt Lake City, Utah, pulling handcarts made of hickory were driven by both economic and religious motives. The handcart immigrants were poor: if they could have afforded to migrate any other way, they would have. They spoke one or more of several languages—German, Welsh, Danish, Swedish—as well as English. And they did not all have so successful a journey as did the pregnant Mrs. Thomas D. Evans. With her one-legged husband, Priscilla Merriman Evans walked the one thousand miles in five months, arriving in Salt Lake City in October 1856, comfortably ahead of the winter weather. In two parties later that year, hundreds died in winter blizzards.

Nine more handcart companies reached the Mormon Zion in the five years after the Evanses' journey. All received rich welcomes with prayers and hymns. Priscilla Merriman Evans concluded her narrative by saying that she always "thanked the Lord for a contented mind, a home and something to eat."

QUESTIONS TO CONSIDER

1. Why did Priscilla Merriman Evans become a Mormon and choose to emigrate?
2. What were the principal difficulties of the trip to Utah?
3. What rewards did Evans find in "Zion"?

I, Priscilla Merriman Evans, born May 4, 1835 at Mounton New Marbeth, Pembrokeshire, Wales, am the daughter of Joseph and Ann James Merriman. About 1839, father moved his family from Mounton up to Tenby, about ten miles distant. Our family consisted of father, mother, Sarah, aged six, and myself, aged four. Tenby was a beautiful place, as are all those Celtic Islands, with remains of old castles, vine- and moss-covered walls, gone to ruin since the time of the Conqueror. . . .

[When] Mother died on the eighth of November 1851 . . . the responsibility of the family rested on my young shoulders. . . . After the death of my mother we were very lonely, and one evening I accompanied my father

Kate B. Carter, comp., *Heart Throbs of the West*, vol. 9 (Salt Lake City: International Society Daughters of Utah Pioneers), 8–13.

to the house of a friend. When we reached there, we learned that they were holding a cottage meeting. Two Mormon Elders were the speakers, and I was very much interested in the principles they advocated. I could see that my father was very worried, and would have taken me away, had he known how. When he became aware that I believed in the Gospel as taught by the Elders, I asked him if he had ever heard of the restored Gospel. He replied, "Oh, yes, I have heard of Old Joe Smith, and his Golden Bible."

When my father argued against the principles taught by the Elders, I said, "If the Bible is true, then Mormonism is true." My father was very much opposed to my joining the Church . . . as he thought the Saints were too slow to associate with. . . . But I had found the truth and was baptized into the Church of Jesus Christ of Latter-day Saints in Tenby, February 26, 1852. My sister Sarah took turns with me going out every Sunday. She would go where she pleased on Sunday, while I would walk seven miles to Stepaside and attend the Mormon meeting. My father was very much displeased with me going out every Sunday. He forbade me to read the Church literature, and threatened to burn all I brought home. . . . I do not think my father was as bitter against the principles of the Gospel as he seemed to be, for many times when the Elders were persecuted, he defended them, and gave them food and shelter. But he could not bear the idea of my joining them and leaving home.

About this time, Thomas D. Evans, a young Mormon Elder, was sent up from Merthyr Tydfil, Wales, as a missionary to Pembrokeshire. He was a fine speaker, and had a fine tenor voice, and I used to like to go around with the missionaries and help with the singing. Elder Evans and I seemed to be congenial from our first meeting, and we were soon engaged. He was traveling and preaching the restored Gospel without purse or script. . . .

I was familiar with the Bible doctrine, and when I heard the Elders explain it, it seemed as though I had always known it, and it sounded like music in my ears. We had the spirit of gathering and were busy making preparations to emigrate.

About that time the Principle of Plurality of Wives was preached to the world, and it caused quite a commotion in our branch. One of the girls came to me with tears in her eyes and said, "Is it true that Brigham Young has nine wives? I can't stand that, Oh, I can't stand it!" I asked her how long it had been since I had heard her testify that she knew the Church was true, and I said if it was then, it is true now. I told her I did not see anything for her to cry about. After I talked to her awhile, she dried her eyes and completed her arrangements to get married and emigrate. She came with us. My promised husband and I went to Merthyr to visit his Mother, brothers, sisters, and friends, preparatory to emigrating. His family did all in their power to persuade him to remain with them. They were all well off, and his brothers said they would send him to school, support his wife, and pay all of his expenses but all to no avail. He bade them all goodbye, and returned to Tenby. . . .

Elder Thomas D. Evans, my promised husband, and I walked the ten miles from Tenby to Pembroke, where we got our license and were married, and walked back to Tenby. We were married on the third of April, 1856. On our return from Pembroke we found a few of our friends awaiting us with supper ready. We visited our friends and relatives and made our preparations to emigrate to Zion. We took a tug from Pembroke to Liverpool, where we set sail on the 17th of April, 1856, on the sailing vessel S.S. *Curling*. Captain Curling said he would prefer to take a load of Saints than others, as he always felt safe with Saints on board. We learned that the next trip across the water that he was loaded with gentiles and his vessel sank with all on board. We were on the sea five weeks; we lived on the ship's rations. I was sick all the way. [Priscilla was then pregnant with their first child.] We landed in Boston on May 23rd, then travelled in cattle cars . . . to Iowa City. We remained in Iowa City three weeks, waiting for our carts to be made.

We were offered many inducements to stay there. My husband was offered ten dollars a day to work at his trade of Iron Roller, but money was no inducement to us, for we were anxious to get to Zion. We learned afterwards that many who stayed there apostatized[1] or died of cholera.

When the carts were ready we started on a three-hundred-mile walk to Winterquarters on the Missouri River. There were a great many who made fun of us as we walked, pulling our carts, but the weather was fine and the roads were excellent and although I was sick and we were tired out at night, we still thought, "This is a glorious way to come to Zion."

We began our journey of one thousand miles on foot with a handcart for each family, some families consisting of man and wife, and some had quite large families. There were five mule teams to haul the tents and surplus flour. Each handcart had one hundred pounds of flour, that was to be divided and [more got] from the wagons as required. At first we had a little coffee and bacon, but that was soon gone and we had no use for any cooking utensils but a frying pan. The flour was self-raising and we took water and baked a little cake; that was all we had to eat.

After months of travelling we were put on half rations and at one time, before help came, we were out of flour for two days. We washed out the flour sacks to make a little gravy.

There were in our tent my husband with one leg,[2] two blind men . . . a man with one arm, and a widow with five children. The widow, her children, and myself were the only ones who could not talk Welsh. My husband was commissary for our tent, and he cut his own rations short many times to help little children who had to walk and did not have enough to eat to keep up their strength.

The tent was our covering, and the overcoat spread on the bare ground with the shawl over us was our bed. My feather bed, and bedding, pillows, all our good clothing, my husband's church books, which he had collected through six years of missionary work, with some genealogy he had collected,

---

1. **apostatized:** Abandoned their faith.
2. Thomas Evans had lost his left leg at the knee as a child, in an industrial accident.

all had to be left in a storehouse. We were promised that they would come to us with the next emigration in the spring, but we never did receive them. It was reported that the storehouse burned down, so that was a dreadful loss to us.

Edward Bunker was the Captain of our Company. His orders of the day were, "If any are sick among you, and are not able to walk, you must help them along, or pull them on your carts." No one rode in the wagons. Strong men would help the weaker ones, until they themselves were worn out, and some died from the struggle and want of food, and were buried along the wayside. It was heart rending for parents to move on and leave their loved ones to such a fate, as they were so helpless, and had no material for coffins. Children and young folks, too, had to move on and leave father or mother or both.

Sometimes a bunch of buffaloes would come and the carts would stop until they passed. Had we been prepared with guns and ammunition, like people who came in wagons, we might have had meat, and would not have come to near starving. President Young[3] ordered extra cattle sent along to be killed to help the sick and weak, but they were never used for that purpose. . . .

In crossing rivers, the weak women and the children were carried over the deep places, and they waded the others. We were much more fortunate than those who came later, as they had snow and freezing weather. Many lost limbs, and many froze to death. President Young advised them to start earlier, but they got started too late. My husband, in walking from twenty to twenty-five miles per day [had pain] where the knee rested on the pad: the friction caused it to gather and break and was most painful. But he had to endure it, or remain behind, as he was never asked to ride in a wagon.

We reached Salt Lake City on October 2, 1856, tired, weary, with bleeding feet, our clothing worn out and so weak we were nearly starved, but thankful to our Heavenly Father for bringing us to Zion. William R. Jones met us on the Public Square in Salt Lake City and brought us to his home in Spanish Fork. I think we were over three days coming from Salt Lake City to Spanish Fork by ox team, but what a change to ride in a wagon after walking 1330 miles from Iowa City to Salt Lake City! We stayed in the home of an ex-bishop, Stephen Markham. His home was a dugout. It was a very large room built half underground. His family consisted of three wives, and seven children. . . . There was a large fireplace in one end with bars, hooks, frying pans, and bake ovens, where they did the cooking for the large family, and boiled, fried, baked, and heated their water for washing.

There was a long table in one corner, and pole bedsteads fastened to the walls in the three other corners. They were laced back and forth with rawhide cut in strips, and made a nice springy bed. There were three trundle beds, made like shallow boxes, with wooden wheels, which rolled under the

---

3. **President Young:** Brigham Young (1801–1877), president of the Church of Jesus Christ of Latter-day Saints from 1847 to 1877.

mother's bed in the daytime to utilize space. There was a dirt roof, and the dirt floor was kept hard and smooth by sprinkling and sweeping. The bed ticks were filled with straw. . . .

Aunt Mary [Markham] put her two children . . . in the foot of her bed and gave us the trundle bed. . . . How delightful to sleep on a bed again, after sleeping on the ground for so many months with our clothes on. We had not slept in a bed since we left the ship *Sam Curling*.

On the 31st of December, 1856, our first daughter was born. . . . My baby's wardrobe was rather meager: I made one night gown from her father's white shirt, another out of a factory lining of an oilcloth sack. Mrs. Markham gave me a square of homemade linsey for a shoulder blanket, and a neighbor gave me some old underwear, that I worked up into little things. They told me I could have an old pair of jean pants left at the adobe yard. I washed them and made them into petticoats. I walked down to the Indian farm and traded a gold pen for four yards of calico that made her two dresses. . . .

Wood and timber were about thirty miles up in the canyon, and when the men went after timber to burn, they went in crowds, armed, for they never knew when they would be attacked by Indians. Adobe houses were cheaper than log or frame, as timber was so far away. Many of the people who had lived in the dugouts after coming from Palmyra got into houses before the next winter. They exchanged work with each other, and in that way got along fine. Mr. Markham had an upright saw, run by water. The next spring they got timber from the canyon, and my husband helped Mr. Markham put up a three-roomed house and worked at farming.

He worked for William Markham a year, for which he received two acres of land. I helped in the house, for which, besides the land, we got our board and keep. The next Spring we went to work for ourselves. We saved our two acres of wheat, and made adobes for a two-roomed house, and paid a man in adobes for laying it up. It had a dirt roof. He got timber from Mr. Markham to finish the doors, windows, floors, shelves, and to make furniture. My husband made me a good big bedstead and laced it with rawhides. There were benches and the frames of chairs with the rawhide seat, with the hair left on; a table, shelves in the wall on either side of the fireplace, which was fitted with iron bars and hooks to hang kettles on to boil, frying pans and bake oven. A tick for a bed had to be pieced out of all kinds of scraps, as there were no stores, and everything was on a trade basis.

If one neighbor had something they could get along without, they would exchange it for something they could use. We were lucky to get factory, or sheeting to put up to the windows instead of glass. We raised a good crop of wheat that fall, for which we traded one bushel for two bushels of potatoes. We also exchanged for molasses and vegetables. We had no tea, coffee, meat, or grease of any kind for seasoning. No sugar, milk, or butter. In 1855–1856 the grasshoppers and crickets took the crops and the cattle nearly all died. They were dragged down in the field west [and left to die].

We bought a lot on Main Street, and my husband gave his parents our first little home with five acres of land. They had a good ox team, two cows, a new wagon, and they soon got pigs, chickens and a few sheep. It wasn't long before they were well off. . . .

It was indeed comfortable to be in a good house with a shingled roof and good floors. He set out an orchard of all kinds of fruit; also currents and gooseberries, planted lucern[4] . . . in a patch by itself for cows and pigs. We had a nice garden spot, and we soon had butter, milk, eggs, and meat. We raised our bread, potatoes, and vegetables. While our fruit trees were growing is when the saleratus[5] helped. When I had the babies all about the same size, I could not get out to gather saleratus as others did; so we went with team and wagon, pans, buckets, old brooms, and sacks down on the alkali land, between Spanish Fork and Springville. The smallest children were put under the wagon on a quilt, and the rest of us swept and filled the sacks, and the happiest time was when we were headed for home. The canyon wind seemed always to blow and our faces, hands and eyes were sore for some time after. We took our saleratus over to Provo, where they had some kind of refining machinery where it was made into soda for bread. It was also used extensively in soap making. We got our pay in merchandise. . . .

. . . My husband had poor luck farming. His farm was in the low land, near the river where the sugar factory now stands. Sometimes it would be high water, sometimes grasshoppers or crickets would take his crop; so he got discouraged with farming, sold his farm and put up a store. We had just got well started in the business and had got a bill of goods, when in the spring of 1875 my husband was called on another mission to England.

Before starting on his mission he sold his team and all available property, also mortgaged our home, for although he was called to travel without purse or scrip,[6] he had to raise enough money to pay his passage and his expenses to his field of labor in Europe. He had too tender a heart for a merchant; he simply could not say no when people came to him with pitiful stories of sickness and privation. He would give them credit, and the consequence was that when he was suddenly called on a mission, the goods were gone and there were hundreds of dollars coming to us from the people, some of which we never got. Everything was left in my hands.

On the 24th of October 1875, after my husband's departure, our daughter Ada was born. . . . I nursed her, along with my little granddaughter Maud, as twins, kept all the books and accounts . . . and was sustained as President and Secretary of the Relief Society Teachers, which office I held through many reorganizations.

During my husband's absence, we had considerable sickness. My little daughter, Mary, came near dying with scarlet fever. To help out, our eldest daughter, Emma, got a position as clerk in the Co-op store. I appreciated that action of the Board very much, as before that time they had not been employing lady clerks and she was the first girl to work in the store. . . .

4. **lucern:** Alfalfa.
5. **saleratus:** A form of baking soda.
6. **scrip:** Any paper substitute for money that is not the legal tender of a state.

In 1877, my twelfth child was born. . . . I have had seven daughters and five sons. . . .

My husband's health was not good after his return from his mission. He had pneumonia twice. We sold our home on Main Street, paid off the mortgage and put up a little house on the five acres of land we had given his parents.

They had left it to us when they died. We have some of our children as near neighbors and are quite comfortable in our new home.

30

GUADALUPE VALLEJO ET AL.

Life in California before the Gold Discovery

It is remarkable to consider that California was once an isolated part of the Mexican northern frontier. The few Americans who journeyed there before the completion of the transcontinental railroad in 1869 faced many weeks of sea travel around the southern tip of South America. The Spanish had begun to settle California in 1769 in response to a growing Russian presence near what is now San Francisco. They converted natives; built four presidios (forts) at San Diego, Monterey, San Francisco, and Santa Barbara; and set up a system of missions and civil pueblos (towns). California, however, remained a distant outpost.

Like the Spanish-speaking Tejanos who were born and raised in Texas, the ranchers and their servants in Alta California had little connection to the government in Mexico City. At independence in 1821, they ceased to be Spanish but remained isolated from Mexico, calling themselves Californios. Also like the Tejanos, they watched as the 1820s, 1830s, and 1840s brought a steady stream of English-speaking settlers into their lives.

When the United States declared war on Mexico in May 1846, José Castro, the Californios' Mexico City–appointed governor, proclaimed all land acquisitions by settlers who were not naturalized Mexicans to be null and void. Anglo settlers organized an armed resistance and on June 9, 1846, they took Mexican general Mariano Vallejo prisoner, lowered the Mexican flag at the center of town, and raised the "Bear Flag," establishing the California Republic. The U.S. Army, which had been hoping to win over the Californios and avoid war in the West, was forced to back "the Bears," as they came to be known. The California Republic lasted for only a month, not enough time to create the kind of nationalist identity the Texans formed with their Alamo martyrs, founding fathers, national congress, and diverse citizenry.

"Life in California before the Gold Discovery," *The Century Magazine*, December 1890, 183, 189, 192–93, 464–76.

With the Treaty of Guadalupe Hidalgo (1848) ending the Mexican War, Mexico lost most of what is now the western United States, but the treaty guaranteed linguistic, cultural, and property rights for Mexicans within this vast territory. Few of these property rights were respected, and Mexicans, Chicanos, and Anglos in the western states continue to debate over linguistic and cultural issues. However, California has remained a meeting ground for Latino and Anglo peoples and cultures.

The following documents are from aging Californios, remembering life before the 1846 "Bear Flag Revolt" and the 1849 gold rush brought tens of thousands of immigrants to California. The first account is by Guadalupe Vallejo, the nephew of the general taken prisoner by "the Bears." The subsequent two accounts are by daughters of some of the important Mexican ranching families, many of whom lost land, animals, and social status to the newly arrived Anglo settlers.

QUESTIONS TO CONSIDER

1. How did the changes brought about by the gold rush and by becoming part of the United States affect what these *Californios* wrote and what they remembered about life in Mexican California?
2. How did these *Californios* feel about the arrival of Americans?
3. Some time in the late nineteenth century, *Californios* seem to have disappeared as a group. What might have happened to them?

GUADALUPE VALLEJO

Ranch and Mission Days in Alta California

It seems to me that there never was a more peaceful or happy people on the face of the earth than the Spanish, Mexican, and Indian population of Alta California before the American conquest. We were the pioneers of the Pacific coast, building towns and Missions while General Washington was carrying on the war of the Revolution, and we often talk together of the days when a few hundred large Spanish ranches and Mission tracts occupied the whole country from the Pacific to the San Joaquin. No class of American citizens is more loyal than the Spanish Californians, but we shall always be especially proud of the traditions and memories of the long pastoral age before 1840. Indeed, our social life still tends to keep alive a spirit of love for the simple, homely, outdoor life of our Spanish ancestors on this coast, and we try, as best we may, to honor the founders of our ancient families, and the saints and heroes of our history since the days when Father Junípero[1] planted the cross at Monterey.

The leading features of old Spanish life at the Missions, and on the large ranches of the last century, have been described in many books of travel, and with many contradictions. I shall confine myself to those details and

---

1. **Father Junípero:** Father Junípero Serra (1713–1784) founded Mission San Carlos Borromeo de Carmelo in Monterey in 1770.

illustrations of the past that no modern writer can possibly obtain except vaguely, from hearsay, since they exist in no manuscript, but only in the memories of a generation that is fast passing away. My mother has told me much, and I am still more indebted to my illustrious uncle, General Vallejo, of Sonoma, many of whose recollections are incorporated in this article.

When I was a child there were fewer than fifty Spanish families in the region about the bay of San Francisco, and these were closely connected by ties of blood or intermarriage. My father and his brother, the late General Vallejo, saw, and were a part of, the most important events in the history of Spanish California, the revolution and the conquest. My grandfather, Don Ygnacio Vallejo, was equally prominent in his day, in the exploration and settlement of the province. The traditions and records of the family thus cover the entire period of the annals of early California, from San Diego to Sonoma.

What I wish to do is to tell, as plainly and carefully as possible, how the Spanish settlers lived, and what they did in the old days. The story will be partly about the Missions, and partly about the great ranches. . . .

A number of trappers and hunters came into Southern California and settled down in various towns. There was a party of Kentuckians, beaver-trappers, who went along the Gila and Colorado rivers about 1827, and then south into Baja California to the Mission of Santa Catalina. Then they came to San Diego, where the whole country was much excited over their hunter clothes, their rifles, their traps, and the strange stories they told of the deserts, and fierce Indians, and things that no one in California had ever seen. Captain Paty was the oldest man of the party, and he was ill and worn out. All the San Diego people were very kind to the Americans. It is said that the other Missions, such as San Gabriel, sent and desired the privilege of caring for some of them. Captain Paty grew worse, so he sent for one of the fathers and said he wished to become a Catholic, because, he added, it must be a good religion, for it made everybody so good to him. Don Pio Pico and Doña Victoria Dominguez de Estudillo were his sponsors. After Captain Paty's death the Americans went to Los Angeles, where they all married Spanish ladies, were given lands, built houses, planted vineyards, and became important people. Pryor repaired the church silver, and was called "Miguel el Platero."[2] Laughlin was always so merry that he was named "Ricardo el Buen Mozo."[3] They all had Spanish names given them besides their own. One of them was a blacksmith, and as iron was very scarce he made pruning shears for the vineyards out of the old beaver traps.

On Christmas night, 1828, a ship was wrecked near Los Angeles, and twenty-eight men escaped. Everybody wanted to care for them, and they were given a great Christmas dinner, and offered money and lands. Some of them staid, and some went to other Missions and towns. One of them who staid was a German, John Gronigen, and he was named "Juan Domingo,"

---

2. **Miguel el Platero:** Miguel the Silversmith.
3. **Ricardo el Buen Mozo:** Ricardo the Good Guy.

or, because he was lame, "Juan Cojo."[4] Another, named Prentice, came from Connecticut, and he was a famous fisherman and otter hunter. After 1828 a good many other Americans came in and settled down quietly to cultivate the soil, and some of them became very rich. They had grants from the governor, just the same as the Spanish people.

It is necessary, for the truth of the account, to mention the evil behavior of many Americans before, as well as after, the conquest. . . .

In those times one of the leading American squatters came to my father, Don J. J. Vallejo, and said: "There is a large piece of your land where the cattle run loose, and your vaqueros[5] have gone to the gold mines. I will fence the field for you at my expense if you will give me half." He liked the idea, and assented, but when the tract was inclosed the American had it entered as government land in his own name, and kept all of it. In many similar cases American settlers in their dealings with the rancheros took advantage of laws which they understood, but which were new to the Spaniards, and so robbed the latter of their lands. Notes and bonds were considered unnecessary by a Spanish gentleman in a business transaction, as his word was always sufficient security.

Perhaps the most exasperating feature of the coming-in of the Americans was owing to the mines, which drew away most of the servants, so that our cattle were stolen by thousands. Men who are now prosperous farmers and merchants were guilty of shooting and selling Spanish beef "without looking at the brand," as the phrase went. My father had about ten thousand head of cattle, and some he was able to send back into the hills until there were better laws and officers, but he lost the larger part. . . .

PRUDENCIA HIGUERA

Trading with the Americans

In the autumn of 1840 my father lived near what is now called Pinole Point, in Contra Costa County, California. I was then about twelve years old, and I remember the time because it was then that we saw the first American vessel that traded along the shores of San Pablo Bay. One afternoon a horseman from the Peraltas, where Oakland now stands, came to our ranch, and told my father that a great ship, a ship "with two sticks in the center," was about to sail from Yerba Buena into San Pablo and Suisun, to buy hides and tallow.

The next morning my father gave orders, and my brothers, with the peons, went on horseback into the mountains and smaller valleys to round up all the best cattle. They drove them to the beach, killed them there, and salted the hides. They tried out the tallow in some iron kettles that my father had bought from one of the Vallejos, but as we did not have any barrels, we followed the common plan in those days. We cast the tallow in round pits

---

4. **Juan Cojo:** Limping Juan.
5. **vaqueros:** Cowboys.

about the size of a cheese, dug in the black adobe and plastered smooth with clay. Before the melted tallow was poured into the pit an oaken staff was thrust down in the center, so that by the two ends of it the heavy cake could be carried more easily. By working very hard we had a large number of hides and many pounds of tallow ready on the beach when the ship appeared far out in the bay and cast anchor near another point two or three miles away. The captain soon came to our landing with a small boat and two sailors, one of whom was a Frenchman who knew Spanish very well, and who acted as interpreter. The captain looked over the hides, and then asked my father to get into the boat and go to the vessel. Mother was much afraid to let him go, as we all thought the Americans were not to be trusted unless we knew them well. We feared they would carry my father off and keep him a prisoner. Father said, however, that it was all right; he went and put on his best clothes, gay with silver braid, and we all cried, and kissed him good-by, while mother clung about his neck and said we might never see him again. Then the captain told her: "If you are afraid, I will have the sailors take him to the vessel, while I stay here until he comes back. He ought to see all the goods I have, or he will not know what to buy." After a little my mother let him go with the captain, and we stood on the beach to see them off. Mother then came back, and had us all kneel down and pray for father's safe return. Then we felt safe.

He came back the next day, bringing four boat-loads of cloth, axes, shoes, fish-lines, and many new things. There were two grindstones and some cheap jewelry. My brother had traded some deerskins for a gun and four tooth-brushes, the first ones I had ever seen. I remember that we children rubbed them on our teeth till the blood came, and then concluded that after all we liked best the bits of pounded willow root that we had used for brushes before. After the captain had carried all the hides and tallow to his ship he came back, very much pleased with his bargain, and gave my father, as a present, a little keg of what he called Boston rum. We put it away for sick people.

After the ship sailed my mother and sisters began to cut out new dresses, which the Indian women sewed. On one of mine mother put some big brass buttons about an inch across, with eagles on them. How proud I was! I used to rub them hard every day to make them shine, using the tooth-brush and some of the pounded egg-shell that my sisters and all the Spanish ladies kept in a box to put on their faces on great occasions. . . .

AMALIA SIBRIAN

A Spanish Girl's Journey from Monterey to Los Angeles

Early in the winter of 1829 my father, who had long expected an appointment under the governor, received a letter from Los Angeles saying that his papers were in the hands of the authorities there, and would only be delivered in person. He decided to take my mother and myself with him and go overland, without waiting for the yearly vessel from Yerba Buena which would soon be due at Monterey, where we were staying. It was nearly Christmas when we began the journey. Word was sent ahead by a man on horseback to some of the smaller ranches at which we meant to stop, so that we were expected. A young American who had reached the coast with letters from the city of Mexico heard of our plans, and came to my father to ask if he might travel with us to Los Angeles, which was easily arranged. He did not know a word of Spanish, and I have often laughed at some of his experiences on the road, owing to his ignorance of our ways and speech. . . .

Our route took us up the Salinas Valley and over the mountains to the coast valleys and the Missions. At San Miguel we found everything prepared for a jubilee over the prosperous year. The men walked about and fired off their carbines and home-made fire works, while the padres' servant swung a burning oaken brand in the air, and lighted a few rockets. Inside the church the Indian choir was singing. We saw it all, until about ten o'clock that night; then the alcalde of the village came with fresh horses, and we went on, as it was very pleasant traveling.

The young American picked up some words in Spanish; he could say "*Gracios*," "*Si, señor*," and a few other phrases. One day we passed a very ugly Indian woman, and he asked me how to ask her how old she was. Out of mischief I whispered, "*Yo te amor*,"[6] which he said at once, and she, poor creature, immediately rose from her seat on the ground and replied, "*Gracios, Señor, pero soy indio*" ("but I am an Indian"), which gave us sport till long after. The next day our companion gave me a lesson in English by way of revenge. It was the day before Christmas, and we had reached San Buenaventura. It was a holiday for every one. After mass all the men and boys assembled on horseback in front of the church, with the padre and the alcalde at their head. They rode about in circles like a circus, fired guns, beat drums, and shouted. I thought it was very fine, and by signs I asked my American friend how he liked it, and he answered, "Damfools!" with such energy that I supposed they were words of praise. Indeed, I used the bad words as very proper English for a year or two, until I learned better, when I was of course much mortified.

When near Los Angeles we had the nearest approach to an adventure of our whole journey. We spent the night at a ranch-house. As I was the young lady of the party, the hostess gave up her own private room to me. At the end of it was an alcove with a window, and in front of the window stood a shrine, with wax figures of the holy Virgin and the child Christ. . . .

To judge from appearances [however] the only shrine to which our host was devoted was the cockpit, for the courtyard of the adobe was fairly lined with rows of the "blooded birds" so popular at that time with many wealthy rancheros, each one tied to a stake by his leg, and being trained for the battlefield. The young American, who, like many other foreigners, took up with our bad customs more easily than with our good ones, was greatly delighted when he saw the rows of fighting cocks in the yard. He offered to buy one, but the owner thought them too precious to sell. At last, by signs, he wagered

6. **Yo te amor:** I love you.

a dollar on the homeliest of the lot. The host, accepting the wager, released his favorite. Instead of fighting, the two birds went through the window into the room I had occupied, and that with such force that there was a crash, and a mixture of feathers, wax saints, and flowers on the floor. Our host turned pale, and rushed in to disentangle his pets, while the American jumped up and down on a porch, shouting, *"Bueno! bueno!"* The birds were now fighting in earnest, but the host separated them, gave them to a servant, mounted the saddled horse which always stood ready, day or night, and, with a faint *"Adios"* to me, disappeared. He knew what he was about, as events proved, for the rage of his wife when she saw the broken shrine was something terrible. The moment she came on the scene she cried out, "Where is he?" and going into the inner courtyard she began to release the game-cocks, which hastened to hide in the nearest shelter. The next morning, when we took our departure, the master of the house had not yet returned, and the mistress was endeavoring to restore the shrine.

31

DAGUERREOTYPE BY JOSEPH B. STARKWEATHER
Miners during the California Gold Rush

Through most of the nineteenth century, no significant legal restrictions prevented immigrants from coming to the United States—and staying. In fact, some states and companies advertised in Europe to attract immigrants. All this changed with the California gold rush.

Globally, the nineteenth century was a time of movement and migration. Political change and agricultural crises drove people to cross continents and oceans looking for higher wages and new economic opportunities, and the discovery of gold in California in late 1848 brought tens of thousands of migrants from all over the United States and the far corners of the world. Until 1860, leaving China was a violation of imperial law that was punishable by death. However, one of the first forty-niners (named after 1849, the first full year of the gold rush) to strike it rich was a Chinese prospector named Chum Ming, whose tale of overnight wealth inspired thousands of Chinese to bribe ship captains and port officials to let them escape a country that had been defeated by the British in the Opium Wars and was declining into political and economic crisis.

Once in California, Chinese immigrants faced a cold welcome. In 1850, nativist attempts to exclude immigrant prospectors yielded the California Foreign Miners

Head of Auburn Ravine, 1852. Courtesy of the California History Room, California State Library, Sacramento, California.

License Law. In a highly multiethnic state with little formal record keeping, it was often difficult to determine who was foreign and who was not. However, everyone agreed that the Chinese were foreigners, and they wound up paying nearly 85 percent of all the license fees collected by the state of California.

As initial gold fever dissipated with the exhaustion of surface gold, and as prospecting fees cut into Chinese miners' incomes, those who stayed in California looked for other work or started small businesses in the booming San Francisco–area economy. They were tolerated as long as the economy was growing and there were jobs for all. A change in Chinese law that enabled migration to the United States, along with the need for laborers to construct the transcontinental railroad in 1864, brought many more Chinese to America and opened opportunities for Chinese businesses and jobs in the shadow of the Central Pacific Railroad, which at one time employed roughly ten thousand Chinese.

The following image is from a daguerreotype made by Joseph B. Starkweather in 1852 at the head of Auburn Ravine in California. It depicts white and Chinese miners standing next to a sluice box, which was used to sort gold from rock and dirt by means of running water.

Miners during the California gold rush, daguerreotype by Joseph B. Starkweather. *Courtesy of the California History Room, California State Library, Sacramento, California*

QUESTIONS TO CONSIDER

1. Many historians have stressed the tremendous isolation that Chinese Americans lived under in their first one hundred years in the United States. In what ways does this photograph confirm or contradict this view?
2. Are these forty-niners prospecting together or separately? What evidence can you find to support your view?
3. How might ethnicity have been important in deciding how these miners shared the sluice, the work, and the gold?

PART FIVE

Reimagining Family, Community, and Society

An Age of Reform

During the second quarter of the nineteenth century, new social forces swept through the American villages, farms, and regions that had once existed in near isolation. Traditional ways of work and life were disrupted. The transportation revolution overcame barriers of distance, as highways, canals, steamships, and railroads linked and transformed established communities and existing markets. Farmers, craftspeople, inventors, and factory owners learned new ways to shape and dominate the physical world. Enterprises like the Lowell mills introduced new work methods as well as novel forms of social organization that changed the lives of workers like Harriet Hanson Robinson.

This new, interconnected American way of life also produced a popular belief in the perfectibility of humankind and the ability to better society. In areas as diverse as property law, public health, and prison reform, the world watched in wonder, and sometimes horror, as Americans created bold new structures and radical procedures for solving everyday problems. Among the most controversial of these reform projects was the Eastern State Penitentiary in Philadelphia—the most expensive and modern prison built at that time, and an early impetus to the new science of penology—about which foreign visitors to America such as Charles Dickens and Frederick Marryat revealed a keen interest, as their travelogues confirm.

One of the key areas in which reformers sought change was women's social status. Rebecca Cox Jackson, a black woman from Philadelphia, defied traditional religious practices when she left her husband to preach the Gospel as an itinerant evangelist. Mary Lois Walker Morris, a young Mormon who lived in the Midwest, questioned her role in a plural marriage even though she believed in the practice. Elizabeth Cady Stanton helped organize the 1848 Seneca Falls Convention and its "Declaration of Sentiments," which asserted that all men *and women* are created equal. These reform efforts were not welcomed by all, however, as is demonstrated in the political cartoon "Bloomerism."

The most controversial reform subject, of course, was slavery. Harriet Jacobs, a one-time slave, published a lengthy account of sexual harassment and abuse suffered at the hands of white slave owners, which fired abolitionist outrage. Visual representations of slavery's evils also excited calls for the end of the peculiar institution, as in the case of "The Auction Sale," an engraving of the human cost of the domestic slave trade found in *Uncle Tom's Cabin* by Harriet Beecher Stowe.

POINTS OF VIEW
The Prison Reform Movement in the Early Republic

32

CHARLES DICKENS

Philadelphia and Its Solitary Prison

The rapid growth in commerce, industry, infrastructure, and urbanism in nineteenth-century America created new wealth and inequality on a scale previously unknown. As the nation expanded and the population became increasingly mobile, crime—particularly theft—was a widespread concern. However, the tiny jails and grotesque instruments of torture and dismemberment that had been the basis of European penal traditions had never been intended for use in a mass society of such diversity and mobility. Moreover, for many Americans, particularly the social reformers of the mid-nineteenth century, traditional methods were inconsistent with the goal of perfecting a new society in a new world. Out of this reform urge came the modern science of penology and the American prison system.

The British had experimented with transporting prisoners to distant lands—first to the southern United States and then, after U.S. independence, to Australia. However,

---

Charles Dickens, *American Notes* (New York: John W. Lovell, 1883), 676–90.

many people considered exile wasteful and expensive, as well as fatalistic in the idea that reforming an individual in his or her own community was impossible. Thus were born the modern science of penology and the two competing American paradigms for rehabilitative imprisonment.

The first experiment, the Auburn Model, inspired Sing Sing prison, which opened in Ossining, New York, in 1826. The Auburn approach centered on group labor that was conducted in complete silence during the day, followed by solitary confinement at night. This view of hard labor without reward, as both punishment and rehabilitation, became the dominant approach in the United States and most European countries.

The other model, far less widely replicated in other countries, was the Pennsylvania (or Separate) system, which forms the basis of the modern-day American practice of solitary confinement. Pioneered in a prison built in 1829 outside Philadelphia, the Pennsylvania system was probably inspired by Quaker beliefs in the inner goodness of the human spirit. The theory was that prisoners might be reformed as people if they were removed from all exterior influences and allowed time for inner reflection through isolation and solitude. Each prisoner had a separate cell with double doors to achieve perfect silence, and a single glass skylight to connect with God. Prisoners were not allowed to see or communicate with one another, and contact with guards was kept to a minimum through use of special food slots in a prisoner's cell door and a daily exercise routine that was staggered so that no two prisoners would ever view each other. A special mask shielded prisoners' eyes and ears, enabling guards to lead them to the garden without distracting them with conversation or the physical infrastructure of the prison.

Eastern State was touted as having running water earlier than the White House. It was a modern wonder that drew social reformers, writers, and government delegations from around the world to see its operation and judge for themselves whether this was the future of prison building. Among the many who visited was the best-selling novelist of the nineteenth century, Charles Dickens (1812–1870), a leader of the English social reform movement. In 1842, at the age of thirty, Dickens, accompanied by his wife, made a trip to America, where he hoped to learn about prison reform, as well as many other aspects of society and daily life. The following passage was written during this trip.

QUESTIONS TO CONSIDER

1. What was Dickens's assessment of the positive and negative aspects of the prison?
2. What evidence did Dickens use to support his conclusions about the value of this type of prison?
3. What preexisting beliefs and prejudices did Dickens reveal?

PHILADELPHIA, AND ITS SOLITARY PRISON

The journey from New York to Philadelphia is made by railroad, and two ferries; and usually occupies between five and six hours. . . .

In the outskirts stands a great prison, called the Eastern Penitentiary: conducted on a plan peculiar to the State of Pennsylvania. The system here is rigid, strict, and hopeless solitary confinement. I believe it, in its effects, to be cruel and wrong.

In its intention I am well convinced that it is kind, humane, and meant for reformation; but I am persuaded that those who devised this system of Prison Discipline, and those benevolent gentlemen who carry it into execution, do not know what it is that they are doing. I believe that very few men are capable of estimating the immense amount of torture and agony which this dreadful punishment, prolonged for years, inflicts upon the sufferers; and in guessing at it myself, and in reasoning from what I have seen written upon their faces, and what to my certain knowledge they feel within, I am only the more convinced that there is a depth of terrible endurance in it which none but the sufferers themselves can fathom, and which no man has a right to inflict upon his fellow-creature. I hold this slow and daily tampering with the mysteries of the brain to be immeasurably worse than any torture of the body: and because its ghastly signs and tokens are not so palpable to the eye and sense of touch as scars upon the flesh; because its wounds are not upon the surface, and it extorts few cries that human ears can hear; therefore I the more denounce it, as a secret punishment which slumbering humanity is not roused up to stay. I hesitated once, debating with myself whether, if I had the power of saying "Yes" or "No," I would allow it to be tried in certain cases, where the terms of imprisonment were short; but now I solemnly declare, that with no rewards or honours could I walk a happy man beneath the open sky by day, or lay me down upon my bed at night, with the consciousness that one human creature, for any length of time, no matter what, lay suffering this unknown punishment in his silent cell, and I the cause, or I consenting to it in the least degree.

I was accompanied to this prison by two gentlemen officially connected with its management, and passed the day in going from cell to cell, and talking with the inmates. Every facility was afforded me that the utmost courtesy could suggest. Nothing was concealed or hidden from my view, and every piece of information that I sought was openly and frankly given. The perfect order of the building cannot be praised too highly, and of the excellent motives of all who are immediately concerned in the administration of the system there can be no kind of question. . . .

Standing at the central point, and looking down these dreary passages, the dull repose and quiet that prevails is awful. Occasionally there is a drowsy sound from some lone weaver's shuttle, or shoemaker's last, but it is stifled by the thick walls and heavy dungeon door, and only serves to make the general stillness more profound. Over the head and face of every prisoner who comes into this melancholy house a black hood is drawn; and in this dark shroud, an emblem of the curtain dropped between him and the living world, he is led to the cell from which he never again comes forth until his whole term of imprisonment has expired. He never hears of wife or children; home or friends; the life or death of any single creature. He sees the prison officers, but, with that exception, he never looks upon a human countenance, or hears a human voice. He is a man buried alive; to be dug out in the slow round of years; and in the meantime dead to everything but torturing anxieties and horrible despair.

His name, and crime, and term of suffering are unknown, even to the officer who delivers him his daily food. There is a number over his cell door, and in a book of which the governor of the prison has one copy, and the moral instructor another: this is the index to his history. Beyond these pages the prison has no record of his existence: and though he live to be in the same cell ten weary years, he has no means of knowing, down to the very last hour, in what part of the building it is situated; what kind of men there are about him; whether in the long winter nights there are living people near, or he is in some lonely corner of the great gaol [jail], with walls, and passages, and iron doors between him and the nearest sharer in its solitary horrors.

Every cell has double doors: the outer one of sturdy oak, the other of grated iron, wherein there is a trap through which his food is handed. He has a Bible, and a slate and pencil, and, under certain restrictions, has sometimes other books, provided for the purpose, and pen and ink and paper. His razor, plate, and can, and basin, hang upon the wall, or shine upon the little shelf. Fresh water is laid on in every cell, and he can draw it at his pleasure. During the day, his bedstead turns up against the wall, and leaves more space for him to work in. His loom, or bench, or wheel is there; and there he labours, sleeps and wakes, and counts the seasons as they change, and grows old.

The first man I saw was seated at his loom, at work. He had been there six years, and was to remain, I think, three more. He had been convicted as a receiver of stolen goods, but even after this long imprisonment denied his guilt, and said he had been hardly dealt by. It was his second offence.

He stopped his work when we went in, took off his spectacles, and answered freely to everything that was said to him, but always with a strange kind of pause first, and in a low, thoughtful voice. He wore a paper hat of his own making, and was pleased to have it noticed and commended. He had very ingeniously manufactured a sort of Dutch clock from some disregarded odds and ends; and his vinegar bottle served for the pendulum. Seeing me interested in this contrivance, he looked up at it with a great deal of pride, and said that he had been thinking of improving it, and that he hoped the hammer and the piece of broken glass beside it "would play music before long." He had extracted some colours from the yarn with which he worked, and painted a few poor figures on the wall. One, of a female, over the door, he called "The Lady of the Lake."

He smiled as I looked at these contrivances to while away the time; but, when I looked from them to him, I saw that his lip trembled, and could have counted the beating of his heart. I forget how it came about, but some allusion was made to his having a wife. He shook his head at the word, turned aside, and covered his face with his hands.

"But you are resigned now?" said one of the gentlemen after a short pause, during which he had resumed his former manner. He answered with a sigh that seemed quite reckless in its hopelessness, "Oh yes, oh yes! I am resigned to it." "And are a better man, you think?" "Well, I hope so: I'm sure I hope I may be." "And time goes pretty quickly?" "Time is very long, gentle-men, within these four walls!"

He gazed about him—Heaven only knows how wearily!—as he said these words; and, in the act of doing so, fell into a strange stare as if he had forgotten something. A moment afterwards he sighed heavily, put on his spectacles, and went about his work again.

In another cell there was a German, sentenced to five years' imprison-ment for larceny, two of which had just expired. With colours procured in the same manner, he had painted every inch of the walls and ceiling quite beautifully. He had laid out the few feet of ground behind with exquisite neatness, and had made a little bed in the centre, that looked, by-the-bye, like a grave. The taste and ingenuity he had displayed in everything were most extraordinary; and yet a more dejected, heart-broken, wretched crea-ture it would be difficult to imagine. I never saw such a picture of forlorn af-fliction and distress of mind. My heart bled for him; and when the tears ran down his cheeks, and he took one of the visitors aside, to ask, with his trem-bling hands nervously clutching at his coat to detain him, whether there was no hope of his dismal sentence being commuted, the spectacle was re-ally too painful to witness. I never saw or heard of any kind of misery that impressed me more than the wretchedness of this man. . . .

There was one man who was allowed, as an indulgence, to keep rabbits. His room having rather a close smell in consequence, they called to him at the door to come out into the passage. He complied, of course, and stood shading his haggard face in the unwonted sun-light of the great window, looking as wan and unearthly as if he had been summoned from the grave. He had a white rabbit in his breast; and when the little creature, getting down upon the ground, stole back into the cell, and he, being dismissed, crept tim-idly after it, I thought it would have been very hard to say in what respect the man was the nobler animal of the two. . . .

My firm conviction is that, independent of the mental anguish it oc-casions—an anguish so acute and so tremendous, that all imagination of it must fall far short, of the reality—it wears the mind into a morbid state, which renders it unfit for the rough contact and busy action of the world. It is my fixed opinion that those who have undergone this punishment MUST pass into society again morally unhealthy and diseased. There are many in-stances on record of men who have chosen, or have been condemned, to lives of perfect solitude, but I scarcely remember one, even among sages of strong and vigorous intellect, where its effect has not become apparent, in some dis-ordered train of thought, or some gloomy hallucination. What monstrous phantoms, bred of despondency and doubt, and born and reared in solitude, have stalked upon the earth, making creation ugly, and darkening the face of Heaven!

Suicides are rare among these prisoners: are almost, indeed, unknown. But no argument in favour of the system can reasonably be deduced from this circumstance, although it is very often urged. All men who have made diseases of the mind their study, know perfectly well that such extreme depression and despair as will change the whole character, and beat down all its powers of elasticity and self-resistance, may be at work within a man, and yet stop short of self-destruction. This is a common case.

That it makes the senses dull, and by degrees impairs the bodily faculties, I am quite sure. I remarked to those who were with me in this very establishment at Philadelphia, that the criminals who had been there long were deaf. They, who were in the habit of seeing these men constantly, were perfectly amazed at the idea, which they regarded as groundless and fanciful. And yet the very first prisoner to whom they appealed—one of their own selection—confirmed my impression (which was unknown to him) instantly, and said, with a genuine air it was impossible to doubt, that he couldn't think how it happened, but he *was* growing very dull of hearing.

That it is a singularly unequal punishment, and affects the worst man least, there is no doubt. In its superior efficiency as a means of reformation, compared with that other code of regulations which allows the prisoners to work in company without communicating together, I have not the smallest faith. All the instances of reformation that were mentioned to me were of a kind that might have been—and I have no doubt whatever, in my own mind, would have been—equally well brought about by the Silent System [the Auburn model]. . . .

It seems to me that the objection that nothing wholesome or good has ever had its growth in such unnatural solitude, and that even a dog, or any of the more intelligent among beasts, would pine, and mope, and rust away beneath its influence, would be in itself a sufficient argument against this system. But when we recollect, in addition, how very cruel and severe it is, and that a solitary life is always liable to peculiar and distinct objections of a most deplorable nature, which have arisen here; and call to mind, moreover, that the choice is not between this system and a bad or ill-considered one, but between it and another which has worked well, and is, in its whole design and practice, excellent; there is surely more than sufficient reason for abandoning a mode of punishment attended by so little hope or promise, and fraught, beyond dispute, with such a host of evils.

33

FREDERICK MARRYAT

A Different View of Solitary Confinement

Frederick Marryat (1792–1848), like Charles Dickens, was a successful English novelist and a social reformer concerned with perfecting human life. However, unlike Dickens, who had found his fame as a writer at a young age, Marryat took up writing and social commentary late in life. After a successful twenty-five-year career in the navy, Marryat retired at the age of thirty-eight and became a writer and magazine editor. He made a trip to America in 1837. Like many Europeans who published travelogues describing a visit to the United States, Marryat found much of American life uncouth and distasteful. His observations from this trip—including the following account of his visit to Eastern State Penitentiary in Philadelphia, the same prison Dickens had toured—were published in his book A Diary in America: With Remarks on Its Institutions *(1839).*

QUESTIONS TO CONSIDER

1. What was Marryat's assessment of the positive and negative features of the prison?
2. What was the core of Marryat's argument? With what evidence did he support his conclusions?
3. What preexisting beliefs did he reveal?

PENITENTIARIES, &c.

. . . There is a great unwillingness to take away life in America, and it is this aversion to capital punishment which has directed the attention of the American community to the penitentiary system. Several varieties of this species of punishment have been resorted to, more or less severe. . . .

The best system is that acted upon in the Penitentiary at Philadelphia, where there is solitary confinement, but with labour and exercise. Mr. Samuel Wood, who superintends this establishment, is a person admirably calculated for his task, and I do not think that any arrangements could be better, or the establishment in more excellent hands. But my object was, not so much to view the prison and witness the economy of it, as to examine the prisoners themselves, and hear what their opinions were.

Capt. Marryat, C. B. *A Diary in America: With Remarks on Its Institutions* (London: Longman, Orme, Brown, Green & Longmans, 1839), 158–69.

The surgeon may explain the operation, but the patient who has undergone it is the proper person to apply to, if you wish to know the degree and nature of the pain inflicted. I requested, therefore, and obtained permission, to visit a portion of the prisoners without a third party being present to prevent their being communicative; selecting some who had been in but a short time, others who had been there for years, and referring also to the books, as to the nature and degree of their offence. I ought to state that I re-examined almost the whole of the parties about six months afterwards, and the results of the two examinations are now given. I did not take their names, but registered them in my notes as No. 1, 2, 3, &c.

No. 1—a man who had been sentenced to twelve years imprisonment for the murder of his wife. He had been bred up as a butcher. (I have observed that when the use of the knife is habitual, the flinching which men naturally feel at the idea of driving it into a fellow-creature, is overcome; and a man who is accustomed to dissect the still palpitating carcasses of animals, has very little compunction in resorting to the knife in the event of collision with his own race.) This fellow looked a butcher; his face and head were all animal; he was by no means intelligent. He was working at a loom, and had already been confined for seven years and a half. He said that, after the first six months of his confinement, he had lost all reckoning of time, and had not cared to think about it until lately, when he enquired, and was told how long he had been locked up. Now that he had discovered that more than half his time had passed away, it occupied his whole thoughts, and sometimes he felt very impatient. . . .

This man had denied the murder of his wife, and still persisted in the denial, although there was no doubt of his having committed the crime. Of course, in this instance there was no repentance; and the Penitentiary was thrown away upon him, further than that, for twelve years, he could not contaminate society.

No. 2—sentenced to four years imprisonment for forgery; his time was nearly expired. This was a very intelligent man; by profession he had been a schoolmaster. He had been in prison before for the same offence. His opinion as to the Penitentiary was, that it could do no harm, and might do much good. The fault of the system was one which could not well be remedied, which was, that there was degradation attached to it. Could punishment undergone for crime be viewed in the same way as repentance was by the Almighty, and a man, after suffering for his fault, re-appear in the world with clean hands, and be admitted into society as before, it would be attended with the very best effects; but there was no working out the degradation. When he was released from his former imprisonment, he had been obliged to fly from the place where he was known. He was pursued by the harshness of the world, not only in himself, but in his children. No one would allow that his punishment had wiped away his crime, and this was the reason why people, inclined to be honest, were driven again into guilt. Not only would the world not encourage them, but it would not permit them to become honest; the finger of scorn was pointed wherever they were known, or found out, and the punishment after release was infinitely greater than that of the prison itself. . . .

No. 3—a very intelligent, but not educated man: imprisoned three years for stealing. He had only been a few months in the Penitentiary, but had been confined for ten years in Sing Sing prison for picking pockets. I asked him his opinion as to the difference of treatment in the two establishments. He replied, "In Sing Sing the punishment is corporal—here it is more mental." In Sing Sing there was little chance of a person's reformation, as the treatment was harsh and brutal, and the feelings of the prisoners were those of indignation and resentment. Their whole time was occupied in trying how they could deceive their keepers, and communicate with each other by every variety of stratagem. Here [in Philadelphia] a man was left to his own reflections, and at the same time he was treated like a man. Here he was his own tormentor; at Sing Sing he was tormented by others. A man was sent to Sing Sing for doing wrong to others; when there, he was quite as much wronged himself. Two wrongs never made a right. Again, at Sing Sing they all worked in company, and knew each other; when they met again, after they were discharged, they enticed one another to do wrong again. He was convinced that no man left Sing Sing a better man than he went in. Here he felt very often that he could become better—perhaps he might. At all events his mind was calm, and he had no feelings of resentment for his treatment. He had now leisure and quiet for self examination, if he chose to avail himself of it. At Sing Sing there was great injustice, and no redress. The infirm man was put to equal labour with the robust, and punished if he did not perform as much. The flogging was very severe at Sing Sing. He once ventured to express his opinion that such was the case, and (to prove the contrary he supposed) they awarded him eighty-seven lashes for the information. That many of this man's observations, in the parallel drawn between the two establishments, are correct, must be conceded; but still some of his assertions must be taken with due reservation, as it is evident that he had no very pleasant reminiscences of his ten years geological studies in Sing Sing.

No. 4—an Irishman; very acute. He had been imprisoned seven years for burglary, and his time would expire in a month. Had been confined also in Walnut Street prison, Philadelphia, for two years previous to his coming here. He said that it was almost impossible for any man to reform in that prison, although some few did. He had served many years in the United States navy. He declared that his propensity to theft was only strong upon him when under the influence of liquor, or tobacco, which latter had the same effect upon him as spirits. He thought that he was reformed now; the reason why he thought so was, that he now liked work, and had learnt a profession in the prison, which he never had before. He considered himself a good workman, as he could make a pair of shoes in a day. He cannot now bear the smell of liquor or tobacco. (This observation must have been from imagination, as he had no opportunity in the Penitentiary of testing his dislike.) He ascribed all his crimes to ardent spirits. He was fearful of only one thing: his time was just out, and where was he to go? If known to have been in the prison, he would never find work. He knew a fact which had occurred, which would prove that he had just grounds for his fear. A tailor, who had been confined in Walnut Street prison with him, had been released as soon as his time was up. He was an excellent workman, and resolved for the future to be honest. He obtained employment from a master tailor in Philadelphia, and in three months was made foreman. One of the inspectors of Walnut Street prison came in for clothes, and his friend was called down to take the measures. The inspector recognized him, and as soon as he left the shop told his master that he had been in the Walnut Street prison. The man was in consequence immediately discharged. He could obtain no more work, and in a few months afterwards found his way back again to Walnut Street prison for a fresh offence. . . .

No. 9—a young woman, about nineteen; confined for larceny; in other respects a good character. She was very quiet and subdued, and said that she infinitely preferred the solitude of the Penitentiary to the company with which she must have associated had she been confined in a common gaol. She did not appear at all anxious for the expiration of her term. Her cell was very neat, and ornamented with her own hands in a variety of ways. I observed that she had a lock of hair on her forehead which, from the care taken of it, appeared to be a favourite, and as I left the cell, [I] said—"You appear to have taken great pains with that lock of hair, considering that you have no one to look at you."—"Yes, sir," replied she; "and if you think that vanity will desert a woman, even in the solitude of a Penitentiary, you are mistaken."

When I visited this girl a second time, her term was nearly expired; she told me that she had not the least wish to leave her cell, and that if they confined her for two years more, she was content to stay. "I am quite peaceful and happy here," said she, and I believe she really spoke the truth. . . .

I entered many other cells, and had conversation with the prisoners; but I did not elicit from them any thing worth narrating. There is, however, a great deal to be gained from the conversation which I have recorded. It must be remembered that observations made by one prisoner, which struck me as important, if not made by others, were put as questions by me; and I found that the opinions of the most intelligent, although differently expressed, led to the same result—that the present system of the Philadelphia Penitentiary was the best that had been invented. As the schoolmaster said, if it did no good, it could do no harm. There is one decided advantage in this system, which is, that they all learn a trade if they had not one before; and, when they leave the prison, have the means of obtaining an honest livelihood, if they wish so to do themselves, and are permitted so to do by others.

FOR CRITICAL THINKING

1. Compare and contrast the way Dickens and Marryat viewed the debate over prison reform.
2. In what ways did Dickens and Marryat use different types of arguments? Which commentator was more interested in the facts? Which one was more interested in principles?

3. Which commentator do you think would be taken more seriously
   today? By whom? Why?

34

HARRIET HANSON ROBINSON
The Lowell Textile Workers

The transportation revolution made the movement of goods easier and cheaper than ever before, greatly increasing the potential market for manufactured products, particularly textiles. The establishment of legal precedents for the modern corporation, moreover, permitted manufacturing concerns and transportation projects to expand. But where would the workers come from?

One answer was the Lowell–Waltham system in Massachusetts in the 1820s, pioneered by industrialist Francis Cabot Lowell. His textile factories recruited young farm women, guaranteeing to their families that their moral conduct would be upheld. "Lowell girls," as they were called, were paid much lower wages than were men, but they were provided accommodation in carefully chaperoned boardinghouses. They were required to attend church as part of the conditions of their employment.

In the 1830s, Lowell reduced wages in response to growing competition from France and England. The Lowell girls fought back, becoming some of America's first and most militant labor leaders. They organized strikes in 1834 and 1836 and founded the Factory Girls Association and the Lowell Female Labor Reform Association, contributing to the success of the ten-hour workday movement. The struggle between Lowell and "his girls" was ended by the Irish potato famine of the 1840s, when hundreds of thousands of starving families arrived in New England and filled Lowell's factories with a new and lower-paid workforce.

Harriet Hanson Robinson (1825–1911) worked in the Lowell mills between 1834 and 1848, with the exception of the two years that she took off to go to high school from age fifteen to seventeen. At age twenty-four she married abolitionist publisher William Robinson and left her work in the mills to be a housewife. In her later years, after the death of her husband, Robinson reemerged in public life fighting for women's right to vote. She wrote Loom and Spindle, *from which the following passages are taken, at the age of seventy-three.*

Harriet Hanson Robinson, *Loom and Spindle; or, Life Among the Early Mill Girls* (New York: Thomas Y. Crowell, 1898), 26–35, 60–63, 65–67, 68–70, 83–86.

QUESTIONS TO CONSIDER

1. Why did Harriet Hanson Robinson work in the mills?
2. What did she like about life at the mills?
3. How did she think mill work affected women's status?
4. Why did the young women go on strike?

CHILD LIFE IN THE LOWELL COTTON-MILLS

In 1831, under the shadow of a great sorrow, which had made her four children fatherless, — the oldest but seven years of age, — my mother was left to struggle alone; and although she tried hard to earn bread enough to fill our hungry mouths, she could not do it, even with the help of kind friends. And so it happened that one of her more wealthy neighbors, who had looked with longing eyes on the one little daughter of the family, offered to adopt me. But my mother, who had had a hard experience in her youth in living amongst strangers, said, "No; while I have one meal of victuals a day, I will not part with my children." . . .

That was a hard, cold winter; and for warmth's sake my mother and her four children all slept in one bed, two at the foot and three at the head, — but her richer neighbor could not get the little daughter; and, contrary to all the modern notions about hygiene, we were a healthful and a robust brood. . . .

Shortly after this [Robinson refers here to an incident at a sewing school she attended] my mother's widowed sister, Mrs. Angeline Cudworth, who kept a factory boarding-house in Lowell, advised her to come to that city. . . .

When we reached Lowell, we were carried at once to my aunt's house, whose generous spirit had well provided for her hungry relations; and we children were led into her kitchen, where, on the longest and whitest of tables, lay, oh, so many loaves of bread!

After our feast of loaves we walked with our mother to the Tremont Corporation, where we were to live, and at the old No. 5 (which imprint is still legible over the door), in the first block of tenements then built, I began my life among factory people. . . .

I had been to school constantly until I was about ten years of age, when my mother, feeling obliged to have help in her work besides what I could give, and also needing the money which I could earn, allowed me, at my urgent request (for I wanted to earn *money* like the other little girls), to go to work in the mill. I worked first in the spinning-room as a "doffer." The doffers were the very youngest girls, whose work was to doff, or take off, the full bobbins, and replace them with empty ones.

I can see myself now, racing down the alley, between the spinning-frames, carrying in front of me a bobbin-box bigger than I was. These mites had to be very swift in their movements, so as not to keep the spinning-frames stopped long, and they worked only about fifteen minutes in every hour. The rest of the time was their own, and when the overseer was kind they were allowed to read, knit, or even to go outside the mill-yard to play.

Some of us learned to embroider in crewels, and I still have a lamb worked on cloth, a relic of those early days, when I was first taught to improve my time in the good old New England fashion. When not doffing, we were often allowed to go home, for a time, and thus we were able to help our mothers in their housework. We were paid two dollars a week; and how proud I was when my turn came to stand up on the bobbin-box, and write my name in the paymaster's book, and how indignant I was when he asked me if I could "write." "Of course I can," said I, and he smiled as he looked down on me.

The working-hours of all the girls extended from five o'clock in the morning until seven in the evening, with one-half hour for breakfast and for dinner. Even the doffers were forced to be on duty nearly fourteen hours a day, and this was the greatest hardship in the lives of these children. For it was not until 1842 that the hours of labor for children under twelve years of age were limited to ten per day; but the "ten-hour law" itself was not passed until long after some of these little doffers were old enough to appear before the legislative committee on the subject, and plead, by their presence, for a reduction of the hours of labor.

I do not recall any particular hardship connected with this life, except getting up so early in the morning, and to this habit, I never was, and never shall be, reconciled, for it has taken nearly a lifetime for me to make up the sleep lost at that early age. But in every other respect it was a pleasant life. We were not hurried any more than was for our good, and no more work was required of us than we were able easily to do.

Most of us children lived at home, and we were well fed, drinking both tea and coffee, and eating substantial meals (besides luncheons) three times a day. We had very happy hours with the older girls, many of whom treated us like babies, or talked in a motherly way, and so had a good influence over us. And in the long winter evenings, when we could not run home between the doffings, we gathered in groups and told each other stories, and sung the old-time songs our mother had sung, . . .

And we told each other of our little hopes and desires, and what we meant to do when we grew up. For we had our aspirations; and one of us, who danced the "shawl dance," as she called it, in the spinning-room alley, for the amusement of her admiring companions, discussed seriously with another little girl the scheme of their running away together, and joining the circus. . . .

I cannot tell how it happened that some of us knew about the English factory children, who, it was said, were treated so badly, and were even whipped by their cruel overseers. But we did know of it, and used to sing, to a doleful little tune, some verses called, "The Factory Girl's Last Day." . . .

In contrast with this sad picture, we thought of ourselves as well off, in our cosey corner of the mill, enjoying ourselves in our own way, with our good mothers and our warm suppers awaiting us when the going-out bell should ring. . . .

THE CHARACTERISTICS OF THE EARLY FACTORY GIRLS

When I look back into the factory life of fifty or sixty years ago, I do not see what is called "a class" of young men and women going to and from their daily work, like so many ants that cannot be distinguished one from another; I see them as individuals, with personalities of their own. This one has about her the atmosphere of her early home. That one is impelled by a strong and noble purpose. The other,—what she is, has been an influence for good to me and to all womankind.

Yet they were a class of factory operatives, and were spoken of (as the same class is spoken of now) as a set of persons who earned their daily bread, whose condition was fixed, and who must continue to spin and to weave to the end of their natural existence. Nothing but this was expected of them, and they were not supposed to be capable of social or mental improvement. That they could be educated and developed into something more than mere work-people, was an idea that had not yet entered the public mind. So little does one class of persons really know about the thoughts and aspirations of another! It was the good fortune of these early mill-girls to teach the people of that time that this sort of labor is not degrading, that the operative is not only "capable of virtue," but also capable of self-cultivation.

At the time the Lowell cotton-mills were started, the factory girl was the lowest among women. In England, and in France particularly, great injustice had been done to her real character; she was represented as subjected to influences that could not fail to destroy her purity and self-respect. In the eyes of her overseer she was but a brute, a slave, to be beaten, pinched, and pushed about. It was to overcome this prejudice that such high wages had been offered to women that they might be induced to become mill-girls, in spite of the opprobrium that still clung to this "degrading occupation." At first only a few came; for, though tempted by the high wages to be regularly paid in "cash," there were many who still preferred to go on working at some more *genteel* employment at seventy-five cents a week and their board.

But in a short time the prejudice against factory labor wore away, and the Lowell mills became filled with blooming and energetic New England women. . . .

In 1831 Lowell was little more than a factory village. Several corporations were started, and the cotton-mills belonging to them were building. Help was in great demand; and stories were told all over the country of the new factory town, and the high wages that were offered to all classes of work-people,— stories that reached the ears of mechanics' and farmers' sons, and gave new life to lonely and dependent women in distant towns and farmhouses. Into this Yankee El Dorado, these needy people began to pour by the various modes of travel known to those slow old days. The stage-coach and the canal-boat came every day, always filled with new recruits for this army of useful people. The mechanic and machinist came, each with his homemade chest of tools, and often times his wife and little ones. The widow came with her little flock and her scanty housekeeping goods to open a boarding-house or variety store, and so provided a home for her fatherless children. Many farmers' daughters came to earn money to complete their wedding outfit, or buy the bride's share of housekeeping articles.

Women with past histories came, to hide their griefs and their identity, and to earn an honest living in the "sweat of their brow." Single young men came, full of hope and life, to get money for an education, or to lift the mortgage from the home-farm. Troops of young girls came by stages and baggage-wagons, men often being employed to go to other States and to Canada, to collect them at so much a head, and deliver them at the factories. . . .

The early factory girls were not all country girls. There were others also, who had been taught that "work is no disgrace." There were some who came to Lowell solely on account of the social or literary advantages to be found there. They lived in secluded parts of New England, where books were scarce, and there was no cultivated society. They had comfortable homes, and did not perhaps need the *money* they would earn; but they longed to see this new "City of Spindles."

The laws relating to women were such, that a husband could claim his wife wherever he found her, and also the children she was trying to shield from his influence; and I have seen more than one poor woman skulk behind her loom or her frame when visitors were approaching the end of the aisle where she worked. Some of these were known under assumed names, to prevent their husbands from trusteeing their wages. It was a very common thing for a male person of a certain kind to do this, thus depriving his wife of *all* her wages, perhaps, month after month. The wages of minor children could be trusteed, unless the children (being fourteen years of age) were given their time. Women's wages were also trusteed for the debts of their husbands, and children's for the debts of their parents. . . .

It must be remembered that at this date woman had no property rights. A widow could be left without her share of her husband's (or the family) property, a legal "incumbrance" to his estate. A father could make his will without reference to his daughter's share of the inheritance. He usually left her a home on the farm as long as she remained single. A woman was not supposed to be capable of spending her own or of using other people's money. In Massachusetts, before 1840, a woman could not legally be treasurer of her own sewing-society, unless some man were responsible for her.

The law took no cognizance of woman as a money-spender. She was a ward, an appendage, a relict. Thus it happened, that if a woman did not choose to marry, or, when left a widow, to re-marry, she had no choice but to enter one of the few employments open to her, or to become a burden on the charity of some relative.

In almost every New England home could be found one or more of these women, sometimes welcome, more often unwelcome, and leading joyless, and in many instances unsatisfactory, lives. The cotton-factory was a great opening to these lonely and dependent women. From a condition approaching pauperism they were at once placed above want; they could earn money, and spend it as they pleased; and could gratify their tastes and desires without restraint, and without rendering an account to anybody. . . .

CHARACTERISTICS (CONTINUED)

One of the first strikes of cotton-factory operatives that ever took place in this country was that in Lowell, in October, 1836. When it was announced that the wages were to be cut down, great indignation was felt, and it was decided to strike, *en masse*. This was done. The mills were shut down, and the girls went in procession from their several corporations to the "grove" on Chapel Hill, and listened to "incendiary" speeches from early labor reformers.

One of the girls stood on a pump, and gave vent to the feelings of her companions in a neat speech, declaring that it was their duty to resist all attempts at cutting down the wages. This was the first time a woman had spoken in public in Lowell, and the event caused surprise and consternation among her audience.

Cutting down the wages was not their only grievance, nor the only cause of this strike. Hitherto the corporations had paid twenty-five cents a week towards the board of each operative, and now it was their purpose to have the girls pay the sum; and this, in addition to the cut in wages, would make a difference of at least one dollar a week. It was estimated that as many as twelve or fifteen hundred girls turned out, and walked in procession through the streets. They had neither flags nor music, but sang songs, a favorite (but rather inappropriate) one being a parody on "I won't be a nun."

> Oh! isn't it a pity, such a pretty girl as I
> Should be sent to the factory to pine away and die?
> Oh! I cannot be a slave.
> I will not be a slave.
> For I'm so fond of liberty
> That I cannot be a slave.

My own recollection of this first strike (or "turn out" as it was called) is very vivid. I worked in a lower room, where I had heard the proposed strike fully, if not vehemently, discussed; I had been an ardent listener to what was said against this attempt at "oppression" on the part of the corporation, and naturally I took sides with the strikers. When the day came on which the girls were to turn out, those in the upper rooms started first, and so many of them left that our mill was at once shut down. Then, when the girls in my room stood irresolute, uncertain what to do, asking each other, "Would you?" or "Shall we turn out?" and not one of them having the courage to lead off, I, who began to think they would not go out, after all their talk, became impatient, and started on ahead, saying, with childish bravado, "I don't care what you do, *I* am going to turn out, whether any one else does or not"; and I marched out, and was followed by the others.

As I looked back at the long line that followed me, I was more proud than I have ever been since at any success I may have achieved, and more proud than I shall ever be again until my own beloved State gives to its women citizens the right of suffrage.

The agent of the corporation where I then worked took some small re-venges on the supposed ringleaders; on the principle of sending the weaker to the wall, my mother was turned away from her boarding-house, that func-tionary saying, "Mrs. Hanson, you could not prevent the older girls from turning out, but your daughter is a child, and *her* you could control."

It is hardly necessary to say that so far as results were concerned this strike did no good. The dissatisfaction of the operatives subsided, or burned itself out, and though the authorities did not accede to their demands, the majority returned to their work, and the corporation went on cutting down the wages.

And after a time, as the wages became more and more reduced, the best portion of the girls left and went to their homes, or to the other employ-ments that were fast opening to women, until there were very few of the old guard left; and thus the *status* of the factory population of New England gradually became what we know it to be to-day.

35

REBECCA COX JACKSON

Religion and the Power to Challenge Society

Born a free African American woman, Rebecca Cox Jackson was one of three children raised by her grandmother and mother in Philadelphia during the early 1800s. There is no record of who her father was. After losing her mother at age thirteen, she moved in with her brother, Joseph Cox, a powerful African Methodist Episcopal (AME) minister, widower, and father of six children. At some point in the next two decades, she married Samuel Jackson and together they lived in the same house as Joseph. Though she had no children of her own, she spent her days caring for Joseph's children and working as a seamstress. Nothing was particularly unusual about Jackson's early life.

Everything changed in 1830, however. Following instructions given to her by a heavenly spirit, Jackson began to host prayer meetings that quickly surged in popularity. She stirred controversy by tossing aside convention and inviting men and women to wor-ship side by side. She earned a temporary reprieve from criticism after a visit by Morris Brown, a future bishop of the AME Church. Brown came to one of Jackson's meetings with the idea of silencing her, but left so thoroughly impressed by her preaching that he ordered her left alone. In 1833 Jackson embarked on a preaching tour outside of Phila-delphia but met with new and greater resistance as she announced ever-bolder views of

"Diary of Rebecca Cox Jackson, January, 1836," in Jean McMahon Humez, *Gifts of Power: The Writings of Rebecca Jackson, Black Visionary, Shaker Eldress* (Amherst, MA: University of Massachusetts Press, 1981), 368–71.

society. Her growing insistence on her right to preach, open refusal to formally join any church, and radical views on sexuality that included celibacy within marriage angered area clerics and, Jackson claimed, motivated some to assault her. Eventually she broke ranks with the free black church movement and joined a Shaker group in Watervliet, New York. In 1851 she returned to Philadelphia and founded a Shaker community composed mainly of black women.

In this 1836 excerpt from her diary, Jackson offers a glimpse of her evolving sacred life.

QUESTIONS TO CONSIDER

1. When Jackson learned to read through the intervention of a heavenly spirit, how did it change her life?
2. In the opening entry for January 31, 1836, Jackson confided that a recent spiritual experience had compelled her to inform her husband that "I had served him many years, and had tried to please him, but I could not" anymore. What did she mean by this statement? How were her religious convictions altering her marriage?
3. According to Jackson, black men and preachers tried to kill her. Why? What was at stake for them?
4. How could religious experience and expression serve as sources of social liberation for black women?

In the first of January 1836, I was about 40 miles west when I dreamt this dream. I thought I came home, and as I came near the house, Samuel came out of the back door, which opened on the east side. He came around on the south side, and met me on the west side, which was where our front door was. And the way he came, was no passage, for a house stood there. And as he came he said, "Here she is now," as if he was aspeaking to somebody in the house. And he turned right around and went back. And when he got to the door, he turned his face to me, as I followed him, and he handed me into the house.

A white man took me by my right hand and led me on the north side of the room, where sat a square table. On it lay a book open. And he said to me, "Thou shall be instructed in this book, from Genesis to Revelations." And then he took me on the west side, where stood a table. And it looked like the first. And said, "Yea, thou shall be instructed from the beginning of creation to the end of time." And then he took me on the east side of the room also, where stood a table and book like the two first, and said, "I will instruct thee—yea, thou shall be instructed from the beginning of all things to the end of all things. Yea, thou shall be well instructed. I will instruct."

When Samuel handed me to this man at my own back door, he turned away. I never saw him any more. When this man took me by the hand, his hand was soft like down. He was dressed all in light drab. He was bareheaded. His countenance was serene and solemn and divine. There was a father and a brother's countenance to be seen in his face.

And then I awoke, and I saw him as plain as I did in my dream. And after that he taught me daily. And when I would be reading and come to a hard word, I would see him standing by my side and he would teach me the word right. And often, when I would be in meditation and looking into things which was hard to understand, I would find him by me, teaching and giving me understanding. And oh, his labor and care which he had with me often caused me to weep bitterly, when I would see my great ignorance and the great trouble he had to make me understand eternal things. For I was so buried in the depth of the tradition of my forefathers, that it did seem as if I never could be dug up. But I bless God who had power and means to affect the good work which He had begun in my soul. And I am a monument of His great mercy and a witness of His truth. And I rejoice to bear witness of His truth, because He counted me worthy. After I saw these three books it was made known to me that they were agoing to be revealed from Heaven by the revelation of God, and I should see them, and at times I would feel to speak of them. This was in 1836.

January 31, 1836

Shortly after this dream I came home. I was commanded to tell Samuel I had served him many years, and had tried to please him, but I could not. "And now from this day and forever, I shall never strive again. But I shall serve God with all my heart, soul, mind, and strength and devote my body to the Lord and Him only. And when I have done it, He will be pleased." This was in the latter part of the same month that I had the dream of the three books. It was January 31, 1836.

I now passed through many sorrows and trying scenes on the account of my faith. My sufferings were so great at times that I did not know what the end would be. So I gave myself to fasting again, as I did at the beginning—then I fasted the three first days of every week. This I done for more than a year without ceasing. And always fasted on Friday for many years, until I learned the true fast. So now I undertook to fast for three weeks, by taking a morsel now and then. But I did not work nor go out nor nobody came in during this time but Samuel. And I never spoke, and he had no power over me, not even to speak to me. And nobody had power to come until the three weeks was ended. I prayed day and night. And at the end of the three weeks (which was on Thursday before Good Friday)—the three last days of the third week, I was told at the close of my prayer to say the Lord's Prayer, which I did for three days and nights. And I prayed on my knees many times in a day. And when I was not kneeling, I was walking the floor back and forth in prayer.

So at the last day I kneeled just at the hour of twelve, which was an hour given me at the beginning. Twelve at night, twelve in the day, and at the break of day—these were my appointed hours. I suffered nothing to hinder me from these hours of prayer. And as I have said in this writing, I "put my hands to work and my heart to God" in secret prayer. So I prayed always and whenever I was moved to leave my work at any time to go and kneel in prayer, I went. I soon found that obedience in all things was the way to salvation.

So, the third day of the last three, which I closed with the Lord's Prayer at twelve o'clock, kneeling with my face to the east, as I said, "Thy kingdom come," I saw a white ball, the color of a white cloud with the sun reflecting in it, which made it the color of gold.

These three days that I said the Lord's Prayer, I saw the Father and the Son in the northeast, in the same place that I saw them when the mountain was in my path. The first day, when I first said the Lord's Prayer, I saw them first. So I saw them three days.

And at the third day as I repeated, "Thy kingdom come," I saw this ball for the first time. It came from the right side of the Father and from the left side of the Son, as the Son was on the right side of the Father. This ball seemed to proceed out of them both. And when I repeated that word, it began to roll from them to me. So when I saw, by the word, "Thy kingdom come," that this ball was coming to me, I kept on saying that, and that only. And it came to me, entered into my heart.

And as soon as it entered it became a man, and my heart became an arch, and a chair in it. He had a mantle on him. He raised himself up three times, wrapping his mantle around him every time. Every time he wrapped his mantle, it caused black specks to rise up out of my heart and pass away into nothing. They were like the cinder of a burnt paper, about the size of mustard seed. And when it was all out, he wrapped his mantle close around him and sat down on this chair. And when he sat down, my heart and soul, spirit, and all that I possessed, sank into a sea of humility, and my soul was filled with the love of God. I was like one buried in a sea of love, peace, quietness, joy, and thankfulness. I was indeed separated from all my kindred. And I then rose from my knees and walked the floor in quietness, praising the Lord in my new heart. And I found myself in the temple, praising God where no man could see me or hear me.

After this I held forth the testimony with greater power and with a better understanding. And my enemies increased like the hairs of my head.

And there was three Methodist ministers that said I ought not to live. These three appointed what death I ought to die. One said I ought to be stoned to death, one said tarred and feathered and burnt, one said I ought to be put in a hogshead, driven full of spikes, and rolled down a hill. These men called themselves preachers of the Gospel of our Lord and Savior, Jesus Christ. But I felt to pity and pray for them, and to continually pray to God, to keep me from thinking hard of them, and to always enable me to feel the worth of their souls at heart. And I can say in truth that God has both heard and answered my prayer. [After passing through ten years of persecution from these men and others,] I never have felt that I could not pray for them as well as I could for any soul on the earth. And I always spoke to them, when I saw them, kindly, and I felt a kind and motherly feeling toward them, for which I both praise and thank God for the gift. For this is the Lord's doing, and it is marvelous in our eyes. And to Him be all the glory.

36

HARRIET JACOBS

The Life of a Female Slave

Harriet Jacobs's Incidents in the Life of a Slave Girl *stands as the classic narrative of a woman slave, a work to rank with the several autobiographies of Frederick Douglass. Published under a pseudonym in 1861, edited by a white abolitionist, and borrowing form and rhetoric from sentimental novels such as Harriet Beecher Stowe's* Uncle Tom's Cabin, *the book remained suspect for 120 years. Only in 1981, when Jean Fagan Yellin published documentary evidence of Jacobs's authorship, "Written by Herself: Harriet Jacobs' Slave Narrative"* (American Literature *[November 1981]: 479–86), was the book recognized as a major work of African American literature, as well as an essential document for the history of slavery.*

Jacobs (1813–1897), writing under the pseudonym Linda Brent, emerges as a remarkably determined woman. To prevent the permanent enslavement of her children, she hid for seven years in the attic of her grandmother's house, a tiny space only three feet high, while deceiving her master into thinking she had run away to the North by smuggling out letters to be mailed from New York City and Boston. Finally she and then her children escaped from slave territory to discover the ambiguities of freedom in the so-called free states.

QUESTIONS TO CONSIDER

1. What does Harriet Jacobs's account of her experience add to our picture of slavery?
2. Did Jacobs see herself as a victim? What did she emphasize about her reaction to the position her master placed her in?
3. How would readers of the time have likely reacted to Jacobs's tale of the experiences of young female slaves?

THE TRIALS OF GIRLHOOD

During the first years of my service in Dr. Flint's family, I was accustomed to share some indulgences with the children of my mistress. Though this seemed to me no more than right, I was grateful for it, and tried to merit the kindness by the faithful discharge of my duties. But I now entered on my fif-

---

Harriet Jacobs, *Incidents in the Life of a Slave Girl* (Boston: Published for the Author, 1861), 44–49, 51–55, 57–67, 82–89.

teenth year—a sad epoch in the life of a slave girl. My master began to whisper foul words in my ear. Young as I was, I could not remain ignorant of their import. I tried to treat them with indifference or contempt. The master's age, my extreme youth, and the fear that his conduct would be reported to my grandmother, made me bear this treatment for many months. He was a crafty man, and resorted to many means to accomplish his purposes. Sometimes he had stormy, terrific ways, that made his victims tremble; sometimes he assumed a gentleness that he thought must surely subdue. Of the two, I preferred his stormy moods, although they left me trembling. He tried his utmost to corrupt the pure principles my grandmother had instilled. He peopled my young mind with unclean images, such as only a vile monster could think of. I turned from him with disgust and hatred. But he was my master. I was compelled to live under the same roof with him—where I saw a man forty years my senior daily violating the most sacred commandments of nature. He told me I was his property; that I must be subject to his will in all things. My soul revolted against the mean tyranny. But where could I turn for protection? No matter whether the slave girl be as black as ebony or as fair as her mistress. In either case, there is no shadow of law to protect her from insult, from violence, or even from death; all these are inflicted by fiends who bear the shape of men. The mistress, who ought to protect the helpless victim, has no other feelings towards her but those of jealousy and rage. The degradation, the wrongs, the vices, that grow out of slavery, are more than I can describe. . . .

Every where the years bring to all enough of sin and sorrow; but in slavery the very dawn of life is darkened by these shadows. Even the little child, who is accustomed to wait on her mistress and her children, will learn, before she is twelve years old, why it is that her mistress hates such and such a one among the slaves. Perhaps the child's own mother is among those hated ones. She listens to violent outbreaks of jealous passion, and cannot help understanding what is the cause. She will become prematurely knowing in evil things. Soon she will learn to tremble when she hears her master's footfall. She will be compelled to realize that she is no longer a child. If God has bestowed beauty upon her; it will prove her greatest curse. That which commands admiration in the white woman only hastens the degradation of the female slave. I know that some are too much brutalized by slavery to feel the humiliation of their position; but many slaves feel it most acutely, and shrink from the memory of it. I cannot tell how much I suffered in the presence of these wrongs, nor how I am still pained by the retrospect. My master met me at every turn, reminding me that I belonged to him, and swearing by heaven and earth that he would compel me to submit to him. . . .

I longed for some one to confide in. I would have given the world to have laid my head on my grandmother's faithful bosom, and told her all my troubles. But Dr. Flint swore he would kill me, if I was not as silent as the grave. Then, although my grandmother was all in all to me, I feared her as well as loved her. I had been accustomed to look up to her with a respect bordering upon awe. I was very young, and felt shamefaced about telling her such impure things, especially as I knew her to be very strict on such sub-jects. Moreover, she was a woman of a high spirit. She was usually very quiet in her demeanor; but if her indignation was once roused, it was not very easily quelled. I had been told that she once chased a white gentleman with a loaded pistol, because he insulted one of her daughters. I dreaded the con-sequences of a violent outbreak; and both pride and fear kept me silent. But though I did not confide in my grandmother, and even evaded her vigilant watchfulness and inquiry, her presence in the neighborhood was some pro-tection to me. Though she had been a slave, Dr. Flint was afraid of her. He dreaded her scorching rebukes. Moreover, she was known and patronized by many people; and he did not wish to have his villany made public. It was lucky for me that I did not live on a distant plantation, but in a town not so large that the inhabitants were ignorant of each other's affairs. Bad as are the laws and customs in a slaveholding community, the doctor, as a profes-sional man, deemed it prudent to keep up some outward show of decency. . . .

I once saw two beautiful children playing together. One was a fair white child; the other was her slave; and also her sister. When I saw them embrac-ing each other, and heard their joyous laughter, I turned sadly away from the lovely sight. I foresaw the inevitable blight that would fall on the little slave's heart. I knew how soon her laughter would be changed to sighs. The fair child grew up to be a still fairer woman. From childhood to woman-hood her pathway was blooming with flowers, and overarched by a sunny sky. Scarcely one day of her life had been clouded when the sun rose on her happy bridal morning. How had those years dealt with her slave sister, the little playmate of her childhood? She, also, was very beautiful; but the flow-ers and sunshine of love were not for her. She drank the cup of sin, and shame, and misery, whereof her persecuted race are compelled to drink.

In view of these things, why are ye silent, ye free men and women of the north? Why do your tongues falter in maintenance of the right? Would that I had more ability! But my heart is so full, and my pen is so weak! There are noble men and women who plead for us, striving to help those who cannot help themselves. God bless them! God give them strength and courage to go on! God bless those, every where, who are laboring to advance the cause of humanity!

THE JEALOUS MISTRESS

I would ten thousand times rather that my children should be the half-starved paupers of Ireland than to be the most pampered among the slaves of America. I would rather drudge out my life on a cotton plantation, till the grave opened to give me rest, than to live with an unprincipled master and a jealous mistress. The felon's home in a penitentiary is preferable. He may repent, and turn from the error of his ways, and so find peace; but it is not so with a favorite slave. She is not allowed to have any pride of character. It is deemed a crime in her to wish to be virtuous. . . .

I had entered my sixteenth year, and every day it became more apparent that my presence was intolerable to Mrs. Flint. Angry words frequently passed between her and her husband. He had never punished me himself, and he would not allow any body else to punish me. In that respect, she was never satisfied; but, in her angry moods, no terms were too vile for her to bestow upon me. Yet I, whom she detested so bitterly, had far more pity for her than he had, whose duty it was to make her life happy. I never wronged her, or wished to wrong her; and one word of kindness from her would have brought me to her feet.

After repeated quarrels between the doctor and his wife, he announced his intention to take his youngest daughter, then four years old, to sleep in his apartment. It was necessary that a servant should sleep in the same room, to be on hand if the child stirred. I was selected for that office, and informed for what purpose that arrangement had been made. By managing to keep within sight of people, as much as possible, during the daytime, I had hitherto succeeded in eluding my master, though a razor was often held to my throat to force me to change this line of policy. At night I slept by the side of my great aunt, where I felt safe. He was too prudent to come into her room. She was an old woman, and had been in the family many years. Moreover, as a married man, and a professional man, he deemed it necessary to save appearances in some degree. But he resolved to remove the obstacle in the way of his scheme; and he thought he had planned it so that he should evade suspicion. He was well aware how much I prized my refuge by the side of my old aunt, and he determined to dispossess me of it. The first night the doctor had the little child in his room alone. The next morning, I was ordered to take my station as nurse the following night. A kind Providence interposed in my favor. During the day Mrs. Flint heard of this new arrangement, and a storm followed. I rejoiced to hear it rage. . . .

The secrets of slavery are concealed like those of the Inquisition. My master was, to my knowledge, the father of eleven slaves. But did the mothers dare to tell who was the father of their children? Did the other slaves dare to allude to it, except in whispers among themselves? No, indeed! They knew too well the terrible consequences. . . .

Southern women often marry a man knowing that he is the father of many little slaves. They do not trouble themselves about it. They regard such children as property, as marketable as the pigs on the plantation; and it is seldom that they do not make them aware of this by passing them into the slavetrader's hands as soon as possible, and thus getting them out of their sight. I am glad to say there are some honorable exceptions.

I have myself known two southern wives who exhorted their husbands to free those slaves towards whom they stood in a "parental relation;" and their request was granted. These husbands blushed before the superior nobleness of their wives' natures. Though they had only counselled them to do that which it was their duty to do, it commanded their respect, and rendered their conduct more exemplary. Concealment was at an end, and confidence took the place of distrust.

Though this bad institution deadens the moral sense, even in white women, to a fearful extent, it is not altogether extinct. I have heard southern ladies say of Mr. Such a one, "He not only thinks it no disgrace to be the father of those little niggers, but he is not ashamed to call himself their master. I declare, such things ought not to be tolerated in any decent society!"

A PERILOUS PASSAGE IN THE SLAVE GIRL'S LIFE

Dr. Flint contrived a new plan. He seemed to have an idea that my fear of my mistress was his greatest obstacle. In the blandest tones, he told me that he was going to build a small house for me, in a secluded place, four miles away from the town. I shuddered; but I was constrained to listen, while he talked of his intention to give me a home of my own, and to make a lady of me. Hitherto, I had escaped my dreaded fate, by being in the midst of people. My grandmother had already had high words with my master about me. She had told him pretty plainly what she thought of his character, and there was considerable gossip in the neighborhood about our affairs, to which the open-mouthed jealousy of Mrs. Flint contributed not a little. When my master said he was going to build a house for me, and that he could do it with little trouble and expense, I was in hopes something would happen to frustrate his scheme; but I soon heard that the house was actually begun. I vowed before my Maker that I would never enter it. . . . What *could* I do? I thought and thought, till I became desperate, and made a plunge into the abyss.

And now, reader, I come to a period in my unhappy life, which I would gladly forget if I could. The remembrance fills me with sorrow and shame. It pains me to tell you of it; but I have promised to tell you the truth, and I will do it honestly, let it cost me what it may. I will not try to screen myself behind the plea of compulsion from a master; for it was not so. Neither can I plead ignorance or thoughtlessness. For years, my master had done his utmost to pollute my mind with foul images, and to destroy the pure principles inculcated by my grandmother, and the good mistress of my childhood. The influences of slavery had had the same effect on me that they had on other young girls; they had made me prematurely knowing, concerning the evil ways of the world. I knew what I did, and I did it with deliberate calculation.

But, O, ye happy women, whose purity has been sheltered from childhood, who have been free to choose the objects of your affection, whose homes are protected by law, do not judge the poor desolate slave girl too severely! If slavery had been abolished, I, also, could have married the man of my choice; I could have had a home shielded by the laws; and I should have been spared the painful task of confessing what I am now about to relate; but all my prospects had been blighted by slavery. I wanted to keep myself pure; and, under the most adverse circumstances, I tried hard to preserve my self-respect; but I was struggling alone in the powerful grasp of the demon Slavery; and the monster proved too strong for me. I felt as if I was forsaken by God and man; as if all my efforts must be frustrated; and I became reckless in my despair.

I have told you that Dr. Flint's persecutions and his wife's jealousy had given rise to some gossip in the neighborhood. Among others, it chanced that a white unmarried gentleman had obtained some knowledge of the circumstances in which I was placed. He knew my grandmother, and often spoke to me in the street. He became interested for me, and asked questions about my master, which I answered in part. He expressed a great deal of sympathy, and a wish to aid me. He constantly sought opportunities to see me, and wrote to me frequently. I was a poor slave girl, only fifteen years old.

So much attention from a superior person was, of course, flattering; for human nature is the same in all. I also felt grateful for his sympathy, and encouraged by his kind words. It seemed to me a great thing to have such a friend. By degrees, a more tender feeling crept into my heart. He was an educated and eloquent gentleman; too eloquent, alas, for the poor slave girl who trusted in him. Of course I saw whither all this was tending. I knew the impassable gulf between us; but to be an object of interest to a man who is not married, and who is not her master, is agreeable to the pride and feelings of a slave, if her miserable situation has left her any pride or sentiment. It seems less degrading to give one's self, than to submit to compulsion. There is something akin to freedom in having a lover who has no control over you, except that which he gains by kindness and attachment. A master may treat you as rudely as he pleases, and you dare not speak; moreover, the wrong does not seem so great with an unmarried man, as with one who has a wife to be made unhappy. There may be sophistry in all this; but the condition of a slave confuses all principles of morality, and, in fact, renders the practice of them impossible.

When I found that my master had actually begun to build the lonely cottage, other feelings mixed with those I have described. Revenge, and calculations of interest, were added to flattered vanity and sincere gratitude for kindness. I knew nothing would enrage Dr. Flint so much as to know that I favored another; and it was something to triumph over my tyrant even in that small way. I thought he would revenge himself by selling me, and I was sure my friend, Mr. Sands, would buy me. He was a man of more generosity and feeling than my master, and I thought my freedom could be easily obtained from him. The crisis of my fate now came so near that I was desperate. I shuddered to think of being the mother of children that should be owned by my old tyrant. I knew that as soon as a new fancy took him, his victims were sold far off to get rid of them; especially if they had children. I had seen several women sold, with his babies at the breast. He never allowed his offspring by slaves to remain long in sight of himself and his wife. Of a man who was not my master I could ask to have my children well supported; and in this case, I felt confident I should obtain the boon. I also felt quite sure that they would be made free. With all these thoughts revolving in my mind, and seeing no other way of escaping the doom I so much dreaded, I made a headlong plunge. Pity me, and pardon me, O virtuous reader! You never knew what it is to be a slave; to be entirely unprotected by law or custom; to have the laws reduce you to the condition of a chattel, entirely subject to the will of another. . . .

The months passed on. I had many unhappy hours. I secretly mourned over the sorrow I was bringing on my grandmother, who had so tried to shield me from harm. I knew that I was the greatest comfort of her old age, and that it was a source of pride to her that I had not degraded myself, like most of the slaves. I wanted to confess to her that I was no longer worthy of her love; but I could not utter the dreaded words.

As for Dr. Flint, I had a feeling of satisfaction and triumph in the thought of telling *him*. From time to time he told me of his intended arrangements, and I was silent. At last, he came and told me the cottage was completed, and ordered me to go to it. I told him I would never enter it. He said, "I have heard enough of such talk as that. You shall go, if you are carried by force; and you shall remain there."

I replied, "I will never go there. In a few months I shall be a mother."

He stood and looked at me in dumb amazement, and left the house without a word. I thought I should be happy in my triumph over him. But now that the truth was out, and my relatives would hear of it, I felt wretched. Humble as were their circumstances, they had pride in my good character. Now, how could I look them in the face? My self-respect was gone! I had resolved that I would be virtuous, though I was a slave. I had said, "Let the storm beat! I will brave it till I die." And now, how humiliated I felt!

I went to my grandmother. My lips moved to make confession, but the words stuck in my throat. I sat down in the shade of a tree at her door and began to sew. I think she saw something unusual was the matter with me. . . . Presently, in came my mistress, like a mad woman, and accused me concerning her husband. My grandmother, whose suspicions had been previously awakened, believed what she said. She exclaimed, "O Linda! has it come to this? I had rather see you dead than to see you as you now are. You are a disgrace to your dead mother." She tore from my fingers my mother's wedding ring and her silver thimble. "Go away!" she exclaimed, "and never come to my house, again." . . . How I longed to throw myself at her feet, and tell her all the truth! But she had ordered me to go, and never to come there again. After a few minutes, I mustered strength, and started to obey her. With what feelings did I now close that little gate, which I used to open with such an eager hand in my childhood! It closed upon me with a sound I never heard before.

Where could I go? I was afraid to return to my master's. I walked on recklessly, not caring where I went, or what would become of me. When I had gone four or five miles, fatigue compelled me to stop. . . . At last, with great effort I roused myself, and walked some distance further, to the house of a woman who had been a friend of my mother. When I told her why I was there, she spoke soothingly to me; but I could not be comforted. I thought I could bear my shame if I could only be reconciled to my grandmother. I longed to open my heart to her. I thought if she could know the real state of the case, and all I had been bearing for years, she would perhaps judge me less harshly. My friend advised me to send for her. I did so; but days of agonizing suspense passed before she came. Had she utterly forsaken me? No. She came at last. I knelt before her, and told her the things that had poisoned my life; how long I had been persecuted; that I saw no way of escape; and in an hour of extremity I had become desperate. She listened in silence. I told her I would bear any thing and do any thing, if in time I had hopes of obtaining her forgiveness. I begged of her to pity me, for my dead mother's sake. And she did pity me. She did not say, "I forgive you," but she looked at me lovingly, with her eyes full of tears. She laid her old hand gently on my head, and murmured, "Poor child! Poor child!"

37

HAMMATT BILLINGS

The Auction Sale

Publicizing the sheer inhumanity of human bondage was foremost in the minds of abolitionists as they whipped up antislavery fervor in the antebellum North. Few books accomplished this as well as Harriet Beecher Stowe's Uncle Tom's Cabin; or, Life Among the Lowly *(1852). Her vivid depiction of slavery's devastating impact on family life and its violent core prompted many Southern legislatures to ban its sale and distribution in their states. A decade after the book was published Stowe met President Lincoln at the White House, and he supposedly quipped, "So you're the little woman who wrote the book that started this great war."*

One unusual feature of Uncle Tom's Cabin *was its use of engravings. Few novels in the 1850s published illustrations of any kind, but Stowe's story featured six full-page engravings by Hammatt Billings (1818–1874). A rising artist and architect from Boston who shared Stowe's politics, Billings had earlier designed the masthead for the* Liberator, *William Lloyd Garrison's famous abolitionist newspaper.*

Each of Billings's engravings depicted a pivotal scene from Uncle Tom's Cabin *and one — "The Auction Sale" — captured the horrors of the domestic slave trade. In this scene, a slave family is being forcibly separated. Tom's master, Haley, is in Kentucky to add to his supply of slaves. Clad in a top hat, white topcoat, and checked pants, Haley puts money down on fourteen-year-old Albert but refuses to purchase Albert's mother despite her pleas to be kept with her son. Haley believes she is too old and not worth much.*

Hammatt Billings, *The Auction Sale.* Engraving from Harriet Beecher Stowe, *Uncle Tom's Cabin; or, Life Among the Lowly.* (Boston: John P. Jewett & Company, 1852), p. 174. © Corbis.

THE AUCTION SALE.   Page 174.

© Corbis

QUESTIONS TO CONSIDER

1. How does Billings portray slavery as a dehumanizing institution?
2. How are blacks and whites represented differently? What do these representations suggest about members of each race in the South?
3. How might this image help us understand why white Southerners would find *Uncle Tom's Cabin* objectionable?

38

MARY LOIS WALKER MORRIS
Marriage and Mormonism

Born in Leeds, England, Mary Lois Walker Morris (1835–1919) immigrated with her parents to St. Louis, Missouri, after they joined the Church of Jesus Christ of Latter-day Saints in the 1840s. Married in 1852 to John Morris, also a Mormon, she soon moved to Cedar City, Utah, and began a family. Then tragedy struck: in short succession, her only child died and her husband succumbed to tuberculosis. Mary was a widow at age 20.

Mary Lois Walker Morris, *Before the Manifesto: the Life Writings of Mary Lois Walker Morris* (Logan, UT: Utah State University Press, 2007) 121–24.

On her husband's deathbed, however, she made a promise that would shape her future. At John's request, she agreed to marry his older brother, Elias, thus becoming his second wife. It was not an easy decision for Mary, despite the church's approval of plural marriages and her strong belief in its sacred legitimacy. As she recorded in her diary, she feared becoming a burden to Elias and interrupting his relationship to his first wife, Mary Parry, and their two children. Her writings reveal a constant internal battle to stay obedient to her faith and accept her role as the second wife.

QUESTIONS TO CONSIDER

1. Why does Mary agree to marry Elias?
2. How does Mary describe her relationship to Elias? Would you describe it as a "happy" marriage?
3. What are the social costs *and* advantages experienced by Mary when she agrees to become Elias's second wife?

TWENTY YEARS OLD

I was twenty years old and in the forty eight years that have elapsed since that winter evening I have never seen a darker hour.

I considered the covenant I had made with my husband on his death bed. I knew that Elias was worth of all the confidence and love that his brother had reposed in him, and I knew that I was all that my departed husband had in the world to look to his interest in the world to come and his eternal increase. God knows that I believed and had accepted the principle that His law required of me. I took a mind's eye view of the other brothers. One was older than Elias and two were younger. The youngest, Hugh, had sent word from California that it was his right to have me. There were also two Apostles, to either of whom I might have been married, but could I have taken either of these and kept my concience perfectly clear before God? Did either of these excel Elias in point of honor, virtue and integrity? Could either of these take the interest in my departed husband that his brother Elias did? Had either of them, except Elias, been asked to perform this sacred duty, though all had known and loved my husband? Was I willing to endure whatever might befall me in this straight and narrow path I had chosen? Yes, I had already counted the cost, had already tasted the bitter cup which I had agreed to drink to the dregs.

A PECULIAR SITUATION

A few months after my husbands death I chanced, one day, to meet his brother Elias, who told me that he and his wife were invited to a wedding to which he would have liked to have taken me, but as the invitation was for only one couple he could not do so.

In the Spring he invited me to attend a party with him and his wife, and told me that at a certain time he would call for me. Being ready in good time and having an opportunity to go with a friend I left before he arrived. Perhaps this was unwise, also unkind to him, as opportunities for showing me any regard were very meager. My motive, however, was principally to save his wife's feelings, and also perhaps, I was prompted by my own natural independence.

In the Spring following the winter that I lived with Elias and his wife, William P. [Price] Jones, the husband of your Aunt Barbara Morris Jones, came home from his Las Vegas mission, and with him came a Brother——, who had formerly beed a drill master in Her Majesty's Army in India. I was told that this gentleman had formed an attachment for me before he saw me, from what he had heard of me. He was a man of refinement, as may be supposed, having occupied such a position, was fine looking, of good address, well acquainted with horsemanship, a very good singer and devout and sincere in the religion he had espoused. I have no idea how he began to come to the house, but he came frequently and took a great deal of pleasure in teaching my brother-in-law sword exercises. He would come also on Sunday evenings and sing for us and afterwards we would all sing together.

A FRIENDLY ADMONITION

When this had continued for some time, a friend of the family who understood my position and sympathized with me, drew me aside one evening and in a very kind manner told me that if I intended to be true to Elias and the covenant I had made, I had better not allow my affections to turn in a channel where I might be led to break my sacred vows. This friend was unmarried and ten years my senior, and he felt that there was danger of my being led in a direction opposed to that of duty, and I must admit that it was me and my God and stirling principle for the battle.

A CALL OF DUTY

Some time afterwards, on a Sunday evening, my brother-in-law asked me to come and sit down at the family hearth, as he wanted to talk about something. Of course I knew upon what subject he wished to converse and sensed my position keenly. It was very embarrassing for all concerned, as there was a third person present, whichever way we might take it, and all had an equal right to be present as all were equally concerned. In honor of the Principle, obedience to which had created the necessity of our coming together as a family, we were obliged to meet in order to discuss the preliminaries which should cause us to enter into a relationship which would place us in a more trying but more exalted position. For how can gold be cleansed from dross except it be placed in the crucible? Imagine how hard it was for a girl, not twenty years old, to be asked if she intended to be true to one of the three persons present, and that in the interest of a fourth person, and he departed this life? And yet how very hard also for the lady who was the third to the two contracting parties, in this particular case? And how hard for this man of God, this loving brother, to take another's wife into his care and to all present appearances break up the happiness of his married life? Nothing but the love he bore his brother and the covenants he had made at the water's edge could have induced him to climb the rugged path, upon which alone now he could ask the Heavenly Father's blessing. And in view of all these circumstances, how very much easier for this girl widow to renounce the sacred covenant she had made with her husband's brother, at the death bed of the former, than to be true to what the law of God required and to the life-long contract she had made? No one was to blame for the circumstances which surrounded us, but this was one of the ordeals we had to meet, as all have their fiery trials to pass through who set their faces like steel to serve God to the end.

There was only one answer that I could make to this solemn and weighty question, and that was that I intended to keep my covenant.

The time now approached for our marriage, according to the date set by President Young a year previous. There was much laborious work to be done to prepare for a journey to Salt Lake City where we were to receive our Endowments in the House of the Lord. We traveled by ox-team, and were two weeks upon the road. It was in the month of May, 1856. Our company consisted of five persons, viz.—Elias and his wife and their two children and myself. Upon our arrivan we stayed at the home of our brother-in-law, Richard V. Morris, which was situated near the City Hall, and often, during the time that we stayed there I went outside that historic structure and prayed that my deceased husband would come in person and tell me if he really did require me to drink this bitter cup.

He came not. I was again left alone, I and my Heavenly Father, for the battle. I talked with my beloved and only sister about the matter. She suggested that perhaps my husband wanted to prove me and know what I should do while standing alone in this dark world. Now, as I look upon things, I think that my Heavenly Father wished to prove how I should stand the trying ordeal.

If I had wished to forsake my husband I should have done so while he was in this life, and could have chosen another help-meet, and I had the power, for I knew that he was not in the best of health. But it was not in my nature to desert an afflicted person. No, and now my duty was clear, I would lay my life's happiness upon the altar of the requirements of the will of God, and trust in him for the future.

There was no one to take me by the hand and give me a word of encouragement at that critical moment, or at least no one did so. All had their trials.

THE CONSUMMATION

So I kneeled on the altar in God's Holy House with the deepest dread in my heart that I had ever known. No physical strength could have drawn me there, had I consulted my own feelings. But God required it. I sensed keenly that it was no my happiness alone that was sacrificed, but it was marring the happiness of others, which rendered the cup doubly bitter. I knew that nothing that I could do would remove the sting that comes to the heart of a first wife when her husband enters into the order of Plural Marriage. I had been so concious of the suffering she must of necessity pass through, that during the time that I had been living with my sister-in-law, I felt that no service was too menial, or labor too great, to serve her, and so strong was my sympathy for her that I felt willing to forego almost everything, except honor, for her sake. There was only one way to relieve the situation and that was to recant, and this I could not, I dared not, do. I would rather have died than have shrunk from my duty. If God is angry with me, I can only leave myself to His Mercy. My motives were as pure as those of an angel.

On our return to Cedar City, we arrived about mid-day and Mother had prepared an excellent repast, set out on a long table. I could not imagine what it was for. It had no charm for me, my heart was too sad in contemplating the future. After many, many long years, however, I have come to the conclusion that our dear mother intended it as a wedding feast.

39

ELIZABETH CADY STANTON
Pioneering Women's Rights

The women's movement before the Civil War was among the most intensely unpopular of the era's reform efforts. The ideal of domesticity, which assigned to women a separate and less-powerful role in the family than that of men, made the reformists' claims for equal rights, especially the right to vote, a violation of social convention and of the religious beliefs of many. Friendships were enormously important in providing the courage and emotional support women needed to oppose the sometimes oppressive institutions of family, religion, and politics. Elizabeth Cady Stanton (1815–1902) was inspired by Lucretia Mott, whose Quaker ministry had given her experience in public speaking that she applied to the antislavery cause. The two had met at an antislavery convention in London in 1840 and, as Stanton was to recall later, "resolved to hold a convention as soon as we returned home, and form a society to advocate the rights of women." Yet eight years elapsed before this resolve bore fruit in the Seneca Falls Woman's Rights Convention. In the interim, Stanton had settled in three different locations, borne three children (she would eventually have seven), and assumed all the other cares of a financially strapped, middle-class household.

Elizabeth Cady Stanton, *Eighty Years and More: Reminiscences, 1815–1897* (London: T. Fisher Unwin, 1898), 79–83, 143–50; copy of the Declaration of Sentiments, courtesy of the Seneca Falls Historical Society, Seneca Falls, NY.

In her autobiography, Eighty Years and More, *published in 1898 when she was eighty-three, and excerpted below, Stanton remained astonished at the avalanche of criticism and sarcasm provoked by the Seneca Falls participants' "Declaration of Sentiments," a document modeled on the U.S. Declaration of Independence and reprinted here. Commenting on the meeting, a Philadelphia newspaper asserted, "A pretty girl is equal to ten thousand men," and sneered, "The ladies of Philadelphia . . . are resolved to maintain their rights as Wives, Belles, Virgins and Mothers, and not as Women." But the women who met at Seneca Falls in upstate New York in 1848 had launched a women's rights movement that would continue, mainly by following Stanton's strategy of making woman suffrage the major objective until that goal was achieved in 1920 with the ratification of the Nineteenth Amendment to the Constitution.*

QUESTIONS TO CONSIDER

1. Why was Stanton's attendance at the antislavery convention in 1840 so important to her development as a women's rights advocate?
2. How did Stanton's life between 1840 and the Seneca Falls Convention of 1848 deepen her commitment to women's rights?
3. What was the relationship between abolitionism and the women's rights movement? Do you think that civil rights movements for women and those for African Americans are natural collaborators or competitors? Explain.
4. What relevance to today's world do you see in the Declaration of Sentiments?

EIGHTY YEARS AND MORE

Our chief object in visiting England at this time was to attend the World's Anti-slavery Convention, to meet June 12, 1840, in Freemasons' Hall, London. Delegates from all the anti-slavery societies of civilized nations were invited, yet, when they arrived, those representing associations of women were rejected. Though women were members of the National Anti-slavery Society, accustomed to speak and vote in all its conventions, and to take an equally active part with men in the whole anti-slavery struggle, and were there as delegates from associations of men and women, as well as those distinctively of their own sex, yet all alike were rejected because they were women. Women, according to English prejudices at that time, were excluded by Scriptural texts from sharing equal dignity and authority with men in all reform associations; hence it was to English minds pre-eminently unfitting that women should be admitted as equal members to a World's Convention. The question was hotly debated through an entire day. My husband made a very eloquent speech in favor of admitting the women delegates.

When we consider . . . [the] many remarkable women . . . [who] were all compelled to listen in silence to the masculine platitudes on woman's sphere, one may form some idea of the indignation of unprejudiced friends, and especially that of such women as Lydia Maria Child, Maria Chapman, Deborah Weston, Angelina and Sarah Grimké, and Abby Kelly,[1] who were impatiently waiting and watching on this side, in painful suspense, to hear how their delegates were received. Judging from my own feelings, the women on both sides of the Atlantic must have been humiliated and chagrined, except as these feelings were outweighed by contempt for the shallow reasoning of their opponents and their comical pose and gestures in some of the intensely earnest flights of their imagination.

The clerical portion of the convention was most violent in its opposition. The clergymen seemed to have God and his angels especially in their care and keeping, and were in agony lest the women should do or say something to shock the heavenly hosts. Their all-sustaining conceit gave them abundant assurance that their movements must necessarily be all-pleasing to the celestials whose ears were open to the proceedings of the World's Convention. . . .

It was really pitiful to hear narrow-minded bigots, pretending to be teachers and leaders of men, so cruelly remanding their own mothers, with the rest of womankind, to absolute subjection to the ordinary masculine type of humanity. I always regretted that the women themselves had not taken part in the debate before the convention was fully organized and the question of delegates settled. It seemed to me then, and does now, that all delegates with credentials from recognized societies should have had a voice in the organization of the convention, though subject to exclusion afterward. However, the women sat in a low curtained seat like a church choir, and modestly listened to the French, British, and American Solons[2] for twelve of the longest days in June, as did, also, our grand Garrison and Rogers[3] in the gallery. They scorned a convention that ignored the rights of the very women who had fought, side by side, with them in the anti-slavery conflict. . . .

As the convention adjourned, the remark was heard on all sides, "It is about time some demand was made for new liberties for women." As Mrs. Mott and I walked home, arm in arm, commenting on the incidents of the day, we resolved to hold a convention as soon as we returned home, and form a society to advocate the rights of women. At the lodging house on Queen Street, where a large number of delegates had apartments, the discussions were heated at every meal, and at times so bitter that, at last, Mr. Birney packed his valise and sought more peaceful quarters. Having strongly opposed the admission of women as delegates to the convention it was rather embarrassing to meet them, during the intervals between the various sessions, at the table and in the drawing room.

These were the first women I had ever met who believed in the equality of the sexes and who did not believe in the popular orthodox religion. The

---

1. Child, Chapman, Weston, the Grimké sisters, and Kelly were famous early feminists.
2. **French, British, and American Solons:** Here Stanton refers sarcastically to the notoriously sage statesman of ancient Greece, Solon.
3. **Garrison and Rogers:** Abolitionists William Lloyd Garrison (see p. 235) and Nathaniel P. Rogers.

acquaintance of Lucretia Mott, who was a broad, liberal thinker on politics, religion, and all questions of reform, opened to me a new world of thought. . . .

In the spring of 1847 we moved to Seneca Falls. Here we spent sixteen years of our married life, and here our other children—two sons and two daughters—were born. . . .

The house we were to occupy had been closed for some years and needed many repairs, and the grounds, comprising five acres, were overgrown with weeds. My father gave me a check and said, with a smile, "You believe in woman's capacity to do and dare; now go ahead and put your place in order." After a minute survey of the premises and due consultation with one or two sons of Adam, I set the carpenters, painters, paper-hangers, and gardeners at work, built a new kitchen and woodhouse, and in one month took possession. Having left my children with my mother, there were no impediments to a full display of my executive ability. In the purchase of brick, timber, paint, etc., and in making bargains with workmen, I was in frequent consultation with Judge Sackett and Mr. Bascom. The latter was a member of the Constitutional Convention, then in session in Albany, and as he used to walk down whenever he was at home, to see how my work progressed, we had long talks, sitting on boxes in the midst of tools and shavings, on the status of women. I urged him to propose an amendment to Article II, Section 3, of the State Constitution, striking out the word "male," which limits the suffrage to men. But, while he fully agreed with all I had to say on the political equality of women, he had not the courage to make himself the laughing-stock of the convention. Whenever I cornered him on this point, manlike he turned the conversation to the painters and carpenters. However, these conversations had the effect of bringing him into the first woman's convention, where he did us good service. . . .

There was quite an Irish settlement at a short distance, and continual complaints were coming to me that my boys threw stones at their pigs, cows, and the roofs of their houses. This involved constant diplomatic relations in the settlement of various difficulties, in which I was so successful that, at length, they constituted me a kind of umpire in all their own quarrels. If a drunken husband was pounding his wife, the children would run for me. Hastening to the scene of action, I would take Patrick by the collar, and, much to his surprise and shame, make him sit down and promise to behave himself. I never had one of them offer the least resistance, and in time they all came to regard me as one having authority. I strengthened my influence by cultivating good feeling. I lent the men papers to read, and invited their children into our grounds; giving them fruit, of which we had abundance, and my children's old clothes, books, and toys. I was their physician, also—with my box of homeopathic medicines I took charge of the men, women, and children in sickness. Thus the most amicable relations were established, and, in any emergency, these poor neighbors were good friends and always ready to serve me.

But I found police duty rather irksome, especially when called out dark nights to prevent drunken fathers from disturbing their sleeping children, or to minister to poor mothers in the pangs of maternity. Alas! alas! who can measure the mountains of sorrow and suffering endured in unwelcome motherhood in the abodes of ignorance, poverty, and vice, where terror-stricken women and children are the victims of strong men frenzied with passion and intoxicating drink?

Up to this time life had glided by with comparative ease, but now the real struggle was upon me. My duties were too numerous and varied, and none sufficiently exhilarating or intellectual to bring into play my higher faculties. I suffered with mental hunger, which, like an empty stomach, is very depressing. I had books, but no stimulating companionship. To add to my general dissatisfaction at the change from Boston, I found that Seneca Falls was a malarial region, and in due time all the children were attacked with chills and fever which, under homeopathic treatment in those days, lasted three months. The servants were afflicted in the same way. Cleanliness, order, the love of the beautiful and artistic, all faded away in the struggle to accomplish what was absolutely necessary from hour to hour. . . .

I now fully understood the practical difficulties most women had to contend with in the isolated household, and the impossibility of woman's best development if in contact, the chief part of her life, with servants and children. . . . The general discontent I felt with woman's portion as wife, mother, housekeeper, physician, and spiritual guide, the chaotic conditions into which everything fell without her constant supervision, and the wearied, anxious look of the majority of women impressed me with a strong feeling that some active measures should be taken to remedy the wrongs of society in general, and of women in particular. My experience at the World's Anti-slavery Convention, all I had read of the legal status of women, and the oppression I saw everywhere, together swept across my soul, intensified now by many personal experiences. It seemed as if all the elements had conspired to impel me to some onward step. I could not see what to do or where to begin—my only thought was a public meeting for protest and discussion.

In this tempest-tossed condition of mind I received an invitation to spend the day with Lucretia Mott, at Richard Hunt's, in Waterloo. There I met several members of different families of Friends, earnest, thoughtful women. I poured out, that day, the torrent of my long-accumulating discontent, with such vehemence and indignation that I stirred myself, as well as the rest of the party, to do and dare anything. My discontent, according to Emerson, must have been healthy, for it moved us all to prompt action, and we decided, then and there, to call a "Woman's Rights Convention." We wrote the call that evening and published it in the *Seneca County Courier* the next day, the 14th of July, 1848, giving only five days' notice, as the convention was to be held on the 19th and 20th. . . . The convention, which was held two days in the Methodist Church, was in every way a grand success. The house was crowded at every session, the speaking good, and a religious earnestness dignified all the proceedings.

These were the hasty initiative steps of "the most momentous reform that had yet been launched on the world—the first organized protest against

the injustice which had brooded for ages over the character and destiny of
one-half the race." No words could express our astonishment on finding,
a few days afterward, that what seemed to us so timely, so rational, and so
sacred, should be a subject for sarcasm and ridicule to the entire press of the
nation. With our Declaration of Rights and Resolutions for a text, it seemed
as if every man who could wield a pen prepared a homily on "woman's
sphere." All the journals from Maine to Texas seemed to strive with each
other to see which could make our movement appear the most ridiculous.
The anti-slavery papers stood by us manfully and so did Frederick Douglass,
both in the convention and in his paper, *The North Star*, but so pronounced
was the popular voice against us, in the parlor, press, and pulpit, that most of
the ladies who had attended the convention and signed the declaration, one
by one, withdrew their names and influence and joined our persecutors. Our
friends gave us the cold shoulder and felt themselves disgraced by the whole
proceeding.

If I had had the slightest premonition of all that was to follow that
convention, I fear I should not have had the courage to risk it, and I must
confess that it was with fear and trembling that I consented to attend another, one month afterward, in Rochester. Fortunately, the first one seemed
to have drawn all the fire, and of the second but little was said. But we had
set the ball in motion, and now, in quick succession, conventions were held
in Ohio, Indiana, Massachusetts, Pennsylvania, and in the City of New York,
and have been kept up nearly every year since.

DECLARATION OF SENTIMENTS, 1848

When, in the course of human events, it becomes necessary for one portion
of the family of man to assume among the people of the earth a position
different from that which they have hitherto occupied, but one to which
the laws of nature and of nature's God entitle them, a decent respect to the
opinions of mankind requires that they should declare the causes that impel
them to such a course.

We hold these truths to be self-evident: that all men and women are created equal; that they are endowed by their Creator with certain inalienable
rights; that among these are life, liberty, and the pursuit of happiness; that
to secure these rights governments are instituted, deriving their just powers
from the consent of the governed. Whenever any form of government becomes destructive of these ends, it is the right of those who suffer from it
to refuse allegiance to it, and to insist upon the institution of a new government, laying its foundation on such principles, and organizing its powers in
such form, as to them shall seem most likely to effect their safety and happiness. Prudence, indeed, will dictate that governments long established should
not be changed for light and transient causes; and accordingly all experience
hath shown that mankind are more disposed to suffer, while evils are suffer-
able, than to right themselves by abolishing the forms to which they were

accustomed. But when a long train of abuses and usurpations, pursuing invariably the same object evinces a design to reduce them under absolute despotism, it is their duty to throw off such government, and to provide new guards for their future security. Such has been the patient sufferance of the women under this government, and such is now the necessity which constrains them to demand the equal station to which they are entitled.

The history of mankind is a history of repeated injuries and usurpations on the part of man toward woman, having in direct object the establishment of an absolute tyranny over her. To prove this, let facts be submitted to a candid world.

He has never permitted her to exercise her inalienable right to the elective franchise.

He has compelled her to submit to laws, in the formation of which she had no voice.

He has withheld from her rights which are given to the most ignorant and degraded men—both natives and foreigners.

Having deprived her of this first right of a citizen, the elective franchise, thereby leaving her without representation in the halls of legislation, he has oppressed her on all sides.

He has made her, if married, in the eye of the law, civilly dead.

He has taken from her all right in property, even to the wages she earns.

He has made her, morally, an irresponsible being, as she can commit many crimes with impunity, provided they be done in the presence of her husband. In the covenant of marriage, she is compelled to promise obedience to her husband, he becoming to all intents and purposes, her master—the law giving him power to deprive her of her liberty, and to administer chastisement.

He has so framed the laws of divorce, as to what shall be the proper causes of divorce, and in case of separation, to whom the guardianship of the children shall be given, as to be wholly regardless of the happiness of women—the law, in all cases, going upon a false supposition of the supremacy of man, and giving all power into his hands.

After depriving her of all rights as a married woman, if single and the owner of property, he has taxed her to support a government which recognizes her only when her property can be made profitable to it.

He has monopolized nearly all the profitable employments, and from those she is permitted to follow, she receives but a scanty remuneration.

He closes against her all the avenues to wealth and distinction, which he considers most honorable to himself. As a teacher of theology, medicine, or law, she is not known.

He has denied her the facilities for obtaining a thorough education—all colleges being closed against her.

He allows her in Church as well as State, but a subordinate position, claiming Apostolic authority for her exclusion from the ministry, and, with some exceptions, from any public participation in the affairs of the Church.

He has created a false public sentiment by giving to the world a different code of morals for men and women, by which moral delinquencies which exclude women from society, are not only tolerated, but deemed of little account in man.

He has usurped the prerogative of Jehovah himself, claiming it as his right to assign for her a sphere of action, when that belongs to her conscience and to her God.

He has endeavored, in every way that he could, to destroy her confidence in her own powers, to lessen her self-respect, and to make her willing to lead a dependent and abject life.

Now, in view of this entire disfranchisement of one-half the people of this country, their social and religious degradation,—in view of the unjust laws above mentioned, and because women do feel themselves aggrieved, oppressed, and fraudulently deprived of their most sacred rights, we insist that they have immediate admission to all the rights and privileges which belong to them as citizens of these United States.

In entering upon the great work before us, we anticipate no small amount of misconception, misrepresentation, and ridicule; but we shall use every instrumentality within our power to effect our object. We shall employ agents, circulate tracts, petition the State and national Legislatures, and endeavor to enlist the pulpit and the press in our behalf. We hope this Convention will be followed by a series of Conventions, embracing every part of the country.

Firmly relying upon the final triumph of the Right and the True, we do this day affix our signatures to this declaration.

40

JOHN LEECH

Bloomerism

Amelia (Jenks) Bloomer (1818–1894), an early advocate for women's rights and temperance, was born and raised in central New York. In 1840 she married David Bloomer and moved to Seneca Falls, where her interest in reform grew. In 1848 she attended the first women's rights convention held in her hometown, and the next year she became the founding editor of the Lily, *a temperance newspaper run mostly by women.*

During her four-year stint as editor, Bloomer befriended Elizabeth Cady Stanton and gradually embraced wider calls for reform. Her newspaper bore witness to her expanding advocacy. By the time Bloomer sold the Lily *in 1853, its circulation had grown from roughly 300 to 4,000. Men and women increasingly looked to it for information about the cause of women's rights. Also driving up sales was Bloomer's public call for*

John Leech, "Bloomerism—An American Custom," *Punch*, 1851. © Chronicle / Alamy.

reform in women's dress, which made her and her newspaper a target for controversy and even scorn.

Bloomer argued that women's clothes should model their cry for greater rights and thus should be less restricting, more comfortable, and more useful to the tasks of daily life. She asked women to model a different kind of fashion, one liberated from corsets and petticoats. Instead they should don loose-fitting trousers cropped at the ankles and topped by a short skirt breaking at the knees and a trim waistcoat. As women tried out the new fashion, both in the United States and in England, detractors quickly christened it the "Bloomer Costume" or simply "Bloomers." It became a short-lived but popular symbol of women's protest for equal rights. It also emerged as a topic of ceaseless ridicule by conservative critics who found the clothing to be unfeminine, unflattering, and unnatural.

The image below appeared in the satirical British magazine Punch *in 1851.*

BLOOMERISM—AN AMERICAN CUSTOM.

QUESTIONS TO CONSIDER

1. In addition to their trousers, skirts, and waistcoats, in what other ways are the women wearing the Bloomer Costume portrayed as different than the other women in the image? What does that suggest to you?
2. What is the role of the children in the image?
3. What are the social and personal dangers suggested by the women dressed in the Bloomer Costume?

PART SIX

The Growing Sectional Controversy
Slavery and Its Discontents

By the mid-nineteenth century, the issue of slavery dominated politics at both the national and the local levels. Its morality, economy, sustainability, and effect upon the nation's soul were fodder for debate in election halls and across family tables. Most Americans, slave or free, came to recognize that the future of the nation depended on how it continued to integrate slavery into daily life—or not.

African Americans themselves generated much of the heat that ignited the controversies over the "peculiar institution" and attracted some sympathetic whites to their cause. Henry "Box" Brown was a slave who, in the early 1800s, executed one of the most famous escapes from bondage in history. He wrote an account of his life under slavery and publicized the abolitionist cause as an entertainer and entrepreneur. David Walker, a free black man, published a scathing account of the peculiar institution that prompted Southern politicians to ban it from their borders. The slave Nat Turner's rebellion in 1831 set off a firestorm of controversy. Abolitionist William Lloyd Garrison saw it as a fitting response to the evils of bondage; his enemies viewed the uprising as a threat to white freedom. Less strident in his antislavery views was Frederick Law Olmsted, who wrote a book about his travels in the slave states that, while ambivalent about the character of Southern slaves, spotlighted the tense state of racial relations.

During the late antebellum era, moderate white opponents of slavery coolly pled their case on the basis of economics and political theory. Carl Schurz, for example, argued that slavery undercut the free labor of men and women.

Defenders of slavery, however, mounted fierce counterattacks. James Henry Hammond penned a passionate defense of slavery in his native South Carolina, claiming that the institution made possible the continued expansion of liberty in America. Few Northerners or Southerners, however, could dispute the physical toll of slavery on slaves' bodies as recorded in new forms of commercial photography developed in the mid-nineteenth century. And few could discount that a day of reckoning between the sections was fast nearing by the late 1850s. Indeed, the 1859 armed insurrection at Harpers Ferry, West Virginia, spearheaded by abolitionist John Brown and recounted here by his African American supporter Osborne Anderson, illuminates how the country was rapidly approaching the point at which compromise on the matter of slavery was impossible.

Nat Turner's Rebellion (1831)

41

NAT TURNER

A Slave Insurrection

Slave owners, especially those in areas with large slave populations, lived in dread of uprisings. Rebellions in South Carolina in 1739, Virginia in 1800, Louisiana in 1811, and South Carolina again in 1822 kept such fears alive. In 1831 Nat Turner (1800–1831), a slave in Southampton County, Virginia, led the most sensational rebellion of all. Beginning on August 21, Turner's revolt lasted only five days, but it claimed the lives of at least fifty whites. In response, terrified white Southerners gunned down slaves and free blacks and increased restrictions on slaves' education, marriage, and freedom to gather together. The rebellion also dealt a serious blow to any chance of the South's voluntarily emancipating its slaves.

The Confessions of Nat Turner, the source of the following excerpts, was published in 1832 by Thomas R. Gray, who interviewed Turner shortly before he was tried and executed. Gray had interviewed several other slaves who had been involved in the

---

The Confessions of Nat Turner, Leader of the Late Insurrection in Southampton, Virginia, as Fully and Voluntarily Made to Thomas R. Gray (Baltimore: Lucas and Deaver, 1831), 7–18.

uprisings, and he was clearly aware of the great commercial potential for a Turner manuscript. Personally believing that Turner was a dangerous fanatic, Gray may have shaped the account in a sensational manner to make the manuscript more saleable. Nonetheless, the account provides a fascinating window into Turner's world, especially his sources of inspiration and motivation for leading the revolt.

QUESTIONS TO CONSIDER

1. What was Nat Turner's revelation? What purpose did he consider himself destined to fulfill?
2. How well planned was the rebellion? Why did it fail?
3. What did Turner and his compatriots expect to achieve by their rebellion?
4. Historians have speculated about which parts of the text are authentically Turner's and which parts represent the voice of Thomas Gray. Can you identify differences?

I was thirty-one years of age the second of October last, and born the property of Benjamin Turner, of this county. In my childhood a circumstance occurred which made an indelible impression on my mind, and laid the groundwork of that enthusiasm which has terminated so fatally to many both white and black, and for which I am about to atone at the gallows. It is here necessary to relate this circumstance—trifling as it may seem, it was the commencement of that belief which has grown with time, and even now, sir, in this dungeon, helpless and forsaken as I am, I cannot divest myself of. Being at play with other children, when three or four years old, I was telling them something, which my mother overhearing, said it had happened before I was born. I stuck to my story, however, and related some things which went in her opinion to confirm it. Others being called on were greatly astonished, knowing that these things had happened, and caused them to say in my hearing, I surely would be a prophet, as the Lord had shown me things that had happened before my birth. And my father and mother strengthened me in this my first impression, saying in my presence, I was intended for some great purpose, which they had always thought from certain marks on my head and breast.

My grandmother, who was very religious, and to whom I was much attached—my master, who belonged to the church, and other religious persons who visited the house, and whom I often saw at prayers, noticing the singularity of my manners, I suppose, and my uncommon intelligence for a child, remarked I had too much sense to be raised—and if I was, I would never be of any service to any one—as a slave. The manner in which I learned to read and write, not only had great influence on my own mind, as I acquired it with the most perfect ease, so much so that I have no recollection whatever of learning the alphabet—but to the astonishment of the family, one day, when a book was shown me to keep me from crying, I began spelling the names of different objects—this was a source of wonder to all in the neighborhood, particularly the blacks—and this learning was constantly improved at all opportunities. When I got large enough to go to work, while employed, I was reflecting on many things that would present themselves to my imagination. I was not addicted to stealing in my youth, nor have never been. Yet such was the confidence of the Negroes in the neighborhood, even at this early period of my life, in my superior judgment, that they would often carry me with them when they were going on any roguery, to plan for them. Growing up among them, with this confidence in my superior judgment, and when this, in their opinions, was perfected by divine inspiration, from the circumstances already alluded to in my infancy, and which belief was ever afterward zealously inculcated by the austerity of my life and manners, which became the subject of remark by white and black. By this time, having arrived to man's estate, and hearing the Scriptures commented on at meetings, I was struck with that particular passage which says: "Seek ye the kingdom of Heaven and all things shall be added unto you." I reflected much on this passage, and prayed daily for light on this subject. As I was praying one day at my plough, the spirit spoke to me, saying "Seek ye the kingdom of Heaven and all things shall be added unto you." *Question*—What do you mean by the Spirit? *Answer*—The Spirit that spoke to the prophets in former days—and I was greatly astonished, and for two years prayed continually, whenever my duty would permit—and then again I had the same revelation, which fully confirmed me in the impression that I was ordained for some great purpose in the hands of the Almighty. Several years rolled round, in which many events occurred to strengthen me in this my belief. . . . I began to direct my attention to this great object, to fulfill the purpose for which, by this time, I felt assured I was intended. Knowing the influence I had obtained over the minds of my fellow servants, (not by the means of conjuring and such like tricks—for to them I always spoke of such things with contempt) but by the communion of the Spirit whose revelations I often communicated to them, and they believed and said my wisdom came from God.

And on the twelfth of May 1828, I heard a loud noise in the heavens, and the Spirit instantly appeared to me and said the Serpent was loosened, and Christ had laid down the yoke he had borne for the sins of men, and that I should take it on and fight against the Serpent, for the time was fast approaching, when the first should be last and the last should be first. *Question*—Do you not find yourself mistaken now? *Answer*—Was not Christ crucified? And by signs in the heavens that it would make known to me when I should commence the great work—and until the first sign appeared, I should conceal it from the knowledge of men—and on the appearance of the sign (the eclipse of the sun last February), I should arise and prepare myself, and slay my enemies with their own weapons. And immediately on the sign appearing in the heavens, the seal was removed from my lips, and I communicated the great work laid out for me to do, to four in whom I had the greatest confidence (Henry, Hark, Nelson, and Sam). It was intended by us to have begun the work of death on the fourth of July last. Many were the plans formed and rejected by us, and it affected my mind to such a degree that I fell sick, and the time passed without our coming to any determination how to commence—still forming new schemes and rejecting them when the sign appeared again, which determined me not to wait longer.

Since the commencement of 1830, I had been living with Mr. Joseph Travis, who was to me a kind master, and placed the greatest confidence in me; in fact, I had no cause to complain of his treatment to me. On Saturday evening, the twentieth of August, it was agreed between Henry, Hark, and myself to prepare a dinner the next day for the men we expected, and then to concert a plan, as we had not yet determined on any. Hark on the following morning brought a pig, and Henry brandy, and being joined by Sam, Nelson, Will, and Jack, they prepared in the woods a dinner, where, about three o'clock, I joined them. . . .

I saluted them on coming up, and asked Will how came he there; he answered his life was worth no more than others, and his liberty as dear to him. I asked him if he thought to obtain it? He said he would or lose his life. This was enough to put him in full confidence. Jack, I knew, was only a tool in the hands of Hark. It was quickly agreed we should commence at home (Mr. J. Travis') on that night, and until we had armed and equipped ourselves, and gathered sufficient force, neither age nor sex was to be spared (which was invariably adhered to). We remained at the feast until about two hours in the night, when we went to the house and found Austin; they all went to the cider press and drank, except myself. On returning to the house, Hark went to the door with an ax, for the purpose of breaking it open, as we knew we were strong enough to murder the family, if they were awakened by the noise; but reflecting that it might create an alarm in the neighborhood, we determined to enter the house secretly, and murder them while sleeping. Hark got a ladder and set it against the chimney, on which I ascended, and hoisting a window, entered and came down stairs, unbarred the door, and removed the guns from their places. It was then observed that I must spill the first blood. On which armed with a hatchet, and accompanied by Will, I entered my master's chamber; it being dark, I could not give a death blow, the hatchet glanced from his head, he sprang from the bed and called his wife, it was his last word. Will laid him dead, with a blow of his ax, and Mrs. Travis shared the same fate, as she lay in bed. The murder of this family, five in number, was the work of a moment, not one of them awoke; there was a little infant sleeping in a cradle, that was forgotten, until we had left the house and gone some distance, when Henry and Will returned and killed it. We got here four guns that would shoot, and several old muskets, with a pound or two of powder. We remained some time at the barn, where we paraded; I formed them in a line as soldiers, and after carrying them through all the maneuvers I was master of, marched them off to Mr. Salathul Francis', about six hundred yards distant. Sam and Will went to the door and knocked. Mr. Francis asked who was there, Sam replied it was him, and he had a letter for him, on which he got up and came to the door; they immediately seized him, and dragging him out a little from the door, he was dispatched by repeated blows on the head; there was no other white person in the family. We started from there for Mrs. Reese's, maintaining the most perfect silence on our march, where finding the door unlocked, we entered, and murdered Mrs. Reese in her bed, while sleeping; her son awoke, but it was only to sleep the sleep of death, he had only time to say who is that, and he was no more. From Mrs. Reese's we went to Mrs. Turner's, a mile distant, which we reached about sunrise on Monday morning. Henry, Austin, and Sam went to the still, where, finding Mr. Pebbles, Austin shot him, and the rest of us went to the house; as we approached, the family discovered us, and shut the door. Vain hope! Will, with one stroke of his ax, opened it, and we entered and found Mrs. Turner and Mrs. Newsome in the middle of a room almost frightened to death. Will immediately killed Mrs. Turner, with one blow of his ax. I took Mrs. Newsome by the hand, and with the sword I had when I was apprehended, I struck her several blows over the head, but not being able to kill her, as the sword was dull. Will turning around and discovering it, dispatched her also. A general destruction of property and search for money and ammunition always succeeded the murders. By this time my company amounted to fifteen, and nine men mounted, who started for Mrs. White-head's (the other six were to go through a byway to Mr. Bryant's and re-join us at Mrs. Whitehead's). . . . As we pushed on to the house, I discovered someone running round the garden, and thinking it was some of the white family, I pursued them, but finding it was a servant girl belonging to the house, I returned to commence the work of death, but they whom I left had not been idle; all the family were already murdered, but Mrs. Whitehead and her daughter Margaret. As I came round to the door I saw Will pulling Mrs. Whitehead out of the house, and at the step he nearly severed her head from her body, with his broad ax. Miss Margaret, when I discovered her had concealed herself in the corner, formed by the projection of the cellar cap from the house; on my approach she fled, but was soon overtaken, and af-ter repeated blows with a sword, I killed her by a blow on the head with a fence rail. By this time, the six who had gone by Mr. Bryant's rejoined us, and informed me they had done the work of death assigned them. We again divided, part going to Mr. Richard Porter's and from thence to Nathaniel Francis', the others to Mr. Howell Harris', and Mr. T. Doyle's. On my reach-ing Mr. Porter's, he had escaped with his family. I understood there that the alarm had already spread.

I proceeded to Mr. Levi Waller's, two or three miles distant. I took my station in the rear, and as it was my object to carry terror and devastation wherever we went, I placed fifteen or twenty of the best armed and most to be relied on in front, who generally approached the houses as fast as their horses could run; this was for two purposes, to prevent their escape and strike terror to the inhabitants—on this account I never got to the houses, after leaving Mrs. Whitehead's, until the murders were committed, except in one case. I sometimes got in sight in time to see the work of death completed, viewed the mangled bodies as they lay, in silent satisfaction, and immediately started in quest of other victims. Having murdered Mrs. Waller and ten children, we started for Mr. William Williams'—having killed him and two little boys that were there; while engaged in this, Mrs. Williams fled and got some distance from the house, but she was pursued, overtaken, and compelled to get up behind one of the company, who brought her back, and after showing her the mangled body of her lifeless husband, she was told to get down and lay by his side, where she was shot dead. I then started for Mr. Jacob Williams', where the family were murdered. Here we found a young man named Drury, who had come on business with Mr. Williams. He was pursued, overtaken, and shot. Mrs. Vaughan's was the next place we visited—and after murdering the family here, I determined on starting for Jerusalem. Our number amounted now to fifty or sixty, all mounted and armed with guns, axes, swords, and clubs. On reaching Mr. James W. Parker's gate, immediately on the road leading to Jerusalem, and about three miles distant, it was proposed to me to call there, but I objected, as I knew he was gone to Jerusalem, and my object was to reach there as soon as possible; but some of the men having relations at Mr. Parker's it was agreed that they might call and get his people. I remained at the gate on the road, with seven or eight; the others going across the field to the house, about half a mile off. After waiting some time for them, I became impatient, and started to the house for them, and on our return we were met by a party of white men, who had pursued our blood-stained track and who had fired on those at the gate and dispersed them, which I knew nothing of, not having been at that time rejoined by any of them. Immediately on discovering the whites, I order my men to halt and form, as they appeared to be alarmed. The white men, eighteen in number, approached us in about one hundred yards, when one of them fired.

I then ordered my men to fire and rush on them; the few remaining stood their ground until we approached within fifty yards, when they fired and retreated. We pursued and overtook some of them who we thought we left dead; after pursuing them about two hundred yards, and rising a little hill, I discovered they were met by another party, and had halted, and were reloading their guns, thinking that those who retreated first, and the party who fired on us at fifty or sixty yards distant, had all only fallen back to meet others with ammunition. As I saw them reloading their guns, and more coming up than I saw at first, and several of my bravest men being wounded, the others became panic struck and squandered over the field; the white men pursued and fired on us several times. Hark had his horse shot under him, and I caught another for him as it was running by me; five or six of my men were wounded, but none left on the field; finding myself defeated here I instantly determined to go through a private way, and cross the Nottoway River at the Cypress Bridge, three miles below Jerusalem, and attack that place in the rear, as I expected they would look for me on the other road, and I had a great desire to get there to procure arms and ammunition. After going a short distance in this private way, accompanied by about twenty men, I overtook two or three who told me the others were dispersed in every direction. After trying in vain to collect a sufficient force to proceed to

Jerusalem, I determined to return, as I was sure they would make back to their old neighborhood, where they would rejoin me, make new recruits, and come down again. On my way back, I called at Mrs. Thomas's, Mrs. Spencer's, and several other places. The white families having fled, we found no more victims to gratify our thirst for blood, we stopped at Major Ridley's quarter for the night, and being joined by four of his men, with the recruits made since my defeat, we mustered now about forty strong. After placing out sentinels, I laid down to sleep, but was quickly roused by a great racket. Starting up, I found some mounted, and others in great confusion; one of the sentinels having given the alarm that we were about to be attacked, I ordered some to ride round and reconnoiter, and on their return the others being more alarmed, not knowing who they were, fled in different ways, so that I was reduced to about twenty again; with this I determined to attempt to recruit, and proceed on to rally in the neighborhood I had left. Dr. Blunt's was the nearest house, which we reached just before day; on riding up the yard, Hark fired a gun. We expected Dr. Blunt and his family were at Major Ridley's, as I knew there was a company of men there; the gun was fired to ascertain if any of the family were at home; we were immediately fired upon and retreated leaving several of my men. I do not know what became of them, as I never saw them afterward. Pursuing our course back, and coming in sight of Captain Harris's, where we had been the day before, we discovered a party of white men at the house, on which all deserted me but two (Jacob and Nat), we concealed ourselves in the woods until near night, when I sent them in search of Henry, Sam, Nelson, and Hark, and directed them to rally all they could at the place we had had our dinner the Sunday before, where they would find me, and I accordingly returned there as soon as it was dark, and remained until Wednesday evening, when discovering white men riding around the place as though they were looking for someone, and none of my men joining me, I concluded Jacob and Nat had been taken, and compelled to betray me. On this I gave up all hope for the present; and on Thursday night, after having supplied myself with provisions from Mr. Travis's, I scratched a hole under a pile of fence rails in a field, where I concealed myself for six weeks, never leaving my hiding place but for a few minutes in the dead of night to get water, which was very near; thinking by this time I could venture out, I began to go about in the night and eavesdrop the houses in the neighborhood; pursuing this course for about a fortnight and gathering little or no intelligence, afraid of speaking to any human being, and returning every morning to my cave before the dawn of day. I know not how long I might have led this life, if accident had not betrayed me, a dog in the neighborhood passing by my hiding place one night while I was out was attracted by some meat I had in my cave, and crawled in and stole it, and was coming out just as I returned. A few nights after, two Negroes having started to go hunting with the same dog, and passed that way, the dog came again to the place, and having just gone out to walk about, discovered me and barked, on which, thinking myself discovered, I spoke to them to beg concealment. On making myself known, they fled from me. Knowing then they would betray me, I immediately left my hiding place, and was pursued almost incessantly until I was taken a fortnight afterward by Mr. Benjamin Phipps, in a little hole I had dug out with my sword, for the purpose of concealment, under the top of a fallen tree. On Mr. Phipps discovering the place of my concealment, he cocked his gun and aimed at me. I requested him not to shoot, and I would give up, upon which he demanded my sword. I delivered it to him, and he brought me to prison. During the time I was pursued, I had many hair breadth escapes, which your time will not permit you to relate. I am here loaded with chains, and willing to suffer the fate that awaits me.

[Gray:] I here proceeded to make some inquiries of him, after assuring him of the certain death that awaited him, and that concealment would only bring destruction of the innocent as well as guilty, of his own color, if he knew of any extensive or concerted plan. His answer was, I do not.

42

WILLIAM LLOYD GARRISON

Who Is to Blame?

Nat Turner's rebellion occurred just when slavery was under attack from other quarters. In 1829, a free black man named David Walker published his incendiary Walker's Appeal, in Four Articles; Together with a Preamble, to the Coloured Citizens of the World, But in Particular, and Very Expressly, to Those of the United States of America, *which quoted the Declaration of Independence in its justification of a slave insurrection. (See Document 44 on page 242.) Then William Lloyd Garrison (1805–1879), who would also cite the Declaration of Independence, broke with the tradition among white abolitionists of calling for gradual emancipation. From the first issue of* the Liberator, *which Garrison edited and first published in Boston on January 1, 1831, Garrison demanded the immediate and unconditional abolition of slavery.*

The Southern states reacted viscerally to Nat Turner's rebellion. In the immediate hysteria, slaves and free blacks were gunned down. The states strengthened the slave system by restricting the rights of free blacks, as well as the right of owners to free slaves. The states not only augmented the patrols that constricted the mobility of the slave population, but also set limits on black religious meetings and ensured that marriage did not restrict the slave trade. And they moved on many fronts to close the South to antislavery propaganda, touching off a national debate by forbidding the federal postal service from delivering antislavery writings such as the Liberator *in Southern states.*

William Lloyd Garrison, "The Insurrection," *Liberator*, September 3, 1831, http://fair-use
.org/the-liberator/1831/09/03/the-insurrection.

QUESTIONS TO CONSIDER

1. Did William Lloyd Garrison approve of Nat Turner's rebellion? Cite evidence in the document to support your answer.
2. What reasons did Garrison give for the uprising?
3. What comparisons did he draw to explain the event to his readers?

THE *LIBERATOR*, SEPTEMBER 3, 1831

What we have so long predicted,—at the peril of being stigmatized as an alarmist and declaimer,—has commenced its fulfillment. The first step of the earthquake, which is ultimately to shake down the fabric of oppression, leaving not one stone upon another, has been made. The first drops of blood, which are but the prelude to a deluge from the gathering clouds, have fallen. The first flash of the lightning, which is to smite and consume, has been felt. The first wailings of a bereavement, which is to clothe the earth in sackcloth, have broken upon our ears. . . .

You have seen, it is to be feared, but the beginning of sorrows. All the blood which has been shed will be required at your hands. At your hands alone? No—but at the hands of the people of New-England and of all the free states. The crime of oppression is national. The south is only the agent in this guilty traffic. But, remember! the same causes are at work which must inevitably produce the same effects; and when the contest shall have again begun, it must be again a war of extermination. In the present instance, no quarters have been asked or given.

But we have killed and routed them now—we can do it again and again—we are invincible! A dastardly triumph, well becoming a nation of oppressors. Detestable complacency, that can think, without emotion, of the extermination of the blacks! We have the power to kill *all*—let us, therefore, continue to apply the whip and forge new fetters!

In his fury against the revolters, who will remember their wrongs? What will it avail them, though the catalogue of their sufferings, dripping with warm blood fresh from their lacerated bodies, be held up to extenuate their conduct? It is enough that the victims were black—that circumstance makes them less precious than the dogs which have been slain in our streets! They were black—brutes, pretending to be men—legions of curses upon their memories! They were black—God made them to serve us!

Ye patriotic hypocrites! ye panegyrists[1] of Frenchmen, Greeks, and Poles! ye fustian[2] declaimers for liberty! ye valiant sticklers for equal rights among yourselves! ye haters of aristocracy! ye assailants of monarchies! ye republican nullifiers! ye treasonable disunionists! be dumb! Cast no reproach upon

---

1. **panegyrists:** People who celebrate a person, group, or deed.
2. **fustian:** Pretentious; pompous.

the conduct of the slaves, but let your lips and cheeks wear the blisters of condemnation!

Ye accuse the pacific friends of emancipation of instigating the slaves to revolt. Take back the charge as a foul slander. The slaves need no incentives at our hands. They will find them in their stripes—in their emaciated bodies—in their ceaseless toil—in their ignorant minds—in every field, in every valley, on every hill-top and mountain, wherever you and your fathers have fought for liberty—in your speeches, your conversations, your celebrations, your pamphlets, your newspapers—voices in the air, sounds from across the ocean, invitations to resistance above, below, around them! What more do they need? Surrounded by such influences, and smarting under their newly made wounds, is it wonderful[3] that they should rise to contend—as other "heroes" have contended—for their lost rights? It is *not* wonderful.

In all that we have written, is there aught [anything] to justify the excesses of the slaves? No. Nevertheless, they deserve no more censure than the Greeks in destroying the Turks, or the Poles in exterminating the Russians, or our fathers in slaughtering the British. Dreadful, indeed, is the standard erected by worldly patriotism! For ourselves, we are horror-struck at the late tidings. We have exerted our utmost efforts to avert the calamity. We have warned our countrymen of the danger of persisting in their unrighteous conduct. We have preached to the slaves the pacific precepts of Jesus Christ. We have appealed to christians, philanthropists and patriots, for their assistance to accomplish the great work of national redemption through the agency of moral power—of public opinion—of individual duty. How have we been received? We have been threatened, proscribed, vilified and imprisoned—a laughing-stock and a reproach. Do we falter, in view of these things? Let time answer. If we have been hitherto urgent, and bold, and denunciatory in our efforts,—hereafter we shall grow vehement and active with the increase of danger. We shall cry, in trumpet tones, night and day,—Wo to this guilty land, unless she speedily repent of her evil doings! The blood of millions of her sons cries aloud for redress! IMMEDIATE EMANCIPATION can alone save her from the vengeance of Heaven, and cancel the debt of ages!

---

3. **wonderful:** Evoking wonder; surprising.

43

JAMES HENRY HAMMOND
Defending Slavery

James Henry Hammond (1807–1864) was a powerful proslavery voice during the ante-bellum era. Born in Newberry District, South Carolina, he graduated from South Carolina College at age 18, studied law and earned admission to the bar ten years later, and quickly became one of his state's leading politicians. He served as a member of the U.S. House of Representatives from 1835 to 1836, as South Carolina's governor from 1842 to 1844, and as a U.S. senator from 1857 until 1860.

Few men became as publicly identified with the defense of slavery as Hammond. He concentrated his thoughts in a private letter written in 1844 to Reverend Thomas Brown of the Free Church of Glasgow, an international advocate of emancipation. Succinct, barbed, and bold in tone, the letter, which is reprinted below, reveals many of the most popular reasons white Americans, especially those living in the South, stubbornly supported slavery and reviled men like William Lloyd Garrison.

QUESTIONS TO CONSIDER

1. How did Hammond use the Bible to defend slavery?
2. Why did he think that freedom for slaves was a terrible idea?
3. According to Hammond, what historical good came of slavery?

LETTER

To The Free Church Of Glasgow, On The Subject Of Slavery.

Executive Department, South Carolina, 21 June 1844

Your memorial, like all that have been sent to me, denounces slavery in the severest terms; as "traversing every law of nature, and violating the most sacred domestic relations, and the primary rights of man." You and your Presbytery are Christians. You profess to believe, and no doubt do believe, that the laws laid down in the Old and New Testaments for the government of man, in his moral, social and political relations, were all the direct revelation of God himself. Does it never occur to you, that in anathematizing [cursing] slavery, you deny this divine sanction of those laws, and repudiate both

---

James H. Hammond, "Reply to a Memorial from the Free Church of Scotland on Slavery. 1844," in *Selections from the Letters and Speeches of Hon. James H. Hammond of South Carolina* (New York: John F. Trow & Co., Printers, 1866), 107–13.

Christ and Moses; or charge God with downright crime, in regulating and perpetuating slavery in the Old Testament, and the most criminal neglect, in not only not abolishing, but not even reprehending it, in the New? If these Testaments came from God, it is impossible that slavery can "traverse the laws of nature, or violate the primary rights of man." What those laws and rights really are, mankind have not agreed. But they are clear to God; and it is blasphemous for any of His creatures to set up their notions of them in opposition to His immediate and acknowledged Revelation. Nor does *our* system of slavery outrage the most sacred domestic relations. Husbands and wives, parents and children, among our slaves, are seldom separated, except from necessity or crime. The same reasons induce much more frequent separations among the white population in this, and, I imagine, in almost every other country.

But I make bold to say that the Presbytery of the Free Church of Glasgow, and nearly all the abolitionists in every part of the world, in denouncing our domestic slavery, denounce a thing of which they know absolutely nothing—nay, which does not even exist. You weep over the horrors of the Middle Passage, which have ceased, so far as we are concerned; and over pictures of chains and lashes here, which have no existence but in the imagination. Our sympathies are almost equally excited by the accounts published by your Committees of Parliament—and therefore true; and which have been verified by the personal observation of many of us—of the squalid misery, loathsome disease, and actual starvation, of multitudes of the unhappy laborers—not of Ireland only, but of England—nay, of Glasgow itself. Yet we never presume to interfere with your social or municipal regulations—your aggregated wealth and congregated misery—nor the crimes attendant on them, nor your pitiless laws for their suppression. And when we see by your official returns, that even the best classes of English agricultural laborers can obtain for their support but seven pounds of bread and four *ounces* of meat per week, and when sick or out of employment, must either starve or subsist on charity, we cannot but look with satisfaction to the condition of our slave laborers, who usually receive as a weekly allowance, fifteen pounds of bread, and three *pounds* of bacon—have their children fed without stint, and properly attended to—are all well clothed, and have comfortable dwellings, where, with their gardens and poultry yards, they can, if the least industrious, more than realize for themselves the vain hope of the great French king, that he might see every peasant in France have his fowl upon his table on the Sabbath—who, from the proceeds of their own crop, purchase even luxuries and finery—who labor scarcely more than nine hours a day, on the average of the year—and who, in sickness, in declining years, in infancy and decrepitude, are watched over with a tenderness scarcely short of parental. When we contemplate the *known* condition of your operatives, of whom, that of your agricultural laborers is perhaps the least wretched, we are not only not ashamed of that of our slaves, but are always ready to challenge a comparison, and should be highly gratified to submit to a reciprocal investigation, by enlightened and impartial judges.

You are doubtless of opinion that all these advantages in favor of the slave, if they exist, are more than counterbalanced by his being deprived of his freedom. Can you tell me what *freedom* is—who possesses it, and how much of it is requisite for human happiness? Is your operative, existing in the physical and moral condition which your own official returns depict—deprived too of every political right, even that of voting at the polls—who is not cheered by the slightest hope of ever improving his lot or leaving his children to a better, and who actually seeks the four walls of a prison, the hulks, and transportation, as comparative blessings—is *he* free—*sufficiently* free? Can you say that this sort of freedom—the liberty to beg or [steal]—to choose between starvation and a prison—does or ought to make him happier than our slave, situated as I have truly described him, without a single care or gloomy forethought?

But you will perhaps say, it is not in the Thing, but in the Name, that the magic resides—that there is a vast difference between being *called a slave* and being *made one*, though equally enslaved by law, by social forms, and by immutable necessity. This is an ideal and sentimental distinction which it will be difficult to bring the African race to comprehend. But if it be true, and freedom is a name and idea, rather than reality, how many are there then entitled even to that name, except by courtesy; and how many are able to enjoy the idea in perfection? Does your operative regard it as a sufficient compensation for the difference between four ounces and three *pounds* of bacon? If he does, he is a rare philosopher. In your powerful kingdom social grade is as thoroughly established and acknowledged as military rank. Your commonalty see among themselves a series of ascending classes, and, rising above them all, many more, composed of men not a whit superior to themselves in any of the endowments of nature, who yet in name, in idea, and in fact, possess greater worldly privileges. To what one of all these classes does *genuine* freedom belong? To the duke, who fawns upon the prince—to the baron, who knuckles to the duke, or to the commoner, who crouches to the baron?

Doubtless you all boast of being ideally free; while the American citizen counts *your* freedom slavery, and could not brook a state of existence in which he daily encountered fellow mortals, acknowledged and privileged as his superiors, solely by the accident of birth. He, too, in turn, will boast of his freedom, which might be just as little to your taste. I will not pursue this topic farther. But I think you must admit that there is not so much in a name; and that ideal or imputed freedom is a very uncertain source of happiness.

You must also agree, that it would be a bold thing for you or any one to undertake to solve the great problem of good and evil—happiness and misery, and decide in what worldly condition man enjoys most, and suifers [suffers] least. Your profession calls on you to teach that his true happiness is seldom found upon the stormy sea of politics, or in the mad race of ambition, in the pursuits of mammon, or the cares of hoarded gain; that, in short, the wealth and honors of this world are to be despised and shunned. Will you then say, that the slave must be wretched, because he is debarred from them? or because he does not indulge in the dreams of philosophy, the wrangling of sectarians, or the soul-disturbing speculations of the skeptic? or because, having never tasted of what is *called* freedom, he is ignorant of its ideal blessings, and as contented with his lot, such as it is, as most men are with theirs?

You and your Presbytery doubtless desire, as we all should, to increase the happiness of the human family. But since it is so difficult, if not impossible, to determine in what earthly state man may expect to enjoy most of it, why can you not be content, to leave him in that respect where God has placed him; to give up the ideal and the doubtful, for the real; to restrict yourselves to the faithful fulfilment of your great mission of preaching "the glad tidings of salvation" *to all classes and conditions*; or, at the very least, sacredly abstain from all endeavors to ameliorate the lot of man by revolution, bloodshed, massacre, and desolation, to which all attempts at abolition in this country, in the present, and, so far as I can see, in any future age, must inevitably lead?

Be satisfied with the improvement which slavery has made, and which nothing but slavery could have made to the same extent, in the race of Ham.[1] Look at the negro in Africa—a naked savage—almost a cannibal, ruthlessly oppressing and destroying his fellows; idle, treacherous, idolatrous, and such a disgrace to the image of his God, in which you declare him to be made, that some of the wisest philosophers have denied him the possession of a soul. See him here—three millions at least of his rescued race—civilized, contributing immensely to the subsistence of the human family, his passions restrained, his affections cultivated, his bodily wants and infirmities provided for, and the true religion of his Maker and Redeemer taught him. Has slavery been a curse to him? Can you think God has ordained it for no good purpose? or, not content with the blessings it has already bestowed, do you desire to increase them still? Before you act, be sure your heavenly Father has revealed to you the means. Wait for the inspiration which brought the Israelites out of Egypt, which carried salvation to the Gentiles.

I have written you a longer letter than I intended. But the question of slavery is a much more interesting subject to us, involving, as it does, the fate of all that we hold dear, than anything connected with John L. Brown[2] can be to you; and I trust you will read my reply with as much consideration as I have read your memorial.

I have the honor to be, very respectfully,

Your obedient servant,
J. H. HAMMOND.

---

1. **race of Ham:** Reference to the biblical Ham and his descendants, black Africans.
2. **John L. Brown:** South Carolina man executed in 1844 for helping a young slave woman, whom he married, escape from her bondage.

FOR CRITICAL THINKING

1. While Turner and Garrison both advocated the speedy abolition of slavery, only Turner called for violence. Why?
2. Turner, Garrison, and Hammond all rooted their particular beliefs about slavery in the need to protect liberty in America. How could these authors all draw upon the idea of liberty to reach such very different points of view?
3. How might Garrison and Hammond have come to a peaceful resolution about the future of slavery in America?

44

DAVID WALKER

An Appeal for Revolution

Few books savaged slavery with greater force than David Walker's Appeal to the Coloured Citizens of the World. *It warned of a day when God would chasten America for its sin of slavery and encouraged blacks to overthrow Southern society. Not surprisingly, its publication in 1829 struck fear in the hearts of slaveholders. Privately printed by the author himself in Boston and distributed up and down the eastern seaboard through an informal network of black sailors, stewards, travelers, and ministers, it so frightened Southern legislators about a pending race revolt that they had copies seized at ports, implemented new antiliteracy laws among black Southerners, and put a price on the author's head. But they had little to fear about future publications. Illness cut short Walker's life in August 1830, and he went to his grave with his dream of immediate emancipation still decades away from being realized.*

There are scarce clues about what inspired Walker to pen such a scathing account of nineteenth-century race relations. Walker (1796–1830) was born near Wilmington, North Carolina, the son of a free African American woman and a slave father (and, therefore, he was legally free under the laws of the day). He left few permanent records behind him, but he wrote of witnessing the horrors of slavery up close, traipsing across different slave states, maintaining a strong connection with the African Methodist Episcopal Church (a leading abolitionist institution), migrating to Charleston, and

David Walker, *Walker's Appeal, in Four Articles; Together with a Preamble, to the Coloured Citizens of the World, but in Particular, and Very Expressly, to Those of the United States of America, Written in Boston, State of Massachusetts, September 28, 1829* (Boston: REVISED AND PUBLISHED BY DAVID WALKER, 1830), 19–21, 41–46. http://docsouth.unc.edu/nc/walker/walker.html.

eventually making his home in Boston, where he supported himself by selling used clothing. The cities he called home at various times during his life all shared histories of violent opposition to slavery, most notably in Charleston where Denmark Vesey's unsuccessful plot in 1822 to recruit a black army, seize the local armory, and sack the city produced hysteria among the white community. In Boston, a major center of antislavery activity in the 1820s, Walker was a sales agent for Freedom's Journal, *a black newspaper, and he fraternized with black and white church members and authors dedicated to opposing the peculiar institution.* Appeal *ranks among the most incendiary indictments of human bondage published in the antebellum era.*

QUESTIONS TO CONSIDER

1. Why does Walker perceive Americans as the most evil of all slaveholders throughout all of history?
2. What is Walker's view of whites and their religion?
3. Describe Walker's prediction for America's future as a nation. In what ways does he foretell the coming of the Civil War?

Are we MEN!!—I ask you, O my brethren! are we MEN? Did our Creator make us to be slaves to dust and ashes like ourselves? Are they not dying worms as well as we? Have they not to make their appearance before the tribunal of Heaven, to answer for the deeds done in the body, as well as we? Have we any other Master but Jesus Christ alone? Is he not their Master as well as ours?—What right then, have we to obey and call any other Master, but Himself? How we could be so *submissive* to a gang of men, whom we cannot tell whether they are *as good* as ourselves or not, I never could conceive. However, this is shut up with the Lord, and we cannot precisely tell—but I declare, we judge men by their works.

The whites have always been an unjust, jealous, unmerciful, avaricious and blood-thirsty set of beings, always seeking after power and authority.—We view them all over the confederacy of Greece, where they were first known to be any thing, (in consequence of education) we see them there, cutting each other's throats—trying to subject each other to wretchedness and misery—to effect which, they used all kinds of deceitful, unfair, and unmerciful means. We view them next in Rome, where the spirit of tyranny and deceit raged still higher. We view them in Gaul, Spain, and in Britain.—In fine, we view them all over Europe, together with what were scattered about in Asia and Africa, as heathens, and we see them acting more like devils than accountable men. But some may ask, did not the blacks of Africa, and the mulattoes of Asia, go on in the same way as did the whites of Europe. I answer, no—they never were half so avaricious, deceitful and unmerciful as the whites, according to their knowledge.

But we will leave the whites or Europeans as heathens, and take a view of them as Christians, in which capacity we see them as cruel, if not more so than ever. In fact, take them as a body, they are ten times more cruel, avaricious and unmerciful than ever they were; for while they were heathens, they were bad enough it is true, but it is positively a fact that they were not quite so audacious as to go and take vessel loads of men, women and children, and in cold blood, and through devilishness, throw them into the sea, and murder them in all kind of ways. While they were heathens, they were too ignorant for such barbarity. But being Christians, enlightened and sensible, they are completely prepared for such hellish cruelties. Now suppose God were to give them more sense, what would they do? If it were possible, would they not *dethrone* Jehovah and seat themselves upon his throne? I therefore, in the name and fear of the Lord God of Heaven and of earth, divested of prejudice either on the side of my colour or that of the whites, advance my suspicion of them, whether they are *as good by nature* as we are or not. Their actions, since they were known as a people, have been the reverse, I do indeed suspect them, but this, as I before observed, is shut up with the Lord, we cannot exactly tell, it will be proved in succeeding generations.—The whites have had the essence of the gospel as it was preached by my master and his apostles—the Ethiopians have not, who are to have it in its meridian splendor—the Lord will give it to them to their satisfaction. I hope and pray my God, that they will make good use of it, that it may be well with them. . . .

But Christian Americans, not only hinder their fellow creatures, the Africans, but thousands of them *will absolutely beat a coloured person nearly to death, if they catch him on his knees, supplicating the throne of grace.* This barbarous cruelty was by all the heathen nations of antiquity, and is by the Pagans, Jews and Mahometans of the present day, left entirely to Christian Americans to inflict on the Africans and their descendants, that their cup which is nearly full may be completed. I have known tyrants or usurpers of human liberty in different parts of this country to take their fellow creatures, the coloured people, and beat them until they would scarcely leave life in them; what for? Why they say "The black devils had the audacity to be found *making prayers and supplications to the God who made them!!!!*" Yes, I have known small collections of coloured people to have convened together, for no other purpose than to worship God Almighty, in spirit and in truth, to the best of their knowledge; when tyrants, calling themselves *patrols,* would also convene and wait almost in breathless silence for the poor coloured people to commence singing and praying to the Lord our God, as soon as they had commenced, the wretches would burst in upon them and drag them out and commence beating them as they would rattle-snakes—many of whom, they would beat so unmercifully, that they would hardly be able to crawl for weeks and sometimes for months. Yet the American minister send out missionaries to convert the heathen, while they keep us and our children sunk at their feet in the most abject ignorance and wretchedness that ever a people was afflicted with since the world began. Will the Lord suffer this people to proceed much longer? Will he not stop them in their career? Does he regard the heathens abroad, more than the heathens among the Americans? Surely the Americans must believe that God is partial, notwithstanding his Apostle Peter, declared before Cornelius and others that he has no respect to persons, but in every nation he that feareth God and worketh righteousness is accepted with him.—"The word," said he, which God sent unto the children of Israel, preaching peace, "by Jesus Christ, (he is Lord of all.")[1] . . .

Have not the Americans the Bible in their hands? Do they believe it? Surely they do not. See how they treat us in open violation of the Bible!! They no doubt will be greatly offended with me, but if God does not awaken them, it will be, because they are superior to other men, as they have represented themselves to be. Our divine Lord and Master said, "all things whatsoever ye would that men should do unto you, do ye even so unto them." But an American minister, with the Bible in his hand, holds us and our children in the most abject slavery and wretchedness. Now I ask them, would they like for us to hold them and their children in abject slavery and wretchedness? No says one, that never can be done—your are too abject and ignorant to do i—you are not men—your were made to be slaves to us, to dig up gold and silver for us and our children. Know this, my dear sirs, that although you treat us and our children now, as you do your domestic beast—yet the final result of all future events are known but to God Almighty alone, who rules in the armies of heaven and among the inhabitants of the earth, and who dethrones one earthly king and sits up another, as it seemeth good in his holy sight. We may attribute these vicissitudes to what we please, but the God of armies and of justice rules in heaven and in earth, and the whole American people shall see and know it yet, to their satisfaction. I have known pretended preachers of the gospel of my Master, who not only held us as their natural inheritance, but treated us with as much rigor as any Infidel or Deist in the world—just as though they were intent only on taking our blood and groans to glorify the Lord Jesus Christ. The wicked and ungodly, seeing their preachers treat us with so much cruelty, they say: our preachers, who must be right, if any body are, treat them like brutes, and why cannot we?—They think it is no harm to keep them in slavery and put the whip to them, and why cannot we do the same!—They being preachers of the gospel of Jesus Christ, if it were any harm, they would surely preach against their oppression and do their utmost to erase it from the country; not only in one or two cities, but one continual cry would be raised in all parts of this confederacy, and would cease only with the complete overthrow of the system of slavery, in every part of the country. But how far the American preachers are from preaching against slavery and oppression, which have carried their country to the brink of a precipice; to save them from plunging down the side of which, will hardly be affected, will appear in the sequel of this paragraph, which I shall narrate just as it transpired. I remember a Camp Meeting in South Carolina, for which I embarked in a Steam Boat at Charleston, and

1. See Acts of the Apostles, chap. x. v.—25–27 (King James Version).

having been five or six hours on the water, we at last arrived at the place of hearing, where was a very great concourse of people, who were no doubt, collected together to hear the word of God, (that some had collected barely as spectators to the scene, I will not here pretend to doubt, however, that is left to themselves and their God.) Myself and boat companions, having been there a little while, we were all called up to hear; I among the rest went up and took my seat—being seated, I fixed myself in a complete position to hear the word of my Saviour and to receive such as I thought was authenticated by the Holy Scriptures; but to my no ordinary astonishment, our Reverend gentleman got up and told us (coloured people) that slaves must be obedient to their masters—must do their duty to their masters or be whipped—the whip was made for the backs of fools. &c. Here I pause for a moment, to give the world time to consider what was my surprise, to hear such preaching from a minister of my Master, whose very gospel is that of peace and not of blood and whips, as this pretended preacher tried to make us believe. What the American preachers can think of us, I aver this day before my God, I have never been able to define. They have newspapers and monthly periodicals, which they receive in continual succession, but on the pages of which, you will scarcely ever find a paragraph respecting slavery, which is ten thousand times more injurious to this country than all the other evils put together; and which will be the final overthrow of its government, unless something is very speedily done; for their cup is nearly full.—Perhaps they will laugh at or make light of this; but I tell you Americans! that unless you speedily alter your course, *you* and your *Country are gone!!!!!!* For God Almighty will tear up the very face of the earth!!! Will not that very remarkable passage of Scripture be fulfilled on Christian Americans? Hear it Americans!! "He that is unjust, let him be unjust still:—and he which is filthy, let him be filthy still: and he that is righteous, let him be righteous still: and he that is holy, let him be holy still."[2]

I hope that the Americans may hear, but I am afraid that they have done us so much injury, and are so firm in the belief that our Creator made us to be an inheritance to them for ever, that their hearts will be hardened, so that their destruction may be sure. This language, perhaps is too harsh for the American's delicate ears. But Oh Americans! Americans!! I warn you in the name of the Lord, (whether you will hear, or forbear,) to repent and reform, or you are ruined!!! Do you think that our blood is hidden from the Lord, because you can hide it from the rest of the world, by sending out missionaries, and by your charitable deeds to the Greeks, Irish, &c.? Will he not publish your secret crimes on the house top? Even here in Boston, pride and prejudice have got to such a pitch, that in the very houses erected to the Lord, they have built little places for the reception of coloured people, where they must sit during meeting, or keep away from the house of God,

---

2. See Revelation, chap. xxii. 11.

and the preachers say nothing about it—much less go into the hedges and highways seeking the lost sheep of the house of Israel, and try to bring them in to their Lord and Master. There are not a more wretched, ignorant, miserable, and abject set of beings in all the world, than the blacks in the Southern and Western sections of this country, under tyrants and devils. The preachers of America cannot see them, but they can send out missionaries to convert the heathens, notwithstanding. Americans! unless you speedily alter your course of proceeding, if God Almighty does not stop you, I say it in his name, that you may go on and do as you please for ever, both in time and eternity—never fear any evil at all!!!!!!!!

45

FREDERICK LAW OLMSTED
A Northern View of the Slave States

It is hard to think of Frederick Law Olmsted (1822–1903) and not associate him with the birth of the urban parks movement in the nineteenth century. Born in Hartford, Connecticut, this son of a wealthy merchant was an early lover of the natural world. Illness kept him out of college, and instead, as a young man he worked as a writer, seafarer, farmer, and journalist who eventually founded the magazine The Nation *in 1857. Olmsted's real talents, however, lay in the emerging discipline of landscape architecture. Along with Calvert Vaux, he designed Central Park in New York City and later public green spaces in California, New York, and Massachusetts. His vision of interlocking parks, pathways, and recreational centers as vital to sustaining an educated and disciplined citizenry still influences artists today.*

Less known about Olmsted is his powerful work as a social critic of the antebellum South. In a lengthy record of his travels across the slave states in the early 1850s, Olmsted penned a vivid account of the region's flora and fauna and people, particularly the relationship between blacks and whites. Published in 1856, A Journey in the Seaboard Slave States: With Remarks on Their Economy *catalogues how black and white Southerners interacted and argues that slavery itself chocked the full potential of the South's economy. It also gives voice to a range of Northern views of black Americans, some of which viewed them as decidedly less human than whites. The following excerpt is from Olmsted's visit to Virginia. He describes a slave funeral and how slaves generally dressed and behaved in public.*

Frederick Law Olmsted, *A Journey in the Seaboard Slave States: With Remarks on Their Economy* (New York: Dix & Edwards, 1856), 24–29.

QUESTIONS TO CONSIDER

1. How does Olmsted describe the voice of the preacher, his use of the Bible, and the song of the audience at the funeral? Why is he so fascinated by these elements of the funeral, and how does he use them to paint a picture of African Americans as less disciplined than whites?
2. In his descriptions of the physical characteristics of African Americans, how does Olmsted create a racial hierarchy among Southern blacks? What does a black "lady" look like?
3. Olmsted identifies black "manliness" as a point of conflict between blacks and whites. What does he mean by this? Why are whites so concerned about black expressions of manliness in public spaces?

A NEGRO FUNERAL.

On a Sunday afternoon I met a negro funeral procession, and followed after it to the place of burial. There was a decent hearse, of the usual style, drawn by two horses; six hackney coaches followed it, and six well-dressed men, mounted on handsome saddle-horses, and riding them well, rode in the rear of these. Twenty or thirty men and women were also walking together with the procession, on the side-walk. Among all there was not a white person.

Passing out into the country, a little beyond the principal cemetery of the city (a neat, rural ground, well filled with monuments and evergreens), the hearse halted at a desolate place, where a dozen colored people were already engaged heaping the earth over the grave of a child, and singing a wild kind of chant. Another grave was already dug, immediately adjoining that of the child, both being near the foot of a hill, in a crumbling bank—the ground below being already occupied, and the graves advancing in irregular terraces up the hill-side—an arrangement which facilitated labor.

The new comers, setting the coffin—which was neatly made of stained pine—upon the ground, joined in the labor and the singing, with the preceding party, until a small mound of earth was made over the grave of the child. When this was completed, one of those who had been handling a spade, sighed deeply and said,

"Lord Jesus have marcy on us—now! you Jim—*you! see yar;* you jes lay dat yar shovel cross dat grave—so fash—dah—yes, dat's right."

A shovel and a hoe-handle having been laid across the unfilled grave, the coffin was brought and laid upon them, as on a trestle; after which, lines were passed under it, by which it was lowered to the bottom.

Most of the company were of a very poor appearance, rude and unintelligent, but there were several neatly-dressed and very good-looking men. One of these now stepped to the head of the grave, and, after a few sentences of prayer, held a handkerchief before him as if it were a book, and pronounced a short exhortation, as if he were reading from it. His manner was earnest, and the tone of his voice solemn and impressive, except that, occasionally, it would break into a shout or kind of howl at the close of a long sentence. I noticed several women near him, weeping, and one sobbing intensely. I was deeply influenced myself by the unaffected feeling, in connection with the simplicity, natural, rude truthfulness, and absence of all attempt at formal decorum in the crowd.

I never in my life, however, heard such ludicrous language as was sometimes uttered by the speaker. Frequently I could not guess the idea he was intending to express. Sometimes it was evident that he was trying to repeat phrases that he had heard used before, on similar occasions, but which he made absurd by some interpolation or distortion of a word; thus, "We do not see the end here! oh no, my friends! there will be a *putrification* of this body!" the context failing to indicate whether he meant purification or putrefaction, and leaving it doubtful if he attached any definite meaning to the word himself. He quoted from the Bible several times, several times from hymns, always introducing the latter with "in the words of the poet, my brethren;" he once used the same form, before a verse from the New Testament, and once qualified his citation by saying, "I *believe* the Bible says that;" in which he was right, having repeated words of Job.

He concluded by throwing a handful of earth on the coffin, repeating the usual words, slightly disarranged, and then took a shovel, and, with the aid of six or seven others, proceeded very rapidly to fill the grave. Another man had, in the mean time, stepped into the place he had first occupied at the head of the grave; an old negro, with a very singularly distorted face, who raised a hymn, which soon became a confused chant—the leader singing a few words alone, and the company then either repeating them after him or making a response to them, in the manner of sailors heaving at the windlass. I could understand but very few of the words. The music was wild and barbarous, but not without a plaintive melody. A new leader took the place of the old man, when his breath gave out (he had sung very hard, with much bending of the body and gesticulation), and continued until the grave was filled, and a mound raised over it.

A man had, in the mean time, gone into a ravine near by, and now returned with two small branches, hung with withered leaves, that he had broken off a beech tree; these were placed upright, one at the head, the other at the foot of the grave. A few sentences of prayer were then repeated in a low voice by one of the company, and all dispersed. No one seemed to notice my presence at all. There were about fifty colored people in the assembly, and but one other white man besides myself. This man lounged against the fence, outside the crowd, an apparently indifferent spectator, and I judged he was a police officer, or some one procured to witness the funeral, in compliance with the law which requires that a white man shall always be present at any meeting, for religious exercises, of the negroes, to destroy the opportunity of their conspiring to gain their freedom.

DRESS OF THE SLAVES.

The greater part of the colored people, on Sunday, seemed to be dressed in the cast-off fine clothes of the white people, received, I suppose, as presents, or purchased of the Jews, whose shops show that there must be considerable importation of such articles, probably from the North, as there is from England into Ireland. Indeed, the lowest class, especially among the younger, remind me much, by their dress, of the "lads" of Donnybrook; and when the funeral procession came to its destination, there was a scene precisely like that you may see every day in Sackville-street, Dublin,—a dozen boys in ragged clothes, originally made for tall men, and rather folded round their bodies than worn, striving who should hold the horses of the *gentlemen* when they dismounted to attend the interment of the body. Many, who had probably come in from the farms near the town, wore clothing of coarse gray "negro-cloth," that appeared as if made by contract, without regard to the size of the particular individual to whom it had been allotted, like penitentiary uniforms. A few had a better suit of coarse blue cloth, expressly made for them evidently, for "Sunday clothes."

DANDIES.

Some were dressed with laughably foppish extravagance, and a great many in clothing of the most expensive materials, and in the latest style of fashion. In what I suppose to be the fashionable streets, there were many more well-dressed and highly-dressed colored people than white, and among this dark gentry the finest French cloths, embroidered waistcoats, patent-leather shoes, resplendent brooches, silk hats, kid gloves, and *eau de mille fleurs,* were quite as common as among the New York "dry-goods clerks," in their Sunday promenades, in Broadway. Nor was the fairer, or rather the softer sex, at all left in the shade of this splendor. Many of the colored ladies were dressed not only expensively, but with good taste and effect, after the latest Parisian mode. Many of them were quite attractive in appearance, and some would have produced a decided sensation in any European drawing-room. Their walk and carriage was more often stylish and graceful than that of the white ladies who were out. About one quarter seemed to me to have lost all distinguishingly African peculiarity of feature, and to have acquired, in place of it, a good deal of that voluptuousness of expression which characterizes many of the women of the south of Europe. I was especially surprised to notice the frequency of thin, aquiline noses.

46

HENRY "BOX" BROWN

A Family Torn Apart by Slavery

Henry "Box" Brown was born a slave on a Virginia plantation around 1815. When he was fifteen, the death of his master broke up his family, and Brown and his sister Martha were sold to a slave owner in Richmond, Virginia. There, his sister did domestic work while he worked for wages in his new master's tobacco factory.

Richmond gave Brown a clear view of the increasingly turbulent and contradictory world of American slavery. He worked for wages with 150 other African Americans, some of whom were free and some of whom were slaves who tendered most of their wages to their masters. Soon after arriving in Richmond, Brown had witnessed the spectacle of whites fleeing in terror of their own slaves, soldiers patrolling the streets, and armed mobs killing and torturing blacks. The occasion had been Nat Turner's slave uprising of 1831.

Brown became a respected member of the Richmond community, marrying, fathering three children, and developing a network of both white and black friends. Despite Brown's remarkable privileges as an employed "town slave," he discovered, in 1849, how little control he had over his life when his master sold his wife and children away from him. The account that follows charts his failed attempts to preserve an ordinary life and keep his family together within the "peculiar institution" of slavery. With his family gone and his life in shambles, there was nothing left tying the resourceful Brown to slavery. Enlisting the help of friends, he climbed into a wooden box and mailed himself to freedom in Philadelphia.

In addition to planning and executing the most famous escape in the history of American slavery, Brown was a gifted self-promoter and entrepreneur. Claiming the name "Box," he published his narrative, from which this account is taken, and went on the antislavery lecture circuit. In his travels he gave speeches, reenacted his escape, and displayed a giant painted canvas panorama called The Mirror of Slavery, *which depicted American history from a black perspective. After the U.S. government passed the Fugitive Slave Act in 1850, Brown was almost captured in Rhode Island by bounty hunters. He fled to England, where he had a brief but successful career as an antislavery entertainer.*

QUESTIONS TO CONSIDER

1. In what way was Brown's life different from the lives of slaves in the countryside?

Henry Box Brown, *Narrative of the Life of Henry Box Brown Written by Himself* (Oxford: Oxford University Press, 1851), 20–50.

2. What does Brown's account say about the negotiations that went on between masters and slaves?
3. What were Brown's views of religion?

I had now been about two years in Richmond city, and not having, during that time, seen, and very seldom heard from, my mother, my feelings were very much tried by the separation which I had thus to endure. I missed severely her welcome smile when I returned from my daily task; no one seemed at that time to sympathise with me, and I began to feel, indeed, that I really was alone in the world; and worse than all, I could console myself with no hope, not even the most distant, that I should ever see my beloved parents again. . . .

I now began to think of entering the matrimonial state; and with that view I had formed an acquaintance with a young woman named Nancy, who was a slave belonging to a Mr. Leigh a clerk in the Bank, and, like many more slaveholders, professing to be a very pious man. We had made it up to get married, but it was necessary in the first place, to obtain our masters' permission, as we could do nothing without their consent.

I therefore went to Mr. Leigh, and made known to him my wishes, when he told me he never meant to sell Nancy, and if my master would agree never to sell me, I might marry her. He promised faithfully that he would not sell her, and pretended to entertain an extreme horror of separating families. He gave me a note to my master, and after they had discussed the matter over, I was allowed to marry the object of my choice. . . .

From the apparent sincerity of his promises to us, we felt confident that he would not separate us. We had not, however, been married above twelve months, when his conscientious scruples vanished, and he sold my wife to a Mr. Joseph H. Colquitt, a saddler, living in the city of Richmond, and a member of Dr. Plummer's church there. This Mr. Colquitt was an exceedingly cruel man, and he had a wife who was, if possible, still more cruel. She was very contrary and hard to be pleased she used to abuse my wife very much, not because she did not do her duty, but because, it was said, her manners were too refined for a slave. At this time my wife had a child and this vexed Mrs. Colquitt very much; she could not bear to see her nursing her baby and used to wish some great calamity to happen to my wife. Eventually she was so much displeased with my wife that she induced Mr. Colquitt to sell her to one Philip M. Tabb, Jr. for the sum of 450 dollars; but coming to see the value of her more clearly after she tried to do without her, she could not rest till she got Mr. Colquitt to repurchase her from Mr. Tabb, which he did in about four months after he had sold her, for 500 dollars, being 50 more than he had sold her for.

Shortly after this Mr. Colquitt was taken sick. . . . He proceeded to sell my wife to one Samuel Cottrell, who wished to purchase her. Cottrell was a saddler and had a shop in Richmond. This man came to me one day and told me that Mr. Colquitt was going to sell my wife, and stated that he wanted a woman to wait upon his wife, and he thought my wife would precisely suit her; but he said her master asked 650 dollars for her and her children, and he had only 600 that he could conveniently spare but if I would let him have fifty, to make up the price, he would prevent her from being sold away from me. I was, however, a little suspicious about being fooled out of my money, and I asked him if I did advance the money what security I could have that he would not sell my wife as the others had done; but he said to me "do you think if you allow me to have that money, that I could have the heart to sell your wife to any other person but yourself, and particularly knowing that your wife is my sister and you my brother in the Lord; while all of us are members of the church? *Oh! no*, I never could have the heart to do such a deed as that."

After he had shown off his religion in this manner, and lavished it upon me, I thought I would let him have the money, not that I had implicit faith in his promise, but that I knew he could purchase her if he wished whether I were to assist him or not, and I thought by thus bringing him under an obligation to me it might at least be somewhat to the advantage of my wife and to me; so I gave him the 50 dollars and he went off and bought my wife and children:—and that very same day he came to me and told me, that my wife and children were now his property, and that I must hire a house for them and he would allow them to live there if I would furnish them with everything they wanted, and pay him 50 dollars, a year; "if you dont do this," he said, "I will sell her as soon as I can get a buyer for her." I was struck with astonishment to think that this man, in one day, could exhibit himself in two such different characters. A few hours ago filled with expressions of love and kindness, and now a monster tyrant, making light of the most social ties and imposing such terms as he chose on those whom, but a little before, had begged to conform to his will.

Now, being a slave, I had no power to hire a house, and what this might have resulted in I do not know, if I had not met with a friend in the time of need, in the person of James C. A. Smith, Jr. He was a free man and I went to him and told him my tale and asked him to go and hire a house for me, to put my wife and children into; which he immediately did. He hired one at 72 dollars per annum, and stood master of it for me; and, notwithstanding the fearful liabilities under which I lay, I now began to feel a little easier, and might, perhaps, have managed to live in a kind of a way if we had been let alone here. But Mr. S. Cottrell had not yet done with robbing us; he no sooner saw that we were thus comfortably situated, than he said my wife must do some of his washing. I still had to pay the house hire, and the hire of my wife; to find her and the children with everything they required, and she had to do his washing beside. Still we felt ourselves more comfortable than we had ever been before. In this way, we went on for some time: I paid him the hire of my wife regularly, whenever he called for it—whether it was due or not—but he seemed still bent on robbing me more thoroughly than he had the previous day; for one pleasant morning, in the month of August, 1848, when my wife and children, and myself, were sitting at table, about to eat our breakfast, Mr. Cottrell called, and said, he wanted some money today, as he had a demand for a large amount. I said to him, you know I have no money to spare, because it takes nearly all that I make for myself, to pay my wife's hire, the rent of my house, my own ties to my master, and to keep ourselves in meat and clothes; and if at any time, I have made anything more than that, I have paid it to you in advance, and what more can I do? Mr. Cottrell, however said, "I want money, and money I will have."

I could make him no answer; he then went away. I then said to my wife, "I wonder what Mr. Cottrell means by saying I want money and money I will have," my poor wife burst into tears and said perhaps he will sell one of our little children, and our hearts were so full that neither of us could eat any breakfast, and after mutually embracing each other, as it might be our last meeting, and fondly pressing our little darlings to our bosoms, I left the house and went off to my daily labour followed by my little children who called after me to come back soon. I felt that life had joys worth living for if I could only be allowed to enjoy them, but my heart was filled with deep anguish from the awful calamity, which I was thus obliged to contemplate, as not only a possible but a highly probable occurrence. . . .

I had not been many hours at my work, when I was informed that my wife and children were taken from their home, sent to the auction mart and sold, and then lay in prison ready to start away the next day for North Carolina with the man who had purchased them. I cannot express, in language, what were my feelings on this occasion. My master treated me kindly but he still retained me in a state of slavery. His kindness however did not keep me from feeling the smart of this awful deprivation. I had left my wife and children at home in the morning as well situated as slaves could be; I was not anticipating their loss, not on account of the feigned piety of their owner, for I had long ago learned to look through such hollow pretences in those who held slaves, but because of the obligation to me for money I had advanced to him, *on the expressed condition that he should not sell her to any person but myself;* such, however was the case. . . . I went to my *Christian* master and informed him how I was served, but he shoved me away from him as if I was not human. I could not rest with this however, I went to him a second time and implored him to be kind enough to buy my wife and to save me from so much trouble of mind; still he was inexorable and only answered me by telling me to go to my work and not bother him any more. I went to him a *third* time, which would be about ten o'clock and told him how Cottrell had robbed me, as this scoundrel was not satisfied with selling my wife and children, but he had no sooner got them out of the town than he took everything which he could find in my house and carried it off to be sold; the things which he then took had cost me nearly three hundred dollars. I begged master to write Cottrell and make him give me up my things, but his answer was Mr. Cottrell is a gentleman I am afraid to meddle with his business. . . . I went sorrowfully back to my own deserted home, and found that what I had heard was quite true; not only had my wife and children been taken away, but every article of furniture had also been removed to the auction mart to be sold.

I then made inquiry as to where my things had been put; and having found this out went to the sheriff's office and informed him, that the things Mr. Cottrell had brought to be sold did not belong to him, but that they were mine, and I hoped he would return them to me. I was then told by the sheriff that Mr. Cottrell had left the things to be sold in order to pay himself a debt of seventeen dollars and twenty-one cents, which he said if I would pay he would let me take away the things. I then went to my good friend Doctor Smith who was always ready and willing to do what he could for me, and having got the money, I paid it to the sheriff and took away the things which I was obliged to do that night, as far as I was able, and what were left I removed in the morning. When I was taking home the last of my things I met Mr. Cottrell, and two of his Christian brethren, in the street. He stopped me and said he had heard I had been to the sheriff's office and got away my things. Yes I said I have been and got away *my things* but I could not get away *my wife and children* whom you have put beyond my power to redeem. He then began to give me a round of abuse, while his two Christian friends stood by and heard him, but they did not seem to be the least offended at the terrible barbarity which was there placed before them.

. . . [W]hen the morning's sun arose I found myself on my way towards my master's house, to make another attempt to induce him to purchase my wife. But although I besought him, with tears in my eyes, I did not succeed in making the least impression on his obdurate heart, and he utterly refused to advance the smallest portion of the 5000 dollars I had paid him in order to relieve my sufferings, and yet he was a church member of considerable standing in Richmond. . . .

My agony was now complete, she with whom I had travelled the journey of life *in chains*, for the space of twelve years, and the dear little pledges God had given us I could see plainly must now be separated from me for ever, and I must continue, desolate and alone, to drag my chains through the world.

O dear, I thought shall my wife and children no more greet my sight with their cheerful looks and happy smiles! for far away in the North Carolina swamps are they henceforth to toil beneath the scorching rays of a hot sun deprived of a husband's and a father's care! Can I endure such agony—shall I stay behind while they are thus driven with the tyrant's rod? I must stay, I am a slave, the law of men gives me no power to ameliorate my condition; it shuts up every avenue of hope; but, thanks be to God, their is a law of heaven which senates' laws cannot control! While I was thus musing I received a message, that if I wished to see my wife and children, and bid them the last farewell, I could do so, by taking my stand on the street where they were all to pass on their way for North Carolina. . . .

These beings were marched with ropes about their necks, and staples on their arms, and, although in that respect the scene was no very novel one to me, yet the peculiarity of my own circumstances made it assume the

appearance of unusual horror. This train of beings was accompanied by a number of wagons loaded with little children of many different families, which as
they appeared rent the air with their shrieks and cries and vain endeavours
to resist the separation which was thus forced upon them, and the cords with
which they were thus bound; but what should I now see in the very foremost
wagon but a little child looking towards me and pitifully calling, father! father! This was my eldest child, and I was obliged to look upon it for the last
time that I should, perhaps, ever see it again in life. . . .

Thus passed my child from my presence—it was my own child—I loved
it with all the fondness of a father; but things were so ordered that I could
only say, farewell, and leave it to pass in its chains while I looked for the approach of another gang in which my wife was also loaded with chains. My
eye soon caught her precious face, but, gracious heavens! that glance of agony may God spare me from ever again enduring! My wife, under the influence of her feelings, jumped aside; I seized hold of her hand while my mind
felt unutterable things, and my tongue was only able to say, we shall meet
in heaven! I went with her for about four miles hand in hand, but both our
hearts were so overpowered with feeling that we could say nothing, and
when at last we were obliged to part, the look of mutual love which we exchanged was all the token which we could give each other that we should
yet meet in heaven.

I now began to get weary of my bonds; and earnestly panted after liberty.
I felt convinced that I should be acting in accordance with the will of God,
if I could snap in sunder those bonds by which I was held body and soul as
the property of a fellow man. I looked forward to the good time which every
day I more and more firmly believed would yet come, when I should walk
the face of the earth in full possession of all that freedom which the finger
of God had so clearly written on the constitutions of man, and which was
common to the human race; but of which, by the cruel hand of tyranny, I,
and millions of my fellow-men, had been robbed.

47

Visualizing the Peculiar Institution

*Visual representations of African Americans in the nineteenth century varied over time
and according to technology and the presuppositions of the beholder. The growing controversy over slavery fostered new images that first appeared before the public in the
1830s. With the advent of photography in 1839, stills and daguerreotypes of slaves
and free blacks were developed for personal and public use. Magazines such as* Harper's
Weekly *illustrated their stories with wood engravings made from these photographs.*

Early photographic processes set certain limits and created specific conventions about the images produced in this era. Bulky equipment, the time required for preparation of a photosensitive surface, and lengthy exposure times often gave nineteenth-century portraiture a solemn character. Movement produced a blur, so people had to set their faces into an expression that they could hold for about thirty seconds.

Such was the case for Delia, a slave in the first image below. "Delia" (1850), a daguerreotype, was put to use by the prominent American scientist Louis Agassiz, who used the image to demonstrate an anthropological theory of the "separate creation" of the different races. Such public displays of non-European bodies were a common spectacle in nineteenth-century North Atlantic societies. Medical researchers combined with promoters to put on photographic as well as sometimes live displays. Images like this one, which clearly violated norms of nineteenth-century public modesty, did not gain widespread condemnation for their depictions of nudity except from abolitionists.

The second image, "Gordon" (1863), is of a runaway slave of the same name who is also without a shirt. As the Civil War unfolded, thousands of Southern slaves fled their homes and made tracks for the Union Army. Realizing that an unprecedented measure of safety and freedom could be had by living under the protective arm of the army, they swelled its ranks and collectively debunked any idea that bondspeople were happy and contented with their lot. While these runaways presented large-scale organizational challenges for generals, they also became a cause célèbre among abolitionists and antislavery soldiers.

Gordon entered Union territory in early 1863. In March of that year he enlisted in the army. During the physical exam required of all new soldiers, the attending physician saw the dense scarring on his back. Two photographers asked him to pose so that they might chronicle the physical cost of slavery. They soon produced Gordon's image as a carte-de-visite, which was a new type of commercial photography in the mid-1800s. About the size of the visiting card used in business and social life—hence its name—the carte-de-viste consisted of an image on a thin piece of photographic paper pasted to a thicker cardboard backing; a message could be inscribed on the back, and frequently was.

"Gordon" quickly became an emblem of slavery's horrors, and Harper's Weekly featured the photograph on its front page on July 4, 1863. The particular carte-de-visite displayed here also featured a message printed on the back that read:

"The Peculiar Institution" Illustrated. Copy of a photograph taken from life at Baton Rouge, La. Ap. 2, '63; the lacerated body—months after the brutal flogging had been inflicted—having healed in the manner represented. The alleged offense was a trifling one. How noble and benignant the countenance of the victim!

QUESTIONS TO CONSIDER

1. Why were Delia and Gordon both photographed naked from the waist up?
2. What stories about slavery does each image suggest?
3. What type of message might Delia and Gordon have hoped to present to the people who viewed their images?

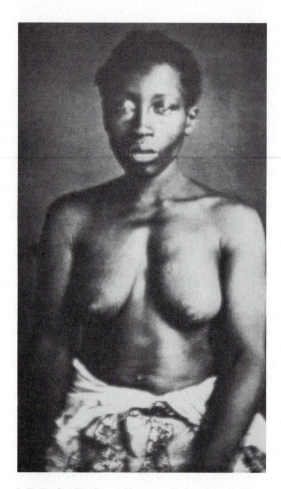

J. T. Zealy, "Delia, a Slave in Columbia, S.C.,
' . . . Country Born of African Parents,'" 1850.
*Private Collection / Peter Newark American
Pictures / Bridgeman Images.*

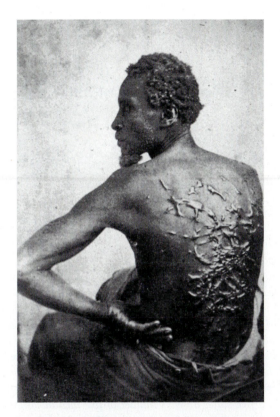

McPherson & Oliver, "'The Peculiar Institution.' Gordon, Escaped from Mississippi," 1863. *Library of Congress, Prints and Photographs Division, LC-USZ62-98515*

48

OSBORNE P. ANDERSON

An African American at Harpers Ferry

In October 1859, fifty-nine-year-old John Brown, a white abolitionist and failed busi-
nessman, launched the ultimate battle in his war against slavery. With five black and
sixteen white followers, two of them his sons, he captured the federal arsenal at Harpers
Ferry, a town (then still in Virginia but today part of West Virginia) about sixty miles
northwest of Washington, D.C. Intending that slaves use arms from the arsenal to rise
up and claim their freedom, Brown planned to set off a spreading slave rebellion that
made use of weapons from other arsenals.

Committed to a Christianity rooted in the Old Testament, Brown had begun his
campaign of armed struggle in Kansas. In 1854, Senator Stephen A. Douglas of Illi-
nois introduced the bill that became the Kansas–Nebraska Act. The measure created
two territories and allowed the inhabitants of each to decide whether, upon achieving
statehood, it should institute or prohibit slavery. Soon after passage of Douglas's bill,
proslavery migrants from Missouri and antislavery partisans from the North descended
on Kansas with the aim of settling there and determining the territory's future. Brown
and several sons participated in the guerrilla warfare over whether the territory would
become a slave or a free state. Brown's murder of five men at Pottawatomie Creek in
retaliation for the killing of an antislavery partisan intensified the violence that erupted
in the territory in the mid-1850s.

The Harpers Ferry raid proved to be a military failure but a political success. Fed-
eral troops overwhelmed Brown and his remaining men and retook the arsenal. How-
ever, Brown used the treason charges to put slavery on trial—and electrified the nation
with his righteous, unrepentant conviction in the face of death by hanging. Widespread
sympathy for Brown in the North, supplemented by a flood of European appeals for par-
don, put already enraged Southerners on the defensive. Brown's last words, handed in
a note to a soldier escorting him to the gallows, proved both prophesy and provocation:
"I, John Brown, am now quite certain that the sins of this guilty land will never be
purged away but with blood." Less than a year later, third party antislavery candidate
Abraham Lincoln would be elected president, and only weeks after his inauguration the
South would secede—the first concrete step toward civil war.

Osborne Perry Anderson (1830–1872) was the only African American survivor of
John Brown's army. Born in Pennsylvania of free parents, he attended Oberlin College
in Ohio, where he met John Anthony Copeland Jr., another of Brown's African American

_____
Osborne P. Anderson, *A Voice from Harper's Ferry: A Narrative of Events at Harper's Ferry* (Boston: 1861), 2, 6, 9–10, 23–25, 31–38, 40–44, 59–62.

raiders. After college Anderson worked as a printer for Mary Ann Shadd, an Afro-Canadian abolitionist newspaper publisher. In 1858 he joined Brown's war on slavery. After the raid, Anderson escaped to the North and, with Shadd's help, wrote and published A Voice from Harper's Ferry, *from which the following narrative is taken. He served as a recruiting officer in the Union Army and fought for black civil rights until his death.*

QUESTIONS TO CONSIDER

1. What reasons did Anderson give for the raid's military failure?
2. What, if any, criticisms did Anderson have of John Brown?
3. Anderson, like many abolitionists, believed that slaves had supported the uprising. Why do you think this was such an important issue?

THE IDEA AND ITS EXPONENTS—JOHN BROWN ANOTHER MOSES

The idea underlying the outbreak at Harper's Ferry is not peculiar to that movement, . . . There is an unbroken chain of sentiment and purpose from Moses of the Jews to John Brown of America; from Kossuth, and the liberators of France and Italy, to the untutored Gabriel, and the Denmark Veseys, Nat Turners and Madison Washingtons of the Southern American States. The shaping and expressing of a thought for freedom takes the same consistence with the colored American—whether he be an independent citizen of the Haytian nation, a proscribed but humble nominally free colored man, a patient, toiling, but hopeful slave— . . . When the Egyptian pressed hard upon the Hebrew, Moses slew him; and when the spirit of slavery invaded the fair Territory of Kansas, causing the Free-State settlers to cry out because of persecution, old John Brown, famous among the men of God for ever, though then but little known to his fellow-men, called together his sons and went over, as did Abraham, to the unequal contest, but on the side of the oppressed white men of Kansas that were, and the black men that were to be. To-day, Kansas is free, and the verdict of impartial men is, that to John Brown, more than any other man, Kansas owes her present position. . . .

He regarded slavery as a state of perpetual war against the slave, and was fully impressed with the idea that himself and his friends had the right to take liberty, and to use arms in defending the same. Being a devout Bible Christian, he sustained his views and shaped his plans in conformity to the Bible; and when setting them forth, he quoted freely from the Scripture to sustain his position. He realized and enforced the doctrine of destroying the tree that bringeth forth corrupt fruit. Slavery was to him the corrupt tree, and the duty of every Christian man was to strike down slavery, and to commit its fragments to the flames. . . .

MORE CORRESPONDENCE—MY JOURNEY TO THE FERRY—A GLANCE AT THE FAMILY

On the 20th, four days after I reached this outpost, Capt. Brown, Watson Brown, Kagi, myself, and several friends, held another meeting, after which, on the 24th, I left Chambersburg for Kennedy Farm. I walked alone as far as Middletown, a town on the line between Maryland and Pennsylvania, and it being then dark, I found Captain Brown awaiting with his wagon. We set out directly, and drove until nearly day-break the next morning, when we reached the Farm in safety. As a very necessary precaution against surprise, all the colored men at the Ferry who went from the North, made the journey from the Pennsylvania line in the night. I found all the men concerned in the undertaking on hand when I arrived, excepting Copeland, Leary, and Merriam; and when all had collected, a more earnest, fearless, determined company of men it would be difficult to get together. . . . There was no milk and water sentimentality—no offensive contempt for the negro, while working in his cause; the pulsations of each and every heart beat in harmony for the suffering and pleading slave. I thank God that I have been permitted to realize to its furthest, fullest extent, the moral, mental, physical, social harmony of an Anti-Slavery family, carrying out to the letter the principles of its antetype, the Anti-Slavery cause. In John Brown's house, and in John Brown's presence, men from widely different parts of the continent met and united into one company, wherein no hateful prejudice dared intrude its ugly self— no ghost of a distinction found space to enter.

LIFE AT KENNEDY FARM

To a passer-by, the house and its surroundings presented but indifferent attractions. Any log tenement of equal dimensions would be as likely to arrest a stray glance. Rough, unsightly, and aged, it was only those privileged to enter and tarry for a long time, and to penetrate the mysteries of the two rooms it contained—kitchen, parlor, dining-room below, and the spacious chamber, attic, store-room, prison, drilling room, comprised in the loft above— who could tell how we lived at Kennedy Farm. . . .

The principal employment of the prisoners, as we severally were when compelled to stay in the loft, was to study Forbes' Manual, and to go through a quiet, though rigid drill, under the training of Capt. Stevens, at some times. At others, we applied a preparation for bronzing our gun barrels—discussed subjects of reform—related our personal history; but when our resources became pretty well exhausted, the *ennui* from confinement, imposed silence, etc., would make the men almost desperate. At such times, neither slavery nor slaveholders were discussed mincingly. . . .

During the several weeks I remained at the encampment, we were under the restraint I write of through the day; but at night, we sallied out for a ramble, or to breathe the fresh air and enjoy the beautiful solitude of the mountain scenery around, by moonlight. . . .

At eight o'clock on Sunday evening, Captain Brown said: "Men, get on your arms; we will proceed to the Ferry." His horse and wagon were brought out before the door, and some pikes, a sledge-hammer and crowbar were placed in it[.] The Captain then put on his old Kansas cap, and said: "Come, boys!" when we marched out of the camp behind him, into the lane leading down the hill to the main road. As we formed the procession line, Owen Brown, Barclay Coppic, and Francis J. Merriam, sentinels left behind to protect the place as before stated, came forward and took leave of us; after which, agreeably to previous orders, and as they were better acquainted with the topography of the Ferry, and to effect the tearing down of the telegraph wires, C. P. Tidd and John E. Cook led the procession. While going to the Ferry, the company marched along as solemnly as a funeral procession, till we got to the bridge. When we entered, we halted, and carried out an order to fasten our cartridge boxes outside of our clothes, when every thing was ready for taking the town.

THE CAPTURE OF HARPER'S FERRY—COL. A. D. STEVENS AND PARTY SALLY OUT TO THE PLANTATIONS— WHAT WE SAW, HEARD, DID, ETC.

As John H. Kagi and A. D. Stevens entered the bridge, as ordered in the fifth charge, the watchman, being at the other end, came toward them with a lantern in his hand. When up to them, they told him he was their prisoner, and detained him a few minutes, when he asked them to spare his life. They replied, they did not intend to harm him; the object was to free the slaves, and he would have to submit to them for a time, in order that the purpose might be carried out.

Captain Brown now entered the bridge in his wagon, followed by the rest of us, until we reached that part where Kagi and Stevens held their prisoner, when he ordered Watson Brown and Stewart Taylor to take the positions assigned them in order sixth, and the rest of us to proceed to the engine house. We started for the engine house, taking the prisoner along with us. When we neared the gates of the engine-house yard, we found them locked, and the watchman on the inside. He was told to open the gates, but refused, and commenced to cry. The men were then ordered by Captain Brown to open the gates forcibly, which was done, and the watchman taken prisoner. The two prisoners were left in the custody of Jerry Anderson and Adolphus Thompson, and A. D. Stevens arranged the men to take possession of the Armory and rifle factory. About this time, there was apparently much excitement. People were passing back and forth in the town, and before we could do much, we had to take several prisoners. After the prisoners were secured, we passed to the opposite side of the street and took the Armory, and Albert Hazlett and Edwin Coppic were ordered to hold it for the time being.

The capture of the rifle factory was the next work to be done. When we went there, we told the watchman who was outside of the building our business, and asked him to go along with us, as we had come to take possession of the town, and make use of the Armory in carrying out our object. He obeyed the command without hesitation. John H. Kagi and John Copeland were placed in the Armory, and the prisoners taken to the engine house. Following the capture of the Armory, Oliver Brown and William Thompson were ordered to take possession of the bridge leading out of town, across the Shenandoah river, which they immediately did. These places were all taken, and the prisoners secured, without the snap of a gun, or any violence whatever.

The town being taken, Brown, Stevens, and the men who had no post in charge, returned to the engine house, where council was held, after which Captain Stevens, Tidd, Cook, Shields Green, Leary and myself went to the country. On the road, we met some colored men, to whom we made known our purpose, when they immediately agreed to join us. They said they had been long waiting for an opportunity of the kind. Stevens then asked them to go around among the colored people and circulate the news, when each started off in a different direction. The result was that many colored men gathered to the scene of action. The first prisoner taken by us was Colonel Lewis Washington. . . .

After making known our business to him [John Allstadt], he went into as great a fever of excitement as Washington had done. We could have his slaves, also, if we would only leave him. This, of course, was contrary to our plans and instructions. He hesitated, puttered around, fumbled and meditated for a long time. At last, seeing no alternative, he got ready, when the slaves were gathered up from about the quarters by their own consent, and all placed in Washington's big wagon and returned to the Ferry.

One old colored lady, at whose house we stopped, a little way from the town, had a good time over the message we took her. This liberating the slaves was the very thing she had longed for, prayed for, and dreamed about, time and again; and her heart was full of rejoicing over the fulfillment of a prophecy which had been her faith for long years. . . .

THE EVENTS OF MONDAY, OCT. 17 — ARMING THE SLAVES — TERROR IN THE SLAVEHOLDING CAMP — IMPORTANT LOSSES TO OUR PARTY — THE FATE OF KAGI — PRISONERS ACCUMULATE — WORKMEN AT THE KENNEDY FARM — ETC.

Monday, the 17th of October, was a time of stirring and exciting events. In consequence of the movements of the night before, we were prepared for commotion and tumult, but certainly not for more than we beheld around us. Gray dawn and yet brighter daylight revealed great confusion, and as the sun arose, the panic spread like wild-fire. Men, women and children could be seen leaving their homes in every direction; some seeking refuge among residents, and in quarters further away, others climbing up the hill-sides, and hurrying off in various directions, evidently impelled by a sudden fear, which was plainly visible in their countenances or in their movements.

Capt. Brown was all activity, though I could not help thinking that at times he appeared somewhat puzzled. He ordered Sherrard Lewis Leary, and four slaves, and a free man belonging to the neighborhood, to join John Henry Kagi and John Copeland at the rifle factory, which they immediately did. . . .

Capt. Brown next ordered me to take the pikes out of the wagon in which he rode to the Ferry, and to place them in the hands of the colored men who had come with us from the plantations, and others who had come forward without having had communication with any of our party. It was out of the circumstances connected with the fulfillment of this order, that the false charge against "Anderson" as leader, or "ringleader," of the negroes, grew.

The spectators, about this time, became apparently wild with fright and excitement. The number of prisoners was magnified to hundreds, and the judgment-day could not have presented more terrors, in its awful and certain prospective punishment to the justly condemned for the wicked deeds of a life-time, the chief of which would no doubt be slaveholding, than did Capt. Brown's operations.

The prisoners were also terror-stricken. Some wanted to go home to see their families, as if for the last time. The privilege was granted them, under escort, and they were brought back again. Edwin Coppic, one of the sentinels at the Armory gate, was fired at by one of the citizens, but the ball did not reach him, when one of the insurgents close by put up his rifle, and made the enemy bite the dust. . . .

After these incidents, time passed away till the arrival of the United States troops, without any further attack upon us. The cowardly Virginians submitted like sheep, without resistance, from that time until the marines came down. Meanwhile, Capt. Brown, who was considering a proposition for release from his prisoners, passed back and forth from the Armory to the bridge, speaking words of comfort and encouragement to the men. "Hold on a little longer, boys," said he, "until I get matters arranged with the prisoners." This tardiness on the part of our brave leader was sensibly felt to be an omen of evil by some of us, and was eventually the cause of our defeat. It was no part of the original plan to hold on to the Ferry, or to parley with prisoners; but by so doing, time was afforded to carry the news of its capture to several points, and forces were thrown into the place, which surrounded us.

At eleven o'clock, Capt. Brown dispatched William Thompson from the Ferry up to Kennedy Farm, with the news that we had peaceful possession of the town, and with directions to the men to continue on moving the things. He went; but before he could get back, troops had begun to pour in, and the general encounter commenced.

RECEPTION TO THE TROOPS—THEY RETREAT TO THE BRIDGE—A PRISONER—DEATH OF DANGERFIELD NEWBY—WILLIAM THOMPSON—THE MOUNTAINS ALIVE—FLAG OF TRUCE—THE ENGINE HOUSE TAKEN

It was about twelve o'clock in the day when we were first attacked by the troops. Prior to that, Capt. Brown, in anticipation of further trouble, had girded to his side the famous sword taken from Col. Lewis Washington the night before, and with that memorable weapon, he commanded his men against General Washington's own State.

When the Captain received the news that the troops had entered the bridge from the Maryland side, he, with some of his men, went into the street, and sent a message to the Arsenal for us to come forth also. We hastened to the street as ordered, when he said—"The troops are on the bridge, coming into town; we will give them a warm reception." He then walked around amongst us, giving us words of encouragement, in this wise:—"Men! be cool! Don't waste your powder and shot! Take aim, and make every shot count!" "The troops will look for us to retreat on their first appearance; be careful to shoot first." Our men were well supplied with firearms, but Capt. Brown had no rifle at that time; his only weapon was the sword before mentioned.

The troops soon came out of the bridge, and up the street facing us, we occupying an irregular position. When they got within sixty or seventy yards, Capt. Brown said, "Let go upon them!" which we did, when several of them fell. Again and again the dose was repeated.

There was now consternation among the troops. From marching in solid martial columns, they became scattered. Some hastened to seize upon and bear up the wounded and dying,—several lay dead upon the ground. They seemed not to realize, at first, that we would fire upon them, but evidently expected we would be driven out by them without firing. Capt. Brown seemed fully to understand the matter, and hence, very properly and in our defence, undertook to forestall their movements. The consequence of their unexpected reception was, after leaving several of their dead on the field, they beat a confused retreat into the bridge, and there stayed under cover until reinforcements came to the Ferry.

On the retreat of the troops, we were ordered back to our former post. . . .

There was comparative quiet for a time, except that the citizens seemed to be wild with terror. Men, women and children forsook the place in great haste, climbing up hill-sides and scaling the mountains. The latter seemed to be alive with white fugitives, fleeing from their doomed city. During this time. Wm. Thompson, who was returning from his errand to the Kennedy Farm, was surrounded on the bridge by the railroad men, who next came up, taken a prisoner to the Wager House, tied hand and foot, and, at a late hour of the afternoon, cruelly murdered by being riddled with balls, and thrown headlong on the rocks.

Late in the morning, some of his prisoners told Capt. Brown that they would like to have breakfast, when he sent word forthwith to the Wager House to that effect, and they were supplied. He did not order breakfast for himself and men, as was currently but falsely stated at the time, as he suspected foul play; on the contrary, when solicited to have breakfast so provided for him, he refused.

Between two and three o'clock in the afternoon, armed men could be seen coming from every direction; soldiers were marching and counter-marching; and on the mountains, a host of blood-thirsty ruffians swarmed, waiting for their opportunity to pounce upon the little band. The fighting commenced in earnest after the arrival of fresh troops. Volley upon volley was discharged, and the echoes from the hills, the shrieks of the townspeople, and the groans of their wounded and dying, all of which filled the air, were truly frightful. The Virginians may well conceal their losses, and Southern chivalry may hide its brazen head, for their boasted bravery was well tested that day, and in no way to their advantage. It is remarkable, that except that one fool-hardy colored man was reported buried, no other funeral is mentioned, although the Mayor and other citizens are known to have fallen. Had they reported the true number, their disgrace would have been more apparent; so they wisely (?) concluded to be silent.

The fight at Harper's Ferry also disproved the current idea that slaveholders will lay down their lives for their property. Col. Washington, the representative of the old hero, stood "blubbering" like a great calf at supposed danger; while the laboring white classes and non-slaveholders, with the marines, (mostly gentlemen from "furrin" parts,) were the men who faced the bullets of John Brown and his men. Hardly the skin of a slaveholder could be scratched in open fight; the cowards kept out of the way until danger was passed, sending the poor whites into the pitfalls, while they were reserved for the bragging, and to do the safe but cowardly judicial murdering afterwards. . . .

After an hour's hard fighting, and when the enemy were blocking up the avenues of escape, Capt. Brown sent out his son Watson with a flag of truce, but no respect was paid to it; he was fired upon, and wounded severely. He returned to the engine house, and fought bravely after that for fully an hour and a half, when he received a mortal wound, which he struggled under until the next day. The contemptible and savage manner in which the flag of truce had been received, induced severe measures in our defence, in the hour and a half before the next one was sent out. The effect of our work was, that the troops ceased to fire at the buildings, as we clearly had the advantage of position.

Capt. A. D. Stevens was next sent out with a flag, with what success I will presently show. . . .

Capt. Stevens was fired upon several times while carrying his flag of truce, and received severe wounds, as I was informed that day, not being myself in a position to see him after. He was captured, and taken to the Wager House, where he was kept until the close of the struggle in the evening, when he was placed with the rest of our party who had been captured.

After the capture of Stevens, desperate fighting was done by both sides. The marines forced their way inside the engine-house yard, and commanded Capt. Brown to surrender, which he refused to do, but said in reply, that he was willing to fight them, if they would allow him first to withdraw his men to the second lock on the Maryland side. As might be expected, the cowardly hordes refused to entertain such a proposition, but continued their assault, to cut off communication between our several parties. The men at the Kennedy Farm having received such a favorable message in the early part of the day, through Thompson, were ignorant of the disastrous state of affairs later in the day. Could they have known the truth, and come down in time, the result would have been very different; we should not have been captured that day. A handful of determined men, as they were, by taking a position on the Maryland side, when the troops made their attack and retreated to the bridge for shelter, would have placed the enemy between two fires. Thompson's news prevented them from hurrying down, as they otherwise would have done, and thus deprived us of able assistance from Owen Brown, a host in himself, and Tidd, Merriam and Coppic, the brave fellows composing that band.

The climax of murderous assaults on that memorable day was the final capture of the engine house, with the old Captain and his handful of associates. This outrageous burlesque upon civilized warfare must have a special chapter to itself, as it concentrates more of Southern littleness and cowardice than is often believed to be true. . . .

THE BEHAVIOR OF THE SLAVES—CAPTAIN BROWN'S OPINION

Of the various contradictory reports made by slaveholders and their satellites about the time of the Harper's Ferry conflict, none were more untruthful than those relating to the slaves. There was seemingly a studied attempt to enforce the belief that the slaves were cowardly, and that they were really more in favor of Virginia masters and slavery, than of their freedom. As a party who had an intimate knowledge of the conduct of the colored men engaged, I am prepared to make an emphatic denial of the gross imputation against them. They were charged specially with being unreliable, with deserting Captain Brown the first opportunity, and going back to their masters; and with being so indifferent to the work of their salvation from the yoke, as to have to be forced into service by the Captain, contrary to their will.

On the Sunday evening of the outbreak, when we visited the plantations and acquainted the slaves with our purpose to effect their liberation, the greatest enthusiasm was manifested by them—joy and hilarity beamed from every countenance. One old mother, white-haired from age, and borne down with the labors of many years in bonds, when told of the work in hand, replied: "God bless you! God bless you!" She then kissed the party at her house, and requested all to kneel, which we did, and she offered prayer to God for His blessing on the enterprise, and our success. At the slaves' quarters, there was apparently a general jubilee, and they stepped forward manfully, without impressing or coaxing. In one case, only, was there any hesitation. A dark-complexioned freeborn man refused to take up arms. He showed the only want of confidence in the movement, and far less courage than any slave consulted about the plan. In fact, so far as I could learn, the free blacks South are much less reliable than the slaves, and infinitely more fearful. In Washington City, a party of free colored persons offered their services to the Mayor, to aid in suppressing our movement. Of the slaves who followed us to the Ferry, some were sent to help remove stores, and the others were drawn up in a circle around the engine-house, at one time, where they were, by Captain Brown's order, furnished by me with pikes, mostly, and acted as a guard to the prisoners to prevent their escape, which they did.

As in the war of the American Revolution, the first blood shed was a black man's, Crispus Attuck's [see Documents 15 and 16], so at Harper's Ferry, the first blood shed by our party, after the arrival of the United States troops, was that of a slave. In the beginning of the encounter, and before the troops had fairly emerged from the bridge, a slave was shot. I saw him fall. Phil, the slave who died in prison, with fear, as it was reported, was wounded at the Ferry, and died from the effects of it. Of the men shot on the rocks, when Kagi's party were compelled to take to the river, some were slaves, and they suffered death before they would desert their companions, and their bodies fell into the waves beneath. Captain Brown, who was surprised and pleased by the promptitude with which they volunteered, and with their manly bearing at the scene of violence, remarked to me, on that Monday morning, that he was agreeably disappointed in the behavior of the slaves; for he did not expect one out of ten to be willing to fight. The truth of the Harper's Ferry "raid," as it has been called, in regard to the part taken by the slaves, and the aid given by colored men generally, demonstrates clearly: First, that the conduct of the slaves is a strong guarantee of the weakness of the institution, should a favorable opportunity occur; and, secondly, that the colored people, as a body, were well represented by numbers, both in the fight, and in the number who suffered martyrdom afterward.

The first report of the number of "insurrectionists" killed was *seventeen*, which showed that several slaves were killed; for there were only *ten* of the men that belonged to the Kennedy Farm who lost their lives at the Ferry, namely: John Henri Kagi, Jerry Anderson, Watson Brown, Oliver Brown, Stewart Taylor, Adolphus Thompson, William Thompson, William Leeman, all eight whites, and Dangerfield Newby and Sherrard Lewis Leary, both colored. The rest reported dead, according to their own showing, were colored. Captain Brown had but seventeen with him, belonging to the Farm, and when all was over, there were four besides himself taken to Charlestown, prisoners, viz: A. D. Stevens, Edwin Coppic, white; John A. Copeland and Shields Green, colored. It is plain to be seen from this, that there was a proper per centage of colored men killed at the Ferry, and executed at Charlestown. Of those that escaped from the fangs of the human bloodhounds of slavery, there were four whites, and one colored man, myself being the sole colored man of those at the Farm.

That hundreds of slaves were ready, and would have joined in the work, had Captain Brown's sympathies not been aroused in favor of the families of his prisoners, and that a very different result would have been seen, in consequence, there is no question. There was abundant opportunity for him and the party to leave a place in which they held entire sway and possession, before the arrival of the troops. And so cowardly were the slaveholders, proper, that from Colonel Lewis Washington, the descendant of the Father of his Country, General George Washington, they were easily taken prisoners. They had not pluck enough to fight, nor to use the well-loaded arms in their possession, but were concerned rather in keeping a whole skin by parleying, or in spilling cowardly tears, to excite pity, as did Colonel Washington, and in that way escape merited punishment. No, the conduct of the slaves was beyond all praise; and could our brave old Captain have steeled his heart against the entreaties of his captives, or shut up the fountain of his sympathies against their families—could he, for the moment, have forgotten them, in the selfish thought of his own friends and kindred, or, by adhering to the original plan, have left the place, and thus looked forward to the prospective freedom of the slave—hundreds ready and waiting would have been armed before twenty-four hours had elapsed. As it was, even the noble old man's mistakes were productive of great good, the fact of which the future historian will record, without the embarrassment attending its present narration. John Brown did not only capture and hold Harper's Ferry for twenty hours, but he held the whole South. He captured President Buchanan and his Cabinet, convulsed the whole country, killed Governor Wise, and dug the mine and laid the train which will eventually dissolve the union between Freedom and Slavery. The rebound reveals the truth. So let it be!

49

CARL SCHURZ

Free Labor, Free Men

Born in Liblar, Germany, to a schoolteacher and a domestic, Carl Schurz (1829–1906) embraced revolutionary politics at a young age. During the political revolutions that swept Europe in the late 1840s, he founded the Bonner Zeitung, *an organ of democratic reform. After the revolts were suppressed, he immigrated to the United States in 1852, settling first in Philadelphia before making a permanent home in Watertown, Wisconsin.*

In the Midwest, Schurz became a lawyer, took up the antislavery cause, and joined the Republican Party. He was an ardent supporter of Abraham Lincoln during Lincoln's

---

"The Free Labor Movement Great Speech of Carl Schurz, of Wis., Delivered at St. Louis, Wednesday Eve. Aug. 1," *Freedom's Champion* (Atchison, Kans.), August 11, 1860, issue [25], col. A.

failed campaign for the Senate in 1858, helping him secure critical support from the community of German immigrants. Schurz served as his state's representative to the Republican National Convention in 1860. His loyalty to Lincoln paid off in later years. As president, Lincoln initially appointed Schurz as ambassador to Spain before commissioning him as a brigadier general in the Union Army.

From his antislavery perspective, Schurz argued that the "peculiar institution" threatened the "free labor" of men. In this excerpt from a speech given in 1860 and reprinted in a local newspaper, he offers a sense that bonded labor not only degraded the dignity of work itself but unfairly competed with the efforts of free men to produce and sell goods.

QUESTIONS TO CONSIDER

1. According to Schurz, why was free labor superior to slavery?
2. Why, in Schurz's view, did slavery endanger the country's future?
3. How did Schurz view the relationship between slave labor and free labor?

Cast your eyes over that great beehive called the free states. See by the railroad and the telegraphic wire every village, almost every backwoods cottage, drawn within the immediate reach of progressive civilization. Look over our grain fields, but lately a lonesome wilderness, where machinery is almost superseding the labor of the human hand; over our workshops, whose aspect is almost daily changed by the magic touch of inventive genius; over our fleets of merchant vessels, numerous enough to make the whole world tributary to our prosperity; look upon our society, where by popular education and the continual change of condition the dividing lines between ranks and classes are almost obliterated; look upon our system of public instruction, which places even the lowliest child of the people upon the high road of progressive advancement; upon our rapid growth and expansive prosperity, which is indeed subject to reverses and checks, but contains such a wonderful fertility of resources, that every check is a mere incentive to new enterprise, every reverse but a mere opportunity for the development of new powers.

To what do we owe all this? First and foremost, to that perfect freedom of inquiry, which acknowledges no rules but those of logic, no limits but those that bound the faculties of the human mind. [Cheers.] Its magic consists in its universality. To it we owe the harmony of our progressive movement in all its endless ramifications. No single science, no single practical pursuit exists in our day independently of all other sciences, all other practical pursuits. This is the age of the solidarity of progress. Set a limit to the freedom of inquiry in one direction and you destroy the harmony of its propelling action. Give us the Roman inquisition, which forbids Galileo Galilei to think that the earth moves around the sun, and he has to interrupt and give up the splendid train of his discoveries, and their influence upon all other branches of science is lost; he has to give it up, or he must fight the inquisition. [Cheers.] Let the slave power or any other political or economic interest tell us that we must think and say and invent and discover nothing which is against its demands—and we must interrupt and give up the harmony of our progressive development, or fight the tyrannical pretension, whatever shape it may assume. [Loud cheers.]

Believing, as we do, that the moral and ideal development of man is the true aim and end of human society, we must preserve in their efficiency the means which serve that end. In order to secure to the freedom of inquiry its full productive power, we must surround it with all the safeguards which political institutions afford. As we cannot set a limit to the activity of our minds, so we cannot muzzle our mouths or fetter the press with a censorship. [Applause.] *We cannot arrest or restrain the discussion of the question, what system of labor, or what organization of society promotes best the moral and intellectual development of man.* [Loud applause.] We cannot deprive a single individual of the privileges which protect him in the free exercise of his faculties and the enjoyment of his right, so long as these faculties are not employed to the detriment of the rights and liberties of others. Our organization of society resting upon equal rights, we find our security in a general system of popular education which fits all for an intelligent exercise of those rights. This is the home policy of free-labor society. This policy in our federal affairs must necessarily correspond. Deeming free and intelligent labor the only safe basis of society, it is our duty to expand its blessings over all the territory within our reach; seeing our own prosperity advanced by the prosperity of our neighbors, we must endeavor to plant upon our borders a system of labor which answers in that respect. Do we recognize the right of the laboring man to the soil he cultivates and shield him against oppressive speculation? Seeing in the harmonious development of all branches of labor a source of progress and power, we must adopt a policy which draws to light the resources of the land, gives work to our workshops and security to our commerce. These are the principles and views governing our policy.

Slaveholders, look at this picture, and at this. Can the difference escape your observation? You may say as many have said, that there is indeed a difference of principles, but not necessarily an antagonism of interests. Look again.

Your social system is founded upon forced labor, ours upon free labor. Slave labor cannot exist together with freedom of inquiry, and so you demand the restriction of that freedom; free labor cannot exist without it, and so we maintain its inviolability. Slave labor demands the setting aside of the safeguards of individual liberty, for the purpose of upholding subordination and protecting slave property; free labor demands their preservation as essential and indispensable to its existence and progressive development. Slavery demands extension by an agressive foreign policy; free labor demands an honorable peace and friendly intercourse with the world abroad for its commerce, and a peaceable and undisturbed development of our resources at home for its agriculture and industry. Slavery demands extension over national territories for the purpose of gaining political power. Free labor demands the national domain for workingmen, for the purpose of spreading the blessing of liberty and civilization. Slavery therefore opposes all measures tending to secure the soil to the actual laborer; free labor therefore recognizes the right of the settlers to the soil, and demands measures protecting him against the pressure of speculation. Slavery demands the absolute ascendency of the planting interest in our economical policy; free labor demands legislation tending to develop all the resources of the land, and to harmonize the agricultural, commercial and industrial interests. Slavery demands the control of the general government for its special protection and the promotion of its peculiar interests; free labor demands that the general government be administered for the purpose of securing to all the blessings of liberty and for the promotion of the general welfare. [Tremendous applause.] Slavery demands the recognition of its divine right; free labor recognizes no divine right but that of the liberty of all men. [Loud cheers.]

With one word, *slavery demands, for its protection and perpetuation, a system of policy which is utterly incompatible with the principles upon which the organization of free labor society rests*. There is the antagonism. That is the essence of the "irrepressible conflict."

PART SEVEN

Civil War and Reconstruction

The Price of War

On April 5, 1861, the United States erupted in civil war. Four years later, when General Robert E. Lee of the Confederate States of America surrendered to General Ulysses S. Grant of the United States at a courthouse in Appomattox, Virginia, slavery was forever ended, and the territorial integrity of the Union preserved. Yet the war had claimed nearly 620,000 lives, wounded or maimed another 281,000, and left great swaths of the South in ruin. Urgent questions arose about the future of democracy and citizenship. How would former slaves be integrated into the nation as free men and women? What role would the federal government play in policing Southern society and ensuring the liberties of blacks? How would the South rebuild its economy and society?

The documents in Part Seven illuminate the crises that the nation faced in this turbulent era. On the eve of the war, Southern lawmakers, among them Robert Toombs and Alexander H. Stephens, debated how to respond to the election of President Abraham Lincoln in November 1860, measuring the threat Lincoln ostensibly represented to slave states and weighing whether to secede. Once war broke out, few were prepared for the extent of death and destruction. The accounts by Union soldier Samuel Cormany and his wife, Rachel, of the Battle at Gettysburg graphically illustrate the impact of war on the Northern army and society. Ellen Leonard's account of the New York antidraft riot in 1863, and black soldiers' letters detailing their difficulties when they were finally accepted into the Union Army in late 1862, expose the dilemma of conflicting visions of the goals of the war.

As the war wound down in 1865, it was clear that the nation was changed forever. The South presented a stark landscape of abandoned fields, twisted rails, and burned buildings; men hobbling about on one leg or dangling an empty sleeve; and former slaves searching for food, shelter, and

275

work—and exploring their new freedom. Photographers like George Barnard and Mathew Brady dutifully registered the human and environmental cost of battle.

The war settled some things: that secession was impossible, slavery was dead, and the South's agricultural, slave-based economy was gone with the wind. Other matters, however, were far less clear. In particular, the Union victory did not resolve questions about race relations in the South. Many white Southerners, like plantation owner Henry William Ravenel, did not know what to make of the changes. His wartime diary reveals profound confusion over the place of ex-slaves in Southern society and alludes to the social tensions between whites and blacks that would severely strain the nation during Reconstruction. New Yorker George Templeton Strong revealed a profound mistrust of Southerners and, after the assassination of President Lincoln, a strong desire to punish them. The road to sectional reconciliation was anything but clear at the war's end and would eventually turn on two fundamental issues: how to integrate black Americans into the Union and what protections to afford their newfound status as citizens.

POINTS OF VIEW
The Gathering Storm (1860)

50

ROBERT TOOMBS

Immediate Secession

Shortly after Abraham Lincoln won the presidency on November 6, 1860, the idea of leaving the Union reached a fever pitch in some corners of the slave states. Many white Southerners tightly associated Lincoln with the growing abolition movement and with rising Northern hostility to laws intended to protect the "peculiar institution," such as the Fugitive Slave Law of 1850. They now feared that the election of a Republican to the White House spelled doom for their way of life. Southern legislators quickly organized special conventions to debate how best to respond to the election. Radicals, often

William W. Freehling and Craig M. Simpson, eds., *Secession Debated: Georgia's Showdown in 1860* (New York: Oxford University Press, 1992), 31–50.

labeled "Fire Eaters," demanded that Southern states secede from the Union. Moderates, however, urged patience, extolling the virtues of reasoned debate and compromise.

The state of Georgia hosted some of the most important convention meetings, at which lawmakers squared off and voiced a range of opinions on secession. Robert Toombs (1810–1885) argued strongly for his home state to cut ties with the Union. Born in the small town of Washington in Wilkes County, Toombs had graduated from Union College in upstate New York and later from the University of Virginia Law School. Admitted to the Georgia bar in 1830, he had quickly turned to politics, serving in the Georgia House of Representatives (1838, 1840–1841, 1843–1844), the United States House of Representatives (1844–1853), and the United States Senate (1851–1861). An ardent supporter of the right to own slaves, Toombs urged his constituents to secede immediately after Lincoln's election and officially resigned his Senate post in January 1861. During the Civil War, Toombs served first as the secretary of state for the Confederacy and later as a brigadier general.

Toombs delivered the following address to the Georgia legislature on November 13, 1860. Mincing few words, he demanded freedom from the North.

QUESTIONS TO CONSIDER

1. What was the effect on Northerners of the Fugitive Slave Act of 1850? Why did the law become such a point of contention between North and South?
2. Why did Lincoln's election represent a dire threat to slaveholding states?
3. According to Toombs, how did the institution of slavery promote liberty?

ROBERT TOOMBS'S SPEECH TO THE GEORGIA LEGISLATURE, NOVEMBER 13, 1860

GENTLEMEN OF THE GENERAL ASSEMBLY: I very much regret, in appearing before you at your request, to address you on the present state of the country, and the prospect before us, that I can bring you no good tidings. The stern, steady march of events has brought us in conflict with our non-slaveholding confederates upon the fundamental principles of our compact of Union. We have not sought this conflict; we have sought too long to avoid it; our forbearance has been construed into weakness, our magnanimity into fear, until the vindication of our manhood, as well as the defense of our rights, is required at our hands. The door of conciliation and compromise is finally closed by our adversaries, and it remains only to us to meet the conflict with the dignity and firmness of men worthy of freedom. We need no declaration of independence. Above eighty-four years ago our fathers won that by the sword from Great Britain, and above seventy years ago Georgia, with the twelve other confederates, as free, sovereign, and independent

States, having perfect governments already in existence, for purposes and objects clearly expressed, and with powers clearly defined, erected a common agent for the attainment of these purposes by the exercise of those powers, and called this agent the United States of America.

The Executive Department of the Federal Government, for forty-eight out of the first sixty years under the present Constitution, was in the hands of Southern Presidents, and so just, fair, and equitable, constitutional and advantageous to the country was the policy which they pursued, that their policy and administrations were generally maintained by the people. Certainly there was no just cause of complaint from the Northern States—no advantage was ever sought or obtained by them for their section of the Republic. They never sought to use a single one of the powers of the Government for the advancement of the local or peculiar interests of the South, and they all left office without leaving a single law on the statute-book where repeal would have affected injuriously a single industrial pursuit, or the business of a single human being in the South. But on the contrary, they had acquiesced in the adoption of a policy in the highest degree beneficial to Northern interests. The principles and policy of these Presidents were marked by the most enlarged and comprehensive statesmanship, promoting the highest interests of the Republic. They enlarged the domains of commerce by treaties with all nations, upon the great principle of equal justice to all nations, and special favors to none. They protected commerce and trade with an efficient navy in every sea. Mr. Jefferson acquired Louisiana, extending from the Balize[1] to the British possessions on the north, and from the Mississippi to the Pacific Ocean—a country larger than the whole United States at the time of the acknowledgement of their independence. He guaranteed the protection of the Federal Government by treaty to all the inhabitants of the purchased territory, in their lives, liberties, property and religion—sanctioned by law the right of all the people of the United States to emigrate into the territory with all of their property of every kind, (expressly including slaves,) to build up new States, and to come into the Union with such constitutions as they might choose to make. Mr. Madison vindicated the honor of the nation, maintained the security of commerce, and the inviolability of the persons of our sailors by the war of 1812. Mr. Monroe acquired Florida from Spain, extending the same guarantee to the inhabitants which Mr. Jefferson had to those of Louisiana. General Jackson compelled France, and other nations of Europe, to do long deferred justice to our plundered merchants. Mr. Tyler acquired Texas by voluntary compact, and Mr. Polk California and New Mexico by successful war. In all their grand additions to the wealth and power of the Republic, these statesmen neither asked nor sought any advantage for their own section; they admitted they were common acquisitions, purchased by the common blood and treasure, and for the common benefit of the people of the Republic, without reference to locality or institutions. Neither these

---

1. **the Balize:** Early French settlement and fort at the mouth of the Mississippi River, located in what today is Louisiana's Placquemines Parish.

statesmen nor their constituents sought in any way to use the Government for the interest of themselves or their section, or for the injury of a single member of the Confederacy. We can to-day open wide the history of their administrations and point with pride to every act, and challenge the world to point out a single act stained with injustice to the North, or with partiality to their own section. This is our record; let us now examine that of our confederates.

The instant the Government was organized, at the very first Congress, the Northern States evinced a general desire and purpose to use it for their own benefit, and to pervert its powers for sectional advantage, and they have steadily pursued that policy to this day. They demanded a monopoly of the business of ship-building, and got a prohibition against the sale of foreign ships to citizens of the United States, which exists to this day.

In 1820, the Northern party, (and I mean by that term now and whenever else it is used, or its equivalent, in these remarks, the Antislavery or Abolition party of the North,) endeavored to exclude the State of Missouri from admission into the Union, because she chose to protect African slavery in the new State. In the House, where they had a majority, they rejected her application, and a struggle ensued, when some half a dozen of Northern men gave way, and admitted the State, but upon condition of the exclusion of slavery from all that country, acquired from France by the treaty of 1802, lying north of thirty-six degrees thirty minutes, north latitude, and outside of the State of Missouri. This act of exclusion violated the express provisions of the treaty of 1802, to which the National faith was pledged; violated the well-settled policy of the Government, at least from Adams's administration to that day, and has, since slavery was adjudicated by the Supreme Court of the United States, violated the Constitution itself. When we acquired California and New-Mexico this party, scorning all compromises and all concessions, demanded that slavery should be forever excluded from them, and all other acquisitions of the Republic, either by purchase or conquest, forever. This position of this Northern party brought about the troubles of 1850, and the political excitement of 1854. The South at all times demanded nothing but equality in the common territories, equal enjoyment of them with their property, to that extended to Northern citizens and their property—nothing more. They said, we pay our part in all the blood and treasure expended in their acquisition. Give us equality of enjoyment, equal right to expansion—it is as necessary to our prosperity as yours. In 1790 we had less than eight hundred thousand slaves. Under our mild and humane administration of the system they have increased above four millions. The country has expanded to meet this growing want, and Florida, Alabama, Mississippi, Louisiana, Texas, Arkansas, Kentucky, Tennessee, and Missouri, have received this increasing tide of African labor; before the end of this century, at precisely the same rate of increase, the Africans among us in a subordinate condition will amount to eleven millions of persons. What shall be done with them? We must expand or perish. We are constrained by an inexorable necessity to accept expansion or extermination. Those who tell you that the territorial question is an abstraction, that you can never colonize another territory without the African slave trade, are both deaf and blind to the history of the last sixty years. All just reasoning, all past history, condemn the fallacy. The North understand it better—they have told us for twenty years that their object was to pen up slavery within its present limits—surround it with a border of free States, and like the scorpion surrounded with fire, they will make it sting itself to death. One thing at least is certain, that whatever may be the effect of your exclusion from the Territories, there is no dispute but that the North means it, and adopts it as a measure hostile to slavery upon this point.

But this is only one of the points of the case; the North agreed to deliver up fugitives from labor. In pursuance of this clause of the Constitution, Congress, in 1797, during Washington's administration, passed a Fugitive Slave law; that act never was faithfully respected all over the North, but it was not obstructed by State legislation until within the last thirty years; but the spirit of hostility to our rights became more active and determined, and in 1850 that act was found totally insufficient to recover and return fugitives from labor; therefore the act of 1850 was passed. The passage of that act was sufficient to rouse the demon of abolition all over the North. The pulpit, the press, abolition societies, popular assemblages, belched forth nothing but imprecations and curses upon the South and the honest men of the North who voted to maintain the Constitution. And thirteen States of the Union, by the most solemn acts of legislation, willfully, knowingly, and corruptly perjured themselves and annulled this law within their respective limits.

Hitherto the Constitution has had on its side the Federal Executive, whose duty it is to execute the laws and Constitution against these malefactors. It has earnestly endeavored to discharge that duty. Relying upon its power and good faith to remedy these wrongs, we have listened to conservative counsels, trusting to time, to the Federal Executive, and to a returning sense of justice in the North. The Executive has been faithful—the Federal judiciary have been faithful. The President has appointed sound judges, sound marshals, and other subordinate officers to interpret and to execute the laws. With the best intentions, they have all failed—our property has been stolen, our people murdered; felons and assassins have found sanctuary in the arms of the party which elected Mr. Lincoln. The Executive power, the last bulwark of the Constitution to defend us against these enemies of the Constitution, has been swept away, and we now stand without a shield, with bare bosoms presented to our enemies, and we demand at your hands the sword for our defense, and if you will not give it to us, we will take it—take it by the divine right of self-defense, which governments neither give nor can take away. Therefore, redress for past and present wrongs demands resistance to the rule of Lincoln and his Abolition horde over us; he comes at their head to shield and protect them in the perpetration of these outrages upon us, and, what is more, he comes at their head to aid them in consummating their avowed purposes by the power of the Federal Government. Their main purpose, as indicated by all their acts of hostility to slavery, is its final and total abolition. . . . They declare their purpose to war against slavery until there shall not be a slave in America, and until the African is elevated to a social and political equality with the white man. Lincoln indorses them and their principles, and in his own speeches declares the conflict irrepressible and enduring, until slavery is everywhere abolished.

Hitherto they have carried on this warfare by State action, by individual action, by appropriation, by the incendiary's torch and the poisoned bowl. They were compelled to adopt this method because the Federal executive and the Federal judiciary were against them. They will have possession of the Federal executive with its vast power, patronage, prestige of legality, its army, its navy, and its revenue on the fourth of March[2] next. Hitherto it has been on the side of the Constitution and the right; after the fourth of March it will be in the hands of your enemy. Will you let him have it? (Cries of "No, no. Never.") Then strike while it is yet today. Withdraw your sons from the army, from the navy, and every department of the Federal public service. Keep your own taxes in your own coffers—buy arms with them and throw the bloody spear into this den of incendiaries and assassins, and let God defend the right. But you are advised to wait, send soft messages to their brethren, to beg them to relent, to give you some assurances of their better fidelity for the future. What more can you get from them under this Government. . . . Then strike while it is yet time.

But we are told that secession would destroy the fairest fabric of liberty the world ever saw, and that we are the most prosperous people in the world under it. The arguments of tyranny as well as its acts, always reenact themselves. The arguments I now hear in favor of this Northern connection are identical in substance, and almost in the same words as those which were used in 1775 and 1776 to sustain the British connection. We won liberty, sovereignty, and independence by the American Revolution—we endeavored to secure and perpetuate these blessings by means of our Constitution. The very men who use these arguments admit that this Constitution, this compact, is violated, broken and trampled under foot by the abolition party. Shall we surrender the jewels because their robbers and incendiaries have broken the casket? Is this the way to preserve liberty? I would as surrender it back to the British crown as to the abolitionists. I will defend it from both. Our purpose is to defend those liberties. What baser fate could befall us or this great experiment of free government than to have written upon its tomb: "Fell by the hands of abolitionists and the cowardice of its natural defenders." If we quail now, this will be its epitaph.

We are said to be a happy and prosperous people. We have been, because we have hitherto maintained our ancient rights and liberties—we will be until we surrender them. They are in danger; come, freemen, to the rescue. If we are prosperous, it is due to God, ourselves, and the wisdom of our State government. We have an executive, legislative, and judicial department at home, possessing and entitled to the confidence of the people. I have already vainly asked for the law of the Federal Government that promotes our prosperity. I

---

2. **fourth of March:** A reference to the date in 1861 when Lincoln would officially assume his duties as president.

have shown you many that retard that prosperity—many that drain our coffers for the benefit of our bitterest foes. I say bitterest foes—show me the nation in the world that hates, despises, vilifies, or plunders us like our abolition "brethren" in the North. There is none. I can go to England or France, or any other country in Europe with my slave, without molestation or violating any law. I can go anywhere except in my own country, whilom [sometimes] called "the glorious Union"; here alone am I stigmatized as a felon; here alone am I an outlaw; here alone am I under the ban of the empire; here alone I have neither security nor tranquility; here alone are organized governments ready to protect the incendiary, the assassin who burns my dwelling or takes my life or those of my wife and children; here alone are hired emissaries paid by brethren to glide through the domestic circle and intrigue insurrection with all of its nameless horrors. My countrymen, "if you have nature in you, bear it not." Withdraw yourselves from such a confederacy; it is your right to do so—your duty to do so. I know not why the abolitionists should object to it, unless they want to torture and plunder you. If they resist this great sovereign right, make another war of independence, for that then will be the question; fight its battles over again—reconquer liberty and independence. As for me, I will take any place in the great conflict for rights which you may assign. I will take none in the Federal Government during Mr. Lincoln's administration.

51

ALEXANDER H. STEPHENS

A Course of Moderation

While secessionists like Toombs would eventually carry the day in Georgia, the state's actions were not foreordained. In contrast to the Fire Eaters, other local politicians vigorously promoted a course of caution and moderation. Leading the call for cooler heads was Alexander Stephens. Although he would later become the vice president of the Confederacy, Stephens squared off against Toombs in November 1860, when he gave the following speech opposing Toombs's appeals for Southern independence.

Stephens (1812–1883) grew up poor in Taliaferro County, Georgia. A graduate of Franklin College (later the University of Georgia), he studied law and passed the state bar in 1832. Four years later he began his political career, serving in the Georgia House of Representatives (1836–1841), the Georgia State Senate (1842), and the United States House of Representatives (1841–1859). Stephens used his political connections to secure

A. D. Candler, ed., *Confederate Records of the State of Georgia*, vol. 1 (Atlanta: Chas. P. Byrd, State Printer, 1909), 183–205.

business for his law practice and by the time of the Civil War owned thirty-four slaves and thousands of acres of land.

Despite his slaveholding background, Stephens urged restraint when Georgia lawmakers argued the merits of secession. Although his pleas for moderation failed to sway the majority of opinion, they signal the diversity of Southern viewpoints on the question of what to do after Lincoln's election.

QUESTIONS TO CONSIDER

1. Why, according to Stephens, was secession not Georgia's best option in late 1860?
2. Why did Stephens believe that Lincoln did not represent a significant threat to slaveholding states?
3. Why didn't more Georgians back Stephens's idea of waiting to see how Lincoln's election would affect South Carolinians and then calling a meeting of lawmakers to decide the course of action for the state?

SPEECH OF ALEXANDER H. STEPHENS, NOVEMBER 14, 1860

Fellow Citizens: I appear before you tonight at the request of Members of the Legislature and others, to speak of matters of the deepest interest that can possibly concern us all, of an earthly character. There is nothing, no question or subject connected with this life, that concerns a free people so intimately as that of the Government under which they live. We are now, indeed, surrounded by evils. Never since I entered upon the public stage, has the country been so environed with difficulties and dangers that threatened the public peace and the very existence of our Institutions as now. I do not appear before you at my own instance. It is not to gratify any desire of my own that I am here. Had I consulted my personal ease and pleasure, I should not be before you; but believing that it is the duty of every good citizen, when called on, to give his counsels and views whenever the country is in danger, as to the best policy to be pursued, I am here. For these reasons, and these only, do I bespeak a calm, patient, and attentive hearing.

The first question that presents itself is, shall the people of Georgia secede from the Union in consequence of the election of Mr. Lincoln to the Presidency of the United States? My countrymen, I tell you frankly, candidly, and earnestly, that I do not think that they ought. In my judgment, the election of no man, constitutionally chosen to that high office, is sufficient cause to justify any State to separate from the Union. It ought to stand by and aid still in maintaining the Constitution of the country. To make a point of resistance to the Government, to withdraw from it because any man has been elected, would put us in the wrong. We are pledged to maintain the Constitution. Many of us have sworn to support it. Can we, therefore, for the mere election of any man to the Presidency, and that, too, in accordance with the prescribed forms of the Constitution, make a point of resistance to the

Government, without becoming the breakers of that sacred instrument ourselves, by withdrawing ourselves from it? Would we not be in the wrong? Whatever fate is to befall this country, let it never be laid to the charge of the people of the South, and especially the people of Georgia, that we were untrue to our national engagements. Let the fault and the wrong rest upon others. If all our hopes are to be blasted, if the Republic is to go down, let us be found to the last moment standing on the deck with the Constitution of the United States waving over our heads. (Applause.) Let the fanatics of the North break the Constitution, if such is their fell purpose. Let the responsibility be upon them. I shall speak presently more of their acts; but let not the South, let us not be the ones to commit the aggression. We went into the election with this people. The result was different from what we wished; but the election has been constitutionally held. Were we to make a point of resistance to the Government and go out of the Union merely on that account, the record would be made up hereafter against us.

But it is said Mr. Lincoln's policy and principles are against the Constitution, and that, if he carries them out, it will be destructive of our rights. Let us not anticipate a threatened evil. If he violates the Constitution, then will come our time to act. Do not let us break it because, forsooth, he may. If he does, that is the time for us to act. (Applause.) I think it would be injudicious and unwise to do this sooner. I do not anticipate that Mr. Lincoln will do anything, to jeopardize our safety or security, whatever may be his spirit to do it; for he is bound by the constitutional checks which are thrown around him, which at this time render him powerless to do any great mischief. This shows the wisdom of our system. The President of the United States is no Emperor, no Dictator—he is clothed with no absolute power. He can do nothing, unless he is backed by power in Congress. The House of Representatives is largely in a majority against him. In the very face and teeth of the majority of Electoral votes, which he has obtained in the Northern States, there have been large gains in the House of Representatives, to the Conservative Constitutional Party of the country, which I here will call the National Democratic Party, because that is the cognomen [name] it has at the North. There are twelve of this Party elected from New York, to the next Congress, I believe. In the present House, there are but four, I think. In Pennsylvania, New Jersey, Ohio, and Indiana, there have been gains. In the present Congress, there were one hundred and thirteen Republicans, when it takes one hundred and seventeen to make a majority. The gains in the Democratic Party in Pennsylvania, Ohio, New Jersey, New York, Indiana, and other States, notwithstanding its distractions, have been enough to make a majority of near thirty, in the next House, against Mr. Lincoln. Even in Boston, Mr. Burlingame,[1] one of the noted leaders of the fanatics of that section, has been defeated, and a Conservative man returned in his stead. Is this the time, then, to apprehend that

---

1. **Mr. Burlingame:** Anson Burlingame (1820–1870), antislavery lawyer and Republican member of the U.S. House of Representatives from Boston, 1855–1861.

Mr. Lincoln, with this large majority of the House of Representatives against him, can carry out any of [these] unconstitutional principles in that body?

In the Senate, he will also be powerless. There will be a majority of four against him. This, after the loss of Bigler,[2] Fitch,[3] and others, by the unfortunate dissensions of the National Democratic Party in their States. Mr. Lincoln can not appoint an officer without the consent of the Senate—he can not form a Cabinet without the same consent. He will be in the condition of George the Third (the embodiment of Toryism), who had to ask the Whigs to appoint his ministers, and was compelled to receive a Cabinet utterly opposed to his views; and so Mr. Lincoln will be compelled to ask of the Senate to choose for him a Cabinet, if the Democracy or that Party choose to put him on such terms. He will be compelled to do this, or let the Government stop, if the National Democratic Senators (for that is their name at the North), the Conservative men in the Senate, should so determine. Then how can Mr. Lincoln obtain a Cabinet which would aid him, or allow him to violate the Constitution? Why, then, I say, should we disrupt the ties of this Union, when his hands are tied—when he can do nothing against us?

My honorable friend who addressed you last night [Mr. Toombs], and to whom I listened with the profoundest attention, asks if we would submit to Black Republican rule? I say to you and to him, as a Georgian, I would never submit to any Black Republican aggression upon our Constitutional rights.

I will never consent myself, as much as I admire this Union, for the glories of the past or the blessings of the present; as much as it has done for civilization; as much as the hopes of the world hang upon it; I would never submit to aggression upon my rights to maintain it longer; and if they can not be maintained in the Union standing on the Georgia Platform, where I have stood from the time of its adoption, I would be in favor of disrupting every tie which binds the States together. I will have equality for Georgia, and for the citizens of Georgia, in this Union, or I will look for new safeguards elsewhere. This is my position. The only question now is, can this be secured in the Union? That is what I am counseling with you tonight about. Can it be secured? In my judgment it may be, yet it may not be; but let us do all we can, so that in the future, if the worst comes, it may never be said we were negligent in doing our duty to the last.

My countrymen, I am not of those who believe this Union has been a curse up to this time. True men, men of integrity, entertain different views from me on this subject. I do not question their right to do so; I would not impugn their motives in so doing. Nor will I undertake to say that this Government of our Fathers is perfect. There is nothing perfect in this world of human origin; nothing connected with human nature, from man himself to any of his works. You may select the wisest and best men for your Judges, and yet

---

2. **Bigler:** William Bigler (1814–1880), Pennsylvania governor (1851–1854) and U.S. senator (1855–1861).
3. **Fitch:** Graham Fitch (1809–1892), Indiana free-soil politician who served in the U.S. House of Representatives (1849–1853) and Senate (1855–1861).

how many defects are there in the administration of justice? You may select the wisest and best men for your Legislators, and yet how many defects are apparent in your laws? And it is so in our Government. But that this Government of our Fathers, with all its defects, comes nearer the objects of all good Governments than any other on the face of the earth, is my settled conviction.

I look upon this country, with our institutions, as the Eden of the World, the Paradise of the Universe. It may be that out of it we may become greater and more prosperous, but I am candid and sincere in telling you that I fear if we yield to passion, and without sufficient cause shall take that step, that instead of becoming greater or more peaceful, prosperous and happy—instead of becoming Gods, we will become demons, and at no distant day commence cutting one another's throats. This is my apprehension. Let us, therefore, whatever we do, meet these difficulties, great as they are, like wise and sensible men, and consider them in the light of all the consequences which may attend our action. Let us see, first clearly, where the path of duty leads, and then we may not fear to tread therein.

Now, upon another point, and that the most difficult, and deserving your most serious consideration, I will speak. That is, the course which this State should pursue toward those Northern States which, by their legislative acts, have attempted to nullify the Fugitive Slave Law.

Northern States, on entering into the Federal Compact, pledged themselves to surrender such fugitives; and it is in disregard of their constitutional obligations that they have passed laws which even tend to hinder or inhibit the fulfillment of that obligation. They have violated their plighted faith. What ought we to do in view of this? That is the question. What is to be done? By the law of nations, you would have a right to demand the carrying out of this article of agreement, and I do not see that it should be otherwise with respect to the States of this Union; and in case it be not done, we would, by these principles, have the right to commit acts of reprisal on these faithless governments, and seize upon their property, or that of their citizens, wherever found. The States of this Union stand upon the same footing with foreign nations in this respect.

Now, then, my recommendation to you would be this: In view of all these questions of difficulty, let a convention of the people of Georgia be called, to which they may all be referred. Let the sovereignty of the people speak. Some think that the election of Mr. Lincoln is cause sufficient to dissolve the Union. Some think those other grievances are sufficient to justify the same; and that the Legislature has the power thus to act, and ought thus to act. I have no hesitancy in saying that the Legislature is not the proper body to sever our Federal relations, if that necessity should arise.

I say to you, you have no power so to act. You must refer this question to the people, and you must wait to hear from the men at the cross-roads, and even the groceries; for the people of this country, whether at the cross-roads or groceries, whether in cottages or palaces, are all equal, and they are the Sovereigns in this country. Sovereignty is not in the Legislature. We, the people, are sovereign. I am one of them, and have a right to be heard; and so has

every other citizen of the State. You Legislators—I speak it respectfully—ar
but our servants. You are the servants of the people, and not their masters.
Power resides with the people in this country. The great difference between
our country and most others, is, that here there is popular sovereignty, while
there sovereignty is exercised by kings or favored classes. This principle of
popular sovereignty, however much derided lately, is the foundation of our
institutions. Constitutions are but the channels through which the popular
will may be expressed. Our Constitutions, State and Federal, came from the
people. They made both, and they alone can rightfully unmake either.

Should Georgia determine to go out of the Union, I speak for one, though
my views might not agree with them, whatever the result may be, I shall bow
to the will of her people. Their cause is my cause, and their destiny is my destiny; and I trust this will be the ultimate course of all. The greatest curse that
can befall a free people, is civil war.

I am for exhausting all that patriotism demands, before taking the last
step. I would invite, therefore, South Carolina to a conference. I would ask
the same of all the other Southern States, so that if the evil has got beyond
our control, which God in his mercy grant may not be the case, we may not
be divided among ourselves; (cheers) but if possible, secure the united coop-
eration of all the Southern States, and then in the face of the civilized world,
we may justify our action, and, with the wrong all on the other side, we can
appeal to the God of Battles, if it comes to that, to aid us in our cause. (Loud
applause.) But do nothing, in which any portion of our people, may charge
you with rash or hasty action. It is certainly a matter of great importance to
tear this government asunder. You were not sent here for that purpose. I
would wish the whole South to be united, if this is to be done; and I believe if
we pursue the policy which I have indicated, this can be effected.

In this way, our sister Southern States can be induced to act with us; and
I have but little doubt, that the States of New York, and Pennsylvania, and
Ohio, and the other Western States, will compel their Legislatures to recede
from their hostile attitude, if the others do not. Then, with these, we would
go on without New England, if she chose to stay out.

I am, as you clearly perceive, for maintaining the Union as it is, if possible. I will exhaust every means, thus, to maintain it with an equality in
it. My position, then, in conclusion, is for the maintenance of the honor,
the rights, the equality, the security, and the glory of my native State in the
Union, if possible; but if these cannot be maintained in the Union, then I am
for their maintenance, at all hazards, out of it. Next to the honor and glory
of Georgia, the land of my birth, I hold the honor and glory of our common
country. In Savannah, I was made to say by the reporters, who very often
make me say things which I never did, that I was first for the glory of the
whole country, and next for that of Georgia. I said the exact reverse of this.
I am proud of Georgia, of her history, of her present standing. I am proud
even of her motto, which I would have duly respected at the present time,
by all her sons—"Wisdom, Justice and Moderation." I would have her rights,
and those of the Southern States maintained now upon these principles.

ow is just what it was in 1850, with respect to the Southern
form, then established, was subsequently adopted by most, if
r Southern States. Now I would add but one additional plank
, which I have stated, and one which time has shown to be
that shall likewise be adopted in substance by all the South-
... ⌐taces, all may yet be well. But, if all this fails, we shall at least have the
satisfaction of knowing that we have done our duty, and all that patriotism
could require.

FOR CRITICAL THINKING

1. How might Robert Toombs have reacted to Alexander Stephens's
   speech about avoiding secession, at least in the short term? What
   might Toombs have pointed out to demonstrate the immediate need
   for Georgia to withdraw from the Union?
2. As you read the orations by Toombs and Stephens delivered in November 1860, what do you think any politician might have said or
   done to avoid war?

52

ELLEN LEONARD

Three Days of Terror: The New York City Draft Riots

*Sixteen major and many lesser riots erupted in New York City between 1834 and 1874.
Almost any reason sufficed to bring out the clubs, guns, and paving stones: Protestants
attacked Catholics, Irish Catholics fought Irish Protestants, slavery-supporting mobs
roughed up abolitionists, rival fire companies and gangs started violence that simply
spread. The underlying complications were many: municipal government was ineffective
and corrupt; the weak and unprofessional New York police often could not maintain
order without calling out the militia; alcohol was cheap, and people habitually drank
to excess; and masses of new immigrants and unskilled laborers lived on the edge of
destitution. With the coming of the Civil War, the city's political conflicts grew sharper
and war-induced inflation worsened the living conditions of the poor.*

*At the war's outbreak, North and South had fielded large armies of patriotic vol-
unteers, but as the fighting continued, both sides turned to conscription. Yet only about
7 percent of those whose names were drawn in draft lotteries actually served. Many*

Ellen Leonard, "Three Days of Terror," *Harper's New Monthly Magazine,* January 1867,
225–33.

simply refused or ran off to another district, and both sides allowed those who were drafted to hire substitutes to fight in their place or to pay a fee of $300 to avoid serving.

With the Union's conscription law vastly unpopular, the Democratic Party press made the draft a major issue. In so doing, the media fanned opposition, particularly among urban Irish American populations who largely opposed the war and who feared competition from freed slaves for the unskilled jobs that provided their meager livelihoods. As soon as actual conscription began in July 1863, rioting broke out in several cities.

Most horrific was the uprising of July 13–16 in New York City. Many of the federal troops usually stationed in the city, who might have put down the riot, were pursuing General Lee's retreating army after the Battle of Gettysburg. Over one hundred people died, most of them rioters gunned down when troop reinforcements arrived to retake control of the streets. In addition to random looting and vandalism, the rioters lynched several blacks; burned down the Colored Orphan Asylum; and attacked Republican newspapers, the homes of prominent Republicans and abolitionists, and businesses that employed blacks. Ellen Leonard's article on the riot, published in Harper's New Monthly Magazine *in 1867 and excerpted below, offers a rare eyewitness account by an innocent visitor accidentally trapped in these dramatic and dangerous events.*

QUESTIONS TO CONSIDER

1. According to Ellen Leonard's account, what seemed to have been the mob's main motivators?
2. How much danger did the mob pose to the city's citizens and to visitors like Leonard?
3. Are you surprised by the ways women behaved during the war? How did their behavior contradict what you know about women's roles during this era?

On the tenth of July, 1863, my mother and myself arrived in the city of New York. . . . We hoped . . . to spend a few days quietly with my brother J., call on various friends and relatives, visit Central Park and a lion or so, shop a little, and move onward at our leisure.

But man proposes and Fate *disposes*, and nothing in New York turned out as we expected. Instead of visiting our friends and meandering leisurely about the city, we were caught in a mob and penned up in our first stopping-place. . . .

Returning thence [after a visit to the Astor Library] at mid-day I first saw signs of disturbance. A squad of policemen passed before me into Third Avenue, clerks were looking eagerly from the doors, and men whispering in knots all up and down the street; but . . . once at home [I] thought no more of it. We were indulging ourselves in siestas after our noonday lunch, when a great roaring suddenly burst upon our ears—a howling as of thousands of wild Indians let loose at once; and before we could look out or collect our thoughts at all the cry arose from every quarter, "The mob! the mob!" "The Irish have risen to resist the draft!"

In a second my head was out the window, and I saw it with my own eyes. We were on a cross-street between First and Second avenues. First Avenue was crowded as far as we could see it with thousands of infuriated creatures, yelling, screaming, and swearing in the most frantic manner; while crowds of women, equally ferocious, were leaning from every door and window, swinging aprons and handkerchiefs, and cheering and urging them onward. The rush and roar grew every moment more terrific. Up came fresh hordes faster and more furious; bareheaded men, with red, swollen faces, brandishing sticks and clubs, or carrying heavy poles and beams; and boys, women, and children hurrying on and joining with them in this mad chase up the avenue like a company of raging fiends. In the hurry and tumult it was impossible to distinguish individuals, but all seemed possessed alike with savage hate and fury. The most dreadful rumors flew through the street, and we heard from various sources the events of the morning. The draft had been resisted, buildings burned, twenty policemen killed, and the remainder utterly routed and discomfited; the soldiers were absent, and the mob triumphant and increasing in numbers and violence every moment.

Our neighborhood was in the greatest excitement. The whole population turned out at once, gazing with terror and consternation on the living stream passing before them, surging in countless numbers through the avenue, and hurrying up town to join those already in action. Fresh yells and shouts announced the union of forces, and bursting flames their accelerated strength and fury. The armory on Twenty-second Street was broken open, sacked, and fired, and the smoke and flames rolled up directly behind us. . . .

Bells were tolling in every quarter. The rioters were still howling in Twenty-second Street, and driving the firemen from the burning armory. The building fell and the flames sunk, and then darkness came all at once and shut out every thing. We gathered gloomily around my brother in the back-parlor. An evening paper was procured, but brought no comfort. It only showed more clearly the nature and extent of this fearful outbreak. It only told us that the whole city was as helpless and anxious as ourselves. . . .

As the clocks struck twelve a great shout startled me, and a light flamed right up before me. A huge bonfire had been kindled in the middle of the street not far below us. Wild forms were dancing about it, and piling on fresh fuel. Great logs and beams and other combustibles were dragged up and heaped upon it. Sleep, now, was of course impossible. From a seat in an upper window I saw it rise and fall, flame up and fade. . . .

[The next day] there was no milk, no ice to be had, and meat and bread were on the wane; and so I ventured out with my sister H. for supplies. We found our street full of people, excitement, and rumors. Men and boys ran past us with muskets in their hands. We heard that a fight was in progress above Twenty-second Street. The mob had seized a gun-factory and many muskets; but the police had driven them off and taken back part of their plunder. It was cheering to find that the police were still alive. . . . Men talked in low, excited tones, and seemed afraid of each other. The stores were mostly closed and business suspended. With difficulty we procured supplies of provisions and a newspaper. . . . The mob were gathering in great force in our vicinity, and things looked every moment more threatening; so we hurried home as fast as possible, and I took my post again at the window.

. . . In the First Avenue the crowd was now very dense and clamorous. The liquor store on the corner was thronged with villainous-looking customers, and the women who had welcomed the mob on their first appearance were again talking loudly as if urging them on to action. "Die *at home!*" was the favorite watch-word which often reached our ears. Every thing indicated that a collision was approaching. We caught, after a time, a glimpse of soldiers, and heard the welcome rattle of musketry, distant at first, then nearer and nearer. The soldiers marched to and through Twenty-second Street and turned down First Avenue. The mob yelled and howled and stood their ground. Women from the roofs threw stones and brickbats upon the soldiers. Then came the volleys; the balls leaped out and the mob gave way at once and fled in every direction. A great crowd rushed through our street, hiding in every nook and corner. We closed doors and blinds, but still peeped out of the windows. The soldiers marched slowly back up the avenue, firing along the way; crossed over into Second Avenue, marched down opposite our street and fired again. Again the mob scattered, and scampered in droves through the street. . . .

The papers brought no encouragement. Fearful deeds of atrocity were recorded. The mob were increasing in power and audacity, and the city was still paralyzed and panic-struck. The small military force available could only protect a few important positions, leaving the greater part defenseless. Our inflammable neighborhood was wholly at the mercy of the mob. . . .

Another day had come, Wednesday, July 15th. . . . The city was not all burned down, we found. The newspapers were still alive, and insisting that more troops were on hand and the mob checked; but we saw no signs of it. The morning indeed passed more quietly. The rioters were resting from the labors of the night; but business was not resumed, and swarms of idle men still hung about the streets and stores. . . .

As night approached we heard drums beating, and gangs of rioters marched up their favorite avenue. . . . Then some one shouted, "They are coming!" and a small band of soldiers appeared marching up our street. The mob seemed to swell into vast dimensions, and densely filled the whole street before them. Hundreds hurried out on the house-tops, tore up brickbats, and hurled them with savage howls at the approaching soldiers. Shots were fired from secret ambushes, and soldiers fell before they had fired. Then they charged bravely into the mob, but their force was wholly inadequate. One small howitzer and a company of extemporized militia could do little against those raging thousands. . . . Some [soldiers] now appeared in sight with a wounded officer and several wounded men, looking from side to side for shelter. Their eyes met ours with mute appeal. There was no time to be lost; the mob might any moment be upon them. There was a moment's consultation, a hasty reference to J., an unhesitating response: "Yes, by all means"; we beckoned them in, and in they came. Doors and windows were at once closed, and the house became a hospital, and seemed filled with armed men. The wounded men were carried into my brother's room; the Colonel was laid on the bed, and the others propped up with pillows. There were a few moments of great commotion and confusion. We flew for fans, ice water, and bandages. Some of the soldiers went out into the fight again, and some remained with the wounded. A surgeon, who had volunteered as a private under his old commander, dressed the wounds of the sufferers. The Colonel was severely wounded in the thigh by a slug made of a piece of lead pipe, producing a compound fracture. The wounds of two others, though less dangerous, were severe and painful.

Twilight was now upon us, and night rapidly approaching. The soldiers had been forced to retreat, leaving the mob in great force and fury. We heard them shouting and raving on the corner, and knew that we were in great danger. Already they were clamoring for the wounded soldiers who had escaped them. We thought of Colonel O'Brien's fate, and could not suppress the thought that our own house might be made the scene of a like tragedy. Could we defend ourselves if attacked? A hurried consultation was held. We had arms and ammunition, and, including J. and the slightly wounded soldiers, half a dozen men able and willing to use them. But we could not "man our lines." We were open to attack at once from the front and rear, the roof, the front basement, and the balcony above it. We might, indeed, retreat to the upper stories, barricade the stairway, and hold it against all the assailants that could crowd into the hall. But if they chose to fire the house below we could not prevent it, and then there would be no escape either for our wounded or ourselves.

The Colonel promptly decided the question; resistance was hopeless, could only make the case worse, and must not be attempted. Not only so, but all signs of the presence of soldiers must be removed. Arms, military apparel, and bloody clothing were accordingly concealed. The Colonel was conveyed to the cellar and placed on a mattress. The young soldier, next to him most severely wounded, was assisted up to the rear apartment on the upper floor and placed in charge of my mother and myself. The soldiers who had remained were then ordered to make their escape from the house as they best could, and to hasten to head-quarters with an urgent request that a force might be sent to our relief. . . .

J., with his bandaged head and disabled arm, was liable to be taken for a wounded soldier, and his wife and her sister, Mrs. P——, insisted that he also should betake himself to the roof. He could render no material assistance if he remained; on the other hand, his presence might precipitate a scene of violence which would not be offered to ladies alone. They did not feel that they were personally in danger—so far there was no report that the lawless violence of the rioters had been directed against women; and if he could get away he might be the means of bringing speedier relief. Very reluctantly he yielded to these considerations, and prepared to accompany the wounded soldier. The mother of the household took refuge in her room on the second-floor. To her daughter-in-law, wife of an absent son, was assigned a post of observation at a front window. The two heroic women, H. and her sister, remained below to confront the mob. . . .

In front the demonstrations were still more alarming. The rioters had taken possession of the street, stationed a guard on both avenues, and were chasing up and down for the soldiers. Then they were seen searching from house to house. . . . Then came a rush up the steps, and the bell rang violently. Not a sound was heard through the house. Again and yet again the bell rang, more and more furiously. Hearts throbbed, nerves quivered, but no one stirred. Then came knocks, blows, kicks, threats, attempts to force the door. Come in they must and would; nothing could stay them.

Having gained for the retreating party all the time she could, Mrs. P—— at length unlocked the door, opened it, passed out, and closing it behind her, stood face to face with the mob, which crowded the steps and swarmed on the sidewalk and the adjacent street. What could she do? She knew that they would come in, that they would search the house, that they would find the men; but she was determined not to give them up without an effort to save them. . . .

"What do you want?" she asked, while the air was yet ringing with the cry that came up from the crowd, "The soldiers! the soldiers!" "Bring out the soldiers!" One who stood near and seemed to be a leader replied, "There were two soldiers went into this house, and we must have them. You must give them up."

"There *were* two that came in, but went out again. They are not here now."

She spoke in a low but perfectly clear and steady voice, that compelled attention, and the crowd hushed its ravings to catch her words.

"Let us see; if they are not here we will not harm you; but we must search the house."

"We can not let you in; there are only women here—some that are old and feeble, and the sight of such a crowd will frighten them to death."

"They shall not all come in," was the reply; and after some further parley it was agreed that half a dozen only should enter and make the search. The leader gave his orders, the door was opened, and the men detailed came in; but before it could be closed the mob surged up, pressed in, and filled the hall. Many of them were armed with the stolen carbines.

"Light the gas!" was the cry.

"My sister has gone for a light."

It came, and the parley was renewed. The leader again demanded the soldiers; insisted that they were there, and said it would be better for themselves if they would give them up. She persisted in the statement she had made.

"She is fooling us, and using up the time while they are getting away by the roof!" cried one, and pressing forward with his musket pointed at her, endeavored to pass her. Very deliberately she took hold of the muzzle and turned it aside, saying, "Don't do that. You know I am a woman, and it might frighten me."

The leader returned to the charge. "We know the men are here, and if you give them up to us you shall not be harmed. But if you do not, and we find them, you know what a mob is. I can not control them; your house will be burned over your heads, and I will not guarantee your lives for five minutes."

"You will not do that," was the reply. "We are not the kind of people whose houses you wish to burn. My only son works as you do, and perhaps in the same shop with some of you, for seventy cents a day."

She did not tell them that her amateur apprentice boy had left his place to go to Pennsylvania and fight their friends the rebels. A young man, whom she had noticed as one of the few of decent appearance, stepped to her side and whispered to her, advising her compliance with the demand, assuring her that the men could not be controlled. The tone more than the words indicated to her that she had made one friend; and she found another, in the same way, a moment later.

Meantime the leaders were consulting whether they should go first above or below, and decided on the latter. Stationing one man with a musket at the door, and one at the stairs, they proceeded, pioneered by H., first to the parlors, and then to the basement, thoroughly examining both. Most fortunately the sentinels were the two young men in whom Mrs. P——felt she had found friends, and she was not slow to improve the opportunity to deepen the impression she had made. But now the crowd outside, thundering at the basement door, burst in the panels, and forcing it open, with terrible oaths and threats rushed in and filled the lower hall. Part joined the searching party, and some hurried up the first-floor. One, crowding past the sentinel, was striding up the stairs. We heard his call to his comrades, "Come on up stairs!" and our hearts sunk within us. But the sentinel's stern command, enforced by his leveled piece, brought him back.

The main party, having ransacked the basement rooms, now turned to the cellar. In a moment a loud shout announced that they had found a victim. The surgeon was dragged up, forced out at the lower door, and delivered over to the crowd outside. A blow from a bludgeon or musket felled him to the earth, inflicting a terrible wound on the head. "Hang him, hang him!" "To the post at the Twenty-second Street corner!" were the cries as they hurried him off. The search within proceeded; a moment more and they had found the Colonel. A new and fiercer shout was sent up. An order from a leader thrilled through the hall, "Come down here some of yees wid yer muskets!"

At the first cry from the cellar Mrs. P——sprung for the basement, intending to make her way at any hazard. A sentinel stood at the head of the stairway; a stalwart brute, reeking with filth and whisky. He seized her, with both arms about her waist, with a purpose of violence quite too evident. She struggled to free herself without raising an alarm, but in vain; then a sudden and piercing shriek, which rung through the house, made him for an instant relax his hold, and, wrenching herself away, she hurried back and sought the protection of the friendly sentinel.

"He will not let me pass; I must go down."

"You must not," he replied; "it is no place for you." And then he added, looking sternly at her, "You have deceived us. You said there was no one here, and there is."

"I would have done the same thing for you if you had been wounded. Look at me; do you not believe me?"

He did look, full in her eye, for an instant; then said: "Yes, I do believe it. You have done right, and I admire your spirit."

"But I must go down. Go with me."

"No; it is no place for you."

"Then go yourself, and save his life."

And turning over his charge to the sentinel at the door, he did go. Meantime the searching party, having found the Colonel, proceeded to question him. He said he was a citizen, accidentally wounded, and had been obliged to seek refuge there.

"Why did you hide, if you are a citizen?"

Because, he said, he was afraid he should be taken for a soldier. They would not believe, but still he insisted on his statement. Then the muskets were sent for, and four pieces leveled at his head, as he lay prostrate and helpless.

"Fire, then, if you will, on a wounded man and a citizen. I shall die, any how, for my wound is a mortal one. But before you fire I wish you would send for a priest."

"What, are you a Catholic?"

"Yes."

This staggered them; and while they were hesitating the sentinel joined the group, and as soon as he looked on the Colonel exclaimed: "I know that man. I used to go to school with him. He is no soldier."

This turned the scale. The leaders were satisfied, and decided to let him go. . . .

Those of the mob who had remained above, disappointed of their prey, with oaths and execrations protested against the action of their leaders, and sent the ruffian at the head of the stairway down to see if it was all right. But the positive statements of the friendly sentinel, which Mrs. P——had the satisfaction of hearing him rehearse, as the two met in the lower hall, disarmed even his suspicions, and the rest could do no otherwise than acquiesce. So well satisfied, indeed, were the leaders, and, as it is not unreasonable to suppose, so impressed with the resolute bearing of the two ladies, that they volunteered to station a guard before the door to prevent the annoyance of any further search. As they had found the two men who had been reported to them as having entered the house, it did not seem to occur to them that there might be still others concealed; and so they took their departure, leaving the upper stories unvisited. . . .

It was now, we thought, past midnight. We had no hope of relief, no thought or expectation but of struggling on alone hour after hour of distress and darkness; but as I was listening in my window to some unusually threatening demonstrations from the mob, I heard the distant clank of a horse's hoof on the pavement.

Again and again it sounded, more and more distinctly; and then a measured tread reached my ears, the steady, resolute tramp of a trained and disciplined body. No music was ever half so beautiful! It might, it must be, our soldiers! Off I flew to spread the good news through the household, and back again to the window to hear the tramp nearer and fuller and stronger, and see a long line of muskets gleam out from the darkness, and a stalwart body of men stop at our door. "Halt!" was cried; and I rushed down stairs headlong, unlocked the door without waiting for orders, and with tears of joy and gratitude which every one can imagine and nobody describe, welcomed a band of radiant soldiers and policemen, and in the midst of them all who should appear but my brother, pale and exhausted, who had gotten off the housetop in some mysterious way and brought this gallant company to our rescue!

53

SAMUEL AND RACHEL CORMANY

The Battle of Gettysburg: On the Field and at Home

In the spring of 1863, with Vicksburg on the Mississippi River under siege and with the possibility of a Confederate victory hanging in the balance, General Robert E. Lee ventured upon a brilliantly daring plan. He would invade southern Pennsylvania, taking the conflict into Union territory to the north of the nation's capital. Achievement might win independence for the Confederacy, if not by total military triumph on the field then by a political success: namely, a deepening of discouragement in the North that would lead to the equivalent to surrender.

By late June, Lee was in Pennsylvania. The immediate task of the newly appointed commander of the Union Army of the Potomac, George Meade, was to counter the Confederate advance. A triumph by Meade in the battle that would follow at Gettysburg in Pennsylvania could not have given the Union total victory in the war; but a defeat, on the other hand, would have come close to total victory for the Confederacy.

The great battle began on July 1. For a time, the Union was on the defensive, clinging to the slope known as Cemetery Ridge. On July 2, under the command of Joshua Chamberlain, the Maine troops holding Little Round Top—now out of ammunition—swept down in a desperate and successful bayonet charge that preserved that point in the Union lines against a powerful Confederate assault. That same day, a handful of Minnesota troops

James C. Mohr, ed., *Franklin County: Diary of Rachel Cormany* and *Franklin County: Diary of Samuel Cormany*, 1863. From *The Cormany Diaries: A Northern Family in the Civil War* (Pittsburgh: University of Pittsburgh Press, 1982).

attacked a rebel force numbering several times their own strength and beat back the Confederates. Together, the Maine and the Minnesota troops were instrumental in keeping the Union position intact.

On July 3, General Lee ordered Confederate general James Longstreet to initiate an attack on the Union center. Led by Virginia general George Pickett, fourteen thousand rebel troops advanced upward on exposed ground against a combination of artillery and infantry fire far heavier than the Confederate officers had expected. The assault briefly touched the Union lines but then wilted against impossible firepower. The repulsion of "Pickett's Charge" effectively ended the Confederate hope of a victory by Lee. Gettysburg was a heartening moment for the Union, intensified by General Ulysses S. Grant's nearly simultaneous capture of Vicksburg.

The writers of the following journal entries, Samuel and Rachel Cormany, were witnesses to the Battle of Gettysburg. Samuel was a soldier in battle, having enlisted in September 1862 as a second lieutenant in the sixteenth Pennsylvania Cavalry. Rachel remained a civilian on the home front, living with the couple's baby, Cora, in a rented space barely twenty-five miles away. Both writers offer glimpses of the everyday grind of the war on everyday people, especially the physical toll exacted by fear, deprivation, and the uncertainty of the future. Note the lack of a strong political viewpoint in either account; indeed, both authors focus on survival more than on any overarching philosophy about slavery.

QUESTIONS TO CONSIDER

1. How did access to information shape people's experiences of the war?
2. How important was it to soldiers to believe they had widespread civilian support?
3. How did living in the shadow of a brutal, bloody battle affect Rachel Cormany's everyday life? What is surprising about her account?

DIARY OF SAMUEL CORMANY

June 30, 1863

Tuesday. We moved out early to within a few miles of Westminster and drew up in line for battle—our advance moved on—and the Reg't supported—met little resistance in taking the City—Took 8 prisoners.

The Regiment halted close to the City—We got some eatables—The people were ecstatic to see our troops driving out and following up the "Johnies."[1] They did all in their power for us—The Rebs had acted awful meanly—Took everything like hats, boots, shoes, clothing &c—The streets and fence corners were strewn with their discarded old ones. Some of them, yes many, were almost able to join in the march, being so full of lice—Soon we were called on to muster for pay—still near town—and at noon took up the march Manchester—I never saw more cherries, ripe and ripening,

---

1. **Johnies:** Slang for Confederate soldiers.

and better crops then are to be seen hereabouts—Lieut Barnes & I got a fine supper at Mr. Bingamins—Fine ladies about. Exultant on our arrival, and almost worshipped us as their protectors—i.e., our soldiers—For the night we picketed and laid ready—I stood Post two hours—

July 1, 1863

Wednesday. I had a fine chicken breakfast—and a feast of other good things. Took up march for Hanover. Very fine rich country—and such fine water—Settlers are Old Style People. Many Dunkerds.[2] We were given any amount to eat all along the way—The Rebs who had passed this way acted very meanly—All around—demanding setters to pay money to exempt horses from being taken and barns and houses from being burned—One old man said he paid $100 to exempt 2 horses—another paid $23 to save his horse—Still another—$100 to save his barn. We found this hideous thing to be quite common—We struck Hanover at dark. Found N.C.R.R.[3] badly torn up—During the day we heard heavy canonading—and later musketry firing—in the direction of Gettysburg. Rumor was, "Theres a Battle on at Gettysburg" and was not hard to believe—Some of our Cavalry had fought desperately here today, early—Charging into the enemy's rear and flanks—Killed some 30 rebs and hustled large forces on their way. So they had to abandon their dead and some of their wounded—We lay on arms in a field for the night—we were well fed, but awfully tired and sleepy. . . .

July 2, 1863

Thursday. More or less Picket firing[4] all night—We were aroused early, and inspection showed a lot of our horses too lame and used up for good action—So first, our good mounts were formed for moving out, and were soon off—with the Brigade and took Reb. Genl. St[u]ar[t] by surprise on the Deardorf Farm—on right and rear of the army line—where St[u]ar[t] was expected to at least annoy the rear of Genl Mead—But our boys charged him—and after severe fighting dealt him an inglorious defeat and later in the day came in and lay on arms in the rear of Meads right—While our mounted men were paying attention to Genl St[u]ar[t], we fellows had our horses cared for and were marched down to the right of the main line—to occupy a gap and do Sharpshooting—at long range, with our Carbines—we soon attracted attention, and later an occasional shell fell conspicuously close—but far enough to the rear of us so we suffered no serious harm. Towards noon firing became more general and in almost all directions—and we were ordered

---

2. **Dunkerds:** Spelled *Dunkards*, referring to a sect of post-reformation Anabaptists, similar in dress and theology to the Amish and Mennonites and concentrated in Pennsylvania and Maryland.
3. **N.C.R.R.:** Northern Central Railroad.
4. **Picket firing:** The firing of rounds by men on watch duty to communicate with one another.

to our horses—and joined our returned heroes, and lay in readiness for any emergency—The general battle increaced in energy—and occasional fierceness—and by 2 P.M. the canonading was most terrific and continued til 5 P.M. and was interspersed with musketry—and Charge-yells and everything that goes to making up the indescribable battle of the best men on Earth, seemingly in the Fight to the Finish—At dark, our Cav Brig—2nd Brig 2" Div—was moved to the left—many wounded came in—Taken as a whole from all one can see from one point—it seems as tho our men—The Union Army—is rather overpowered and worsted—Lay on arms to rest—Little chance to feed and eat.

July 3, 1863

Friday. Canonading commenced early—and battle was on again in full intensity at 10 ock we were ordered to the Front and Center, but immediately removed to the right of the Center—had some skirmishing. Pretty lively—Our squadron almost ran into a Rebel Battery with a Brigade of Cavalry maneuvering in the woods. They didn't want to see us, but moved leftward and we held the woods all P-M.—All seemed rather quiet for several hours—From 1 1/2 til 4 P.M.—there was the heaviest canonading I ever have heard—One constant roar with rising and falling inflections.

July 4, 1863

Saturday. The great battle closed and quieted with the closing day—Some firing at various points—

Our Regt layed on arms with Pickets out—on the ground where we had put in most of the day—Rather expecting attack momentarily—Rained furiously during the night—We had fed, eaten, and were standing "to horse" when about 6 ock NEWS CAME—"The Rebs are falling back!" and "Our Forces are following them" and our Regt went out towards Hunterstown reconnoitering. We found some confederates who had straggled, or were foraging, not knowing yet what had happened and was taking place—Of course, our Boys took them in—Making a little detour I captured two. Sergt. Major J. T. Richardson and Private Cox 9th Va Cav—disarming them and bringing them in—I guarded them—while the Regt gathered in some others—P.M. Captain Hughes came along and paroled them—and we were ordered to camp near Hanover—where we first lay on arriving near Gettysburg—Evening awfully muddy and disagreeable—I saw much of the destructiveness of the Johnies today—

July 5, 1863

Sunday. Rained awfully during the night. I got very wet—

Early we took up the march for Chambersburg—Crossing the battlefield—Cemitary Hill—The Great Wheat Field Farm, Seminary ridge—and other places where dead men, horses, smashed artillery, were strewn in utter confusion, the Blue and The Grey mixed—Their bodies so bloated—distorted—discolored on account of decomposition having set in—that they were utterly unrecognizable, save by clothing, or things in their pockets— The scene simply beggars description—Reaching the west side of the Field of Carnage—we virtually charged most of the way for 10 miles—to Cashtown—Frequently in sight of the Rebel rear guard—taking in prisoners—in bunches—We captured some 1,500 wounded men, and 300 stragglers—we went as far as Goodyears Springs, where we rested [*unclear:*] for the night. (I had to guard a Reb all night.)

July 6, 1863

Monday. Had a good breakfast. Turned my prisoner over to others. We took up the march—via Fayeteville for Quincy—I told Corp. Metz I intended going on—To Chambersburg—To see wife and Baby—and would report in the morning again. He understood and I slipped away—and was soon making time for home—I got a fine "10 oclock piece" at Heintzelmans—on approaching Chambersburg I was assured there were still squads of rebs about town—Near town I was met by townfolk inquiring about the battle. I was the first "blue coat" they had seen—and the first to bring direct news of the Enemy's defeat—as communications had been cut. As I struck the edge of town, I was told "The Rebel rear-guard had just left the Diamond." So I ventured out 2nd Street and ventured to strike Main near where Darling and Pussy[5] lodged—and behold They were at the door—had been watching the Reb Rear leaving town—and Oh! The surprise and delight thus to meet after the awful battle they had been listening to for passing days—My horse was very soon stabled. My Cavalry outfit covered with hay—and myself in my citazens clothes—So should any final "rear" come along, I would not be discovered—To attempt to describe my joy and feelings at meeting and greeting my dear little family must prove a failure—We spent the P.M. and evening very sweetly and pleasantly, but only we had a few too many inquiring callers.

DIARY OF RACHEL CORMANY

June 16, 1863

Retired at 11 oclock. All was very quiet, so we concluded that all those reports must be untrue about the Reb's being so near, or that they had struck off in some other direction. Mr. Plough took his horse away so as to be on the safe side. So Annie and I were all alone. At 11 1/2 I heard the clattering of horses hoofs. I hopped out of bed & ran to the front window & sure enough there the Greybacks were going by as fast as their horses could take them down to the Diamond. Next I heard the report of a gun then they

---

5. **Darling and Pussy:** Terms of endearment popular in the mid-nineteenth century, in this case referring to the writer's wife and daughter.

came back faster if possible than they came in. But a short time after the whole body came, the front ones with their hands on the gun triggers ready to fire & calling out as they passed along that they would lay the town in ashes if fired on again. It took a long time for them all to pass, but I could not judge how many there were—not being accustomed to seeing troops in such a body—At 2 oclock A.M. all was quiet again save an occasional reb. riding past. We went to bed again & slept soundly until 5 the morning. All seemed quiet yet. We almost came to the conclusion that the reb's had left again leaving only a small guard who took things quite leasurely. Soon however they became more active. Were hunting up the contrabands[6] & driving them off by droves. O! How it grated on our hearts to have to sit quietly & look at such brutal deeds—I saw no men among the contrabands—all women & children. Some of the colored people who were raised here were taken along—I sat on the front step as they were driven by just like we would drive cattle. Some laughed & seemed not to care—but nearly all hung their heads. One woman was pleading wonderfully with her driver for her children—but all the sympathy she received from him was a rough "March along"—at which she would quicken her pace again. It is a query what they want with those little babies—whole families were taken. Of course when the mother was taken she would take her children. I suppose the men left thinking the women & children would not be disturbed. I cannot describe all the scenes—now—Noon—The Rebel horses with just enough men to take care of them & their teams, have just pased through town again on the retreat. Wonder what all this means. . . .

June 17, 1863

. . . All was so quiet during the night that I veryly thought the Reb's had left—but they are still here. All forenoon they were carrying away mens clothing & darkeys. shortly after dinner their horses & wagons were taken on the retreat again. Yes Generals and all went. Saw Gen [Albert] Jenkins, he is not a bad looking man—Some of the officers tipped their hats to us. I answered it with a curl of the lip. I knew they did it to taunt us. The one after he had tipped his hat most graciously & received in answer a toss of the head & curl of the lip took a good laugh over it. There were a few real inteligent good looking men among them. What a pity that they are rebels. After the main body had passed the news came that our soldiers were coming & just then some 1/2 doz reb's flew past as fast as their horses could take them. we learned since that one of them fired Oaks warehouse & that he was very near being shot by the citizens. Among the last to leave were some with darkeys on their horses behind them. How glad we are they are gone—None of our Soldiers came.

* * *

6. **contrabands:** Escaped slaves.

June 20, 1863

Went to bed early & slept well all night. This morning there is great excitement again. The report came last night that 40,000 or 50,000 infantry & some artillery have taken possession of Hagerstown—that the camps extend nearly to Greencastle—things surely look a little dubious. If we could only have regular mails. a mail came last night—but was not opened until this morning—Got a letter from My Samuel. it is but short. He is still safe—but were under marching orders again. it has been over a week on the way—I almost feel like getting out of this to some place where the mail is uninterupted, but then I fear, My Samuel might chance to come here & I would not see him so I shall stay—Will write to him now.

* * *

June 26, 1863

12 1/2 oclock Cannon-waggons & men have been passing since between 9 & 10 this morning—42 Cannon & as many amunition waggons have passed—so now there are 62 pieces of artillery between us & Harrisburg & between 30,000 & 40,000 men. O it seems dreadful to be thus thrown into the hands of the rebbels & to be thus excluded from all the rest of the world—I feel so very anxious about Mr. Cormany—& who knows when we will hear from any of our friends again. It is no use to try to get away from here now—we must just take our chance with the rest—trusting in God as our Savior then come life come death if reconciled with God all is well—My God help me—I do wish to be a real true & living christian. Oh for more religion. . . .

June 27, 1863

Got up early & wakened Annie. And we flew round & put away our best bed-clothes—before I got my things in order again Mrs. Clippinger came to go to Hokes where we got syrup & sugar. I also got me a lawn dress. Before we got started the rebels poured in already. they just marched through. Such a hard looking set I never saw. All day since 7 oclock they have been going through. Between 30 & 40 pieces of canno—& an almost endless trail of waggons. While I am writing thousands are passing—such a rough dirty ragged rowdyish set one does not often see—Gen's Lee & Longstreet passed through today. A body would think the whole south had broke loose & are coming into Pa. It makes me feel too badly to see so many men & cannon going through knowing that they have come to kill our men—Many have chickens as they pass—There a number are going with honey—robed some man of it no doubt—they are even carrying it in buckets. The report has reached us that [Union generals Joseph] Hooker & [Daniel] Sickel & [George] Stoneman are after them. & at Harisburg the north has congregated en masse to oppose the invaders. Many think this the best thing in the wor[l]d to bring the war to close—I hope our men will be strong enough to completely whip them—. . .

June 28, 1863

Slept well. Nowadays our cooking does not take much time—nowadays being we do all our eating by piecing. At 8 A.M. the rebels commenced coming again. Ga. troops. I was told this morning of some of their mean tricks of yesterday & before. They took the hats & boots off the men—Took that off Preacher Farney. Took $50. off Dr. Sneck & his gold watch valued very highly—took the coats off some, totally stripped one young fellow not far from town—Mr. Skinner. We have to be afraid to go out of our houses. A large wagon train & 500 or 600 Cavalry have just passed & it is now about 3 1/2 oclock. hope all are through now. Many of the saddles were empty, & any amount of negroes are along. This does not seem like Sunday. No church.

* * *

June 30, 1863

Nothing special transpired today. The Rebs are still about doing all the mischief they can. They have everything ready to set fire to the warehouses & machine shops—Tore up the railroad track & burned the crossties—They have cleared out nearly every store so they cannot rob much more—Evening—Quite a number of the young folks were in the parlor this evening singing all the patriotic & popular war songs. Quite a squad of rebels gathered outside to listen & seemed much pleased with the music—"When this cruel war is over" nearly brought tears from some. they sent in a petition to have it sung again which was done. they then thanked the girls very much & left—they acted real nicely.

* * *

July 2, 1863

At 3 A.M. I was wakened by the yells & howls of this dirty ragged lousy trash—they made as ugly as they could—all day they have been passing—part of the time on the double quick. At one time the report came that our men had come on them & that they were fighting—the excitement was high in town—but it was soon found out to be untrue—but the shock was so great that I got quite weak & immagined that I could already see My Samuel falling—I feel very uneasy about him—I cannot hear at all—They had quite a battle with Stuart[7]—I almost fear to hear the result in who was killed & who wounded—still I want to know.

---

7. **Stuart:** J. E. B. Stuart, Confederate States of America army general.

July 3, 1863

Started out with Cora & a little basket on the hunt for something to eat out of the garden. I am tired of bread & molasses—went to Mammy Royers & got some peas & new potatoes—Cora got as many raspberries as she could eat. Came home put Cora to sleep then went to Mrs McG's for milk. got a few cherries to eat also a few for Cora when I got back Daddy Byers was standing at the gate. he came to see how I was getting along & told me how the rebels acted—they robbed him of a good deal—they wanted the horse but he plead so hard for him that they agreed to leave him & while one wrote a paper of securety others plundered the house. I guess Samuels silk hat & all that was in the box is gone. took Ellies best shoes—took towels sheets &c &c—After they were gone others came & took the horse too yet—they did not care for his security. Other of their neighbors fared worse yet. He would not stay for dinner. After dinner Henry Rebok came—he walked part of the way had an old horse but feared to bring him in—they were robbed of their horses and cattle up there—many had their horses sent away—one of J. Cormanys horses was taken. Henry wanted me to go along home with him but I could not think of leaving now—Samuel might come this way & if I were out there I would not get to see him. . . .

July 4, 1863

At daybreak the bells were rung—Then all was quiet until about 8 oclock when a flag was hoisted at the diamond. Soon after the band made its appearance & marched from square & played national airs—two rebels came riding along quite leisurely thinking I suppose to find their friends instead of that they were taken prisoners by the citizens—some 13 more footmen came and were taken prisoners. . . .

July 5, 1863

I was roused out of sleep by Mr Early coming into Wampler & telling him something about wounded prisoners. so I got up took a bath dressed & went for a pitcher of water when I was told that 10, 4 or 6 horse waggons filled with wounded from the late battle were captured by citizens & brought to town—the wounded were put into the hospitals & the waggons & drivers were taken on toward Harisburg. Was also told that a great many more were out toward Greencastle—some went out to capture those but found that it was a train 20 miles long. P.M. A report has reached us that the whole rebel army is on the retreat—later that they are driven this way & are expected on soon—Have church S. School here today—seems like Sunday again Evening. At or after 4 P.M. I dressed myself & little girl and went to Mrs. Sulenbargers & while there we heard a fuss outside & when we got out lo our (Union of course) soldiers were coming in—she came along upstreet then to see them. They are of Milroys men—Just at dusk they went out the Green-castle road enroute to capture the waggon train which is trying to get over the river again. It is frightful how those poor wounded rebels are left to suf-fer. they are taken in large 4 horse waggons—wounds undressed—nothing to eat. Some are only about 4 miles from town & those that are here are as dirty and lousy as they well can be. The condition of those poor rebels all along from Getysburg to as far as they have come yet is reported dreadful. I am told they just beg the people along the road to help them—many have died by the way.

July 6, 1863

I was sitting reading, Pussy playing by my side when little Willie Wampler came running as fast as he could to tell me a soldier had come to see me & sure enough when I got to the door Mr Cormany just rode up. I was so very glad to see him that I scarcely knew how to act. He was very dirty & sweaty so he took a bath & changed clothes before he got himself dressed A. Holler & Barny Hampshire called—next Rev. Dixon & Dr Croft & others. Eve we went down into the parlor to hear some of the girls play—Mr. C was very much pleased with the music.

54

BLACK UNION SOLDIERS

Fighting for the Union

The Civil War began with limited aims. The South sought independence to expand the plantation system to uncultivated lands to the west, while the North sought to preserve the Union and contain slavery. At first both sides wanted to limit the conflict to avoid disruption of the businesses, families, and institutions spread across the divide. This objective meant, among other things, excluding blacks from military service and leaving slavery intact.

Although African Americans had served in every war in U.S. history, an old militia law was invoked that left them out of the first Civil War battles. Frederick Douglass and other abolitionists argued that excluding blacks was a mistake and that the guerrilla war in "bleeding Kansas" in the 1850s showed the conflict to be a life-or-death battle between two different economic systems and two contrasting ways of life. They

Edwin S. Redkey, ed., *A Grand Army of Black Men* (New York: Cambridge University Press, 1992).

counseled Lincoln to end the war quickly by involving the four million enslaved African Americans in crippling the Southern economy by abandoning their masters to join the Union Army. More moderate voices, however, claimed that slaves were too servile and too dependent on their masters to be reliable soldiers. Regardless of what Lincoln believed personally, his strategy was to preserve the Union by not antagonizing the five "border states" that had slavery but remained loyal to the Union. Maintaining these states' loyalty meant continuing slavery, keeping blacks out of the military, and reversing the actions of generals, like abolitionist David Hunter, who freed slaves taken in battle.

By 1862, however, states were struggling to provide enough soldiers to fight, and so they started swearing in African Americans. Later that year Congress repealed the ban on blacks in the U.S. Army, and on January 1, 1863, Lincoln's Emancipation Proclamation signaled that the Civil War had become a war against slavery. African Americans deserted their masters by the thousands, swelling the Union Army by two hundred thousand soldiers, or 10 percent of the fighting force.

Black soldiers were poorly equipped and trained, paid less than white soldiers, and given the worst tasks. In the beginning they were excluded from combat, but after the heroic assault on Fort Wagner in July 1863 by the black 54th Massachusetts Regiment (portrayed in the movie Glory*), they became widely known as some of the Union Army's bravest soldiers. Lincoln described their services as "the heaviest blow yet dealt to the rebellion." The Confederacy even came to recognize the central role of black slaves in the conflict, authorizing their enlistment on February 18, 1865.*

The letters that follow are a small selection of the thousands written by black soldiers in the Union Army to friends and family, officers and officials, and African American newspapers in the North. They reveal how black soldiers shared the anxiety, dread, and fear experienced by their white comrades, but also afford a glimpse of how African Americans tied the war to ideals of freedoms and just government.

QUESTIONS TO CONSIDER

1. What do the letters suggest about the concerns and hopes of African Americans serving in the Union Army? How might these perspectives have influenced their performance in battle?
2. By 1865, there were roughly two hundred thousand African Americans in the Union Army. What impact do you think their presence had on white Northerners' and Southerners' views of the war?
3. How did their army experience change African Americans' outlook on their place in society?

Near Petersburge [Virginia][1] August 19th 1864

Dear Madam   I receave A letter from You A few day Ago inquir in regard to the Fait of Your Son I am sarry to have to inform You that thear is no dobt of his Death he Died A Brave Death in Trying to Save the Colors of Rige[ment]

---

1. Bracketed notes were provided by the original editor of these sources, Edwin S. Redkey.

in that Dreadful Battil Billys Death was unevesally [mourned] by all but by non greatter then by my self ever sins we have bin in the Army we have bin amoung the moust intimoat Friend wen every our Rige[ment] wen into Camp he sertan to be at my Tent and meney happy moment we seen to gether Talking about Home and the Probability of our Living to get Home to See each other Family and Friend But Providence has will other wise and You must Bow to His will You and His Wife Sister and all Have my deepust Simppathy and trust will be well all in this Trying moment.

You Inquired about Mr Young He wen to the Hospetol and I can not give You eney other information in regard to Him.

Billys thing that You requested to inquired about I can git no informa of us in the bustil of the Battil every thing was Lost.

Give my Respects to Samual Jackson and Family not forgetting Your self and Family I remain Your Friend.

G. H. Freeman

[Benton Barracks Hospital, St. Louis, Missouri, September 3, 1864. Spotswood Rice was an African American soldier writing to his children in captivity.]

My Children I take my pen in hand to rite you A few lines to let you know that I have not forgot you and that I want to see you as bad as ever now my Dear Children I want you to be contented with whatever may be your lots be assured that I will have you if it cost me my life on the 28th of the mounth. 8 hundred White and 8 hundred blacke solders expects to start up the rivore to Glasgow and above there thats to be jeneraled by a jeneral that will give me both of you when they Come I expect to be with, them and expect to get you both in return. Dont be uneasy my children I expect to have you. If Diggs dont give you up this Government will and I feel confident that I will get you Your Miss Kaitty said that I tried to steal you But I'll let her know that god never intended for man to steal his own flesh and blood. If I had no confidence in God I could have confidence in her But as it is If I ever had any Confidence in her I have none now and never expect to have And I want her to remember if she meets me with ten thousand soldiers she [will?] meet her enemy I once [thought] that I had some respect for them but now my respects is worn out and have no sympathy for Slaveholders. And as for her cristianantty I expect the Devil has Such in hell You tell her from me that She is the frist Christian that I ever hard say that a man could Steal his own child especially out of human bondage.

You can tell her that She can hold to you as long as she can I never would expect to ask her ain to let you come to me because I know that the devil has got her hot set against that that is write now my Dear children I am a going to close my letter to you Give my love to all enquiring friends tell them all that we are well and want to see them very much and Corra and Mary receive the greater part of it you sefves and dont think hard of us not sending you any thing I you father have a plenty for you when I see you Spott &

Noah sends their love to both of you Oh! My Dear children how I do want to see you.

[Spotswood Rice]

March 13, 1864

To the *Christian Recorder*

It is with pleasure that I now seat myself to inform you of our last battle . . .

The battle took place in a grove called Olustee, with the different regiments as follows: First there was the 8th U.S. [Colored Infantry]; they were cut up badly, and they were the first colored regiment in the battle. The next was the 54th Mass., which I belong to. . . . The firing was very warm, and it continued for about three hours and a half. The 54th was the last off the field. . . .

Now it seems strange to me that we do not receive the same pay and rations as the white soldiers. Do we not fill the same ranks? Do we not cover the same space of ground? Do we not take up the same length of ground in a grave-yard that others do? The ball does not miss the black man and strike the white, nor the white and strike the black. But sir, at that time there is no distinction made; they strike one as much as another. The black men have to go through the same hurling of musketry, and the same belching of cannonading as white soldiers do.

E.D.W. [Private]

[In August 1864 African American soldiers who had been free before the war began receiving equal pay. Units made up of former slaves did not receive full back pay until March 1865.]

June 20, 1864

To the *Weekly Anglo-African*

. . . Since I last wrote, almost half of the 5th Massachusetts Cavalry have been in several engagements, and about thirty have been killed and wounded. The first notice I had of going into the engagement was about 1 o'clock, a.m., Wednesday, the 15th. We heard the bugle, and sprang to our arms, and, with two days rations, we started towards Petersburg, and when about four miles on our way toward that city, at a place called Beatty's House, we came in front of the rebels' works. Here we formed a line of battle, and started for the rebs' works. I was with some thirty of my Company. We had to pass through the woods; but we kept on, while the shell, grape and canister came around us cruelly. Our Major and Col. [Henry F.] Russell were wounded, and several men fell—to advance seemed almost impossible; but we rallied, and after a terrible charge, amidst pieces of barbarous iron, solid shot and shell, we drove the desperate greybacks from their fortifications, and gave three cheers for our victory. But few white troops were with us. Parts of the 1st, 4th, 6th and 22nd [United States Colored Infantry] were engaged.

The colored troops here have received a great deal of praise. The sensations I had in the battle were, coolness and interest in the boys' fighting. They shouted, "Fort Pillow,"[2] and the rebs were shown no mercy.

[Private Charles Torrey Beman]

August 21, 1864

To the *Christian Recorder*

... I will say something about the prejudice in our own regiment when we returned from Olustee to Jacksonville. One of our captains was sick, and there was no doctor there excepting our hospital steward, who administered the medicines and effected a cure; he was a colored man, Dr. [Theodore] Becker, and a competent physician, and through the exertions of this recovered captain, there was a petition got up for his promotion. All the officers signed the petition but three, Captain [Charles] Briggs, and two lieutenants; they admitted he was a smart man and understood medicine, but he was a negro, and they did not want a negro Doctor, neither did they want negro officers. The Colonel, seeing so much prejudice among his officers, destroyed the document; therefore the negro is not yet acknowledged.

Notwithstanding all these grievances, we prefer the Union rather than the rebel government, and will sustain the Union if the United States will give us our rights. We will calmly submit to white officers, though some of them are not so well acquainted with military matters as our orderly sergeants, and some of the officers have gone so far to say that a negro stunk under their noses. This is not very pleasant, but we must give the officers of Company B of the 54th Massachusetts regiment, their just dues; they generally show us the respect due to soldiers, and scorn any attempt to treat us otherwise....

"Fort Green" [54th Massachusetts Infantry]

October, 1865

To the *Weekly Anglo-African*

I have never before attempted to pen a line for your columns, but in this case I am compelled to, because I have been waiting patiently to see if I could see anything in regard to our noble Regiment, and have seen nothing. We have fought and captured Blakesly's Fort. We were only ten days on the siege, and had nothing to eat but Parched Corn. But as luck would have it, I crept out of my hole at night and scared one of the Jonnys so bad that he left his rifle

---

2. At Fort Pillow in April 1864, Confederate troops shot prisoners, especially African Americans, who had surrendered. [Redkey's note.]

pit, gun and accouterments, also one corn dodger and about one pint of buttermilk, all of which I devoured with a will, and returned to my hole safe and sound. After sleeping the remainder of the night, about day I was awakened by our turtlebacks that were playing with the enemy's works. At that time I forgot myself and poked my head out of my hole, and came very near getting one of Jonny's cough pills.[3] We had to keep our heads down all the time or else run the risk of getting shot. So me and my friend of whom I was speaking had it all that day, shooting at each other. Finally, he got hungry and cried out to me, "Say, Blacky, let's stop and eat some Dinner." I told him, "All right." By the time I thought he was done eating, I cried, "Hello, Reb." He answered, "What do you want?" I said, "Are you ready" "No, not yet," he said. Then I waited for awhile. I finally got tired and cried for a chew of tobacco. He then shot at me and said, "Chew that!" I thanked him kindly and commenced exchanging shots with him.

I must not take too much time in relating all the incidents, for Parched Corn takes the day also. We have accomplished all undertakings, and excel in the drill. We ask nothing now but to be mustered out.

[Sergeant Cassius M. Clay Alexander]

April 12, 1865

To the *Christian Recorder*

I have just returned from the city of Richmond; my regiment was among the first that entered that city. I marched at the head of the column, and soon I found myself called upon by the officers and men of my regiment to make a speech, with which, of course, I readily complied. A vast multitude assembled on Broad Street, and I was aroused amid the shouts of ten thousand voices, and proclaimed for the first time in that city freedom to all mankind. After which the doors of all the slave pens were thrown open, and thousands came out shouting and praising God, and Father, or Master Abe, as they termed him. In this mighty consternation I became so overcome with tears that I could not stand up under the pressure of such fullness of joy in my own heart. I retired to gain strength, so I lost many important topics worthy of note.

Among the densely crowded concourse there were parents looking for children who had been sold south of this state in tribes, and husbands came for the same purpose; here and there one was singled out in the ranks, and an effort was made to approach the gallant and marching soldiers, who were too obedient to orders to break ranks.

We continued our march as far as Camp Lee, at the extreme end of Broad Street, running westwards. In camp the multitude followed, and everybody could participate in shaking the friendly but hard hands of the poor slaves. Among the many broken-hearted mothers looking for their children

---

3. **Jonny's cough pills:** Confederate bullets.

who had been sold to Georgia and elsewhere, was an aged woman, passing through the vast crowd of colored, inquiring for [one] by the name of Garland H. White, who had been sold from her when a small boy, and was bought by a lawyer named Robert Toombs, who lived in Georgia. Since the war has been going on she has seen Mr. Toombs in Richmond with troops from his state, and upon her asking him where his body-servant Garland was, he replied: "He ran off from me at Washington, and went to Canada. I have since learned that he is living somewhere in the State of Ohio." Some of the boys knowing that I lived in Ohio, soon found me and said, "Chaplain, here is a lady that wishes to see you." I quickly turned, following the soldier until coming to a group of colored ladies. I was questioned as follows: "What is your name, sir?"

"My name is Garland H. White."

"What was your mother's name?"

"Nancy."

"Where was you born?"

"In Hanover County, in this State."

"Where was you sold from?"

"From this city."

"What was the name of the man who bought you?"

"Robert Toombs."

"Where did he live?"

"In the State of Georgia."

"Where did you leave him?"

"At Washington."

"Where did you go then?"

"To Canada."

"Where do you live now?"

"In Ohio."

"This is your mother, Garland, whom you are now talking to, who has spent twenty years of grief about her son."

I cannot express the joy I felt at this happy meeting of my mother and other friends. But suffice it to say that God is on the side of the righteous, and will in due time reward them. I have witnessed several such scenes among the other colored regiments . . .

[Chaplain Garland H. White]

May 18, 1865

To the *Christian Recorder*

It is the first time in the history of my life that one so humble as myself ever attempted to write anything for publication through the columns of your most worthy journal; and it is with great reluctance that I attempt it on the present occasion, owing to my short stay at home in Park Co[unty], Ind[iana], on a furlough, where I found many friends to rejoice over, and many disadvantages upon the part of the colored people to mourn over. It seems very strange to me that the people of Indiana are so very indifferent about removing from their statute books those Black Laws, which are a curse to them in the eyes of God and man, and above all things in life, the most grievous to be borne by any people.

Shall the history of the old 28th [United States Colored Infantry], which was raised in that State, stand upon the great record of the American army second to none? Shall these brave sons return home after periling their lives for several years in the storm of battle for the restoration of the Union and to vindicate the honor and dignity of that fair Western State which is classed among the best composing this great nation, but to be treated as slaves? Shall it be said by the nations of the earth that any portion of the United States treated her brave defenders thus? I hope never to see the day; yet it is fast approaching.

Have we no friends at home among the whites to look this great injustice in the face, and bid its sin-cursed waves forever leave? Have we no colored friends at home who feel tired of the burden and are willing to pray to the thinking public to lighten it? As for us, we have done our duty and are willing to do it whenever the State and country call us; but after responding, are you not willing to pay the laborer for his hire? It is to be seen in all past history that when men fought for their country and returned home, they always enjoyed the rights and privileges due to other citizens. We ask to be made equal before the law; grant us this and we ask no more. Let the friends of freedom canvass the country on this subject. Let the sound go into all the earth. . . .

William Gibson, Corporal

55

HENRY WILLIAM RAVENEL

A Slave Owner's Journal at the End of the War

In a letter of August 26, 1865, Henry William Ravenel (1814–1887) summarized the immediate effects of the Confederacy's collapse as well as anyone ever has:

> *A new era opens before us, but alas! with what great changes. Our country is in ruins, and our people reduced to poverty. . . . We had no money but Confederate and*

Arney Robinson Childs, ed., *The Private Journal of Henry William Ravenel, 1859–1887* (Columbia: University of South Carolina Press, 1947), 202–3, 206–7, 210–21 passim, 228–29, 237, 239–40.

that is now worthless . . . all our securities and investments are bankrupt. . . . There is little money in the country, little cotton and other produce, so there is no business or employment for those who are anxiously seeking to make a living. . . .

As Ravenel documented, the changes in Southern life were nothing short of staggering. Emancipation had altered social relations. The Confederacy's fall and then Reconstruction were transforming Southern politics. The war and emancipation had upset every economic arrangement, making currency worthless, land unsalable, and credit—previously based on chattel mortgages on slave "property"—scarcely to be obtained.

Ravenel belonged to a prominent South Carolina slaveholding family. In addition to managing a plantation, he became an important self-trained naturalist whose studies of American fungi achieved international renown. After the war he supported his family by selling seeds and parts of his collections of fungi to collectors and later worked as a naturalist for the U.S. Department of Agriculture.

Ravenel began his journal, from which the following excerpts come, in 1859, and he continued it to within weeks of his death in 1887. The journal shows how one thoughtful and well-placed member of the Southern elite struggled to understand the collapse of his familiar world.

QUESTIONS TO CONSIDER

1. How did Henry William Ravenel interpret the war's causes and outcome?
2. What did he expect to happen to former slaves? How did he explain their behavior?
3. What is surprising about Ravenel's reactions as a slaveholder?

November [1864]

F. 18   The Augusta paper of this morning has startling intelligence from Atlanta. There is no doubt that [General William T.] Sherman has burned Rome, Decatur & Atlanta, & has commenced a move with 4 or 5 army corps (40 to 50,000) in the direction of Macon & Augusta. The Northern papers say his intention is to move through to Charleston & Mobile, destroy the rail road & bridges behind him & feed his army from the country. I have been apprehending just such a move since Hood's army was withdrawn. It is a bold stroke, & if successful, would bring untold evils upon us, in the destruction of property & the means of subsistence. . . .

Sunday 20   [General P. G. T.] Beauregard telegraphs the people to be firm & resolute—to obstruct his [Sherman's] passage by cutting the woods in his front & flank—to destroy all provisions which cannot be carried away—to remove all negroes, horses & cattle, & leave a scene of desolation in his front, instead of in his rear as it would be if he passed. . . . Should Sherman succeed in taking Augusta, his march will be onward toward Charleston, & his track will be a scene of desolation. I await the developments of the next few days with anxiety, chiefly on account of my negroes. If I send them away &

the farm & house is left without protection, my house will be robbed & despoiled of every thing, whether the enemy passes here or not. I must wait before removing them, until I am very sure the enemy will succeed in his designs upon Augusta—& then perhaps it may be too late.

M. 21   I have had a talk with my negroes on the subject, & explained to them the true state of affairs—that should the enemy pass through this place they must escape & take care of themselves for a while until the danger is passed. I am well satisfied from their assurances, that they are really alarmed at the idea of being seized & taken off by the Yankees, & that they will not desert me.

F. 25   We are now at the gloomiest period of the war which for nearly four years has afflicted our land. I cannot conceal from myself the many discouraging features of our situation & the perilous straits in which we stand. . . .

February [1865]

Sunday 19   Dr. Frank Porcher dined here today. He thinks we should remain where we are. The upper country is in danger of famine, & will soon be without salt, now the coast is given up. . . . Charleston was occupied by the enemy yesterday at 10 A.M.—Columbia has been captured. We hear of a great fire in Charleston yesterday, but no particulars yet. Exciting times!

M. 20   In a few days the last of our army will have crossed the Santee, the bridge burnt behind them—& we then become an evacuated & conquered region. We fall under Yankee rule & the laws & authority of the U. States are established during the continuance of the war. What new relations between us & our negroes will be established we cannot tell but there is no doubt it will be a radical change. I do not apprehend destructive raids, or personal violence to citizens who remain, but we will be compelled to conform to the new conditions under which we are placed, as a conquered people. I suppose all the cotton will be seized & confiscated to the use of the U. S. govt,—& probably a system of culture will be adopted & enforced the profits from which will accrue to them. I think it the duty of all slave owners & planters who remain, to be with their negroes. They have been faithful to the last, & they deserve in turn, confidence from him, protection, attention & care. . . .

T. 21   I think masters who are within these lines of the enemy, should remain on their plantations among their negroes;—the first change of conditions should not be volunteered by us. We have always believed we were right in maintaining the relation of master & slave for the good of the country & also for the benefit of the negro. If we have believed firmly in the Divine sanction which the Bible affords to this relation, we should not be the first to sever it, by abandoning them. They have grown up under us, they look to us for support, for guidance & protection—They have faithfully done their duty during this trying time, when the great temptations were offered to leave us. In the sight of God, we have a sacred duty to stand by them as long as they are faithful to us. We know that if left to themselves, they cannot maintain their happy condition. We must reward their fidelity to us by the same care & consideration we exercised when they were more useful. . . .

T. 28   David returned with a cart from PineVille last night, & said Rene told him the Yankees had been, or were, in PineVille, taking poultry & whatever they wanted. The negroes on many places have refused to go to work. . . . I have spoken to some of them here & intend to give them advice as a friend to continue on the plantation, & work—Of course there must be great care & judgement used in preserving discipline & I have advised with the overseer. I think for their own good & the good of the country, it would be best for the present organization of labor to go on, so that all may get a subsistance, the old & young, the sick & disabled, & the other non producers. . . . The freed & idle negroes who are not kept now under discipline or fear will give us trouble. I feel great anxiety for the future. . . .

March [1865]

Th. 2   Half past two o'clock A.M. Night of horrors! How can I describe the agonizing suspense of the past six hours! Thank God who has protected us all we are still alive & have lost nothing but property.—About half past 8 oclock I was standing in the back piazza, when I heard the discharge of 3 or 4 fire arms. The negroes soon came running up to inform us that the Yankees were in the negro yard. They soon after entered the house, (4 or 5 colored men) armed & demanded to see the owner of the house. I called to Pa & he walked up to the back door where they were. They told him that they had come for provisions, corn, bacon, poultry & whatever they wanted—demanded his horses & wagons, his guns, wine &c. That they had come to tell the negroes they were free & should no longer work for him. They used very threatening language with oaths & curses. They then proceeded to the stable & took my pair & Renes horse—Took the 2 sets harness & put in the horses, into the two wagons & Lequeax buggy. They then emptied the smoke house, store room & meat house, giving to the negroes what they did not want. They then took from the fowl house what poultry they wanted, took the two plantation guns, & used great threats about the wine & brandy. To our great relief they did not enter the house again, & at 1.30 A.M. drove off. They told the negroes if they worked for their master again they would shoot them when they came back. What the future is to be to us God only knows. I feel that my trust is still unshaken in his all protecting Providence. I have all confidance in the fidelity of the negroes & their attachment to us if they are not restrained from showing it. We are all up for the night as the excitement is too great to permit sleep—9 A.M. at the usual hour this morning the house negroes came in—They seemed much distressed & said the troops told them last night if they came to the yard or did anything for us, they would shoot them—That a large troop would come today. We told them to go back & not bring trouble upon themselves, until we could see the Commanding officer. The fidelity & attachment of some who have come

forward is very gratifying. The girls have been cooking our simple breakfast & we have taken our first meal under the new regime. I long for a visit
from some officer in authority, that we may know our future condition &
whether the negroes will be allowed to hire themselves to us or not. . . .

S. 4   Inauguration of Presdt. Lincoln today for his 2d term of 4 years.
Will any thing come out of it in respect to the war? The negroes are completely bewildered at the change of their condition. Many are truly distressed, some of the younger ones delirious with the prospect of good living &
nothing to do. Some are willing to remain & work, but object to gang
work,—all is in a chaotic state. When they were told that they were free,
some said they did not wish to be free, & they were immediately silenced
with threats of being shot. I fear this region will be a desolate waste in one
year hence, if this state of things continue. . . .

M. 6   The events of the past week have brought up vividly before us
the horrors of the French Revolution. . . . We are in a fearful & trying crisis.
If those who had unsettled the present order of things in the name of Humanity, were consistent, they would make some effort to order the freed negroes for their good, & ought to take some steps toward restoring order &
recommanding & enforcing some plan by which such a large number may
escape the horrors of insubordination, violence & ultimately starvation. The
negroes are intoxicated with the idea of freedom. Many of them are deluded
into the hope that their future is to be provided for by the U S. Govt.—&
hence they do not feel the necessity of work. Many are disposed to remain,
but perhaps will insist on terms which are incompatable with discipline &
good management. It is a fearful crisis.

T. 7   No disposition evinced among the negroes to go to work. There
seems to be sullenness which I dislike to see. I think those who are disposed
to work or to do for us, are restrained. I hear that many of the negroes are
armed with pistols & guns. Some were at Black Oak last night firing off pistols. This is a bad feature in this fearful period.—Oh, Humanity! what crimes
are committed in thy name. One week ago we were in the midst of a peaceful, contented & orderly population—now all is confusion, disorder, discontent, violence, anarchy. If those who uprooted the old order of things had
remained long enough to reconstruct another system in which there should
be order restored, it would have been well, but they have destroyed our system & left us in the ruins. . . .

W. 8   We heard guns again last night, but cannot learn from the negroes who fired them. The disordered state of affairs keeps us anxious. . . . On
this day a week ago the old system of slave labour was in peaceful operation. The breath of Emancipation has passed over the country, & we are
now in that transition state between the new & the old systems—a state of
chaos & disorder. Will the negro be materially benefitted by the change? Will
the condition of the country in its productive resources, in material prosperity be improved? Will it be a benefit to the landed proprietors? These are
questions which will have their solution in the future. They are in the hands
of that Providence which over-ruleth all things for good. It was a strong

conviction of my best judgement that the old relation of master & slave, had received the divine sanction & was the best condition in which the two races could live together for mutual benefit. There were many defects to be corrected & many abuses to be remedied, which I think would have been done if we had gained our independence & were freed from outside pressure. Among these defects I will enumerate the want of legislation to make the marriage contract binding—to prevent the separation of families, & to restrain the cupidity of cruel masters. Perhaps it is for neglecting these obligations that God has seen fit to dissolve that relation. I believe the negro must remain in this country & that his condition although a freed-man, must be to labour on the soil. Nothing but necessity will compel him to labour. Now the question is, will that necessity be so strong as to compel him to labour, which will be profitable to the landed proprietors. Will he make as much cotton, sugar, rice & tobacco for the world as he did previously? They will now have a choice *where* to labour. This will ensure good treatment & the best terms. The most humane, the most energetic & the most judicious managers have the best chances in the race for success. I expect to see a revolution in the ownership of landed estates. Those only can succeed who bring the best capacity for the business. Time will show. . . .

Sunday 12   Some of the very peculiar traits of negro character are now exhibited. . . . There are two exhibitions of character which have surprised us, & which were never anticipated. 1st. On many places where there was really kind treatment & mutual attachment, the exciting events of the last week or two, & the powerful temptations brought to bear upon them, have seemed to snap the ties suddenly. Some have left their comfortable homes & kind masters & friends, & gone off with the army, thinking to better their conditions. We must be patient & charitable in our opinions—They are ignorant of what they have to encounter, mere children in knowledge & experience, excitable, impulsive & have fallen under the tempting delusions presented to them in such glowing terms—Some who are disposed to take a proper view of their condition, & to return to work, are intimidated & kept back by threats from the more strong & overbearing. They do not clearly comprehend this situation—they have been told they are free, & their idea of freedom is associated with freedom from work & toil. In many places there was bad discipline & little care for the negroes. These are generally the foremost in all the acts of disorder,—& their example & word keep back others. We are astonished at this defection when we do not expect it, but on reflection the causes at work are sufficient to account for it. 2nd. Had we been told four years ago, that our negroes would have withstood the temptation to fidelity which have been constantly before them during the war, we would have doubted the possibility—& had we been told further of the events of the last two weeks, the incitements to acts of violence both by the example & the precepts of the black troops all throughout this region, we would have shuddered for the consequences. Except from the black soldiers, I have not heard of a single act of violence, or even of rude or uncivil language. Their behaviour is perfectly civil so far, & I believe, with a judicous course on the part of the whites, will continue so. This whole revolution from its commencement has developed in its progress, a course of events which no human sagacity on either side, ever foresaw. . . .

May [1865]

May M. 1   Gen Lees surrender took place on the 9th.ult,[1] but it only reached us through our papers & the returning prisoners about a week ago. . . . [This] means the loss of our Independence for which we have been struggling for four years with immense loss of life & property. But the fate of nations is controlled & over-ruled by a wise Providence, which sees the end from the beginning, & orders all things in the highest wisdom. Whatever therefore may be the will of God regarding our destiny, I accept His decision as final & as eminently good. I have honestly believed we were right in our revolution, & would receive the divine sanction—if I have erred, I pray God to forgive me the error, & I submit with perfect satisfaction to His decree, knowing that He cannot err.

M. 22   We begin now to realize the ruin to property which the war has entailed upon us. All classes & conditions of men will suffer who had property, except the small farmers who owned no negroes. Confederate securities, I consider a total loss. Bank stock, confederation & private bonds, are all more or less dependent for their availability upon Confed securities, & upon the value of negro property; both of which are lost. The Rail road companies are nearly all ruined by the destruction of their roads & the heavy debt they must incur to rebuild. The only money now in possession of our people is coin in small quantities which had been hoarded through the war, & some bills of the local banks. There will be but little means of increasing this amount for some time to come, as provisions are scarce, & the cotton has been mostly burnt, captured or sold. The financial prospect is a gloomy one, & there will be much distress before our conditions can improve. . . .

M. 29   I went in to Aiken this morning & called at the hotel to inquire if any officer in Aiken was authorized to administer the Oath of Allegiance. They expected in a day or two to have it done here. It is necessary now in order to save property, have personal protection, or exercise the rights of citizenship, or any business calling. Every one who is allowed, is now taking the oath, as the Confederate govt. is annulled, the state govt. destroyed, & the return into the Union absolutely necessary to our condition as an organized community. As Gen. [Quincy] Gillmore's order based upon Chief Justice [Salmon] Chase's opinion announces the freedom of the negroes there is no further room to doubt that it is the settled policy of the country. I have today formally announced to my negroes the fact, & made such arrangements with each as the new relation rendered necessary. Those whose whole time we need, get at present clothes & food, house rent & medical attendance. The

---

1. **ult:** *ultimo*, Latin for "last month"; that is, April 9.

others work for themselves giving me a portion of their time on the farm in lieu of house rent. Old Amelia & her two grandchildren, I will spare the mockery of offering freedom to. I must support them as long as I have any thing to give.

T. 30   My negroes all express a desire to remain with me. . . . But in course of time we must part, as I cannot afford to keep so many, & they cannot afford to hire for what I could give them. As they have always been faithful & attached to us, & have been raised as family servants, & have all of them been in our family for several generations, there is a feeling towards them somewhat like that of a father who is about to send out his children on the world to make their way through life. Those who have brought the present change of relation upon us are ignorant of these ties. They have charged us with cruelty. They call us, man stealers, robbers, tyrants. The indignant denial of these charges & the ill feelings engendered during 30 years of angry controversy, have culminated at length in the four years war which has now ended. It has pleased God that we should fail in our efforts for independance—& with the loss of independance, we return to the Union under the dominion of the abolition sentiment. The experiment is now to be tried. The negro is not only to be emancipated, but is to become a citizen with all the right & priviledges! It produces a financial, political & social revolution at the South, fearful to contemplate in its ultimate effects. Whatever the result may be, let it be known & remembered that neither the negro slave nor his master is responsible. It has been done by those who having political power, are determined to carry into practice the sentimental philanthropy they have so long & angrily advocated. Now that is fixed. I pray God for the great issues at stake, that he may bless the effort & make it successful—make it a blessing & not a curse to the poor negro.

56

GEORGE TEMPLETON STRONG

A Northerner's View of the Confederacy's End

One of the Civil War era's most prolific diarists, George Templeton Strong (1820–1875) was a powerful lawyer, socialite, and patrician from New York City. Closely identified with conservative institutions of great wealth and power in his city, Strong was a trustee of Columbia College, his alma mater, and Trinity Church on Wall Street, the center of worship for the Episcopal elite. During the war, he helped found the United States

Allan Nevins, ed., *The Diary of George Templeton Strong* (New York: Macmillan, 1962), 581–84.

Sanitary Commission, the Union's largest and most important voluntary relief agency that commanded millions of dollars in aid and thousands of workers. As treasurer and a member of the ruling body of the Sanitary Commission, Templeton labored tirelessly to raise money, set policy, and coordinate relief efforts around the country. Closer to home, he organized the Union League Club of New York that raised financial and political support for the Republican Party and specifically Lincoln.

A keen-eyed observer of Northern culture, Strong left an invaluable record of popular reactions to the war as it evolved. In painstaking detail, he registered the public's shifting moods and ambitions. The following passage from his diary captures the surging emotions of Northerners as the war came to a close, reveals how they viewed Southerners, and explores how they came to terms with Lincoln's assassination.

QUESTIONS TO CONSIDER

1. What was the popular opinion of the South among Northerners as the war came to a close?
2. In what ways did Northerners interpret Lincoln's killing? How did they begin to frame the historical legacy of the former president?
3. How did Lincoln's assassination affect Northerners' view of the terms of peace and reconstruction?

People hold the war virtually ended. It looks so. Lee is out of the game. Napoleon could hardly save Joe Johnston's army. . . . When Joe Johnston is disposed of, Lincoln should announce by proclamation that from and after the——day of——next, the Confederacy will be no longer practically recognized as a belligerent power, and that men thereafter taken in arms against the country will be treated as criminals and not as prisoners of war. He might properly do so forthwith, for the so-called Confederate government seems to have abdicated and to be concealing itself with intent to avoid the service of process. That power is reported to have emerged from a railroad car at Danville, Virginia, Monday evening (3rd instant), represented by Davis *Imperator* and two of his pals, all three dusty, deliquescent,[1] and much demoralized. Since that date we know nothing of it. . . .

A rather lively theoretical controversy has arisen of and concerning Jeff Davis: Shall we hang him, when and if we catch him, or shall we let him run? Weight of opinion is clearly for hanging him, but he will save his neck somehow. Justice requires his solemn public execution. Sound policy would probably let him live, in prison or exile. I should vote to hang him. "We'll hang Jeff Davis on a sour apple tree, as we go marching on."

This choral promise and vow, so often repeated by so many thousand soldiers and civilians, should be performed at the first opportunity. Bidwell has long predicted that Jeff Davis, when finally cornered, would kill himself.

1. **deliquescent:** of or like a fluid.

The best disposition destiny can make of the scoundrel would be to let him be grabbed by some one of the organized bands of deserters and refugees who hold the hill country of North Carolina and Virginia. They would award him a high gallows and a short shrift, and so dispose of a troublesome question.

Even the *World* and the *Daily News* say that Secessia is now conquered, crushed, subjugated, and under our feet. They whine for forbearance and magnanimity toward their friends and fellow-consipirators. To be sure, we should be as merciful as we *safely* can be. The punishment already inflicted on the Southern people is fearful to think of. The death of their best (or worst) and bravest; the devastation, the breaking up of their social system, general destitution, the bitterest humiliation of the most arrogant of mankind, the most splendid and confident expectations disappointed, universal ruin, bereavement, and shame—these are among the terms of the sentence God has pronounced and is executing on rebellious slaveholders. Never, in modern times, at least, has so vast a territory been so scourged. Think, for example, of the scores of hundreds of families, prouder than Lucifer, worth their millions only *four* years ago, whose women and children and old men are now sustaining life on the rations of Yankee charity, whose plantation homesteads have been plundered and burned, whose husbands, brothers, sons, cousins have been killed, and who have to see soldiers that were once "their niggers" mounting guard in the streets of Savannah, Charleston, or Richmond, and prepared to suppress every Southern lady or "high-toned" gentleman who walks his or her own streets without a pass from some Yankee mudsill provost marshal.

April 12. Letter from Ellie at Washington. She has had a glorious time at City Point and Richmond. . . .

April 15, SATURDAY. Nine o'clock in the morning. *LINCOLN AND SEWARD ASSASSINATED LAST NIGHT!!!!*

The South has nearly filled up the measure of her iniquities at last! Lincoln's death not yet certainly announced, but the one o'clock despatch states that he was then dying. Seward's side room was entered by the same or another assassin, and his throat cut. It is unlikely he will survive, for he was suffering from a broken arm and other injuries, the consequence of a fall, and is advanced in life. Ellie brought this news two hours ago, but I can hardly *take it in* even yet. *Eheu*[2] A. Lincoln!

I have been expecting this. I predicted an attempt would be made on Lincoln's life when he went into Richmond; but just now, after his generous dealings with Lee, I should have said the danger was past. But the ferocious malignity of Southerners is infinite and inexhaustible. I am stunned, as by a fearful personal calamity, though I can see that this thing, occurring just at this time, may be overruled to our great good. Poor Ellie is heartbroken, though never an admirer of Lincoln's. We shall appreciate him at last.

---

2. **Eheu:** Alas.

UP WITH THE BLACK FLAG NOW!

Ten P.M. What a day it has been! Excitement and suspension of business even more general than on the 3rd instant. Tone of feeling very like that of four years ago when the news came of Sumter. This atrocity has invigorated national feeling in the same way, almost in the same degree. People who pitied our misguided brethren yesterday, and thought they had been punished enough already, and hoped there would be a general amnesty, including J. Davis himself, talk approvingly today of vindictive justice and favor the introduction of judges, juries, gaolers, and hangmen among the dramatis personae. Above all, there is a profound, awe-stricken feeling that we are, as it were, in immediate presence of a fearful, gigantic crime, such as has not been committed in our day and can hardly be matched in history.

Faulkner, one of our Kenzua directors, called for me by appointment at half-past nine, and we drove to the foot of Jane Street to inspect apparatus for the reduction of gold ore by amalgamation, which he considers a great improvement on the machinery generally used for that purpose. Returned uptown and saw Bellows to advise about adjournment of our Sanitary Commission meeting next week. Thence to Wall Street. Immense crowd. Bulletins and extras following each other in quick, contradictory succession. Seward and his Fred had died and had not. Booth (one of the assassins, a Marylander, brother of Edwin Booth) had been taken and had not. So it has gone on all day. Tonight the case stands thus:

Abraham Lincoln died at twenty-two minutes after seven this morning. He never regained consciousness after the pistol ball fired at him from behind, over his wife's shoulder, entered his brain. Seward is living and may recover. The gentleman assigned to the duty of murdering him did his butchery badly. The throat is severely lacerated by his knife, but it's believed that no arteries are injured. Fred Seward's situation is less hopeful, his skull being fractured by a bludgeon or sling shot used by the same gentleman. The attendant who was stabbed, is dead. (Is not.)

The temper of the great meeting I found assembled in front of the Custom House (the old Exchange) was grim. A Southerner would compare it with that of the first session of the Jacobins after Marat's death. I thought it healthy and virile. It was the first great patriotic meeting since the war began at which there was no talk of concession and conciliation. It would have endured no such talk. Its sentiment seemed like this: "Now it is plain at last to everybody that there can be no terms with the woman-flogging aristocracy. Grant's generous dealing with Lee was a blunder. The *Tribune*'s talk for the last fortnight was folly. Let us henceforth deal with rebels as they deserve. The rose-water treatment does not meet their case." I have heard it said fifty times today: "These madmen have murdered the two best friends they had in the world!" I heard of three or four men in Wall Street and near the Post Office who spoke lightly of the tragedy, and were instantly set upon by the bystanders and pummelled. One of them narrowly escaped death. It was Charles E. Anderson, brother of our friend Professor Henry James Anderson, father of pretty Miss Louisa. Moses H. Grinnell and the police had hard work to save him. I never supposed him a secessionist.

57

GEORGE N. BARNARD AND MATHEW BRADY
The Aftermath of the Civil War

The Civil War was the first modern war. Guns with rifled barrels could send a bullet accurately for long distances, and cannons loaded with grapeshot could kill and maim many men at one time. Railroads enabled armies to transport troops and supplies over vast distances, greatly increasing the size of battles—and the number of casualties. Not simply fought between professional armies, the war scarred large proportions of the population on both sides.

The technical limits of what the camera could depict shaped the way people of the times imagined battle. The photographic process was too cumbersome to allow "action" photographs: there are no Civil War photographs of actual battles.* Nonetheless, skilled photographers such as George N. Barnard and Mathew Brady followed the Union Army closely, catching the preparations for battle, the sites where battles were fought, and the dreadful aftermaths of these events.

The first photograph is from a portfolio of images of Sherman's march by Barnard, one of the best field photographers of the Civil War. Barnard followed General Sherman's army as it fought its way through the South, photographing when the army paused long enough for him to take pictures, sketching when it moved too quickly for his bulky equipment. After the war, Barnard retraced the army's route, photographing "the principal events and most interesting localities" that he had not been able to capture during the actual march. Included in Photographic Views of Sherman's Campaign, *a portfolio of views that Barnard published in 1866, his photographs suggest both the power and the limits of the era's photography for evoking a vision of war. The publication remains a classic pictorial history of the war.*

The second image also records the toll of the war. Having traveled with Grant's army when it finally broke down Confederate defenses protecting Petersburg, Virginia, Brady provides an account of the war's final days. Taken just six days before Lee surrendered, "Dead Confederates in the trenches of Fort Mahone, April 3, 1865" testifies to the war's power to devalue human life and scar the landscape.

---

*Subjects had to be stationary to be captured clearly on film.

George N. Barnard, *Photographic Views of Sherman's Campaign* (1866; New York: Dover Publications, 1977), Plate 60; Mathew Brady, *Dead Confederates in the trenches of Fort Mahone, April 3, 1865.* Library of Congress Prints and Photographs Division Washington, D.C. 20540 USA. Library of Congress Reproduction Number LC-DIG-ppmsca-32918.

QUESTIONS TO CONSIDER

1. How do the photographers create a sense of desolation in their work?
2. Why do the photographers pose only one or two person in each image? How does this technique affect how we view the landscape?
3. The South did not have the resources to support a photographic industry on the scale that was achieved by the North, and thus almost all our photographs of the war come from Northern sources. How might pictures taken by Southerners have been different? How might we view the war differently if there were large numbers of photographs taken by Southerners?
4. How might audiences today view these images differently from Southern and Northern audiences immediately following the war? Why?

"Ruins in Charleston, South Carolina," 1865 or 1866, by George N. Barnard.
Musee d'Orsay, Paris, France / © RMN-Grand Palais / Art Resource, NY.

"Dead Confederates in the trenches of Fort Mahone, April 3, 1865," by Mathew Brady and his field staff. *Library of Congress, Prints and Photographs Division, LC-B8184-10004.*

ACKNOWLEDGMENTS *(continued from p. iv)*

Bracketed numbers indicate selection numbers.

[1] "Dispatches of the Conquest from the New World." From Anthony Pagden, ed. and trans., *Hernán Cortés: Letters from Mexico*. Copyright © 1971 by Anthony Pagden. Revised edition copyright © 1986 by Yale University Press. Reprinted by permission of Yale University Press.

[2] "A Nahua Account of the Conquest of Mexico." From James Lockhart, ed., *We People Here: Nahuatl Accounts of the Conquest of Mexico* (Berkeley, CA: University of California Press, 1993), 90–104. Reprinted by permission of James Lockhart.

[5] "Travel to the New World." From "A True Reportory of the Wreck and Redemption of Sir Thomas Gates, Knight, upon and from the Islands of the Bermudas." July 15, 1610. Reprinted by permission of Virtual Jamestown.

[13] "Daughter, Wife, Mother, and Planter." From Walter Muir Whitehall, ed., *The Letterbook of Eliza Lucas Pinckney, 1739–1762*, 5–8, 15–17, 22, 34–35, 96–97, 146–49, 164–65. Reprinted by permission of the South Carolina Historical Society.

[20] "Secret Correspondence of a Loyalist Wife." From H. O. H. Vernon-Jackson, ed., "A Loyalist's Wife: Letters of Mrs. Philip Van Cortlandt, December 1776–February 1777," *History Today* 14 (1964): 574–80. Used by permission of the publisher, History Today.

[25] "A Native American Commander in the War of 1812." *The Journal of Major John Norton, 1816*, The Publications of the Champlain Society (Toronto: The Champlain Society, 1970), 289–95. Reprinted with permission from University of Toronto Press (www.utpjournals.com).

[26] "Crossing the Continent." Excerpts from *The Journal of Lewis and Clark,* edited by Bernard DeVoto. Copyright © 1953 by Bernard DeVoto. Copyright © renewed 1981 by Avis DeVoto. Reprinted by permission of Houghton Mifflin Harcourt Publishing Company. All rights reserved.

[28] "The Trail of Tears." *The Papers of Chief John Ross* by ROSS, JOHN. Reproduced with permission of UNIVERSITY OF OKLAHOMA PRESS in the format Republish in a book via Copyright Clearance Center.

[35] "Religion and the Power to Challenge Society." Reprinted from *Gifts of Power: The Writings of Rebecca Jackson*. Copyright © 1987 by the University of Massachusetts Press and published by the University of Massachusetts Press.

[38] "Marriage and Mormonism." *Before the Manifesto: The Life Writings of Mary Lois Walker Morris* by Morris, Mary Lois Walker; Milewski, Melissa Lambert. Reproduced with permission of Utah State University Press in the format Republish in a book via Copyright Clearance Center.

[44] "An Appeal for Revolution." North Carolina Collection, Wilson Special Collections Library, UNC-Chapel Hill Description: quotes from pp. 19–21, 41–46.

[53] "The Battle of Gettysburg: On the Field and at Home." Excerpts from *The Cormany Diaries: A Northern Family in the Civil War,* edited by James C. Mohr, © 1982. Reprinted by permission of the University of Pittsburgh Press.

[54] "Fighting for the Union." From Edwin S. Redkey, ed., *A Grand Army of Black Men.* Copyright © 1992 Cambridge University Press. Reprinted with the permission of Cambridge University Press.

[55] "A Slave Owner's Journal at the End of the War." From Arney Robinson Childs, ed., *The Private Journal of Henry William Ravenel, 1859–1887* (Columbia: University of South Carolina Press, 1947), 202–3, 206–7, 210–21 passim, 228–29, 237, 239–40. Reprinted by permission of the University of South Carolina Press.

[56] "A Northerner's View of the Confederacy's End." Reprinted with the permission of Scribner, a Division of Simon & Schuster, Inc., from THE DIARY OF GEORGE TEMPLETON STRONG by Allan Nevins and Milton Halsey Thomas. Copyright © 1952 by Macmillan Publishing Company, renewed © 1980 by Milton Hasley Thomas. All rights reserved.